D1609343

The Programmable Logic Device Handbook

To my children
Cami E. Burton
and
Charles E. Burton

The Programmable Logic Device Handbook

Von L. Burton

 TAB Professional and Reference Books

Division of TAB BOOKS Inc.

Blue Ridge Summit, PA

Notices

A + Plus	Altera Corp.	**CADAT**	HHB Softron, Inc.
ABEL	Data I/O Corp.	**IBM**	International Business Machines, Inc.
DASH-ABEL			
Data I/O		**APEEL**	International CMOS Technology, Inc.
FutureDesigner			
GATES		**PEEL**	
Logic Fingerprint			
LogicPak		**GAL**	Lattice Semiconductor, Inc.
PLDtest		**CUPL**	Logical Devices, Inc.
Unisite			
VAX	Digital Equipment Corp.	**PAL**	Monolithic Memories, Inc.
		PALASM	
DASH	FutureNet, a Data I/O company	**Logic Cell**	Xilinx
FutureNet			
PLD CADAT		**Logic Fingerprint test circuit**	U.S. patent 4,571,723

TPR books are published by TAB Professional and Reference Books, a division of TAB BOOKS Inc. The TPR logo, consisting of the letters "TPR" within a large "T," is a registered trademark of TAB BOOKS Inc.

FIRST EDITION
FIRST PRINTING

Library of Congress Cataloging in Publication Data

Burton, Von L.
    The programmable logic device handbook / by Von L. Burton.
        p.   cm.
    ISBN 0-8306-3140-2
    1. Programmable logic devices.   I. Title.
    TK7872.L64B87 1989
    621.39′5—dc20   89-20135
                                                     CIP

TAB BOOKS Inc. offers software for sale. For information and a catalog, please contact TAB Software Department, Blue Ridge Summit, PA 17294-0850.

Questions regarding the content of this book should be addressed to:

    Reader Inquiry Branch
    TAB BOOKS Inc.
    Blue Ridge Summit, PA 17294-0214

Vice-President/Editorial Director: Larry Hager
Book Editor: Sandra L. Johnson
Book Design: Jaclyn B. Saunders
Production: Katherine Brown

Contents

Introduction

The purpose of this book is to provide foundational knowledge and reference data for what has come to be known as *Programmable Logic Devices* (PLDs). A full discussion of all popular PLD architectures is provided as well as technology tradeoff data from which proper decisions can be made regarding the implementation of a PLD device into a circuit design. Software tools and programming hardware are given full coverage as an indication of the technology advancements in these areas that will assist in the circuit design process. Several applications are provided to give an overview of the capabilities inherent in PLD devices. The applications cover a wide range from the direct to the highly sophisticated. Finally, the current trends in PLD technology are discussed as an indication of what can be expected in the future.

The data contained in the tables are provided to give an indication of the many PLDs that are currently on the market and a first level cut at their architecturally-related characteristics, as well as other parameters related to their respective current requirements, propagation delay, and the like. The intent of this data is not to replace data books provided by the several manufacturers of PLDs, but to at least direct the user to the proper data book based upon the design requirements, the available architectures and technology preferences. The parts listing contains approximately 80% of the various PLD devices currently in production which represents a reasonably good sampling from the total population of parts. As manufacturers are continuously adding and dropping various parts, any parts listing prepared from a query of the manufacturers could never contain a 100% listing and any claims to this effect would suggest that the PLD industry is static and provide no recognition of the factors that contribute to the dynamics of the industry.

Needless to say, this undertaking would have been impossible without the aid of other experts, and I am very fortunate to have received help from the several semiconductor manufacturers, software development personnel, and the manufacturers of programming hardware. Appreciation is offered to Texas Instruments for the technical notes on PALs. I found this material and examples to be quite helpful, and a considerable amount is included in Chapter 1. The book has benefited greatly from the excellent paper on logic synthesis provided by the people at Data I/O. A special appreciation is offered for the excellent discussion of the historical chronology of logic synthesis (included in the same paper), as the forecast of the direction in which this technology is headed.

I am highly grateful to Signetics for the material they provided on their semiconductor products and software tools to support these products. Equally, I am grateful to the people at International CMOS Technology for similar material for their semiconductor devices and development system that is used to program these devices.

The book has benefited also from Lattice Semiconductor for providing materials on their line of products. Altera's cooperative efforts are highly appreciated and I feel users of this book will benefit from the information provided regarding their semiconductor products and supporting software and hardware. I would also like to thank Dr. William J. Barksdale of SouthTec Associates who looked over the logic tutorial in Appendix A and offered comments and suggestions. I could continue this recognition of the many companies that, in spite of the burdens of their busy schedules, took the necessary time to contribute to this effort; and I am deeply grateful to all who have contributed and warmly appreciate their interest, but in doing so I am not shrinking from this responsibility for the whole book.

Special appreciation is offered to the people at "The Fast Word" of Huntsville, Alabama, who typed the tables and entire manuscript, the several revisions required and the numerous letters to the various companies that contributed material to this book.

Lastly, recognition is offered to my wife, Cleola Colter Burton, whose continuous inspiration I found highly motivating.

The user of this book will not need to be told that the preparation of this book has cost me a great deal of toil. What has sustained me throughout this effort, aside from an intrinsic interest in the subject, is the belief that such a book was highly needed. It is this spirit in which it was written, and I hope that all users will benefit greatly from the material that it contains.

1

PLD Architectural Characteristics

The need for logic devices has its antecedents in the development of computers. Early computers employing algebra developed by George Boole and switching logic developed by Claude Shannon used vacuum tubes. Switching speeds of 10,000 times per second, however, could only be obtained from tubes of this type, and the attendant heat generation problems proved quite formidable in the construction of large computers such as the Eniac.

A significant improvement was made with the development of the transistor by Shockley, Bardeen, Brattain, and others permitting higher switching speeds and the elimination of the heat generation problems. An even greater improvement was contributed by the invention of the Integrated Circuit by Robert Noyce of Fairchild Semiconductors, and Jack Kilby of Texas Instruments, wherein several transistors could be placed on a single IC permitting gates (9 or 10) to be placed on a single chip. The number of transistors and consequently gates that can be placed on a single IC has grown exponentially which has let to Small Scale Integration (SSI), Large Scale Integration (LSI), and Very Large Scale Integration (VLSI) permitting thousands of gates to be placed on a single chip. These ICs have given circuit designers two choices for the construction of digital circuits. One choice is *fixed-function devices* or "Catalog Logic" such as the 7400 series of circuits and the other choice is *custom integrated circuits*. The development of the PLD has provided the circuit designer with a third option that is between fixed function devices and custom integrated devices.

The PLD can be defined as a device with an uncommitted logic array. In this regard, several designers consider it to be a semicustom device because the designer can program it to his own specifications. The most popular known PLDs are *Programmable Read Only Memories* (PROMs), *Field Programmable Logic Arrays* (FPLA), and *Programmable Array Logic* (PAL) devices. The time has arrived however where other devices must be added to this list such as *Erasable Programmable Logic Devices* (EPLDs), *Programmable Electrically*

Erasable Logic (PEELs), *Generic Array Logic* (GALs), *CMOS Programmable Logic* (CPL), *Programmable Macro Logic* (PML), and other architectures and devices that presently remain in the development stages.

To facilitate the understanding of PLDs, a special convention has been adopted. Figure 1-1 shows a 3-input AND gate using conventional notation. Figure 1-2 shows the same AND gate using PLD notation. Note that the gate has only one input line. This line is commonly referred to as the product line. Lines A, B, and C perpendicular to the product line are the considered inputs A, B, and C respectively. More specifically FIG. 1-2 shows a gate with all three fuses on the product line blown. Figure 1-3 shows a gate with all fuses intact while FIG. 1-4 shows a gate unused and all fuses intact.

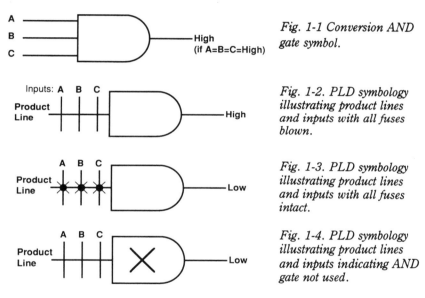

Fig. 1-1 Conversion AND gate symbol.

Fig. 1-2. PLD symbology illustrating product lines and inputs with all fuses blown.

Fig. 1-3. PLD symbology illustrating product lines and inputs with all fuses intact.

Fig. 1-4. PLD symbology illustrating product lines and inputs indicating AND gate not used.

An asterisk (∗) represents an intact fuse that makes that input part of the product term. The absence oı an ∗ represents a blown fuse eliminating that input from the product term.

In FIG. 1-5 the symbology has been extended to develop a simple 2-input programmable AND array feeding an OR gate. The inputs contain buffers which provide both true and complement outputs to the product lines. The intersection of the input terms form a 4×3 (4 input terms and 3 AND gates) programmable AND array. From FIG. 1-5's symbology, the output of the OR gate is programmed to the following equations $F = A\overline{B} + \overline{A}B$. The output of the OR gate is a logic level 1. Because from FIG. 1-5 the condition does not exist where all fuses are blown, the out of each AND gate is logic level 0. The bottom AND gate has an X marked inside the gate symbol, meaning all fuses are left intact which results in that product line not having any effect on the sum term. In other words, the output of this AND gate is logic level 0. As recalled, when all logic level 0 are input into an OR gate, the output is a logic level 1.

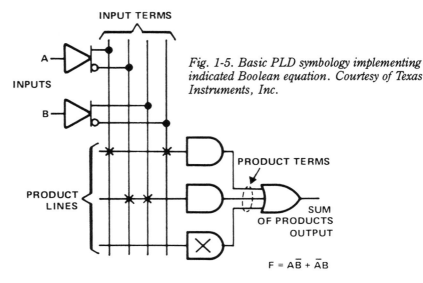

Fig. 1-5. Basic PLD symbology implementing indicated Boolean equation. Courtesy of Texas Instruments, Inc.

$$F = A\bar{B} + \bar{A}B$$

ARCHITECTURE OF A PROM

A PROM is a logic device that is comprised of a fixed AND array and a programmable OR array as shown in FIG. 1-6. The character of this device has found widespread applications in data storage tables, character generators and converters. In general, a PROM can find application in any design that requires the complete decodability of all inputs. However, full decoding of all its inputs can be considered limiting to wider applications for the following reasons.

First, the PROM by design provides the circuit designer with more decodability than is required for certain applications. Because all terms are decoded, those terms over and above what the designer requires can be considered in general surplus. Ideally for some applications, the designer receives no benefit from those product terms that were not derived from a truth table or some other input source. For example, consider a Boolean equation containing 5 inputs that decode into 32 unique combinations. The logic design reduced to its minimal form might only require 3 of the 32 combinations (or *terms* when they are fed to the OR array) which does not suggest an efficient utilization of resources.

The second weakness related to the PROM is that it is prohibitively limited to what has been referred to as a small number of input variables. Consider the function

$$f(n) = 2^n$$

which describes the growth in the size of the PROM fuse matrix for a given number of n inputs. For example consider a PROM with 5 inputs:

$$f(5) = 2^5 = 32 \text{ possible input combinations}$$

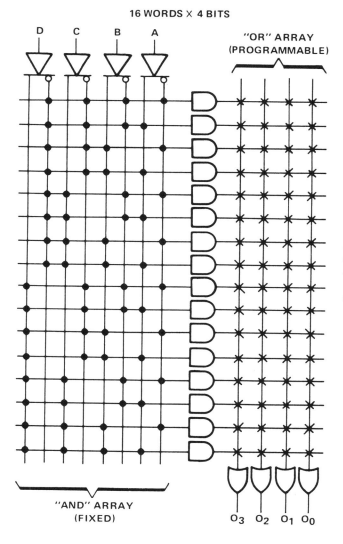

16 WORDS × 4 BITS

"OR" ARRAY (PROGRAMMABLE)

"AND" ARRAY (FIXED)

O_3 O_2 O_1 O_0

Fig. 1-6. Basic architecture of a Programmable Read-Only Memory (PROM) device. Courtesy of Texas Instruments, Inc.

An increase by three and four inputs respectively would cause growth in possible combinations to 256 and 512 respectively. For each variable added, the size of the fuse matrix doubles.

The nomenclature of a PROM might prove helpful which is commonly given as:

(Number of input combinations X number of outputs)

or

(2^n X number of outputs)

Consider a PROM with 5 inputs and a 8-term output word

$$2^5 \times 8 \text{ or } (32 \times 8)$$

This PROM would require 32 fixed AND gates to fully decode its 5 inputs.

By comparison consider a PROM with 9 inputs and an 8-term output word:

$$2^9 \times 8 \text{ or } (512 \times 8)$$

When compared with the above PROM that required only 5 inputs this PROM would require 512 fixed AND gates to fully decode its 9 inputs. An increase in word size by 4 bits caused an increase from the requirement of 32 AND gates to 512 AND gates. This growth rate for a marginal increase in the number of input variables is prohibitive for more than 12 input variables.

A PROM's fixed AND array and programmable OR array makes it ideal for storage of program data. The AND array provides fixed addresses by which data programmed into the OR array can be accessed. PROM's can also implement sum-of-products logic.

ARCHITECTURE OF A FPLA

The above limitations on the PROM caused circuit designers to produce an architecture wherein both the AND array and the OR array would be programmable for maximum flexibility. This capability gave rise to the FPLA (Field Programmable Logic Array) architecture as shown in FIG. 1-7. This device would permit the design engineer to utilize (program) only those product terms required for a specific application. The 2^n growth problem would be lessened for larger word sizes because full decodability would be removed. However, two penalties emerge when both the AND plane and the OR plane are programmable.

The first penalty relates to increased propagation delay times while the second penalty lies in additional silicon cost. True, the FPLA gives maximum flexibility, but the designer must determine if the additional flexibility sufficient for the particular application to justify an increase in the added propagation delay. The propagation delay increases because the high and low pulses are required to move over greater distances resulting from the added circuit complexity to complete a function.

The second penalty results from the cost overhead of additional silicon that is necessary for the added complexity. When this penalty is combined with the above penalty, a different type of PLD device might be more applicable.

ARCHITECTURE OF A PAL

The design of the PAL (comprised of a programmable AND array and fixed OR array, as shown in FIG. 1-8, was considered a proper trade between the FPLA architecture and the PROM architecture and (for quite a while) the PAL, and to some extent continues to account for a large quantity of PLD sales. The

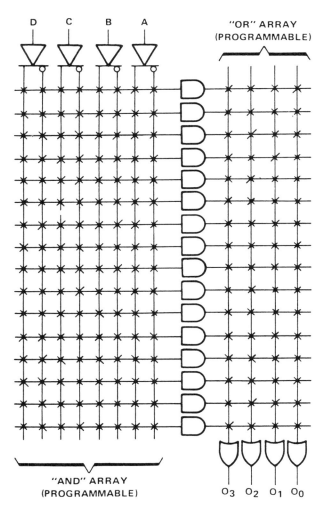

Fig. 1-7. Basic architecture of a Field Programmable Logic Array (FPLA) device. Courtesy of Texas Instruments, Inc.

reason for this is that the PAL strikes a clean balance between the additional complexity to a device, propagation delay and silicon cost.

Figure 1-9 shows the logic diagram of the TIBPAL16L8. It has the basic architecture (programmable AND array and fixed OR array), but with the addition of some special circuit features that can facilitate a broader understanding of a PAL device. The PAL has 10 dedicated inputs, inputs 1 through 11 excluding pin 10 which is ground. (Pin 20, not shown, is tied to V_{CC}.) In addition, 6 of the outputs (13 through 18) operate as I/O ports that permit a feedback into the AND array. An AND gate in each of these product terms controls each 3-state output. The architecture used in this PAL makes it very useful. A variety of combinational logic implementations can be made with this device; output 12 represents a combinatorial output without feedback.

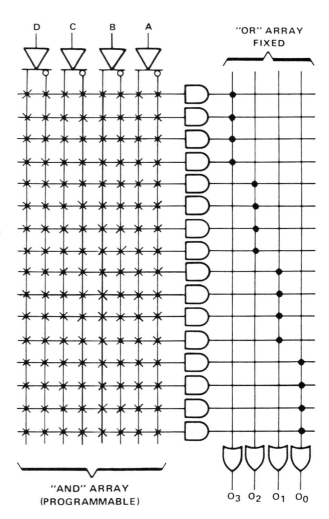

Fig. 1-8. Basic architecture of a Programmable Array Logic (PAL) device. Courtesy of Texas Instruments, Inc.

The basic concept of the TIBPAL16L8 can be expanded further to include D-type flip-flops on the outputs. Figure 1-10 shows which permits it to be used as a TIBPAL16R8 which contains D-type flip-flops as a counter, simple storage register, or similar clocked function. PALs contains a variety of output mixtures of combinatorial and resigned output.

PALs in general offer a great deal of versatility. For example the polarity of the output can be selected via the fuse shown in FIG. 1-11. Figure 1-12 shows an example of input register being fuse programmed. An intact fuse allows data to enter on a low-high transition of the clock. A blown fuse permits the register to become permanently transparent and is equivalent to a normal input buffer.

PALs equipped with input latches offers additional versatility—the input latches can be fuse programmable. Figure 1-13 shows an example of this type of input. An intact fuse permits data to enter while the control input is high. When

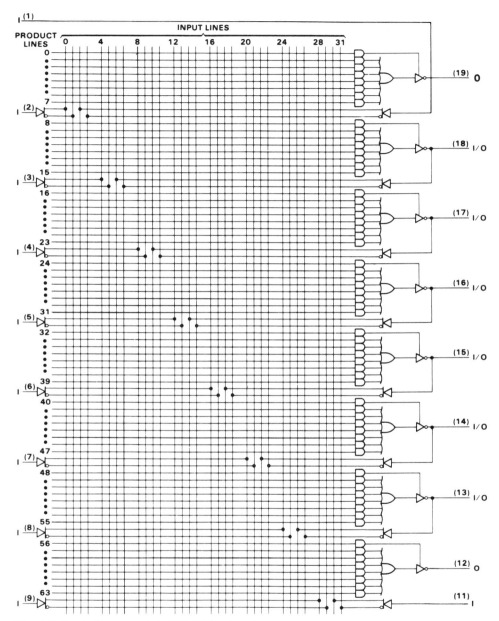

Fig. 1-9. Logic diagram of the TIBPAL 16L8. Courtesy of Texas Instruments, Inc.

the control input is low, the data that was present when the control input went low will be saved. If the fuse is blown, the latch becomes permanently transparent and is equivalent to a normal input buffer.

As noted in FIG. 1-10, a specific fuse to be located anywhere in the fuse matrix via the numbered product and input line. When the device is in the pro-

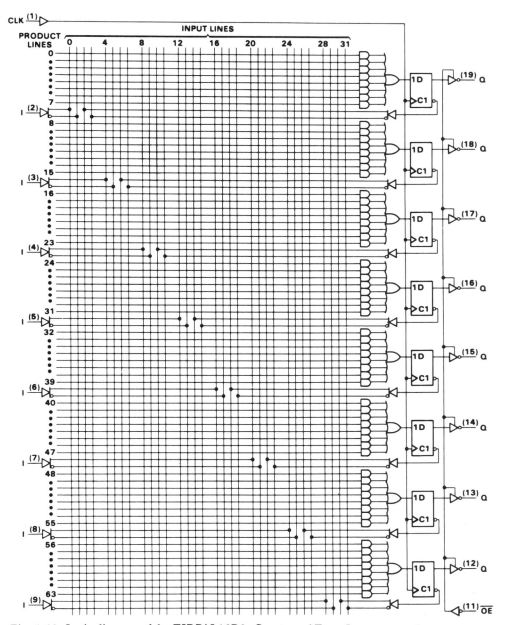

Fig. 1-10. Logic diagram of the TIBPAL16R8. Courtesy of Texas Instruments, Inc.

gramming mode (as defined in the device data sheet), the individual product and input lines can be selected. The fuse at the intersection of these lines can then be blown (programmed) with the defined programming pulse. The user however seldom has to get involved with these actual details of programming,

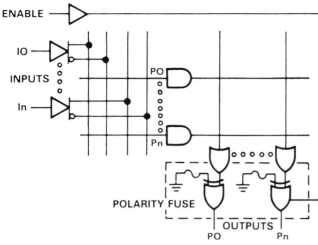

Fig. 1-11. *Logic diagram illustrating polarity selection. Courtesy of Texas Instruments, Inc.*

INTACT: OUTPUT = PO + P1 + ... + Pn
BLOWN: OUTPUT = $\overline{PO} \cdot \overline{P1} \cdot ... \cdot \overline{Pn}$

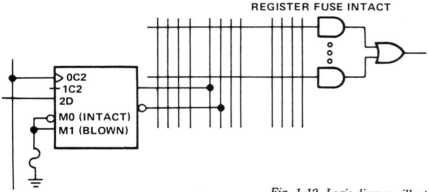

Fig. 1-12. *Logic diagram illustrating input register selection. Courtesy of Texas Instruments, Inc.*

D-TYPE REGISTER FUNCTION TABLE

CLOCK	D	Q	$\overline{Q}$
↑	H	H	L
↑	L	L	H
L	X	Q_0	$\overline{Q}_0$

Q_O = THE STATE OF Q BEFORE CLOCK ↑

because several commercially available programmers can handle this function as discussed in Chapter 5.

The actual blowing of the fuses is not a problem, but what fuses need to be blown to generate a particular function is. Fortunately, this problem has also

LATCH FUSE INTACT

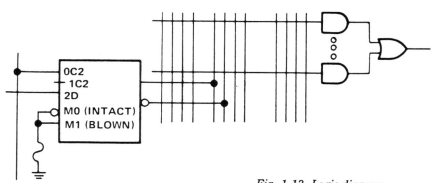

Fig. 1-13. Logic diagram illustrating input latch selection. Courtesy of Texas Instruments, Inc.

TRANSPARENT LATCH
FUNCTION TABLE

ENABLE	D	O	$\overline{Q}$
H	L	L	H
H	H	H	L
L	X	Q_0	$\overline{Q}_0$

Q_0 = THE LEVEL OF Q BEFORE ENABLE ↓

been greatly simplified by recent advances in computer software packages discussed in Chapter 3.

Design engineers are rapidly becoming aware of the many benefits that the PLD has as compared to preconfigured off-the-shelf logic devices. Engineers who are familiar with standard TTL logic understand that TTL logic devices are specified to worst-case conditions for the given application. However, because PALs can be programmed to perform many different applications, their device specifications must also include this versatility. It is this versatility which can cause misunderstandings when interpreting PAL specifications.

In the following paragraphs, the four major categories for logic device specification are discussed to highlight how PALs differ from standard logic devices:

1. Electrical characteristics
2. Absolute maximum ratings
3. Recommended operating conditions
4. Switching characteristics
   a. Propagation delay time calculation
   b. Maximum operating frequency calculation

Electrical characteristics. The method used in specifying DC electrical parameters for PALs does not deviate from the conventional method of specifying standard logic. However, one unique feature of PALs is in the supply current (I_{CC}) specification. The amount of supply current consumed is a function of the total number of fuses blown in the device. For example, a TIBPAL16L8-15 device typically consumes 130 mA of current (at 25°C) with all the fuses intact. The same device with all the fuses blown, typically consumes 70 mA. Power consumption can be minimized by blowing all product lines feeding unused OR terms. Supply current for PALs is specified with all the fuses intact. It is important to remember that the actual system supply current is related to the number of fuses blown for that given function.

Absolute maximum ratings. It is most important that the design engineer does not violate any of the maximum system input/output conditions. The maximum ratings ensure device reliability, as well as guarantee that the programming circuitry will not interfere with normal device operations. In situations where heavy duty outputs are driving long lead lengths (only terminated with very high impedances), excessive overshoot and undershoot can result. This excessive overshoot and undershoot can affect normal PAL operations calculation.

Switching characteristics. The main area where PAL specifications differ from standard logic specifications is in the AC switching characteristics. As a general rule, the PAL device should be viewed as a building block device. Typically, its architecture is made up of several AND-OR, AND-OR-REGISTER, or similar type logic cells. Some device types, such as the TIBPAL16R4, offer a combination of both cell types in the same package. The phrase *building block* describes a logic cell that can be connected by feedback to another logic cell. It is this building block concept which causes PAL specifications of maximum operating frequency (f_{max}) and propagation delay time t_{pd}) based on its given function. Because a PAL device can be configured in a number of different ways, the maximum operating frequency and propagation delay times for a given device will vary. This is dependent on the particular device used and the number of feedback paths used in the application. It is for this reason that these devices are specified by their individual building blocks. This allows the designer to calculate the t_{pd} and the f_{max} for his particular application. The following examples use four different configurations of the TIBPAL16R4 device to show how t_{pd} and f_{max} are calculated.

Propagation delay time calculation. Figure 1-14 shows an example of two different propagation delay paths t_{pd} from I1 to $I/0_1$ and t_{pd2} from 12 to $I/0_2$. The first, t_{pd1} represents the basic input-to-output building block as specified in the data sheet. The second, t_{pd2} is made up of two basic building blocks and is calculated as follows:

$t_{pd1} = (t_{pd}$ I to $I/0_1) = 15$ ns max
$t_{pd2} = (t_{pd}$ I to $I/0_1) + (t_{pd}$ I/O to $I/0_2)$
        $= 15$ ns $+ 15$ ns $= 30$ ns max

Maximum operating frequency calculation. The example in FIG. 1-15 shows the TIBPAL16R4 device, configured as a quad D-type register connected to a common clock. Each path shown represents the basic building block for which f_{max} is specified. Because no feedback paths are being used, f_{max} is the

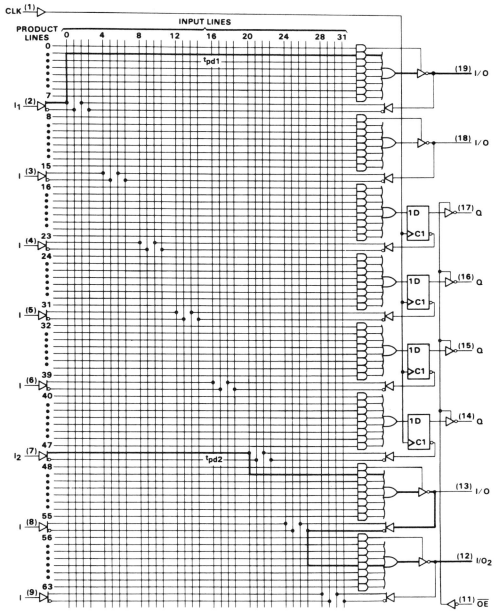

Fig. 1-14. Logic diagram illustrating TIBPAL16R4. Courtesy of Texas Instruments, Inc.

guaranteed data sheet maximum of 50 MHz (assuming the data setup times and hold times are not violated).

Figure 1-16 shows an example where the input signal passes through the array three times before being clocked into the register. Using the building

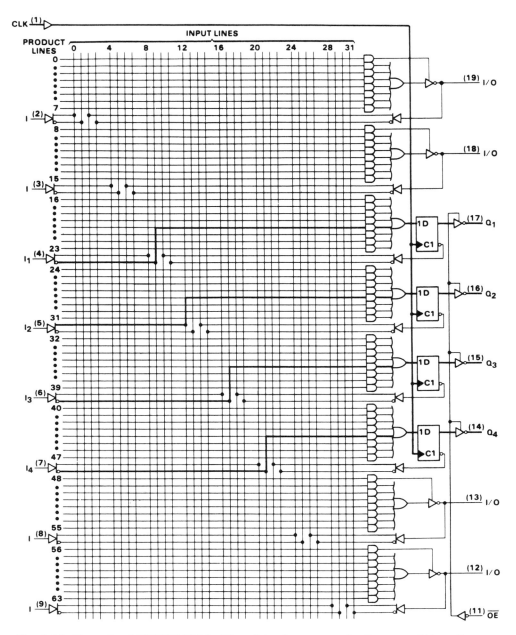

Fig. 1-15. Example of TIBPAL16R4 with registered outputs only. Courtesy of Texas Instruments, Inc.

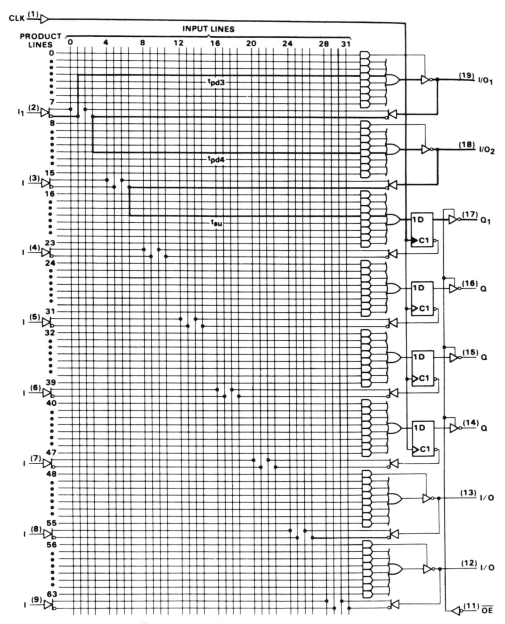

Fig. 1-16. TIBPAL16R4 Tsu example with feedback. Courtesy of Texas Instruments, Inc.

block concept, it is clear the t_{pd3}, t_{pd4}, and t_{su} must be considered when calculating f_{max}. At this point, there must exist a clear understanding of the setup time (t_{su}) specification. Setup time for PALs (data before clock and feedback before clock) is typically made up of two major components; the actual register setup

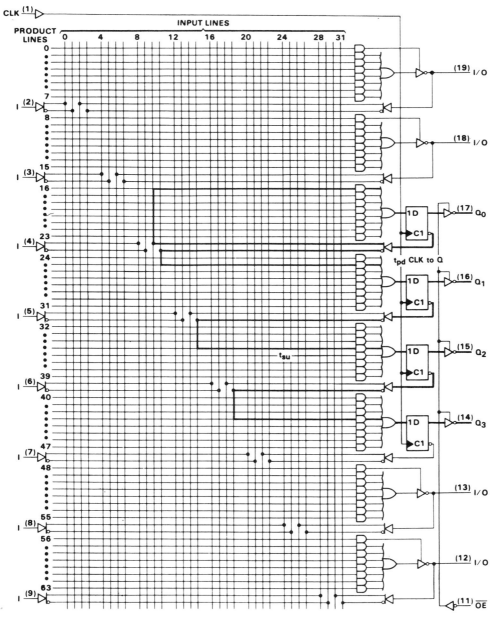

Fig. 1-17. TIBPAL16R4 configured as a 4-bit synchronous counter. Courtesy of Texas Instruments, Inc.

time and the time it takes the data to get through the AND/OR array to the register input. In other words, the setup time also includes the propagation delay through the AND/OR array. Knowing this, it is a simple task to calculate f_{max}:

$$t_{su} \text{ (Register Q1)} = t_{pd3} + t_{pd4} + t_{su} \text{ (Q1)}$$
$$= 15 \text{ ns} + 15 \text{ ns} + 15 \text{ ns} = 45 \text{ ns}$$
$$\text{Thus } f_{max} = 1/45 \text{ ns} = 22.2 \text{ MHz}$$

Figure 1-17 shows a typical application where the TIBPAL16R4 device is configured as a 4-bit synchronous counter. The outputs Q0, Q1, and Q2 are fed back into the array to determine the next state of the counter. Because the clock is common to all four registers, the counter's f_{max} is determined by the clock-to-Q output propagation delay and the feedback setup time. In order to properly calculate f_{max}, it must be understood that the feedback, setup time specification does not include the clock-to-Q output propagation delay:

$$f_{max} = 1/(t_{pd} \text{ clock-to-Q} + t_{su} \text{ feedback before clock})$$
$$= 1/(12 \text{ ns} + 15 \text{ ns}) = 1/27 \text{ ns} = 37 \text{ MHz}$$

It should be noted that the f_{max} of any 2-bit or greater counter (with a configured common clock) is determined by t_{pd} of clock-to-Q output and the feedback setup time. Therefore, the f_{max} for a 6-bit counter using TIBPAL16R6 and an 8-bit counter using TIBPAL16R8 is also 37 MHz. The f_{max} for devices with programmable/independent clock lines varies according to the application.

PALs, with a programmable AND array and fixed OR array, lend themselves to easy implementation of sum-of-products logic equations.

PALs can be thought of as comprised of families—a 20-pin family and a 24-pin family. Within each family are basic combinatorial logical devices as well as registered families with feedback options. Table 1-1 list members of the 20-pin

Table 1-1. Members of the 20-pin small PAL device family.

Part Number	No. of Inputs	No. of Outputs	No. of I/Os	No. of Registers	Output Polarity	Functions
10H8	10	8			AND-OR	AND-OR Array
12H6	12	6			AND-OR	AND-OR Array
14H6	14	4			AND-OR	AND-OR Array
16HL	16	2			AND-OR	AND-OR Array
10L8	10	8			AND-NOR	AND-OR Invert Array
12L6	12	6			AND-NOR	AND-OR Invert Array
14L6	14	4			AND-NOR	AND-OR Invert Array
16L6	16	2			AND-NOR	AND-OR Invert Array
16C1	16	1			AND-OR/NOR	AND-OR/AND-OR Invert Array
16L8	10	8	6		AND-NOR	AND-OR Invert Array
16R8	8	8		8	AND-NOR	AND-OR Invert Register
16R6	8	8	2	6	AND-NOR	AND-OR Invert Array Register
16R4	8	8	4	4	AND-NOR	AND-OR Invert Array Register

Table 1-2. Members of the 24-pin medium PAL device family.

Part Number	No. of Inputs	No. of Outputs	No. of I/Os	No. of Registers	Output Polarity	Functions
12L10	12	10			AND-NOR	AND-OR Invert Gate Array
14L8	14	8			AND-NOR	AND-OR Invert Gate Array
16L6	16	6			AND-NOR	AND-OR Invert Gate Array
18L4	18	4			AND-NOR	AND-OR Invert Gate Array
20L2	20	2			AND-NOR	AND-OR Invert Gate Array
20L8	14	2	6		AND-NOR	AND-OR Invert Gate Array
20L10	12	2	8		AND-NOR	AND-OR Invert Gate Array
20R8	12	8		8	AND-NOR	AND-OR Invert w/Registers
20R6	12	6	2	6	AND-NOR	AND-OR Invert w/Registers
20R4	12	4	4	4	AND-NOR	AND-OR Invert w/Registers
20X10	10	10		10	AND-NOR	AND-OR-XOR Invert w/Registers
20X8	10	8	2	8	AND-NOR	AND-OR-XOR Invert w/Registers
20X4	10	4	6	4	AND-NOR	AND-OR-XOR Invert w/Registers

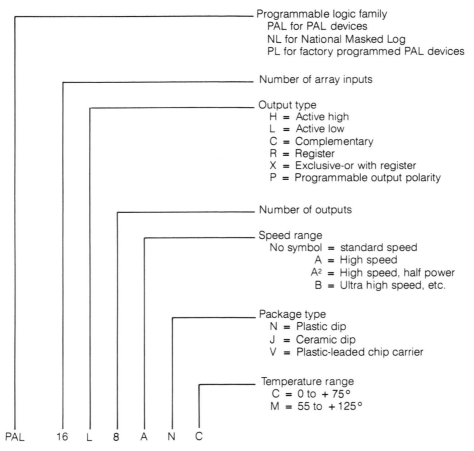

Fig. 1-18. PAL device part number interpretation. Courtesy of National Semiconductor Corporation.

Table 1-3. Texas Instruments, Incorporated, PALs, FPLAs, programmable state machines, programmable sequence generator, programmable logic sequencer.

Part Number	Part Types	Prog Arrays	Prod Terms	Speed (nsec)	Current (mA)	No. of Inputs	Comb Output	Reg Out	Macro Cells
TIBPAL16L8-7	Bipolar PLD	1	64	7.5	200	16	8	8	
TIBPAL16L8-7	Bipolar PLD	1	64	7.5	200	16		8	
TIBPAL16L8-7	Bipolar PLD	1	64	7.5	200	16	2	6	
TIBPAL16L8-7	Bipolar PLD	1	64	7.5	200	16	4	4	
TIBPAD16N8-7	Bipolar PLD	1	8	7	180	16	8		
TIBPAD18N8-6	Bipolar PLD	1	8	6	180	18	8		
TIBPAL16L8-10	Bipolar PLD	1	64	10	180	16	8		
TIBPAL16R8-10	Bipolar PLD	1	64	10	180	16		8	
TIBPAL16R6-10	Bipolar PLD	1	64	10	180	16	2	6	
TIBPAL16R4-10	Bipolar PLD	1	64	10	180	16	4	4	
TIBPAL16L8-12	Bipolar PLD	1	64	12	210	16	8		
TIBPAL16R8-12	Bipolar PLD	1	64	12	210	16		8	
TIBPAL16R6-12	Bipolar PLD	1	64	12	210	16	2	6	
TIBPAL16R4-12	Bipolar PLD	1	64	12	210	16	4	4	
TIBPAL16L8-15	Bipolar PLD	1	64	15	180	16	8		
TIBPAL16R8-15	Bipolar PLD	1	64	15	180	16		8	
TIBPAL16R6-15	Bipolar PLD	1	64	15	180	16	2	6	
TIBPAL16R4-15	Bipolar PLD	1	64	15	180	16	4	4	
TIBPAL16L8-25	Bipolar PLD	1	64	25	100	16	8		
TIBPAL16R8-25	Bipolar PLD	1	64	25	100	16		8	
TIBPAL16R6-25	Bipolar PLD	1	64	25	100	16	2	6	
TIBPAL16R4-25	Bipolar PLD	1	64	25	100	16	4	4	
TIBPALR19L8	Bipolar PLD	1	64	25	210	19	8		
TIBPALR19R8	Bipolar PLD	1	64	25	210	19		8	
TIBPALR19L6	Bipolar PLD	1	64	25	210	19	2	6	
TIBPALR19R4	Bipolar PLD	1	64	25	210	19	4	4	
TIBPAL20L10-20	Bipolar PLD	1	30	20	165	20	10		
TIBPAL20X10-20	Bipolar PLD	1	30	20	180	20		10	
TIBPAL20X8-20	Bipolar PLD	1	30	20	180	20	2	8	
TIBPAL20X4-20	Bipolar PLD	1	30	20	180	20	6	4	
TIBPAL20L10-30	Bipolar PLD	1	30	30	165	20	10		
TIBPAL20X10-30	Bipolar PLD	1	30	30	180	20		10	
TIBPAL20X8-30	Bipolar PLD	1	30	30	180	20	2	8	
TIBPAL20X4-30	Bipolar PLD	1	30	30	180	20	6	4	
TIBPAL20L8-15	Bipolar PLD	1	64	15	180	20	8		
TIBPAL20R8-15	Bipolar PLD	1	64	15	180	20		8	
TIBPAL20R6-15	Bipolar PLD	1	64	15	180	20	2	6	
TIBPAL20R4-15	Bipolar PLD	1	64	15	180	20	4	4	
TIBPAL20L8-20	Bipolar PLD	1	64	25	105	20	8		
TIBPAL20R8-25	Bipolar PLD	1	64	25	105	20		8	
TIBPAL20R6-25	Bipolar PLD	1	64	25	180	20	2	6	
TIBPAL20R4-25	Bipolar PLD	1	64	25	180	20	4	4	
TIBPAL22V10	Bipolar PLD	1	120	35	180	22			10
TIBPAL22V10A	Bipolar PLD	1	120	25	180	22			10
TIBPAL22VP10-20	Bipolar PLD	1	120	20	210	22			10
LOGIC SEQUENCERS									
TIFPLA839	FPLA	2	32	20	180	14	6		
TIFPLA840	FPLA	2	32	25	180	14	6		
TIB82S105B	PROG STATE MACH	2	48	50 MHz	180	16		8	
TIB82S167B	PROG STATE MACH	2	48	50 MHz	180	14		6	
TIBPSG507	PROG SEQ GEN	2	80	50 MHz	180	13		8	
TIBPLS506	PROG LOGIC SEQ	2	97	50 MHz	180	13		8	

Table 1-3. Continued.

Part Number	Part Types	Prog Arrays	Prod Terms	Speed (nsec)	Current (mA)	No. of Inputs	Comb Output	Reg Out	Macro Cells
ECL PALS									
TIEPAL10HI6P8-6	ECL PLD	1	64	6	220	16	8		
TIEPAL10016P8-6	ECL PLD	1	64	6	220	16	8		
ERASABLE, ZERO STANDBY POWER CMOS PALS									
TICPAL16L8-55	ZERO PWR, CMOS	1	64	55	100 uA	16	8		
TICPAL16R8-55	ZERO PWR, CMOS	1	64	55	100 uA	16		8	
TICPAL16R6-55	ZERO PWR, CMOS	1	64	55	100 uA	16	2	6	
TICPAL16R4-55	ZERO PWR, CMOS	1	64	55	100 uA	16	4	4	
TICPAL18V8Z-25	ZERO PWR, CMOS	1	64	25	100 uA	18			8
TICPAL22V10Z-35	ZERO PWR, CMOS	1	64	55	100 uA	22			10

Table 1-4. National Semiconductor Corporation PALs and GALs.

Family and Series	Part Number	tPD1 (max)	Icc (max)	Outputs Combinatorial	Registered
20-Pin Small PAL (Standard) Speed)	PAL10H8	35	90	8	-
	PAL10L8	35	90	8	-
	PAL12H6	35	90	6	-
	PAL12L6	35	90	6	-
	PAL14H4	35	90	4	-
	PAL14L4	35	90	4	-
	PAL16H2	35	90	2	-
	PAL16L2	35	90	2	-
	PAL16C1	35	90	1	-
20-Pin Small PAL Series-A	PAL10H8A	25	90	8	-
	PAL10L8A	25	90	8	-
	PAL12H6A	35	90	6	-
	PAL12L6A	35	90	6	-
	PAL14H4A	25	90	4	-
	PAL14L4A	25	90	4	-
	PAL16H2A	25	90	2	-
	PAL16L2A	25	90	2	-
	PAL16C1A	30	90	1	-
20-Pin Small PAL Series-A2	PAL10H8A2	35	45	8	-
	PAL10L8A2	35	45	8	-
	PAL12H6A2	35	45	6	-
	PAL12L6A2	35	45	6	-
	PAL14H4A2	35	45	4	-
	PAL14L4A2	35	45	4	-
	PAL16H2A2	35	45	2	-
	PAL16L2A2	35	45	2	-
	PAL16C1A2	40	45	1	-
20-Pin Medium PAL (Standard)	PAL16L8	35	180	8	-
	PAL16R4	35	180	4	4
	PAL16R6	35	180	2	6
	PAL16R6	35	180	-	8
20-Pin Medium PAL Series-A	PAL16L8A	25	180	8	-
	PAL16R4A	25	180	4	4

Table 1-4. Continued.

Family and Series	Part Number	tPD1 (max)	Icc (max)	Outputs Combinatorial	Registered
	PAL16R6A	25	180	2	6
	PAL16R6A	25	180	-	8
20-Pin Medium PAL	PAL16L8A2	35	90	8	-
Series-A2	PAL16R4A2	35	90	4	4
	PAL16R6A2	35	90	2	6
	PAL16R6A2	35	90	-	8
20-Pin Medium PAL	PAL16L8B	15	180	8	-
Series-B	PAL16R4B	15	180	4	4
	PAL16R6B	15	180	2	6
	PAL16R8B	15	180	-	8
20-Pin Medium PAL	PAL16L8B2	25	90	8	-
Series-B2	PAL16R4B2	25	100	4	4
	PAL16R6B2	25	100	2	6
	PAL16R8B2	25	100	-	8
20-Pin Medium PAL	PAL16L8D	10	180	8	-
Series-D	PAL16R4D	10	180	4	4
	PAL16R6D	10	180	2	6
	PAL16R8D	10	180	-	8
24-Pin Small PAL	PAL12L10	40	100	10	-
(Standard Speed)	PAL14L8	40	100	8	-
	PAL16L6	40	100	6	-
	PAL18L4	40	100	4	-
	PAL20L2	40	100	2	-
	PAL20C1	40	100	1	-
24-Pin Small PAL	PAL12L10A	25	100	10	-
Series-A	PAL14L8A	25	100	8	-
	PAL16L6A	25	100	6	-
	PAL18L4A	25	100	4	-
	PAL20L2A	25	100	2	-
	PAL20C1A	25	100	1	-
24-Pin XOR PAL	PAL20L10	50	165	10	-
(Standard)	PAL20X4	50	180	6	4
	PAL20X8	50	180	2	8
	PAL20X10	50	180	-	10
24-Pin XOR PAL	PAL20L10A	30	165	10	-
Series-A	PAL20X4A	30	180	6	4
	PAL20X8A	30	180	2	8
	PAL20X10A	30	180	-	10
24-Pin Medium PAL	PAL20L8A	25	210	8	-
Series-A	PAL20R4A	25	210	4	4
	PAL20R6A	25	210	2	6
	PAL20R8A	25	210	-	8
24-Pin Medium PAL	PAL20L8B	15	210	8	-
Series-B	PAL20R4B	15	210	4	4
	PAL20R6B	15	210	2	6
	PAL20R8B	15	210	-	8
24-Pin Medium PAL	PAL20L8D	10	210	8	-
Series-D	PAL20R4D	10	210	4	4
	PAL20R6D	10	210	2	6
	PAL20R8D	10	210	-	8
24-Pin Polarity PAL	PAL20P8B	15	210	8	-
Series-B	PAL20RP4B	15	210	4	4
	PAL20RP6B	15	210	2	6
	PAL20RP8B	15	210	-	8

Table 1-4. Continued.

Family and Series	Part Number	tPD1 (max)	Icc (max)	Outputs Combinatorial	Registered
Register	PAL16RA8	30	170	-	8
Asynch.	PAL20RA10	30	200	-	10
E² CMOS					
20-Pin Generic Array	GAL16V8-20L	20	90	-	8
Logic	GAL16V8-25Q	25	45	-	8
	GAL16V8-25L	25	90	-	8
	GAL16V8-30Q	30	45	-	8
	GAL16V8-30L	30	90	-	8
20-Pin Generic Array	GAL16V8A-10	10	115	-	8
Logic Series-A	GAL16V8A-12	12	115	-	8
	GAL16V8A-15	15	115	-	8
	GAL16V8A-20	20	115	-	8
24-Pin Generic Array	GAL20V8-20L	20	90	-	8
Logic	GAL20V8-25Q	25	45	-	8
	GAL20V8-25L	25	90	-	8
	GAL20V8-30Q	30	45	-	8
	GAL20V8-30L	30	90	-	8
20-Pin Generic Array	GAL20V8A-10	10	115	-	8
Logic Series-A	GAL20V8A-12	12	115	-	8
	GAL20V8A-15	15	115	-	8
	GAL20V8A-20	20	115	-	8
ECL					
Combinatorial	PAL1016P8	6	-240	8	-
	PAL10016P8	6	-240	8	-
Registered	PAL1016RD8	6	-280	-	8
	PAL10016RD8	6	-280	-	8
	PAL1016RC8	6	-280	-	8
	PAL10016RC8	6	-280	-	8
	PAL1016RD4	6	-260	4	4
	PAL10016RD4	6	-260	4	4
	PAL1016RC4	6	-260	4	4
	PAL10016RC4	6	-260	4	4
Latched	PAL1016LD8	6	-260	-	8
	PAL10016LD8	6	-260	-	8
	PAL1016LD4	6	-260	4	4
	PAL10016LD4	6	-260	4	4
Combinatorial Series-A	PAL1016P4A	4	-220	4	-
	PAL10016P4A	4	-220	4	-
	PAL1012C4A	4	-220	4	-
	PAL10012C4A	4	-220	4	-
Registered Series-A	PAL1016RM4A	4	-220	-	4
	PAL10016RM4A	4	-220	-	4
Latched Series-A	PAL1016LM4A	4	-220	-	4
	PAL10016LM4A	4	-220	-	4

small PAL devices and the 20-pin medium PAL devices. Table 1-2 list the 24-pin PAL devices.

Special conventions shown in FIG. 1-18 have been adopted to identify a specific PAL device type. One input array in the 16L8PAL (FIG. 1-18) may be thought of as the termination points of each complemented and uncomplemented output. Note that in FIG. 1-14, both the 16-input arrays and the 8 outputs can be identified. Table 1-3 presents a line of PALs (and other logic devices) offered by Texas Instruments while TABLE 1-4 presents PAL products offered by National Semiconductor.

ARCHITECTURE OF A GAL

The Generic Array Logic (GAL) family of programmable logic devices employs a programmable AND array and fixed OR array similar to bipolar PAL architecture. It is manufactured using a state-of-the-art Electronically Erase-able CMOS (E^{2}CMOS) process that permits Lattice Semiconductor Corporation to test every characteristic of the PLD before it is shipped. These PLDs, for example the GAL16V8A and GAL20V8A, post impressive speeds of 10 ns.

The electrically erasable (EE) matrix, unlike previous PLD matrix technologies (bipolar fuse-link and UV-erasable PROM), permits full testing of the programmability and reprogrammability of each and every matrix cell. The ability to pattern the actual matrix is extremely significant, because it also allows Lattice to test the functionality of each of the macrocell logic blocks, under various worst-case configurations. This test approach is referred to at Lattice as Actual Test. Test conclusively verifies AC and DC performance of every cell in every GAL device.

Consider the 20-pin GAL16V8 shown in FIG. 1-19 which features 8 programmable Output Logic Macrocells (OLMC)s allowing each output to be configured by the user. Additionally, the GAL 16V8 in a functional/fuse map/parametric compatible device is capable of emulating all common 20-pin PAL device architectures.

Programming is accomplished using readily available hardware and software tools. Lattice guarantees a minimum 100 erase/write cycles and that data retention exceeds 20 years.

Unique test circuitry and reprogrammable cells allow complete AC, DC, cell, and functionality testing during manufacture. Therefore, Lattice guarantees 100% field programmability and functionality of the GAL devices. In addition, electronic signature is available to provide positive device ID. A security circuit is built-in, providing proprietary designs with copy protection.

Output Logic Macrocell (OLMC)

The following discussion pertains to the configuration of the outputs logic macrocell. It should be noted that actual implementation is accomplished by development software/hardware and is completely transparent to the user.

The outputs of the AND array are fed into an OLMC, where each output can be individually set to active high or active low with either combinational (asynchronous) or registered (synchronous) configurations. A common output enable can be connected to all outputs, or separate inputs or product terms can be used to provide individual output enable controls. The output logic macrocell provides the designer with maximal output flexibility in matching signal requirements, thus providing more functions than possible with existing 20-pin PAL devices.

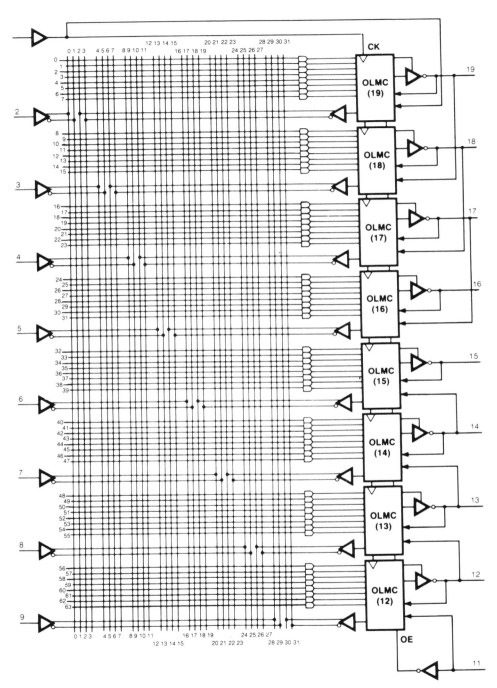

Fig. 1-19. GAL 16V8 logic diagram. Courtesy of Lattice Semiconductor Corporation.

The various configurations of the output logic macrocell are controlled by programming certain cells (SYN, ACO, AC1(n), and the XOR(n) polarity bits) within the 82-bit architecture control word. The SYN bit determines whether or not a device will have registered output capability or will have purely combinational outputs. It also replaces the ACO bit in the two outermost macrocells, OLMC (12) and OLMC (19). When first setting up the device architecture, this is the first bit to choose.

Architecture control bit ACO and the eight AC(n) bits direct the outputs to be wired always on always off (as an input), have common OE control (pin 11), or to be three-state controlled separately from a product term. The architecture control bits also determine the source of the array feedback term through the FMUX, and select either combinational or registered outputs.

The five valid macrocell configurations are shown in each of the macrocell equivalent diagrams. In all cases, the eight XOR(n) bits individually determine each output's polarity. The truth table associated with each diagram shows the bit values of the SYN, ACO, and AC1(n) that set the macrocell to the configuration shown.

Row Address Map Description

Figure 1-20 shows a block diagram of the row address map. A total of 36 unique row addresses are available to the user when programming the GAL 16V8 devices. Row addresses 0-31 each contain 64 bits of input term data. This

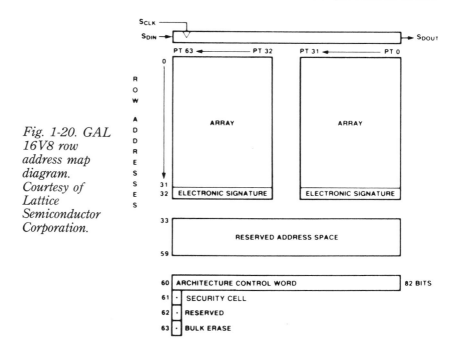

Fig. 1-20. GAL 16V8 row address map diagram. Courtesy of Lattice Semiconductor Corporation.

is the user array where the custom logic pattern is programmed. Row 32 is the electronic signature word. It has 64 bits available for any user-defined purpose. Rows 33-59 are reserved by the manufacturer and are not available to users.

Row 60 contains the architecture and output polarity information. The 82 bits within this word are programmed to configure the device for a specific application. Row 61 contains a one-bit security cell that when programmed prevents further programming verification of the array. Row 63 is the row that is addressed to perform a bulk erase of the device, resetting it back to a virgin state. Each of these functions is described in the following sections.

Electronic Signature Word

An electronic signature word is provided with every GAL 16V8 device. It resides at row address 32 and contains 64 bits of reprogramming memory that can contain user-defined data. Some uses include user ID codes, revision numbers, or inventory control. The signature data is always available to the user independent of the state of the security cell.

Architecture Control Word

All of the various configurations of the GAL 16V8 devices are controlled by programming cells within the 82-bit architecture control word that resides at row 60. The location of specific bits within the architecture control word is shown in the control word diagram in FIG. 1-20. The function of the SYN, ACO and AC1(n) bits have been explained in the output logic macrocell description. The eight polarity bits determine each output's polarity individually will be selectively correct logic. The numbers below the XOR(n) and AC1(n) bits in the architecture control word diagram shows the output device pin number that the polarity bits control.

Security Cell

Row address 61 contains the security cell (one bit5). The security cell is provided on all GAL 16V8 devices as a deterrent to unauthorized copying of the array configuration patterns. Once programmed, the circuitry enabling array access is disabled, preventing further programming or verification of the array (rows 0-31). The cell can be erased only in conjunction with the array during a bulk erase cycle, so the original configuration can never be examined once this cell is programmed. Signature data is always available to the user.

Bulk Erase Mode

By addressing row 63 during the programming cycle, a clear function performs a bulk erase of the array and the architecture word. In addition, the electronic signature word and the security cell are erased. This mode resets a previously configured device back to its virgin state.

Bulk erase is automatically performed by the programming hardware. No special erase operation is required.

Output Register Preload

When testing state machine designs, all possible states and state transitions must be verified in the design, not just those required in the normal machine operations. This is because in system operation, certain events occur that might throw the logic into an illegal state (power-up, line voltage glitches, brownouts, etc.). To test a design for proper treatment of these conditions, a way must be provided to break the feedback paths, and force any desired (i.e., illegal) state into the registers. Then the machine can be sequenced and the outputs tested for correct next state conditions.

The GAL 16V8 device includes circuitry that allows each registered output to be synchronously set either high or low. Thus, any present state condition can be forced for test sequencing. Figure 1-21 shows the pin functions necessary to preload the registers. The register preload timing and pin voltage levels necessary to perform the function are shown. This test mode is entered by raising PRLD to V_{IES}, which enables the serial data in (S_{DIN}) buffer and the serial data out (S_{DOUT}) buffer. Data is then serially shifted into the registers on each rising edge of the clock, DCLK. Only the macrocells with registered output

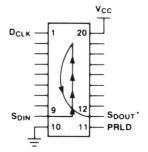

Fig. 1-21. Output register preload pinout. Courtesy of Lattice Semiconductor Corporation.

configurations are loaded. If only 3 outputs have registers, then only 3 bits need be shifted in. The registers are loaded from the bottom up, as shown in FIG. 1-21.

Input Buffers

GAL devices are designed with TTL-level compatible input buffers. These buffers, with their characteristically high impedance, load driving logic much less than traditional bipolar devices. This allows for a greater fan out from the driving logic.

GAL devices do not posses active pull-ups within their input structures. As a result, Lattice recommends that all unused inputs and 3-stated I/O pins be connected to another active input, V_{CC}, or GND. Doing this will tend to improve noise immunity and reduce I_{CC} for the device.

Circuitry within the GAL 16V8 provides a reset signal to all registers during power-up. All internal registers have their Q outputs set low after a specified time (t_{RESET}). As a result, the state on the registered output pins (if they are enabled through OE) is always high on power-up, regardless of the programmed polarity of the output pins. This feature can greatly simplify state machine design by providing a known state on power-up.

The timing diagram for power-up is shown in FIG. 1-22. Because of asynchronous nature of system power-up, some conditions must be met to guarantee a valid power-up reset of the GAL 16V8. First, the V_{CC} rise must be

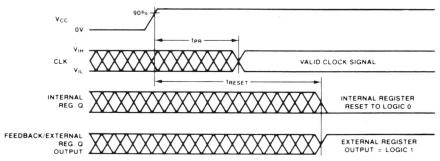

Fig. 1-22. Timing diagram for power-up. Courtesy of Lattice Semiconductor Corporation.

monotonic. Second, the block input must become a proper TTL level within the specified time (T_{PR}). The registers will reset within a maximum of t_{RESET} time. As in normal system operation, avoid clocking the device until all input and feedback path setup times have been met.

Although it is possible to program GAL device manually, Lattice strongly recommends the use of approved programming hardware and software. Programming on unapproved equipment generally voids all guarantees.

Approved equipment includes Lattice programming algorithms that program the array, automatically configure the architecture control word, and track the number of program cycles each devices has experienced (this information is stored within each GAL device). This in turn assures data retention and reliability. Contact the factory for specific conditions which must be met to gain programming equipment approval, the current list of approved GAL programming equipment, or other current programming information. GALs can be programmed with standard software packages such as CUPL and ABEL and programmers from Data I/O. Table 1-5 presents GAL devices offered by Lattice Semiconductor Corporation.

ARCHITECTURE OF A PML

PML (Programmable Macro Logic) was introduced at WESCON '85 by Signetics Corporation in an attempt to overcome what has been termed the two-level AND-OR bottleneck and provide the user with a higher level of logic transformation to implement combination logic in sum-of-products (SOP) form.

Table 1-5. Lattice Semiconductor Corporation GALs.

Part Type Selection Guide

Part Number	Part Types	Package Type	Family/ Pinout Codes	Program- mable Arrays	Product/ Sum Terms	Speed (ns)	Current (mA)
GAL16V8A-10LJ	GAL	PLCC	36/55	AND	64/8	10	115
GAL16V8A-10LP	GAL	DIP	36/55	AND	64/8	10	115
GAL16V8-15LJ	GAL	PLCC	36/55	AND	64/8	15	90
GAL16V8-15LP	GAL	DIP	36/55	AND	64/8	15	90
GAL16V8-20QJ	GAL	PLCC	36/55	AND	64/8	20	45
GAL16V8-20QP	GAL	DIP	36/55	AND	64/8	20	45
GAL20V8A-10LJ	GAL	PLCC	36/57	AND	64/8	10	115
GAL20V8A-15LJ	GAL	DIP	36/57	AND	64/8	10	115
GAL20V8-15LJ	GAL	PLCC	36/57	AND	64/8	15	90
GAL20V8-15LP	GAL	DIP	36/57	AND	64/8	15	90
GAL20V8-20QJ	GAL	PLCC	36/57	AND	64/8	20	45
GAL20V8-20QP	GAL	DIP	36/57	AND	64/8	20	45
GAL6001-30J	GAL	PLCC	36/44	AND/OR	75/36	30	150
GAL6001-30P	GAL	DIP	36/44	AND/OR	75/36	30	150
ispGAL16Z8-25LJ	GAL	PLCC	N/A	AND	64/8	25	90
ispGAL16Z8-25LP	GAL	DIP	N/A	AND	64/8	25	90
18V8-10LJ	GAL	PLCC		AND	64/8	10	115
18V8-10LP	GAL	DIP		AND	64/8	10	115
18D8-6LJ	GAL	PLCC		AND	8/0	6	90
18D8-6LP	GAL	DIP		AND	8/0	6	90
18U8A-15LJ	GAL	PLCC		AND	120/10	15	125
18U8A-15LP	GAL	DIP		AND	120/10	15	125
isp18UAZ8-15LJ	GAL	PLCC		AND	120/10	15	125
isp18UAZ8-15LP	GAL	DIP		AND	120/10	15	125
22V8-10LJ	GAL	PLCC		AND	64/8	10	115
22V8-10LP	GAL	DIP		AND	64/8	10	115
22D8-6LJ	GAL	PLCC		AND	8/0	6	90
22D8-6LP	GAL	DIP		AND	8/0	6	90
22UA10-15LJ	GAL	PLCC		AND	120/10	15	125
22UA10-15LP	GAL	DIP		AND	120/10	15	125
isp22UAZ10-15LJ	GAL	PLCC		AND	120/10	15	125
isp22UAZ10-15LP	GAL	DIP		AND	120/10	15	125
22V10-15LJ	GAL	PLCC		AND	132/10	15	130
22V10-15LP	GAL	DIP		AND	132/10	15	130

The more popular PLDs (PROM, PAL, and PLA) differ primarily in the programmability of the AND-OR gate chain which, by being irrevocably interposed as a two-level logic link between on-chip macros and I/O paths, often can turn into a design liability.

For example, as discussed previously in PROMs, the exponential increase in AND array size with number of inputs is a severe drawback which limits their contention in the logic application arena.

In PAL-type devices, the fixed inputs to the OR array confine their architectures to essentially a composite of AND-OR, AND-OR-REGISTER logic slices defining independent I/O paths through the chip. This causes duplication of common product terms and waste of unused AND gates in each slice (the mutually exclusive product term sharing of later PALs is only a partial solution).

Also, because each slice is dedicated to an output pin, devices with registered, programmable I/O pins entail an even greater waste of on-chip logic resources when configured in register-bypass or fixed input modes. Moreover, no single-level logic function can be constructed, except dedicated on-chip control functions.

Finally, even as the twin programmability of the AND-OR arrays in current PLA-type devices lends greater flexibility and might circumvent some of the above problems, it does pose difficult process, design, and performance compromises in migrating toward more complex structures.

This AND-OR bottleneck can be broken by relying instead on a single NAND-gate array to implement SOP logic functions, and to provide a central programmable "interconnect" site supporting a periphery of multilevel macros on a chip.

The PML architecture is intended to provide users a higher level of logic integration as an economical alternative to gate arrays. The current popular PLD architecture, such as PAL, has a group of AND gates that are hard-wired to an OR gate that is hard-wired to a macro which in turn is connected to an I/O pin. Such architecture has its resources partitioned and committed to different pins of the device. If only part of the resources connected, a certain pin is used, the unused portion is wasted. For example, as shown in FIG.1-23, if an I/O pin of a registered part is used as an input, the output buffer, polarity control circuitry, the flip-flop, and the entire AND-OR matrix are wasted. If a combinatorial output is needed, the flip-flop cannot provide anything else other than what is in the output. The more features that are incorporated in the macro, the more resources are wasted. For low complexity devices, the user simply has to design around those inconveniences. But at a much higher level of complexity, such architecture is evidently too inefficient to provide any meaningful increase in levels of logic integration. Compared to the PAL architecture, the PML architecture is much more efficient in utilizing its resources because all of its macros are independent of all other resources. In addition, resources in the NAND array are shared by all macros. Therefore, it permits more efficient usage of the NAND terms. The feedbacks of the NAND terms enable the user to implement complex logic functions without using up precious I/O pins and without the additional propagation delays of the I/O circuitries. Figure 1-24 illustrates the using of the NAND array to implement different logic functions. For some applications where a single level of logic is sufficient, instead of the AND-OR structure of PAL and PLA, the user now can use a single level of logic and achieve minimum propagation delay.

The architecture of PML consists of different *macrocells* (hereafter called *macros*) and a programmable network that connects macros to each other. The core of PML is the programmable interconnect which is a NAND array that has a large number of NAND terms. The output of every NAND term feeds back to the inputs of the NAND array. Therefore, every NAND term is connected to the outputs of all other NAND terms through programmable elements. Each NAND term has a large number of inputs—inputs from other macros to the NAND array plus feedbacks from the NAND array itself. The basic structure of

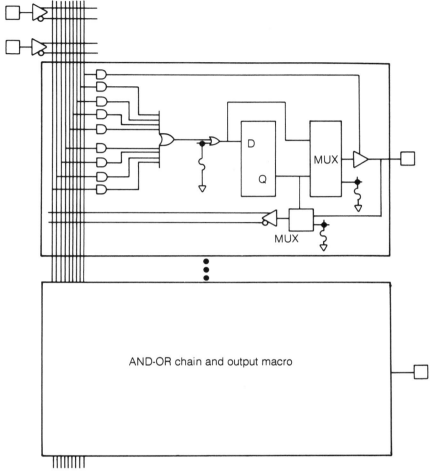

Fig. 1-23. Schematic outline of a registered PAL. Courtesy of Signetics Corporation.

the PML NAND array is shown in FIG. 1-25 where each vertical line represents the inputs of a NAND term, the solid horizontal lines represent driving lines with square dots which are connected to the vertical lines indicate that the vertical lines perform the logic function of NAND and the dotted lines are not connected to any other line. Outputs of the NAND array are connected to other macros such as output macros or process macros (i.e., flip-flop, counters, shift registers, etc.) via NAND terms while inputs to the NAND array are indicated as additional horizontal lines coming from outside of the array as shown in FIG. 1-26.

The general architecture of a PML device is shown in FIG. 1-27 as a foundation for PML.

PML consists of various logic *access* and *progress* macros coupled via a primitive, central programmable structure establishing a uniform discipline in

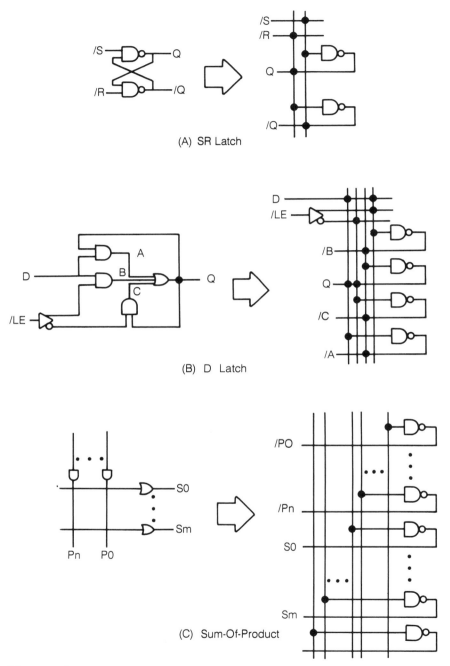

(A) SR Latch

(B) D Latch

(C) Sum-Of-Product

Fig. 1-24. Implementation of various logic applications. Courtesy of Signetics Corporation.

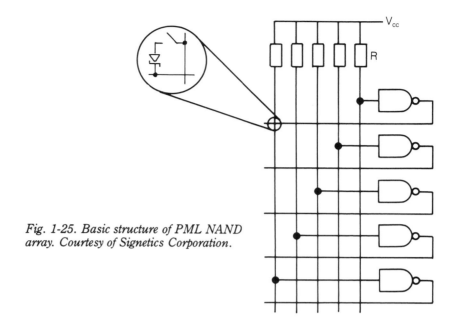

Fig. 1-25. Basic structure of PML NAND array. Courtesy of Signetics Corporation.

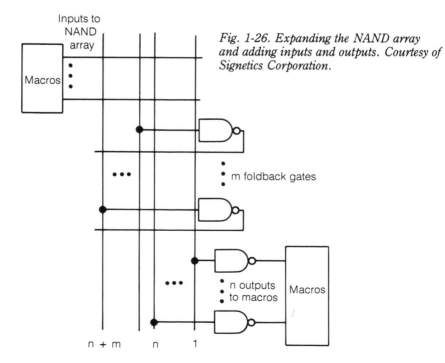

Fig. 1-26. Expanding the NAND array and adding inputs and outputs. Courtesy of Signetics Corporation.

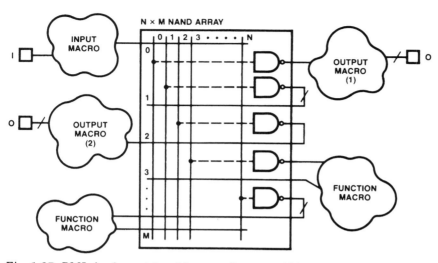

Fig. 1-27. PML fundamental architecture. Courtesy of Signetics Corporation.

the on-chip interconnect system. Macros can have various local intelligence which in turn can be fixed or variable by means of programmable options also embedded in the central programmable core.

The first PML device available is the PLHS501, which is a 52-pin gate bucket. As shown in FIG. 1-28, the device has 72 NAND terms, 24 dedicated inputs (I_0 to I_{23}), 8 bidirectional I/Os (B_0 to B_7), 8 XOR outputs (X_0 to X_7), 8 dedicated outputs O_0 to O_7, 2 V_{cc} and 2 GND pins. B_0 to B_3 are fuse-programmable bidirectional I/Os with active low outputs while B_4 to B_7 are logic-controlled bidirectional I/Os with active high tristate outputs. The XOR outputs have tristate outputs which pair together to share one tristate controlling AND term per pair. The dedicated outputs O_0 to O_3 have active low tristate output buffers while outputs O_4 to O_7 have active high tristate output buffers. Each of the tristate controlling AND terms of O_0 to O_7 controls a pair of output buffers. This device provides up to 1300 equivalent gates. It comes in a 52-pin PLCC package. Its wide NAND input capability makes it ideal for high-speed address decoding and bus interface applications.

Notice that each one of the outputs B_0 to B_3 is controlled a single AND term that is connected to the NAND array. This feature enables the user to configure any of these four outputs as open collector outputs.

The second device in the PML family is the PLHS502 which, in addition to the features in PLHS501, has 16 edge-triggered flip-flops. A logic diagram of the device is shown in FIG. 1-29. In the PLHS502, all 16 flip-flops can be clocked separately or by the same system clock. The clock inputs of the flip-flops are generated from a small subset of the NAND array so that propagation delays and skewing can be kept to a minimum. Notice that the four I/CK pins can be used as inputs and/or as clocks to the flip-flops. This device can accommodate a variety of applications including synchronous and asynchronous state machines.

The PLHS501 is ideal for the applications of asynchronous machines due to the availability of asynchronous machines due to the availability of a large number of gates and feedback paths. The internal feedback paths provide delays which can be used as short term memory elements that can be used in state machine applications. Figure 1-30 illustrates the similarities between the classic synchronous state machine model and a model of asynchronous state machine using feedback delays as memory elements. An example of an asynchronous machine is the 74120, a pulse synchronizer that generates a single pulse or a train of pulses synchronizes with the system clock. An implementation of the synchronizer using PML is shown in FIG.1-31.

Another example of an asynchronous state machine is the asynchronous input change detector which takes two inputs, ARM and INPUT, and one output, TRIGGER_OUT. TRIGGER_OUT is set to 1 when ARM equals 0. While ARM is at 1, the first change occurring to INPUT sets TRIGGER_OUT from 1 to 0. It stays at 0 until ARM becomes 0. The detector is implemented using PML devices as shown in FIG. 1-32.

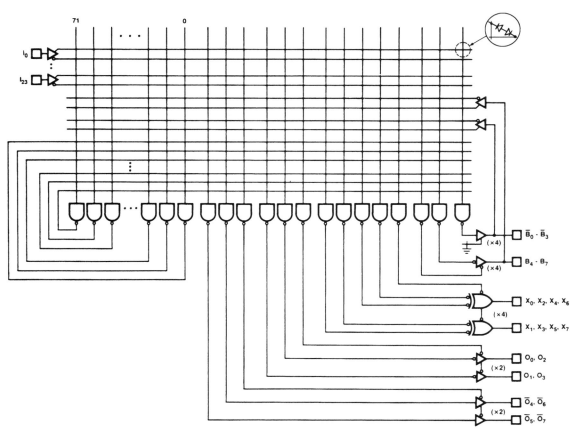

Fig. 1-28. PLHS501 logic diagram. Courtesy of Signetics Corporation.

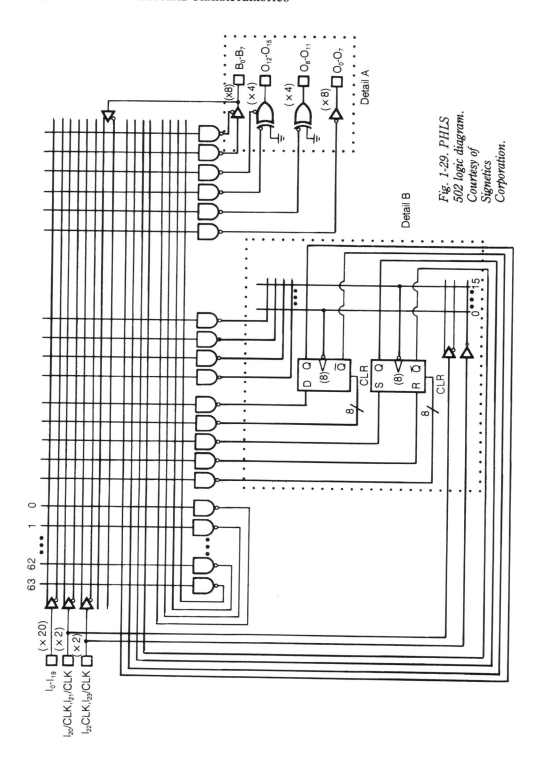

Fig. 1-29. PHLS 502 logic diagram. Courtesy of Signetics Corporation.

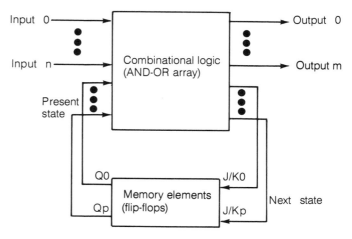

(a) Model of synchronous state machines

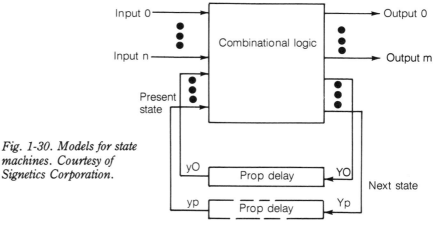

Fig. 1-30. Models for state machines. Courtesy of Signetics Corporation.

(b) Model of asynchronous state machines using propagation delays of the feedback path as memory elements

The advantage of asynchronous machine is that it is not paced by a system clock and therefore can run as fast as its internal logic permits. Another advantage of the asynchronous state machine approach is that it can accommodate asynchronous inputs without having to observe setup and hold time requirements of flip-flops, which usually impose on the system designer to add external flip-flops to the state machine or design the state machine to look for a particular asynchronous input at particular states. Both approaches slow the system down considerably.

Programmable Logic Sequencers such as the PLUS405 have a unique architecture that employs buried registers to store intermediate values. This

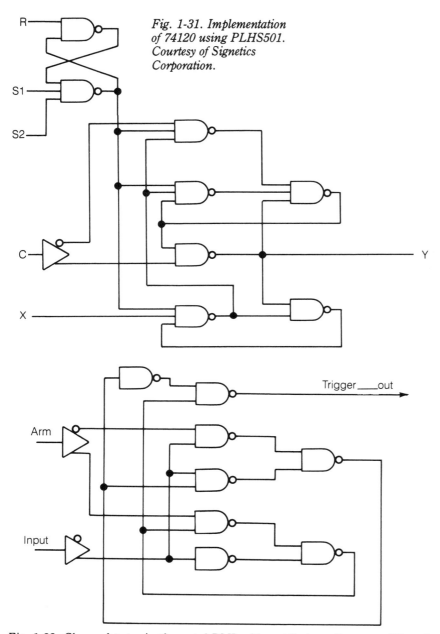

Fig. 1-31. Implementation of 74120 using PLHS501. Courtesy of Signetics Corporation.

Fig. 1-32. Charge detector implemented PML with architecture. Courtesy of Signetics Corporation.

results in greater silicon and pin utilization with increased functionality. Advanced state machine designs become easy with Signetics sequencers. The architecture provided by Signetics makes complex IF-THEN-ELSE statements possible. Connecting any AND term to any OR term (Product term sharing) eliminate redundant state transition terms. And JK or SR registers optimize the logic used in generating state transitions.

Table 1-6 presents a product selection guide for the various logic devices offered by Signetics.

In addition to the previous discussion of architectures, the development of EPLDs and PEELs and CPLs are discussed in the following sections. There

Table 1-6. Signetics Corporation FPGAs, FPADs, FPLAs, FPLSs, and FPMLs.

Signetics PN	Architecture	Package	Total Inputs (# Dedicated)	Product Terms	Internal State Registers	Outputs	T_{pd}	I_{cc}
						C, I/O, R, R/O	(Typical Values)[1,2]	
	FPGA							
PLS103	16 X 9 X 9	28 pin	16	9	0	9C	20 ns	120 mA
PLS151	18 X 15 X 12	20 pin	18(6)	15	0	12 I/O	15 ns	130 mA
	FPAD							
PLS162	16 X 5	24 pin	16	5	0	5C	20 ns	120 mA
PLS163	12 X 9	24 pin	12	9	0	9C	20 ns	120 mA
	FPLA							
PLS100	16 X 48 X 8	28 pin	16	48	0	8C	35 ns	120 mA
PLS153	18 X 42 X 10	20 pin	18(8)	42	0	10 I/O	30 ns	130 mA
PLS153A	18 X 42 X 10	20 pin	18(8)	42	0	10 I/O	20 ns	130 mA
PLHS153**	18 X 42 X 10	20 pin	18(8)	42	0	10 I/O	15 ns	150 mA
PLUS153**	18 X 42 X 10	20 pin	18(8)	42	0	10 I/O	9 ns	175 mA
PLS161	12 X 48 X 8	24 pin	12	48	0	8C	35 ns	120 mA
PLC173	22 X 42 X 10	24 pin	22(12)	42	0	10 I/O	20 ns	150 mA
PLUS173**	22 X 42 X 10	24 pin	22(12)	42	0	10 I/O	35 ns	25 mA
PLHS473	20 X 24 X 11	24 pin	20(11)	24	0	2C & 9 I/O	15 ns	140 mA
PLC473**	20 X 24 X 11	24 pin	20(11)	24	0	2C & 9 I/O	30 ns	25 mA
PLHS18P8A	18 X 72 X 8	20 pin	18(10)	72	0	8 I/O	15 ns	120 mA
	FPLS							
PLS105	16 X 48 X 8	28 pin	16	48		8R	60 ns	120 mA
PLS105A	16 X 48 X 8	28 pin	16	48		8R	45 ns	120 mA
PLC105**	16 X 48 X 8	28 pin	16	48		8R	50 ns	40 mA
PLUS405**	16 X 64 X 8	28 pin	16	64		8R	15 ns	160 mA
PLUS155	16 X 45 X 12	20 pin	16(4)	45		8 I/O & 4 R I/O	55 ns	150 mA
PLS157	16 X 45 X 12	20 pin	16(4)	45		6 I/O & 6 R I/O	55 ns	150 mA
PLS159	16 X 45 X 12	20 pin	16(4)	45		4 I/O & 8 R I/O	55 ns	150 mA
PLS167	14 X 48 X 6	24 pin	14	48	6 plus 2*	6 R	60 ns	120 mA
PLS167A	14 X 48 X 6	24 pin	14	48	6 plus 2*	6 R	45 ns	120 mA
PLS168	12 X 48 X 8	24 pin	12	48	6 plus 4*	8 R	60 ns	120 mA
PLS168A	12 X 48 X 8	24 pin	12	48	6 plus 4*	8 R	45 ns	120 mA
PLS179	20 X 45 X 12	24 pin	20(8)	45	8*	4 R I/O & 8 R I/O	45 ns	145 mA
PLUS155	16 X 45 X 12	20 pin	16(4)	45		8 I/O & 4 R I/O	55 ns	150 mA
PLS157	16 X 45 X 12	20 pin	16(4)	45		6 I/O & 6 R I/O	55 ns	150 mA
PLS159	16 X 45 X 12	20 pin	16(4)	45		4 I/O & 8 R I/O	55 ns	150 mA
PLS167	14 X 48 X 6	24 pin	14	48	6 plus 2*	6 R	60 ns	120 mA
PLS167A	14 X 48 X 6	24 pin	14	48	6 plus 2*	6 R	45 ns	120 mA

Table 1-6. Continued.

Signetics PN	Architecture	Package	Total Inputs (# Dedicated)	Product Terms	Internal State Registers	Outputs	T_{pd}	I_{cc}
PLS168	12 X 48 X 8	24 pin	12	48	6 plus 4*	8 R	60 ns	120 mA
PLS168A	12 X 48 X 8	24 pin	12	48	6 plus 4*	8 R	45 ns	120 mA
PLS179	20 X 45 X 12	24 pin	20(8)	45	8*	4 I/O & 8 R I/O	45 ns	145 mA
PLHS501	32 X 72 X 24	52 pin	32	72	0	16C and 8 I/O	20 ns	250 mA
PLHS502	32 X 64 X 24	52 pin	32(24)	64	16	16C or R and 8 C or R I/O	15/30 ns	250 mA

C = Combinatorial output
R = Registered output
I/O = Combinatorial I/O
R I/O = Registered I/O
* State registers shared with output registers
** Under development
NOTES:
1. $T_{PD} = T_{IS} + T_{CKO}$ for registered devices
2. For worst case specifications refer to data sheets for individual product.

appears to be no limit to this complexity and capability (EPLDs, for example, are erased by UV light while PEELs are erased electrically). From the basic combinatorial output to macrocell registers, the PEEL architecture has proven to be quite feasible and finds many applications.

ARCHITECTURE OF A PEEL DEVICE

Architecturally flexible PEEL devices can emulate other conventional PLDs (PALs, EPLDs, FPLAs). The PEEL 18CV8 alone can functionally emulate over 20 PAL and EPLD devices (see TABLE 1-7). Converting existing designs to PEEL devices can easily be done with the free PEEL Evaluation Kit software translator offered by International CMOS Technologies. Using PEEL

Table 1-7. PLD devices that can be emulated by the 18CV8.

20-pin PAL

Output Type	Part Number and I/O Capacity							
Combinatorial-High	10H8	12H6	14H4	16H2			16H8	16HD8
Combinatorial-Low	10L8	12L6	14L4	16L2			16L8	16LD8
Combinatorial-Polarity							16P8	18P8
Registered-Low					16R4	16R6	16R8	
Registered-Polarity					16RP4	16RP6	16RP8	

Altera
  EP 300/310

devices for functional replacements allows existing designs to take advantage of the many benefits of CMOS PEEL technology including low power, high noise-immunity, lower operating temperature, reprogrammability, and higher quality levels.

As previously discussed, two basic architectures are used in most programmable logic devices. Programmable AND-type devices feed logical inputs to a programmable AND array that in turn drives a fixed array of OR gates. Programmable-AND/OR devices use a programmable AND array and a programmable OR array. Each architecture has its own unique benefits. The PEEL family offers devices with both programmable-AND and programmable-AND/OR architectures. Besides emulation, PEEL devices have enhanced architectures that allow for completely new functions and configurations not supported by conventional PLDs (see TABLE 1-8). For example, the PEEL 18CV8 incorporates a 12-configuration I/O macrocell. Their equivalent circuits are listed in FIG. 1-33. Only 4 of these configurations are possible among all the architectures provided by standard PAL device types. The PEEL I/O macrocell provides 8 additional configurations.

Other architecture enhancements include independent output enables and additional product terms for both logic and control purposes. Such flexibility

Table 1-8. International CMOS Technology, Inc., PEELs.

Part Number	Part Type	Package	Pin Outcode	Pin	Inputs	I/O's	Regs	Macro Configs
153	PEEL	Dip	8C/85	20	8	10	0	2
173	PEEL	Dip	8D/76	24	12	10	0	2
18CV8	PEEL	Dip	8D/3A	20	10	8	8	12
20CG10	PEEL	Dip	8D/56	24	12	10	10	4
20CG10Z	PEEL	Dip	TBD	24	12	10	10	12
22CV10	PEEL	Dip	8D/28	24	10	10	10	4
22CV10Z	PEEL	Dip	8D/A3	24	12	10	10	12
253	PEEL	Dip	8D/85	20	8	10	0	2
273	PEEL	Dip	8D/86	24	12	10	0	2

Part Number	Prog. Arrays	Product/Sum Terms	Prop Delay		Supply Current	
			co(nS)	pd(ns)	Icc(mA)	Z-Mode
153	AND/OR	42/10	N/A	30-40	35 + 1.0/MHz	no
173	AND/OR	42/10	N/A	20-40	35 + 1.0/MHz	no
18CV8	AND	74	15-25	25-50	15 + 0.7/MHz	no
20CG10	AND	90	15-20	25-35	45 + 0.7/MHz	no
20CG10Z	AND	92	15-20	25-35	45 + 1.0/MHz	yes
22CV10	AND	132	15-20	25-35	45 + 0.7/MHz	no
22CV10Z	AND	132	15-20	25-35	45 + 0.7/MHz	yes
253	AND/OR	42/20	N/A	30-40	35 + 1.0/MHz	no
273	AND/OR	42/20	N/A	30-40	35 + 1.0/MHz	no

permits an engineer to focus on the design at hand rather than on the restrictions of a fixed architecture.

Consider for example the PEEL 18CV8 (FIG. 1-34) from International CMOS Technology. A great amount of architectural flexibility is provided by the PEEL 18CV8's reconfigurable I/O macrocells and independently controlled

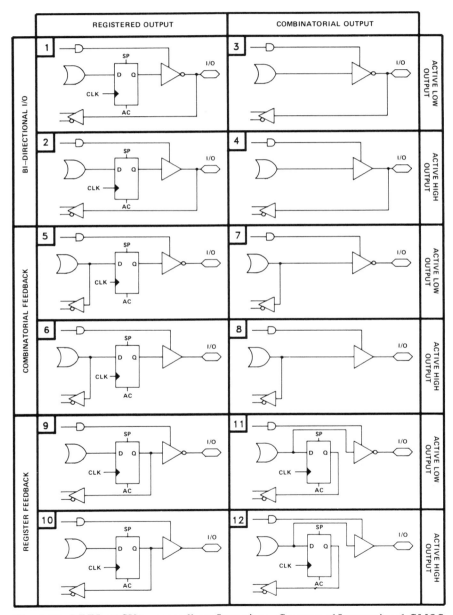

Fig. 1-33. PEEL 18CV8 macrocell configurations. Courtesy of International CMOS Technology, Inc.

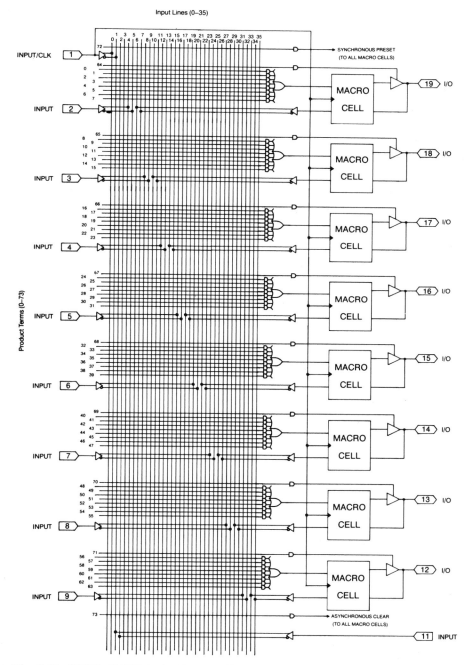

Fig. 1-34. PEEL 18CV8 logic diagram. Courtesy of International CMOS Technology, Inc.

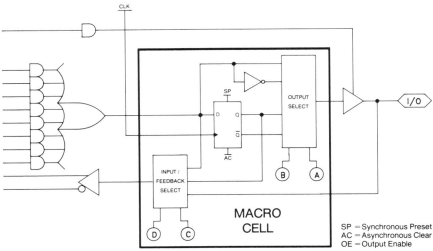

Fig. 1-35. PEEL 18CV8 macrocell diagram. Courtesy of International CMOS Technology, Inc.

output enables. A closer look at the I/O macrocell, FIG. 1-35, shows that it consists of a D-type flip-flop and two signal select multiplexers.

The D-type flip-flop operates similarly to standard TTL D flip-flops to the extent that the D input is latched on the rising edge (low to high transition) of the CLK input and Q or Q̄ output signals can be used. Two additional inputs are controlled by the asynchronous clear and synchronous preset terms.

When the asynchronous clear product term is asserted (high) the Q output is immediately set to a low regardless of the clock state. When the synchronous preset term is asserted (high), the Q output is set to a high on the following rising edge (low to high transition) of the CLK input. Priority is given to the asynchronous clear signal if both asynchronous clear and synchronous preset have been asserted. Upon power-up, the asynchronous clear function is automatically performed setting the Q outputs of all macrocell flip-flops to low.

The two signal select multiplexers of each macrocell are controlled by four E^2PROM programmable bits (A,B,C and D) that determine which of the 12 possible configurations the macrocell will assume. This independent flexibility allows a single PEEL 18CV8 to implement a combination of configurations among its 8 macrocells. The configurations include various arrangements for bidirectional I/O, registered or combinatorial feedback, registered or combinatorial output, and output polarity control.

The versatility of the PEEL makes it an effective alternative to conventional methods of logic design over a broad range of applications.

As an SSI/MSI logic replacement, the PEEL enhances the design process with increased flexibility, higher performance, faster development time, and design security. Manufacturing benefits are also realized by requiring fewer components and interconnects resulting in more efficient use of space, simplified inventory control, and higher reliability.

As a bipolar PAL replacement, the PEEL has comparable speed yet offers several advantages including enhanced design flexibility, simplified inventory control, reduced power consumption, reprogrammability, and 100% factory testability for function and programming.

Design flexibility is of particular importance because the PEEL 18CV8 not only emulates the majority of the 20-pin devices (see TABLE 1-9) but also allows functions found among several PAL device types to be combined. In addition, completely new functions, not supported by the standard PAL devices, can be implemented. This flexibility means a designer can focus on the design rather than on the restrictions of a fixed architecture. Reprogrammability is also a key benefit over one time programmable PALs. This feature adds convenience and cost savings in development prototyping and field retrofitting of systems. Converting existing PAL designs to the PEEL 18CV8 for plug-in replacement is easily accomplished using the PEEL evaluation or development tools.

As a design alternative to low-density gate arrays, one or more PEEL 18CV8s offer a cost-effective and low-risk option. With its architectural flexibility and equivalent gate density of approximately 300 gates, designs traditionally employing low-density gate arrays can be implemented quickly at no factory development (NRE) cost. Unlike the lead times encountered with gate arrays, the PEEL 18CV8 is off-the-shelf available. Furthermore, if a design error is made or an upgrade is necessary, the changes can simply be reprogrammed.

Similar to SSI/MSI logic, PALs and low-density gate arrays, applications of the PEEL 18CV8 cover all the primary areas of system design including data processing, communications, industrial, consumer, military, and transportation. Specific functions implemented using the PEEL 18CV8 range from basic logic

Table 1-9. Gould Electronics, Inc., PEELs.

Part Number	Part Type	Package	Pin Outcode	Pin	Inputs	I/O's	Regs	Macro Configs
173	PEEL	Dip	8D/76	24	12	10	0	2
18CV8	PEEL	Dip	8D/3A	20	10	8	8	12
20CV10	PEEL	Dip	-1-	24	12	10	10	4
20CV10Z	PEEL	Dip	-1-	24	12	10	10	4
253	PEEL	Dip	8D/85	20	8	10	0	2
273	PEEL	Dip	8D/86	24	12	10	0	2

Part Number	Prog. Arrays	Product/Sum Terms	Prop Delay		Supply Current	
			tco(ns)	tpd(ns)	Icc(mA)	Z-Mode
173	AND/OR	42/20	N/A	30-40	35 + 0.5/MHz	no
18CV8	AND	74	15-25	25-50	25 + 0.7/MHz	no
20CV10	AND	90	15-20	25-35	35 + 0.7/MHz	no
20CV10Z	AND	132	15-20	25-35	45 + 1.0/MHz	yes
253	AND/OR	42/20	N/A	30-40	35 + 0.5/MHz	no
273	AND/OR	42/20	N/A	30-40	35 + 0.5/MHz	no

and system support circuitry to stand-alone controllers. In addition, PEELs can emulate the following PLDs:

PEEL DEVICE	Can Emulate These PLDs							
•PEEL18CV8	10H8	12H6	14H4	16H2	16L8	16R4	16R6	16R8
	10L8	12L6	14L4	16L2	16P8	16RP4	16RP6	16RP8
		16HD8	16LD8	18P8	EP310	EP320	16V8	
•PEEL18CV8Z	All of the above plus EP320 (in Zero-Power Mode)							
•PEEL20CG10	12L10	14L4	16L6	18L4	20L2	20L10		
	20L8	20R4	20R6	20R8	20V8	20CG10		
•22CV10(Z)	All of the above plus 22V10							
•PEEL153/253	PLS153	(82S153)	16C1					
•PEEL173/273	PLS173	(82S173)	12L10	20L8	20L10			

ARCHITECTURE OF A CPL

The CPL devices have a programmable AND array followed by a nonprogrammable OR array. Samsung's CPL (CMOS Programmable Logic) devices use a state-of-the-art CMOS EPROM technology that emphasizes complete testability. Figure 1-36 shows the logic diagram of the CPL20L10. The 1.2 micron advanced CMOS process provides high performance, which was previously achieved only with bipolar processes at a much lower power. Testability is inherent to the technology because it allows devices to be programmed and erased, thus facilitating 100% programming, AC, and functional testing.

The first generation of CPL devices are CMOS implementations of the industry standard PAL devices. The CPL devices offer significant advantages over TTL logic, 100% user-programmability, design flexibility, chip-count and pin-count reduction, and pattern duplication prevention (security bit).

The CPL family also offers additional features and benefits which can be attributed to the CMOS EPROM technology 100% programming, AC, and functional testing, increased reliability, easier, lower-cost prototyping with reprogrammable CPL devices (windowed, CERDIP), and lower power consumption over bipolar PALs with matched performance.

The CPL EPROM cells are programmed by charging a floating gate with electrons and unprogrammed by irradiating the cells with ultraviolet (UV) light, making complete testing of all circuitry possible before shipping. On the other hand, bipolar devices that use fuse-programmable cells can be programmed only once, making 100% testing impossible. Special on-chip test arrays also allow additional functional and AC testing without having to program the CPL devices.

CPL devices that are contained in windowed CERDIP packages can be programmed and erased at the customer site. This allows the designer to develop, test, and fine-tune the logic without having to replace each programmed device.

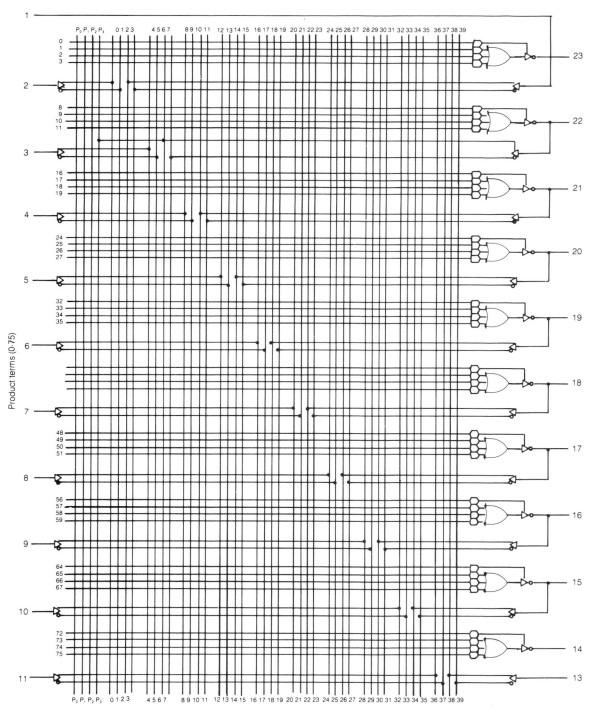

Fig. 1-36. Logic diagram of the CPL20L10. Courtesy of Samsung Semiconductor Corporation.

The CPL family offers the system designer an alternative to the standard bipolar PLDs. The devices function and contains pinouts compatible with their respective PAL predecessors. They can be designed into existing PAL sockets without changing the board layout or the PLD equations. The propagation delays of the CPL devices are 25 ns or 35 ns with 45 mA or 70 mA (max) I_{CC}. Thus, the CPL devices provide bipolar speeds at a fraction of the bipolar power consumption, reducing the system's power requirements and increasing its reliability. The CPL devices utilize the basic PLA (Programmable Logic Array) structure. This structure consists of an AND array followed by an OR array. The CPL devices, like the PAL devices which they might replace, have a programmable AND array followed by a nonprogrammable OR array. Such a structure offers PLA flexibility while decreasing silicon complexity. In comparison, a FPLA (Field Programmable Logic Array) structure has both arrays programmable but occupies more silicon area.

The CPL devices that have a basic PLA structure lend themselves to easy implementation of Boolean transfer functions. These functions are expressed in the sum-of-products form. This allows quick and easy implementation of logic functions of varying complexity.

The CPL devices allow the designer to configure complex interconnections within the chip as opposed to configuring them on the PC board. The design, therefore, becomes more efficient and takes less time to complete. Furthermore, the interconnections made by writing into EPROM cells can be easily modified during prototype testing, saving lengthy and costly printed circuit board changes.

One CPL device can implement logic functions that require four or more conventional logic packages and reduce IC inventories while increasing board savings.

While all CPL devices are based on the PLA structure, they differ in their output structure combinations. The CPL devices feature a variety of output structures including combinatorial outputs, registered outputs, and programmable macrocells (see TABLE 1-10).

Combinational Outputs

There are two types of combinational outputs. The simplest one is a combinatorial output without feedback. It is used in the CPL16L8, CPL20L8, and CPL20L10 devices. This output sums several product terms (P-terms) into an active low signal. One additional P-term is used to individually enable/disable the output signal.

Another type of combinatorial output is the programmable combinatorial I/O. When enabled, this output stage acts like the simple combinatorial output with the addition of a feedback path into the AND array. When disabled, the output stage allows the I/O pin to act as an input into the CPL AND array. This flexibility allows variable input/output ratios as well as bidirectional parts. The programmable combinatorial I/O output is used in all CPL20 and CPL24 devices with the exception of the CPL16R8 and CPL20R8.

Table 1-10. Samsung Semiconductor Corporation CPLs.

Part Number	Part Type	Package	Pin Outcode	Pins	Array Inputs	Dedi- cated Inputs	I/O's	Outputs		Total
								Combi- natorial	Regis- tered	
16L8	CPL	Dip	9D/17	20	16	10	6	8	0	8
16R4	CPL	Dip	9D/24	20	16	8	4	4	4	8
16R6	CPL	Dip	9D/24	20	16	8	2	2	6	8
16R8	CPL	Dip	9D/24	20	16	8	0	0	8	8
20L10	CPL	Dip	9D/06	24	20	12	8	10	0	10
20L8	CPL	Dip	9D/26	24	20	14	6	8	0	8
20R4	CPL	Dip	9D/27	24	20	12	4	4	4	8
20R6	CPL	Dip	9D/27	24	20	12	2	2	6	8
20R8	CPL	Dip	9D/27	24	20	12	0	0	8	8
22V10	CPL	Dip	-	24	22	12	10	Programmable Macrocell Outputs		10
22V10	CPL	Dip	-	20	16	10	8	Programmable Macrocell Outputs		8

Part Number	Max Speed (ns)[1,2]		Max 1cc (mA)	
	− 25	− 35	Low Power	Std Power
16L8	$t_{PD}=25$	$t_{PD}=35$	45	70
16R4	$t_{PD}/t_{CO}=25/15$	$t_{PD}/t_{CO}=35/25$	45	70
16R6	$t_{PD}/t_{CO}=25/15$	$t_{PD}/t_{CO}=35/25$	45	70
16R8	$t_{CO}=15$	$t_{CO}=25$	45	70
20L10	$t_{PD}=25$	$t_{PD}=35$	45	70
20L8	$t_{PD}=25$	$t_{PD}=35$	45	70
20R4	$t_{PD}/t_{CO}=25/15$	$t_{PD}/t_{CO}=35/25$	45	70
20R6	$t_{PD}/t_{CO}=25/15$	$t_{PD}/t_{CO}=35/25$	45	70
20R8	$t_{CO}=15$	$t_{CO}=25$	45	70
22V10	$t_{PD}/t_{CO}=25/15$	$t_{PD}/t_{CO}=35/25$	55	90
16V8	$t_{PD}/t_{CO}=25/15$	$t_{PD}/t_{CO}=35/25$	55	90

[1]The above specifications are for the commercial temperature range of 0 to 70°C. All power supplies are V_{CC} =5V ± 10%

[2]Military product in the temperature ranges of −55°C to +125°C is also available. Speed and power selections may vary from those above. See data sheet.

[3]PLCC and SOIC packages are available. Please contact factory.

Registered Outputs

This type of output features a data register with registered feedback. Each product term is summed into the data input of a D-type flip-flop. The flip-flop records the state of its input on the rising edge of the clock. The Q output of the flip-flop is gated to the output pin through a three-state buffer and is also fed back to the CPL AND array as an input term. This feature allows the CPL device to implement a state machine. The clock and output enable/disable signals are common to all registered outputs of a single device. Registered outputs are used in all CPL20 and CPL24 devices with the exception of CPL16L8, CPL20L8, and CPL20L10.

Programmable Macrocell I/O

The programmable macrocell is a very flexible structure that allows the designer to define the architecture of each I/O separately. Each I/O structure can be configured to be a combinatorial or registered output. Each output features an individually programmable output enable/sizable function as well as an individually programmable polarity function. Common clock, reset, and preset signals facilitate preload, power reset, and state-machine operations. Programmable macrocells are used in the CPL16V8 and CPL22V10 devices.

ARCHITECTURE OF AN EPLD

The Altera Corporation founded in 1983 was the first supplier to overcome these problems of bipolar programmable logic when it introduced its Erasable Programmable Logic Device (EPLD) line of user-programmable logic devices incorporating CMOS floating-gate technology.

Altera's EPLDs are manufactured with high-speed complementary metal oxide semiconductor (CMOS) technology. Compared to bipolar fuse technology, CMOS provides lower power dissipation and a cooler operating temperature which enables designers to pack a greater number of logic functions onto a chip.

EPLDs utilize an EPROM programming mechanism. This technology, used in MOS memories since the early 1970s, brings further advantages. It enables the devices to be reprogrammed in the event of any design changes. The fact that programming can be erased also permits thorough testing during the manufacturing process.

An important aspect of the Altera approach to design tool support is to eliminate the necessity of mastering the inner complexities of EPLD architectures. The user might work in a familiar environment, such as TTL macro functions or a high-level state machine language, and the software automatically translates the design into the format required to fit the EPLD architecture.

Altera's General Purpose EPLDs provide dedicated input pins, user configurable I/O pins, and programmable flip-flop and clock options to insure maximum flexibility for the integration of random logic functions. Many of these features are also present on Altera function-specific EPLDs such as BUSTER.

Within an EPLD, an AND array creates product terms. A product term is simply an n-input AND gate, where n is the number of connections. EPLD schematics use a shorthand *AND-array* notation to represent several large AND gates with common inputs.

An Altera EPLD MacroCell consists of such a programmable AND-array, supporting typically 8 product terms, combined with an 8-input OR gate, a tri-state buffer driving the I/O pin, with a sequential logic block between the OR gate and output buffer. This sequential logic block consists of a flip-flop (either toggle or D-type, depending on device) combined with programmable multiplexers used to control output, and selection of registered or combinatorial output and feedback. Programmable feedback is supported, either from internal logic or from the I/O pin. Some EPLDs provide a dual-feedback option allowing both internal logic and the I/O pin to be buried within the MacroCell and simultaneously use the I/O pin as an additional dedicated input pin. Because each MacroCell can have a different configuration, MacroCell groups provide a powerful logic design base (see TABLE 1-11).

The logic array uses a programmable AND, fixed OR PLA structure. Inputs to the AND array come from the true and complement of the dedicate input and clock pins and from the internal feedback paths.

Connections within the logic array are made using the AND array. At the intersection point of an input signal and a product term (AND gate) is an EPROM connection. In the erased state, all connections are made. This means both the true and complement of all inputs are connected to each product term.

Connections are opened during the programming process. Therefore, any product term can be connected to the true and complement of any array input signal. When both the true and complement of any signal is left intact, a logical false results on the output of the product term. If both the true and complement connection are open, then a logical "don't care" results for that input. If all

Table 1-11. Altera Corporation EPLDs.

ALTERA EPLD PRODUCT SELECTOR GUIDE

General Purpose EPLDs (EP Series).   Random Logic/TTL/PAL Integration

EPLD	Package (1)	Temp (2)	Speed Option	Process (3)	fMAX MHz (4)	Tpdl nS	Icc3 mA (5)	Icc2 mA (6)	Icc1 mA Standby (7)	Macrocells (Registers) (A)	Dedicated Inputs	I/O	Number of Pins	Altera Military Drawing (8)	Status (9)
EP1810	J,L,G	C				30				48	16	48	68		Dev.
EP1810	J,L,G	C	-35		40.0	35	120	45	0.15	48	16	48	68		Prod.
EP1810	J,L,G	I	-40			40	120	45	0.15	48	16	48	68		Prod.
EP1810	J,L,G	C,I,M	-45		33.3	45	120	45	0.15	48	16	48	68		Prod.
EP1810	J,G	M		B	33.3	45	120	45	0.15	48	16	48	68		Dev.
EP1800	J,L,G	C	-2		20.8	65	140	30	0.15	48	16	48	68		Prod.
EP1800	J,L,G	C,I	-3		18.5	75	140 (180)	30 (40)	0.15	48	16	48	68		Prod.
EP1800	J,L,G	C,I,M	—		16.1	85	140 (180)	30 (40)	0.15	48	16	48	68		Prod.
EP1800	J,G	M		883B	18.2	75	180	NA	NA	48	16	48	68	02D-00205	Prod.
EP910	D,P,J,L	C				25				24	12	24	D,P-40 J,L-44		Dev.
EP910	D,P,J,L	C	-30		41.7	30	80	20	0.10	24	12	24	D,P-40 J,L-44		Prod.
EP910	D,P,J,L	C,I	-35		37.0	35	80	20	0.10	24	12	24	D,P-40 J,L-44		Prod.
EP910	D,P,J,L	I	-40		32.3	40	80	20	0.10	24	12	24	D,P-40 J,L-44		Prod.
EP910	D,J	M	-45		28.6	45	100	20	0.15	24	12	24	D-40 J-44		Prod.
EP910	D,J	M		B	28.6	45	100	20	0.15	24	12	24	D-40 J-44		Dev.
EP900	D,P,J,L	C	-2		26.3	45	75	15	0.15	24	12	24	D,P-40 J,L-44		Prod.
EP900	D,P,J,L	C	-3		23.8	50	75	15	0.15	24	12	24	D,P-40 J,L-44		Prod.
EP900	D,P,J,L	C,I,M	—		21.7	55	75 (100)	15 (25)	0.15	24	12	24	D,P-40 J,L-44		Prod.
EP900	D,J	M		883B	20.0	60	100	NA	NA	24	12	24	D,P-40 J-44	02D-00210	Prod.
EP610	D,P,J,L	C				20				16	4	16	D,P-24 J,L-28		Dev.
EP610	D,P,J,L	C	-25		47.6	25	60	10	0.10	16	4	16	D,P-24 J,L-28		Prod.
EP610	D,P,J,L	C,I	-30		41.7	30	60	10	0.10	16	4	16	D,P-24 J,L-28		Prod.

Table 1-11. Continued.

EPLD	Package (1)	Temp (2)	Speed Option	Process (3)	fMAX MHz (4)	Tpdl nS	Icc3 mA (5)	Icc2 mA (6)	Icc1 mA Standby (7)	Macrocells (Registers) (A)	Dedicated Inputs	I/O	Number of Pins	Altera Military Drawing (8)	Status (9)
EP610	D,P,J,L	I	-35		37.0	35	60	10	0.10	16	4	16	D,P-24 J,L-28		Prod.
EP610	D,P,J,L	M	-40		31.3	40	75	15	0.15	16	4	16	D-24 J-28		Prod.
EP610	D,P,J,L	M		B	31.3	40	75	15	0.15	16	4	16	D-24 J-28		Dev.
EP600	D,P,J,L	C,I	-3		26.3	43	50 (60)	10 (15)	0.15	16	4	16	D,P-24 J,L-28		Prod.
EP600	D,P,J,L	C,I,M	—		23.3	53	50 (60)	10 (15)	0.15	16	4	16	D,P-24 J,L-28		Prod.
EP600	D,J	M		883B	22.2	55	60	NA	NA	16	4	16	D-24 J-28	02D-00194	Prod.
8686401LX	D	M		DESC	22.2	55	60	NA	NA	16	4	16	D-24		Prod.
8686401XX	J	M		DESC	22.2	55	60	NA	NA	16	4	16	J-28		Dev.
EP512	D,P	C	-25		25					12					Smple.
EP512	D,P	C	-30		30					12					Smple.
EP320	D,P	C	-1		45.5	29	30	5	0.15	8	10	8	20		Prod.
EP320	D,P	C	-2		40.0	34	30	5	0.15	8	10	8	20		Prod.
EP320	D,P	C,I,M	—		30.3	44	30 (40)	5 (15)	0.15	8	10	8	20		Prod.
EP320	D	M		883B	30.3	45	40	NA	NA	8	10	8	20	02D-00209	Prod.
EP310	D	C	-2		35.7	35		40	30	8	10	8	20		Prod.
EP310	D	C	-3		33.3	40		40	30	8	10	8	20		Prod.
EP310	D	C,I,M	—		31.3	50		40	30 (35)	8	10	8	20		Prod.
EP310	D	M		883B	31.3	50		40	NA	8	10	8	20	02D-00179	Prod.

(A) All EPLD Macrocell flip-flops can be configured as D,JK,SR or T. (The EP310 and EP320 are available with D-type flip-flops only.)

ALTERA MAX EPLD PRODUCT SELECTOR GUIDE

General Purpose EPLDs (MAX Series).   Register Intensive Random Logic/TTL/PAL Integration

EPLD	Package (1)	Temp. (2)	Speed Option	fMAX MHz (4)	Tpd1 nS	Icc3 mA	Icc1 mA Standby	Macrocells (Registers) (A)	Maximum Latches(B)	Dedicated Inputs	I/O	Number of Pins	Status (8)
EPM5128	J,L,G	C	-2	50.0	30	155	150	128	256	8	52	68	Smple.
EPM5128	J,L,G	C	—	40.0	35	155	150	128	256	8	52	68	Smple.
EPM5128	J,L,G	I,M						128	256	8	52	68	Dev.
EPM5127	D,P,J,L	C	-2	50.0	30	155	150	128	256	8	28	D,P-40 J,L-44	Dev.
EPM5127	D,P,J,L	C	—	40.0	35	155	150	128	256	8	28	D,P-40 J,L-44	Dev.
EPM5127	D,P,J,L	I,M						128	256	8	28	D,P-40 J,L-44	Dev.
EPM5064	D,P,J,L	C	-2		25			64	128	8	28	D,P-40 J,L-44	Dev.
EPM5064	D,P,J,L	C	—		35			64	128	8	28	D,P-40 J,L-44	Dev.
EPM5064	D,P,J,L	I,M						64	128	8	28	D,P-40 J,L-44	Dev.
EPM5032	D,P,J,L	C	-2	83.3	20	125	120	32	64	8	16	D,P-28 J,L-28	Smple.
EPM5032	D,P,J,L	C	—	71.4	25	125	120	32	64	8	16	D,P-28 J,L-28	Smple.
EPM5032	D,P,J,L	I,M						32	64	8	16	D,P-28 J,L-28	Dev.
EPM5024	D,P,J,L	C	-2		15			24	48	8	12	24	Dev.
EPM5024	D,P,J,L	C	—		25			24	48	8	12	24	Dev.
EPM5024	D,P,J,L	I,M						24	48	8	12	24	Dev.
EPM5016	D,P	C	-2		15			16	32	8	8	20	Dev.
EPM5016	D,P	C	—		25			16	32	8	8	20	Dev.
EPM5016	D,P	I,M						16	32	8	8	20	Dev.

(A) All MAX EPLD Macrocell flip-flops can be configured as D, JK, SR or T.
(B) Calculated when all Expander Product Terms are used to implement latches.

(1) See Product Ordering Information for appropriate package configuration descriptions.
(2) C = Commercial (0°C to +70°C), I = Industrial (-40°C to +85°C) and M = Military (-55°C to +125°C).
(3) Standard Altera reliability flows exept where noted:
883B - Processed to MIL-STD-883, Rev. C, Class B specifications
B   - Military operating temperature with 160 hour burn-in.
DESC- DESC Standard Military Drawing (SMD) device.
(4) The fMAX values shown represent the highest frequency for pipelined data
(5) Turbo mode. Figures in () pertain to industrial and military temperature versions.

(6) Non-turbo, active mode. Figures in () pertain to industrial and military temperature version.
(7) Non-turbo, standby mode. Figures in () pertain to industrial and military temperature versions.
(8) A Military Product Drawing, prepared in accordance with appropriate military specification formats, is available to provide guidance for the preparation of Source Control Drawings (SCD). Please contact Altera Marketing at (408) 984-2800 x101 to obtain 883 Product drawings.
(9) Dev. = In development; Prod. = In Production.
Smple. = Sample — product available in limited quantities.

inputs for the product term are programmed opened, a logical true results on the output of the product term.

For increased flexibility, general purpose EPLDs provide programmable I/O architectures. Both the macrocell output and feedback selection can be independently configured. Their operation is controlled by a multiplexer whose selection is determined by the programmed state of EPROM cells as shown in FIG. 1-37. Each macrocell I/O architecture can be individually configured.

A macrocell and its associated I/O pin can act as a combinatorial output, a registered output, an input, a combinatorial output with combinatorial feedback, or a registered output with registered feedback. (EP310 provides combinatorial output with registered feedback and registered output with combinatorial feedback.) In addition, certain devices allow dual feedback on the outputs, allowing

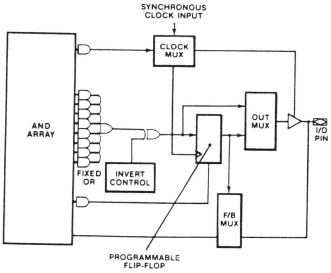

Fig. 1-37. Input/output macrocell. Courtesy of Altera Corporation.

the macrocell to be used as an embedded register and, at the same time, function as an input pin.

Programmable flip-flops are used in many Altera EPLDs to create a variety of logic functions in an efficient manner. Each flip-flop can be programmed to provide a conventional D-type, JK, Toggle, or SR function. This is coded into the JEDEC file by A+PLUS design software. The designer merely sets bits to perform three functions:

1) Inversion Control (De Morgan's theorem).
2) Selection of register type.
3) Distribution of product terms.

Selection of inversion controls is determined from results of A+PLUS computations to decide whether true or complement forms of logic will yield reduced demand for product terms. Figure 1-38 illustrates a function that would require six product terms as drawn. Fortunately, De Morgan's theorem allows reduction to just one product term. The OR gate can be transformed into a NAND gate using De Morgan's conversion:

$$A+B+C+D+E+F \ = \ /(/A*/B*/C*/D*/E*/F)$$

This conversion from OR to AND allows translation of the desired equation and reduces the number of fixed OR terms required in the logic array. This conversion must be done by hand when using most programmable logic tools before the equation can be entered for device programming. Altera software tools automatically apply De Morgan's translations to optimize use of the EPLD array.

The next programmable function is selection of the flip-flop type. A classical view of flip-flop types presents the JK flip-flop as the master configuration from which many others can be constructed. Figure 1-39 illustrates Toggle, D-type, and SR flops derived from the JK type. From this it would be a natural approach to build a basic JK flip-flop and program it to provide the simpler derivations. This technique has been used in some early generation PLDs, but suffers from a major limitation because there is no provision to distribute product terms between J and K inputs. An additional programmable OR array provided this product term allocation. However, this carries the penalty of additional propagation delay.

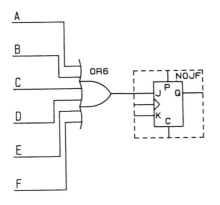

Fig. 1-38. Function that requires six product terms. Courtesy of Altera Corporation.

Altera EPLDs use a flip-flop that is programmed by a single EPROM bit to operate either as a D or Toggle flip-flop. This allows the EPLD to be programmed as a JK with provisions for inversion control and product term distribution. Figure 1-40 shows the Toggle flip-flop used to produce the JK function. The additional gating (for this or other possible flip-flop types) is automatically selected by the A+PLUS design processor, which also handles distribution of terms automatically. This approach does not require the additional programmable logic array, thus eliminating a speed penalty.

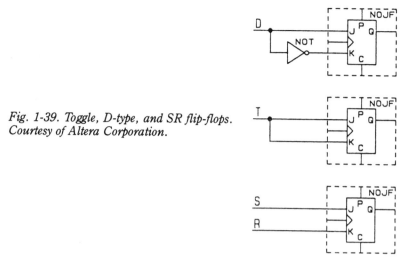

Fig. 1-39. Toggle, D-type, and SR flip-flops.
Courtesy of Altera Corporation.

In general purpose EPLDs (except the 310 and 1210), each internal flip-flop can be clocked independently or in user-defined groups. Any input or internal logic function can be used as a clock. These clock signals are activated by driving the flip-flop clock input with a clock buffer primitive (CLKB). In this mode, flip-flops can be configured for positive or negative edge triggered operation.

External pins which can be programmed as input clocks are provided in certain devices. Direct connection gives enhanced clock-to-output delay times

Function Table

J	K	Qn	Qn + 1
0	0	0	0
0	0	1	1
0	1	0	0
0	1	1	0
1	0	0	1
1	0	1	1
1	1	0	1
1	1	1	0

Fig. 1-40. Toggle flip-flop used to produce JK function. Courtesy of Altera Corporation.

compared to internally generated clock signals. System clocks are positive edge-triggered with data transitions occurring on the rising edge of the clock.

The output configuration EPROM bits include support for an output enable function for each output pin. Microcoded SAM devices provide a bit in the microcode to enable or disable the output on each microcode step.

CMOS technology generally implies lower power dissipation than older bipolar technology. However, the Altera EP600 pioneered true "zero-standby" power operation. Utilizing a unique input-transition detection scheme, the device requires only microamp currents during quiescent periods. Using this feature saves power in applications clocked at low to medium frequencies. Each input is connected to a transition-detection circuit consisting of an exclusive OR, delay element, and OR gate. The trigger output of the OR gate activates logic array power on any transition, allowing new input conditions to propagate to device outputs. The logic array is then automatically powered-down to await the next transition. The transition-detection circuitry does add a 30-40% additional delay in the device input/output path. A programmable Turbo bit is provided to disable the input transition detection circuitry and permanently enable the logic array, giving the user the choice of extra speed versus power consumption. The device also exhibits better system noise rejection characteristics in the Turbo mode, and this mode should be used where noisy environments are a problem. These Turbo bits are included in the JEDEC programming file and programmed like any other EPROM bit.

In the past, all programmable logic products were implemented using bipolar fuse technology. These products eliminated the lead time and development cost penalties of the mask customized solutions previously mentioned, but brought with them their own inherent limitations:

- Bipolar fuse technology, with its high power dissipation, cannot provide the integration density required.
- Bipolar fuse programming does not allow complete testing at the factory and is inefficient in silicon utilization according to some industry experts.
- The devices can only be programmed once; therefore, mistakes in development result in scrap, a significant penalty with high-density parts.
- Some of the programming software and development tools are primitive and tedious to use.

Consider, the EP1800 (FIG. 1-41) Series of CMOS EPLD from Altera offer LSI density, TTL equivalent speed performance, and low power consumption. Each device is capable of implementing over 2100 equivalent gates of SSI, MSI, and custom logic circuits. The EP1800 series is packaged a 68-pin J-leaded chip carrier and pin grid array, available in ceramic (erasable) and plastic (one-time-programmable) versions.

The EP1800 series is designed as an LSI replacement for traditional low power Schottky TTL logic circuits. Its speed and density also make it suitable for high-performance complex functions such as dedicated peripheral controllers and intelligent support chips. IC count and power requirements can be

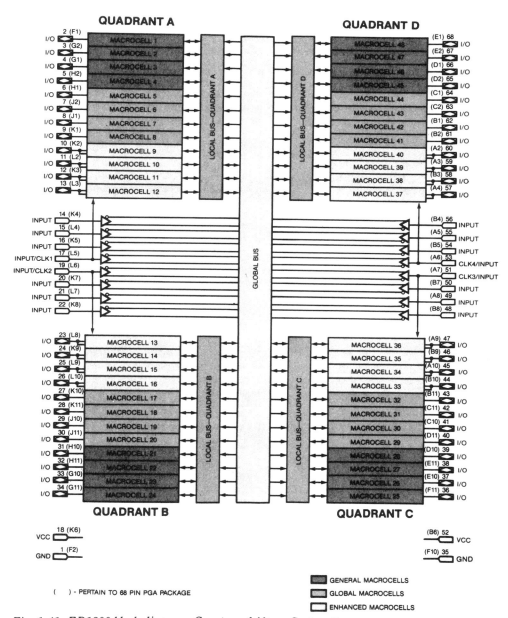

Fig. 1-41. EP1800 block diagram. Courtesy of Altera Corporation.

reduced by several orders of magnitude allowing similar reduction in total size and cost of the system, with significantly enhanced reliability.

The EP1800 architecture has been configured to facilitate design with conventional TTL, SSI, and MSI building blocks as well as simple, optimized gate and flip-flop elements. Schematic descriptions of these functions are stored in a library. The desired TTL logic functions are selected and interconnected on-screen with a low-cost, personal-computer-based workstation. The Design Processor within Altera's A+PLUS Development System then automatically places the functions in appropriate locations within the EPLDs internal structure. Also included in the Development System is EPLD programming hardware and software. A+PLUS is available for the IBM Personal Computer (and compatibles) and VAX environments.

INTEL 5C060 H-EPLD

The Intel 5C060 H-EPLD (H-series Programmable Logic Device) is capable of implementing over 600 equivalent gates of user-customized logic functions through programming. The device can be used to replace low-end gate arrays, multiple programmable logic arrays, and LS, TTL, and 74HC (CMOS) SSI and MSI logic devices. The 5C060 can also be used as a direct, low-power replacement for most common 24-pin fuse-based programmable logic devices. With its revolutionary programmable I/O architecture, the device has advanced functional capabilities beyond that of typical programmable logic (see TABLE 1-12).

The 5C060 H-EPLD uses CHMOS EPROM (floating gate) cells as logic control elements instead of fuses. The CHMOS EPROM technology reduces power consumption of H-EPLDs to less than 20% of a comparable bipolar device without sacrificing speed performance. In addition, Intel's advanced CHMOS II-E EPROM process technology enables greater logic densities to be achieved with superior speed and low-power performance over other comparable devices. Intel's H-EPLDs add the benefits of ''zero'' stand-by power not available on other programmable logic devices. EPROM technology allows these devices to be 100% factory tested by programming and erasing all the EPROM logic control elements.

The erasability of EPLDs introduces the designer to a new concept in hardware design called *Modular EPLD Logic Design* (MELD). Just as modular software design speeds development time and reduces errors by isolating them to a specific module, the MELD philosophy aids in hardware design. A designer can develop a modular design on the Intel Programmable Logic Development System II (iPLDS II) and test individual modules for functionality. If one of the modules has a design flaw, the designer merely erases the part and starts anew (because the 5C060 is EPROM-based, there is no waste associated with modular design as there would be in fuse-based PLDs).

The architecture of the 5C060 is based on the sum-of-products PLA (Programmable Logic Array) structure with a programmable AND array feeding into a fixed OR array. The device accommodates combinational and sequential logic functions. A proprietary programmable I/O architecture provides individual selection of either combinatorial or registered output and feedback signals all with selectable polarity.

A feature unique to the 5C060 is the ability to individually program the output registers as a D-, T-, SR-, or JK-type flip-flop without sacrificing the utilization of programmable AND logic. Additionally, each output register can be individually clocked from any of the input or feedback paths available within the AND array. With these features, a wide variety of logic functions can be simultaneously implemented—all on the same device.

Architecture Description

Externally, the 5C060 has 4 dedicated data input pins, 16, I/O pins that can be configured, for input, output, or bidirectional operations, and 2 synchronous clock inputs. The 5C060 is contained in a 24-pin windowed package (0.3 inch wide) or 28-lead J-leaded chip carrier package and contains 16 programmable registers.

The basic macrocell architecture for the 5C060 is shown in FIG. 1-42. The 5C060 has 16 of these macrocells (one for each I/O pin). The macrocell is organized in the familiar sum-of-products structure with a programmable AND array attached to a fixed OR term. The inputs to the programmable AND array originate from the true and complement signals form each of the dedicated input pins and each of the I/O control blocks. The 40-input AND array of the 5C060 feeds 160 AND gates (product terms) that are distributed among the 16 available macrocells within that device. The global device architecture is shown in FIG. 1-43.

The macrocells contain ten product terms total. Eight of the ten product terms (AND gates) are dedicated for logic implementation. One product term on each macrocell is used for RESET control to the output register associated with the macrocell. The final product term is used for Output Enable/Asynchronous Clock implementation.

Within the AND array, there is an EPROM connection at every intersection of an input signal (true and complement) and a product term to a given macrocell. Before programming an erased device, every EPROM connection is made at every intersection. But during the programming process, these connections are opened so that only the desired connections remain. Therefore, the true or complement of any input signal can be connected to any product term. If both the true and complement connections of any signal are left intact, a logical false results on the output of the AND gate. However, if both the true and complement connections are open, then a logic "don't care" results on the AND gate. Lastly, if all the inputs of a product term are programmed open, then a logical true results on the output of the AND gate.

The 5C060 has two dedicated clock inputs to provide synchronous clock signals to the internal registers. Each of the clock signals controls half the total registers within the given device. For example, CLK1 provides synchronous clocking to the registers in macrocells in the left half of the array while CLK2 controls the registers associated with macrocells in the right half of the array.

Table 1-12. Intel Corporation EPLDs.

Part Type Selector Guide

Part Number	Part Types	Pins	Package Type	Family/ Pinout Codes	(# of Macrocells) Programmable Arrays	Total # of (Product Terms) Product/ Sum Terms	tpd Speed (ns)	Current (mA)
5C031	EPLD	20	DIP	55/50	8	74	40	40
5C032	EPLD	20	DIP	55/95	8	72	25	25
5C032	EPLD	20	PDIP	55/95	8	72	25	25
5C060	EPLD	24	DIP	55/59	16	160	45	15
5C060	EPLD	24	PDIP	55/59	16	160	45	15
5C060	EPLD	24	PLCC	55/59	16	160	45	15
5C090	EPLD	40	DIP	55/96	24	240	50	25
5C090	EPLD	40	PDIP	55/96	24	240	50	25
5C090	EPLD	44	JLCC	055/796	24	240	50	25
5C090	EPLD	44	PLCC	055/796	24	240	50	25
5C121	EPLD	40	DIP	55/97	28	263	50	50
5C180	EPLD	68	JLCC	55/9A	48	480	70	45
5C180	EPLD	68	PLCC	55/9A	48	480	70	45
5AC312	EPLD	24	DIP		12	200	25	50
5AC312	EPLD	24	PDIP		12	200	25	50
5AC312	EPLD	28	PLCC		12	200	25	50
5AC324	EPLD	40	DIP		24	394	35	50
5AC324	EPLD	40	PDIP		24	394	35	50
5AC324	EPLD	44	JLCC		24	394	35	50

Table 1-12. Continued.

Part Number	Part Types	Number of Inputs	Macrocell I/O Configuration											
			Registered Output						Combinatorial Output					
			Bidirectional Input/Output		Combinational Feedback		Register Feedback		Bidirectional Input/Output		Combinational Feedback		Register Feedback	
			AL	AH	AL	AH	AL	AH	AL	AH	AL	AH	AL	AH
5C031	EPLD	18 (10 dedicated 8 I/O)	X	X	X	X	X	X	X	X	X	X	X	X
5C032	EPLD	18 (10 dedicated 8 I/O)	X		X	X		X	X	X				
5C060	EPLD	20 (4 dedicated 16 I/O)	X	X			X	X	X	X				
5C060	EPLD	20 (4 dedicated 16 I/O)	X	X			X	X	X	X				
5C090	EPLD	36 (12 dedicated 24 I/O)	X	X			X	X	X	X				
5C090	EPLD	36 (12 dedicated 24 I/O)	X	X			X	X	X	X				
5C121	EPLD	36 (12 dedicated 24 I/O)	X	X			X	X	X	X			X	X
5C180	EPLD	64 (16 dedicated 48 I/O)	X	X			X	X	X	X	X	X		
5AC312	EPLD	22 (10 dedicated 12 I/O)	X	X			X	X	X	X	X	X		
5AC312	EPLD	22 (10 dedicated 12 I/O)	X	X			X	X	X	X	X	X		
5AC324	EPLD	36 (12 dedicated 12 I/O)	X	X			X	X	X	X	X	X		
5AC324	EPLD	36 (12 dedicated 12 I/O)	X	X			X	X	X	X	X	X		

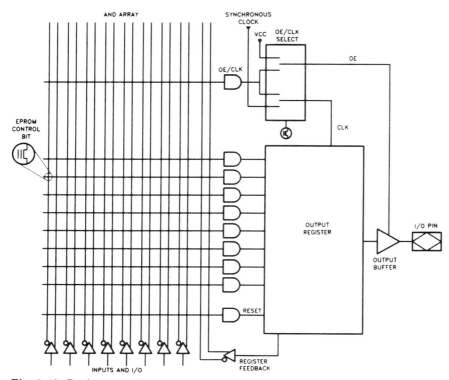

Fig. 1-42. Basic macrocell architecture of the 5C060. Courtesy of Intel Corporation.

The advanced I/O architecture allows for any number of the registers to be synchronously clocked (from none to all). Both of the dedicated clock inputs latch the data into a given register when triggered on a positive edge.

Macrocell Architecture Selection

The 5C060 architecture provides each macrocell with over 50 different possible I/O register configurations. Each I/O pin can be configured for combinatorial or registered output (true or complement) with feedback. In addition, 4 different types of output registers can be implemented into every I/O pin without any additional logic requirements. The feedback mechanism for each register back into the AND array can be programmed to provide for either registered feedback from the macrocell or input feedback (treating the pin as an input). Another advantage of the advanced I/O capability of the 5C060 is the ability to individually clock each internal register from asynchronous clock signals.

Output Enable (OE) Clock Selection. Two modes of operation are provided by the OE/CLK Select Multiplexer as a part of each macrocell. One mode provides for three-state buffering of outputs. In the other mode, the outputs are always enabled. The operation of the OE/CLK Select Multiplexer sets the mode within a given macrocell. Therefore, the output mode can be selected

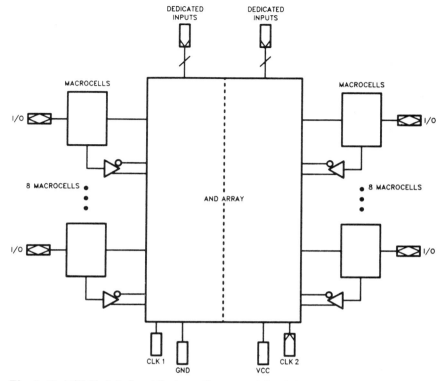

Fig. 1-43. 5C060 global architecture. Courtesy of Intel Corporation.

individually on every output. Figure 1-44 illustrates the two modes of OE/CLK operation.

Mode 0: Three-State Buffering. In Mode 0, the three-state output buffer is controlled by a single product term originating from the AND array. The output is enabled when the product term is a logical true. Conversely, the output appears as high impedance when the product term is a logical false as shown in TABLE 1-13. In Mode 0, the macrocell flip-flop is connected to its associated synchronous clock (either CLK1 or CLK2 depending upon the macrocell's location within the device). Thus, the macrocell flip-flop can be clocked by its respective synchronous clock but its output will not become valid until the output is enabled.

Mode 1: Output Buffer Enabled. In Mode 1, the output buffer is always enabled. In addition, the macrocell flip-flop is connected to the AND array. The macrocell flip-flop can now be triggered from an asynchronous clock signal generated by the AND array logic to the OE/CLK multiplexable term. Mode 1 allows the macrocell flip-flops to be clocked individually from any of the available signals in the AND array. Because both true and complement values appear in the AND array, the flip-flop can be configured to trigger on positive or negative clock edges. Gated clock structures can be created because the flip-flop clock is created by a product term.

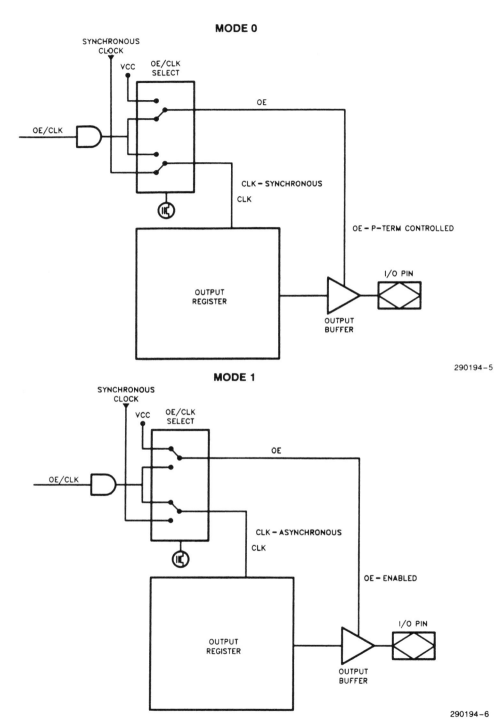

Fig. 1-44. Output enable/clock configuration. Courtesy of Intel Corporation.

Product Term	Output Buffer
FALSE	Three-State
TRUE	Enabled

Table 1-13. Mode O output selection.

Invert Select EPROM Bit. The Invert Select EPROM bit is used to invert the product term input into the register. This applies to all inputs including double inputs on the JK and SR registers.

Register Selection

The advanced I/O architecture of the 5C060 allows four different register types along with combinatorial output as illustrated in FIG. 1-45. The register types include T, D, JK, or SR flip-flop and each macrocell I/O structure can be independently configured. In addition, all registers have an individual asynchronous RESET control from a dedicated product term derived in the AND array. When this dedicated product term is a logical one, the macrocell register is immediately cleared to a logical zero independent of the register clock. The RESET function occurs automatically on power-up.

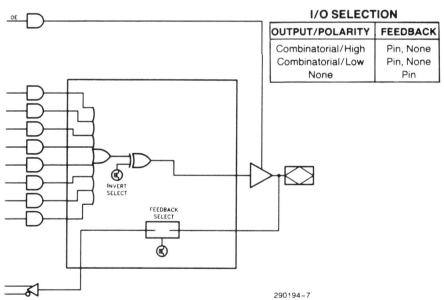

I/O SELECTION	
OUTPUT/POLARITY	**FEEDBACK**
Combinatorial/High	Pin, None
Combinatorial/Low	Pin, None
None	Pin

290194-7

Fig. 1-45. Combinatorial I/O configuration. Courtesy of Intel Corporation.

Output Register Configuration. The four different register types are shown in FIGS. 1-46 through 1-49.

D- or T-type flip-flops. When either a D- or T-type flip-flop is configured as part of the I/O structure, all eight of the product terms into the macrocell are ORed together and fed into the register input.

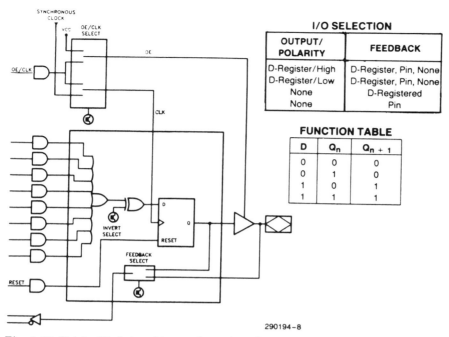

I/O SELECTION

OUTPUT/ POLARITY	FEEDBACK
D-Register/High	D-Register, Pin, None
D-Register/Low	D-Register, Pin, None
None	D-Registered
None	Pin

FUNCTION TABLE

D	Q_n	Q_{n+1}
0	0	0
0	1	0
1	0	1
1	1	1

290194-8

Fig. 1-46. D-type flip-flop register configuration. Courtesy of Intel Corporation.

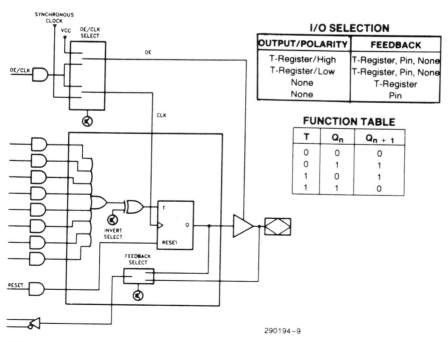

I/O SELECTION

OUTPUT/POLARITY	FEEDBACK
T-Register/High	T-Register, Pin, None
T-Register/Low	T-Register, Pin, None
None	T-Register
None	Pin

FUNCTION TABLE

T	Q_n	Q_{n+1}
0	0	0
0	1	1
1	0	1
1	1	0

290194-9

Fig. 1-47. Toggle flip-flop register configuration. Courtesy of Intel Corporation.

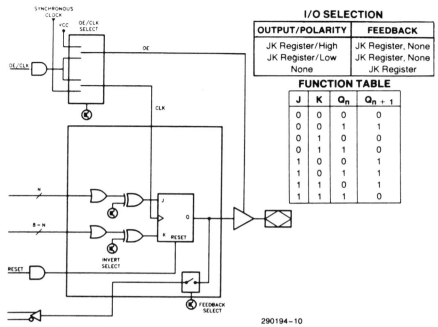

I/O SELECTION

OUTPUT/POLARITY	FEEDBACK
JK Register/High	JK Register, None
JK Register/Low	JK Register, None
None	JK Register

FUNCTION TABLE

J	K	Q_n	Q_{n+1}
0	0	0	0
0	0	1	1
0	1	0	0
0	1	1	0
1	0	0	1
1	0	1	1
1	1	0	1
1	1	1	0

290194-10

Fig. 1-48. JK flip-flop register configuration. Courtesy of Intel Corporation.

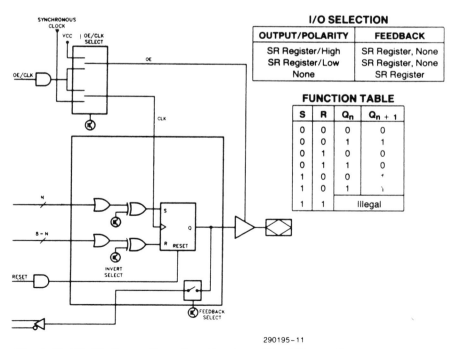

I/O SELECTION

OUTPUT/POLARITY	FEEDBACK
SR Register/High	SR Register, None
SR Register/Low	SR Register, None
None	SR Register

FUNCTION TABLE

S	R	Q_n	Q_{n+1}
0	0	0	0
0	0	1	1
0	1	0	0
0	1	1	0
1	0	0	1
1	0	1	1
1	1	Illegal	

290195-11

Fig. 1-49. SR flip-flop configuration. Courtesy of Intel Corporation.

JK or SR Registers. When either a JK or SR register is configured, the eight product terms are shared among two OR gates (one for the J or S input and the other for the K or R input). The allocation for these product terms for each of the register inputs is optimized by the iPLDS II development software.

Output/Feedback

The Output Select Multiplexer allows for either registered, combinatorial, or no output.

The Feedback Select Multiplexer EPROM bit enables registered, I/O (Using the pin for bidirectional input or just input), or no feedback to the AND array. The Feedback Select is also important for building product terms with more than eight products. The eight-product product term of a macrocell can be fed back into the AND array and combined with still more signals to create a much larger product term (of more than eight-inputs). In addition, if the feed-back product term is not to be output, then the iPLDS II *reserves* the associated macrocell pin and indicate it in the REPORT file. A reserved pin should be left floating (no connect) when assembled onto a circuit board.

Any I/O pin can be configured as a dedicated input by selecting no output and pin feedback through the appropriate multiplexers.

Prior to programming or after erasing, the I/O structure is configured for combinatorial active low output with input (pin) feedback.

Erasure Characteristics

Erasure characteristics of the device are such that erasure begins to occur upon exposure to light with wavelengths shorter than approximately 4000 A. It should be noted that sunlight and certain types of fluorescent lamps have wavelengths in the 3000 A – 4000 A. Data shows that constant exposure to room level fluorescent lighting could erase the typical device in approximately three years, while it would take approximately one week to cause erasure when exposed to direct sunlight. If the 5C060 is to be exposed to these types of lighting conditions for extended periods of time, conductive opaque labels should be placed over the device window to prevent unintentional erasure.

The recommended erasure procedure for the 5C060 is exposure to short-wave ultraviolet light with a wavelength of 2537 A. The integrated dose (i.e., UV intensity × exposure time) for erasure should be a minimum of 15 Wsec/cm^2. The erasure time with this dosage is approximately 15 to 20 minutes using an ultraviolet lamp with a 12,000 uW/cm^2 power rating. The 5C060 should be placed within one inch of the lamp tubes during erasure. The maximum integrated dose the 5C060 can be exposed to without damage is 7258 Wsec/cm^2 (1 week at 12,000 W/cm2). Exposure to high intensity UV light for longer periods may cause permanent damage to the device.

Programming Characteristics

Initially and after erasure, all the EPROM control bits of the 5C060 are connected (in the 1 state). Each of the connected control bits are selectively disconnected by programming the EPROM cells into their 0 state. Programming voltage and waveform specifications are available by request from Intel to support programming of the 5C060.

The 5C060 supports the intelligent Programming Algorithm which rapidly programs Intel H-EPLDs (and EPROMs) using an efficient and reliable method. The Intelligent Programming Algorithm is particularly suited to the production programming environment. This method greatly decreases the overall programming time while programming reliability is ensured as the incremental program margin of each bit is continually monitored to determine when the bit has been successfully programmed.

Functional Testing

Because the logical operation of the 5C060 is controlled by EPROM elements, the device is completely testable. Each programmable EPROM bit controlling the internal logic is tested using application-independent test program patterns. After testing, the devices are erased before shipment to customers. No post-programming tests of the EPROM array are required.

The testability and reliability of EPROM-based programmable logic devices is an important feature over similar devices based on fuse technology. Fuse-based programmable logic devices require a user to perform post-programming tests to insure proper programming. These tests must be done at the device level because of the cumulative error effect. For example, a board containing 10 devices each possessing a 2% device fallout translates into an 18% fallout at the board level. (It should be noted that programming fallout of fuse-based programmable logic devices is typically 2% or higher.)

Design Recommendations

For proper operation, it is recommended that all input and output pins be constrained to the voltage range $GND < (V_{IN}$ or $V_{OUT}) < V_{CC}$. Unused inputs should be tied to an appropriate logic level (e.g., either V_{CC} or GND) to minimize device power consumption. Reserved pins (as indicated in the logic compiler REPORT file) should be left floating (no connect) so that the pin can attain the appropriate logic level. A power supply decoupling capacitor of at least 0.2 F must be connected directly between V_{CC} and GND pins of the device.

As with all CMOS devices, ESD handling procedures should be used with the 5C060 to prevent damage to the device during programming, assembly, and test.

Design Security

A single EPROM bit provides a programmable design security feature that controls the access to the data programmed into the device. If this bit is set, a proprietary design within the device cannot be copied. This EPROM security bit enables a higher degree of design security than fused-based devices because programmed data with EPROM cells is invisible even to microscopic evaluation. The EPROM security bit, along with all the other EPROM control bits, is reset by erasing the device.

Automatic Standby Mode

The 5C060 contains a programmable bit, the Turbo Bit, that optimizes operation for speed or for power savings. When the Turbo Bit is programmed (TURBO = ON), the device is optimized for maximum speed. When the Turbo Bit is not programmed (TURBO = OFF), the device is optimized for power savings by entering standby mode during periods of inactivity.

Figure 1-50 shows the device entering standby mode approximately 100 ns after the last input transition. When the next input transition is detected, the device returns to active mode. Wakeup time adds an additional 25 ns to the propagation delay through the device as measured from the first input. No delay occurs if an output is dependent on more than one input and the last of the inputs changes after the device has returned to active mode.

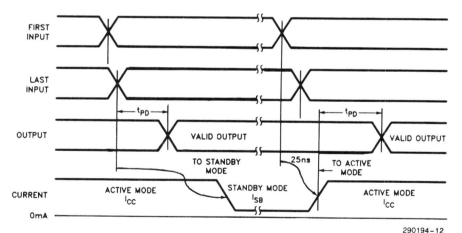

290194–12

Fig. 1-50. 5C060 standby and active mode transitions. Courtesy of Intel Corporation.

After erasure, the Turbo Bit is unprogrammed (OFF), and the automatic standby mode is enabled. When the Turbo Bit is programmed (ON), the device never enters standby mode.

Latch-Up Immunity

All of the input, I/O, and clock pins of the 5C060 have been designed to resist latch-up, which is inherent in inferior CMOS structures. The 5C060 is designed with Intel's proprietary CHMOS II-E EPROM process. Thus, each of the pins will not experience latch-up with currents up to 100 mA and voltages ranging from $-V$ to $V_{CC} + 1$ V. Furthermore, the programming pin is designed to resist latch-up to the 13.5 V maximum device limit.

CYPRESS SEMICONDUCTOR CMOS EPLD FAMILY

Cypress Semiconductor's EPLD family offers the user the next generation in Erasable Programmable Logic Devices (EPLD) based on a high performance 0.8 CMOS process. These devices offer the user the power saving of a CMOS-based process, with delay times equivalent to those previously found only in bipolar devices. No fuses are used in Cypress' EPLD family (shown in TABLE 1-14) rather all devices are based on an EPROM cell to facilitate programming. By using an EPROM cell instead of fuses, programming yields of 100% can be expected because all devices are functionally tested and erased prior to packaging. Therefore, no programming yield loss can be expected by the user.

Table 1-14. Cypress EPLs.

Part Number	Technology	$t_{Pd}1$ (ns)	Icc (mA)	Inputs	Outputs Comb	Reg
16L8	CMOS	25	70	16	8	
16R8	CMOS	25	70	16		8
16R6	CMOS	25	70	16	2	6
16R4	CMOS	25	70	16	4	4
20G10	CMOS	35	70	13	Programmable Macrocell, 4 Registered, 4 Combinatorial	
CY7C330	CMOS	20	120	11	12 I/O Programmable Macrocells	
CY7C331	CMOS	25	120	13	12 I/O Programmable Macrocells	
CY7C332	CMOS	20	120	25	12 I/O Programmable Macrocells	
22V10	CMOS	15 to 35	90	13	Programmable Macrocells	

The EPROM cell used by Cypress serves the same purpose as the fuse used in most bipolar PLD devices. Before programming, the AND gates or product terms are connected via the EPROM cells to both the true and complement inputs. When the EPROM cell is programmed, the inputs from a gate or product term are disconnected. Programming alters the transistor threshold of each cell so that no conduction can occur, which is equivalent to disconnecting the input from the gate or product terms. This is similar to ''blowing'' the fuses of a bipolar device which disconnects the input gate from the product term. Selective programming of each of these EPROM cells enables the specific logic function to be implemented by the user.

The programmability of Cypress' EPLDs allows the users to customize every device in a number of ways to implement their unique logic requirements. Using EPLDs in the place of SSI or MSI components results in more effective utilization of board space, reduced cost, and increased reliability. The flexibility afforded by these EPLDs allows the designer to implement quickly and effectively a number of logic functions ranging from random logic gate replacement to complex combinatorial logic functions.

The EPLD family implements the familiar sum-of-products logic by using a programmable AND array with output terms that feed a fixed OR array. The sum of these can be expressed in a Boolean transfer function and is limited only by the number of product terms available in the AND-OR array. A variety of different sizes and architectures are available. This allows for more efficient logic optimization by matching input, output, and product terms to the desired application.

PLD Circuit Configurations

Cypress EPLDs have several different output configurations that cover a wide spectrum of applications. The available output configurations offer the user the benefits of both lower package counts and reduced costs when used. This approach allows the designer to select a PLD that best fits the needs of his application. An example of some of the configurations that are available are listed in following paragraphs.

Programmable I/O

Programmable I/O offered in the Cypress EPLD family allows product terms to directly control the outputs of the device. One product term is used to directly control the three-state output buffer, which then gates the summation of the remaining terms to the output pin. The output of this summation can be fed back into the PLD as an input to the array. This programmable I/O feature allows the PLD to drive the output pin when the three-state output is enabled, or the I/O pin can be used as an input to the array when the three-state output is disabled.

Registered Outputs with Feedback

Registered output capability, which is offered on a number of the Cypress EPLDs, allows this circuit to function as a state sequencer. The summation of the product terms is stored in the D-type output flip-flop on the rising edge of the system clock. The Q output of the flip-flop can then be gated to the output pin by enabling the three-state output buffer. The output of the flip-flop can also be fed back into the array as an input term. The output feedback feature allows the PLD to remember and then alter its function based upon that state. This circuit can be used to execute such functions as counting, skip, shift, and branch.

Buried Register Feedback

A number of Cypress EPLDs provide registers that might be buried or hidden to create registers for state machine implementation without sacrificing the use of the associated device pin. The device pin normally associated with the register can still be used as a device input. The proprietary CY7C330 Reprogrammable Synchronous State Machine macrocell illustrated in FIG. 1-51, the use of buried registers with provision for saving the I/O pin for use as an input. If the feedback path is selected by the feedback multiplexer, the Q of the register is fed back to the array as an external input by use of a special multiplexer shown in FIG. 1-52 provided for that purpose for each of the six macrocell pairs.

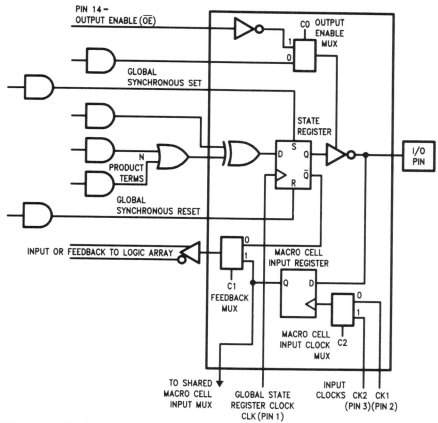

Fig. 1-51. CY7C330 I/O macrocell. Courtesy of Cypress Semiconductor Corporation.

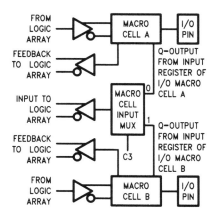

Fig. 1-52. CY7C330 I/O macrocell shaved input MUX. Courtesy of Cypress Semiconductor Corporation.

A special configuration bit, C3, selects the input register output from one of the I/O pins of the pair of macrocell I/O pins that is to be fed to the array as an external input. By proper placement of the buried registers adjacent to I/O macrocells used as normal registered outputs without feedback, maximum use of the buried macrocell I/O pins for inputs can be achieved. The CY7C330 also contains four dedicated buried or hidden registers with no external output, illustrated in FIG. 1-53, that are used as additional state register resources for creation of high-performance state machines.

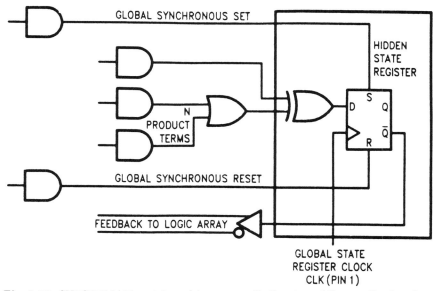

Fig. 1-53. CY7C330 hidden state register macrocell. Courtesy of Cypress Semiconductor Corporation.

Asynchronous Register Control

Cypress also offers EPLDs which may be used in asynchronous systems in which register clock, set, and reset are controlled by the outputs of the product term array. The clock is created by the processing of external inputs and/or internal feedback by the logic of the product term array and is then routed to the register clock. The register set and reset are similarly controlled by product term outputs and can be triggered at any time independent of the clock in response to external and/or feedback inputs processed by the logic array. The proprietary CY7C331 Asynchronous Registered EPLD, for which the I/O macrocell is illustrated in FIG. 1-54, is an example of such a device. The register clock, set, and reset functions of the CY7C331 are all controlled by product terms and enable their respective functions dependent only on input signal timing and combinatorial delay through the device logic array.

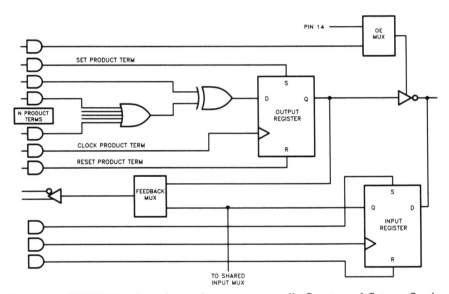

Fig. 1-54. CY7C330 registered asynchronous macrocell. Courtesy of Cypress Semiconductor Corporation.

Programmable Macrocell

The programmable macrocells provide the capability of defining the architecture of each output individually. Each of the potential outputs may be specified to be registered or combinatorial. Polarity of each output can also be individually selected allowing complete flexibility of output configuration. Further configurability is provided through array configurable output enable for each potential output. This feature allows the outputs to be reconfigured as inputs on an individual basis or alternately used as a bidirectional I/O controlled by the programmable array.

Input Register Cell

Other Cypress EPLDs provide input register cells, allowing capture for processing of short duration inputs that would not otherwise be present at the inputs, for sufficient time to allow the device to respond. Both the proprietary CY7C330 Reprogrammable Synchronous State Machine and the proprietary CY7C332 Combinatorial EPLD provide these input register cells. Input can be provided from one of two external clock input pins selectable by a configuration bit, C4, dedicated for this purpose for each input register. This choice of input register clock allows signals to be captured and processed from two independent system sources each controlled by its own independent clock. These input register cells are provided within I/O macrocells, as well as for dedicated input pins.

The PLD C 20G10 shown in FIG. 1-55 is a generic 24-pin device that can be programmed to logic functions that include but are not limited to 20L10, 20L8, 20R8, 20R5, 20R4, 12L10, 14L8, 16L6, 18L4, 20L2, and 20V8. Thus, the PLD C 20G10 can provide significant design, inventory, and programming flexibility over dedicated 24-pin devices. It is executed in a 24-pin 300 mil molded DIP and a 300 n Mil windowed Cerdip. It provides up to 22 inputs and 101 outputs. When the windowed Cerdip is exposed to UV light, the 20G10 is erased and then can be reprogrammed.

The programmable output cell provides the capability of defining the architecture of each output individually. Each of the 101 output cells can be configured with registered or combinatorial outputs, active high or active low outputs, and product term or pin 13 generated output enables.

The CY7C330 shown in FIG. 1-56 is a high-performance, erasable, programmable, logic device (EPLD) with architecture optimized to enable the user to construct easily and efficiently very high-performance synchronous state machines.

The unique architecture of the CY7C330, consisting of the user-configurable output macrocell, bidirectional I/O capability, input registers, and three separate clocks, enables the user to design high-performance state machines

20G10

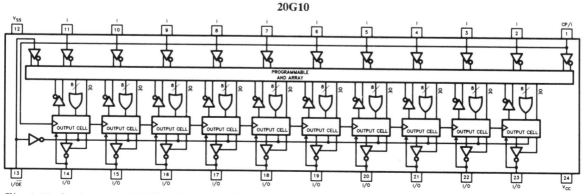

Fig. 1-55. Logic symbol 20G10. Courtesy of Cypress Semiconductor Corporation.

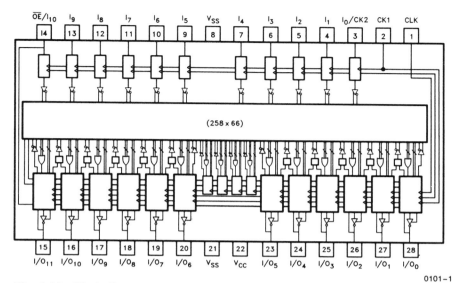

0101-1

Fig. 1-56. Block diagram of CY7C330. Courtesy of Cypress Semiconductor Corporation.

that can communicate either with each other or with microprocessors over bidirectional parallel busses of user-definable widths.

The three separate clocks permit independent, synchronous state machines to be synchronized to each other. The two input clocks, C1 and C2, enable the state machine to sample input signals that might be generated by another system and that might be available on its bus for a short period of time.

The user-configurable state register flip-flops enable the designer to designate JK, SR, T, or D type devices, so that the number of product terms required to implement the logic is minimized.

The CY7C331 shown in FIG. 1-57 is the most versatile PLD available for asynchronous designs. Central resources include 12 full D-type flip-flops with separate set, reset, and clock capability. For increased utility, XOR gates are provided at the D-inputs and the product term allocation per flip-flop is variably distributed.

The CY7C332 as shown in FIG. 1-58 is a versatile combinatorial PLD with I/O registers onboard. There are 25 array inputs; each has a macrocell that can be configured as a register, latch, or simple buffer. Outputs have polarity and tristate control product terms. The allocation of product terms to I/O macrocells is varied so that functions of up to 19 product terms can be accommodated.

RICOH EPL SERIES 20A/B

The Ricoh EPL Series 20A/B are field-programmable logic arrays made possible by CMOS EPROM process technology. Two product groups make up the EPL Series 20A/B family. Group I consists of AND-FIXED OR, XOR arrays, (EPL 10P8, 12P6, 14P4, and 16P2) available in 55 ns or 35 ns versions.

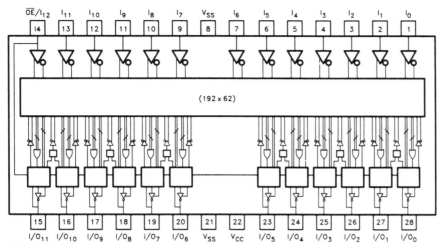

Fig. 1-57. Block diagram of CY7C331. Courtesy of Cypress Semiconductor Corporation.

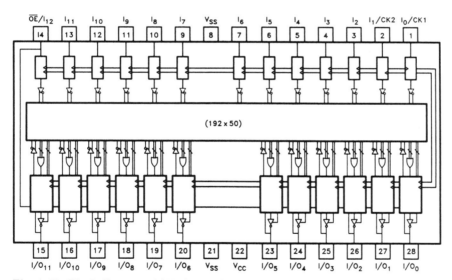

Fig. 1-58. Block diagram of CY7C332. Courtesy of Cypress Semiconductor Corporation.

Group II consists of AND-FIXED OR, XOR array (EPL 16P8) and three registered AND-FIXED OR, XOR arrays, (EPL 16RP8, 16RP6, and 16RP4). EPL Series 20A/B devices allow users to program by writing into EPROM memory cells. Series 20A/B are available in both one-shot plastic packages and reprogrammable Cerdip window packages. Therefore, it is possible to shorten the development time and check and correct the circuits easily.

The EPL241 shown in FIG. 1-59 is a field-programmable logic array with CMOS-EPROM processing and AND-OR (fixed)-register configuration.

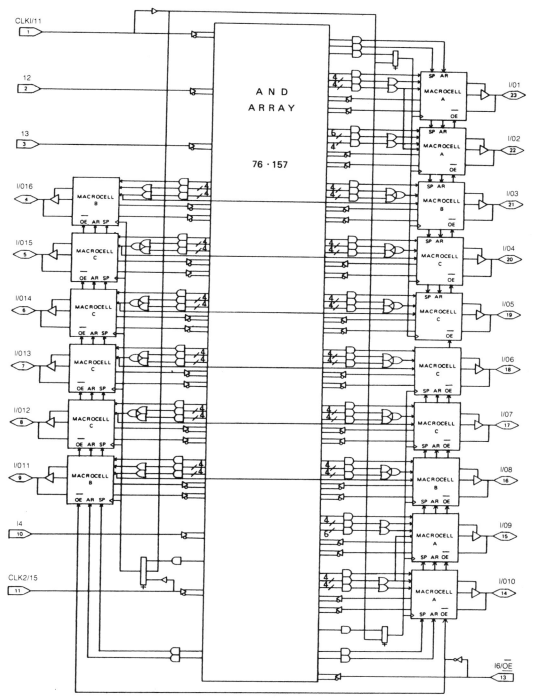

Fig. 1-59. Block diagram of EPL241E. Courtesy of RICOH Company, Ltd.

Table 1-15. PLX Technology, Inc., PLD Product Selector Guide.

CMOS Electronically Programmable Logic

	Model Name	Configuration	Power Supply	Max. power voltage Operation	Standby	Max. Access Time	Max. Operating Freq.	Compatible Products
G I	EPL10P8 B	10 input 8 output AND-OR/XOR Array						PAL10L8, 10H8
	EPL12P8 B	12 input 6 output AND-OR/XOR Array						PAL12L6, 12HA
	EPL14P4 B	14 input 4 output AND-OR/XOR Array		50mA*	40mA*			PAL14L8, 14H4
	EPL16P2 B	16 input 2 output AND-OR/XOR Array						PAL16L2 16H2
G II	EPL16P8 B	10 input 6 input/output AND-OR/XOR Array				35ns	10MHz	PAL18L8,
	EPL16RP8 B	8 input 8 feedback 8 output 8 register AND-OR/XOR Array	5V + 5%					PAL16R8
	EPL16RP8 B	8 input 6 feedback 2 input/output 6 output, 6 register AND-OR/XOR Array		70mA	60mA			PAL16R6
	EPL16RP4B	8 input 4 feedback 4 input/output 4 output, 4 register AND-OR/XOR Array						PAL16R4
	EPL241ED/	6 input 16 input/output 16 microcell built-in clock select asychronous reset attached/6 register		140mA**	120mA**	25ns	20MHz	22V10 & others

Programming is handled by writing to the EPROM memory cells arranged on the array. This programming technique shortens the development period greatly and simplifies circuit corrections.

Each output configuration is individually defined using 16 programmable macro I/O cells that permit the designer to specify either combination output or register output, and the polarity. Each macrocell has two feedback signals, so the designer can simultaneously feedback both the combination and register outputs or feedback one of the combination and register outputs while using an I/O pin as an input pin. The power consumption varies with the product term use efficiency (40 mA when 35% use).

Table 1-15 presents the available products offered by Ricoh.

PLX 464 CMOS PLD

For high drive current (64 mA) in applications for bus interface, consider the PLX 464. The PLX 464 is a CMOS programmable logic device designed to implement a broad range of bus protocol functions. Figure 1-60 shows the logic

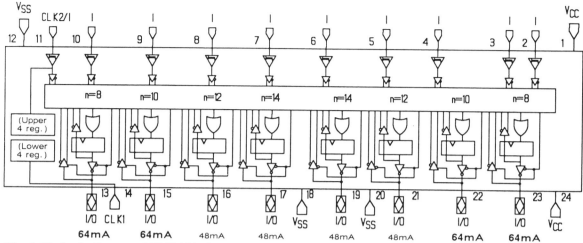

Fig. 1-60. Logic diagram of PLX 464. Courtesy of PLX Technology, Inc.

diagram of this device. The device includes a programmable logic array plus many common elements of bus interface circuitry, including four 64 mA Quad-state drivers, four 48 mA three-state drivers, metastable hardened registers, and inputs with hysteresis. In addition, to implement common bus logic structures, the device includes dynamic bidirectional I/Os, extra input paths to monitor bus levels, buried register capability to build state machines without wasting I/O pins, and two clock inputs for arbitration of asynchronous inputs.

Among the distinctive features of this device are integrated 48 mA and 64 mA drivers, which meet drive requirements for many VME, VSB, MBI, MBII, Micro Channel, NuBus, and other leading bus specification signals. In addition 64 mA quad-state drivers are individually programmable to open collector or three-state configurations. Dynamic bidirectional I/O capability provides additional input path which monitors bus level when output is high impedance. Also metastable hardened registers allow implementation of asynchronous arbiters and synchronizers. Buried register and buried combinatorial feedback capability is supported, and low power UV erasable/reprogrammable CMOS, 80 mA max I_{cc} is employed. The high-speed version (-25) has max input to high current output time (t_{PD}) of 25 ns. There are two independent clock inputs, and input hysteresis allows this device to monitor input signals directly from the bus.

The PLX 464 programmable output macrocell shown in FIG. 1-61, configuration is determined by the architecture bits C_0, $C_1 1$, C_2, and the output enable ($\overline{OE}$) product term.

The user can program each macrocell to a registered or combinatorial configuration with bit C_0. C_1 determines the output polarity (Active High or Active Low). With C_2, the user can individually program the 64 mA outputs (pins 13, 15, 22, and 23) to open collector or three-state configurations.

The $\overline{OE}$ disables and enables both the output buffer and the input path (path B). When one is enabled, the other is disabled and vice versa. The OE

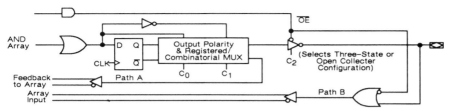

Fig. 1-61. PLX 464 programmable output macrocell. Courtesy of PLX Technology, Inc.

state may be selected permanently or dynamically. The operation of the output buffer and the path B buffer are similar to that of a bidirectional transceiver. With $\overline{OE}$ low, the output buffer is enabled and path B is disabled. In this case, path B is tied to V_{cc}; it does not float. With $\overline{OE}$ high, the output buffer is disabled and goes to a high impedance state. Path B is enabled and acts as an input to the array.

In a typical application, the user will monitor the $\overline{OE}$ term of a macrocell to determine if path B is enabled or disabled. Note that the output is enabled by the logical OR or the inputs to the $\overline{OE}$ product term.

The PLX Product Selection Guide is given in TABLE 1-16.

GALLIUM ARSENIDE PROGRAMMABLE DEVICES

Gallium Arsenide (GaAs) is a compound of two elements that are common mining byproducts. Initially considered an alternative to gernamium transistors during the 1950s, it was overshadowed by silicon which was easier to process. Several new product families, however, resulted from GaAs research including LEDs for displays, laser diodes, and transistors for microwave circuits.

New interest in 1970 by various federal programs has stimulated intense work on GaAs for space communications and very high-speed ICs, Commercial interest was found in the need for digital GaAs for supercomputers during the early 1980s.

Over the last decade, heavy government investment has pushed development of GaAs devices because of their speed and inherent reliability in several military and space applications. Aerospace companies have produced a GaAs, 32-bit microprocessor chip set under government contract. Also, a Colorado company, Prisma, is developing a high-speed computer for aerospace applications based on GaAs logic.

There are basically two advantages to GaAs ICs. First, at relatively low field values, electrons move three times faster in GaAs than in silicon and have four times the mobility. This leads to the advantage that GaAs ICs can operate much faster than silicon devices at an equivalent speed of some of the fastest silicon TTLs, but at lower power levels. Consequently GaAs makes possible circuits that operate reliably over a wider temperature range than can be obtained with silicon (see FIGS. 1-62 and 1-63). A second advantage of GaAs IC

Table 1-16. PLX Technology PLD Product Selector Guide.

Part Number	Package	Count	Buffers	Inputs/Outputs	P Terms	Features
PLX 448	300 mil DIP	24	48 mA with Quad state driver open collector feature	19/8	Variable 8 to 14	1. Metastable hardened registers 2. Input schmitt trigger buffers 3. Dual clocks
PLX 464	300 mil DIP	24	64 mA with Quad state driver open collector feature	19/8	Variable 8 to 14	1. Metastable hardened registers 2. Input schmitt trigger buffers 3. Dual clocks
PLX 448J	JLCC surface mount	28	48 mA with Quad state driver open collector feature	19/8	Variable 8 to 14	1. Metastable hardened registers 2. Input schmitt trigger buffers 3. Dual clocks
PLX 464J	JLCC surface mount	28	64 mA with Quad state driver open collector feature	19/8	Variable 8 to 14	1. Metastable hardened registers 2. Input schmitt trigger buffers 3. Dual clocks
PLX 448P	300 mil plastic DIP	24	48 mA with Quad state driver open collector feature	19/8	Variable 8 to 14	1. Metastable hardened registers 2. Input schmitt trigger buffers 3. Dual clocks
PLX 464P	300 mil plastic DIP	24	64 mA with Quad state driver open collector feature	19/8	Variable 8 to 14	1. Metastable hardened registers 2. Input schmitt trigger buffers 3. Dual clocks

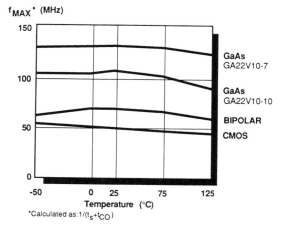

Fig. 1-62. Comparison of GaAs with silicon. Courtesy of Gazelle Microcircuits, Inc.

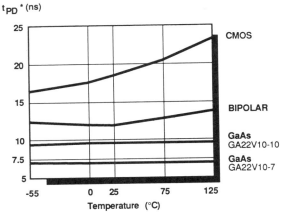

Fig. 1-63. Comparison of GaAs with silicon. Courtesy of Gazelle Microcircuits, Inc.

* Combinatorial Input to Output Delay Time:

relates to their reliability in that they have a higher tolerance to radiation encountered by satellites and other space-related equipment than silicon.

There were initially two disadvantages to GaAs ICs. First, unlike silicon, GaAs cannot be readily doped by the diffusion process that was used to build transistors since the 1950s. Secondly, GaAs ingots could not be grown with a round section and the full-size wafers sliced from the ingots had a "O" shape that was incompatible with commercial equipment for handling silicon wafers. However, GaAs are now practical because new techniques for crystal growth that produce large, symmetric ingots and the advent of ion implantation for silicon circuit surmounted the two major barriers that impeded development. Notably, the tight control of doping profiles afforded by ion implantation allows fabrication on planar GaAs transistors, which are structurally similar to conventional silicon MOSFETS.

Gazelle Microcircuits, Inc., by coupling a proprietary methodology for circuit design with refinements in GaAs processing, can build large-scale, high-performance ICs for such mainstream applications as engineering workstations, minicomputers, and data communications equipment. Other manufacturers of GaAs logic have instead concentrated on simple functions and ultimate speed for niche applications. By leveraging GaAs technology, Gazelle builds standard TTL devices that have a speed-power product one-third that of the best available silicon parts. In addition, Gazelle devices require no special design considerations for system use, and all operate from single 5-V supplies.

Initially, only depletion-mode transistors proved feasible for GaAs ICs. Such transistors continually flow current between their source and drain until a negative bias voltage is applied to turn them off. Although the depletion-mode GaAs transistors could switch much faster than the best silicon transistors, their power consumption prohibited large-scale integration. Within the past two years, enhancement/depletion processes have been implemented by virtually all GaAs foundries; now, nearly 30 in all. The E/D processes dramatically cut power consumption and, consequently, enabled construction of LSI and VLSI devices that offer substantial performance improvements over silicon circuits of like complexity.

Unfortunately, enhancement-mode transistors exhibit wide threshold variations across a wafer that exceeds the parametric tolerances of fundamental circuit forms employed for logic design by most GaAs IC manufacturers. As a result of the mismatch between design assumptions and process characteristics, yields are too low to justify competitive prices in mainstream markets. The firms have no choice but to pursue high-end, niche applications that can bear premium prices.

In contrast, Gazelle proprietary circuits forms are insensitive to threshold variations in available processes. By eliminating parametric discrepancies between circuit designs and processes, Gazelle realizes high yields of GaAs LSI devices from the foundries it engages in strategic relationships. Gazelle presently offers the industry standard 22V10 PLD and a GA23S8 with variations (see TABLE 1-17).

Table 1-17. Gazelle Microcircuits, Inc., Product Selection Guide.

Part Number	Speed	Tpd	Ts	Too	Fmax1	Fmax2	Icc
GA22VP10	−7	7.5ns	3.0ns	6.0ns	110 MHz	200 MHz	225 mA
	−10	10.0ns	3.6ns	7.5ns	90 MHz	178 MHz	215 mA
GA22V10	−7	7.5ns	3.0ns	6.0ns	110 MHz	200 MHz	220 mA
	−10	10.0ns	3.6ns	7.5ns	90 MHz	178 MHz	210 mA
GA23S8	−7	7.5ns	4.0ns	6.5ns	95 MHz	166 MHz	225 mA
	−10	10.0ns	4.5ns	7.5ns	83 MHz	153 MHz	220 mA
GA23SV8	−7	7.5ns	4.0ns	6.5ns	95 MHz	166 MHz	225 mA
	−10	10.0ns	4.5ns	7.5ns	83 MHz	153 MHz	220 mA

Part Number	Product Terms	Buried Registers	Dedicated Inputs	I/O*
GA22VP10	120	0	12	10
	120	0	12	10
GA22VP10	120	0	12	10
	120	0	12	10
GA23S8	124	6	9	8
	124	6	9	8
GA23SV8	124	6	9	8
	124	6	9	8

*Bidirectional I/O
The GA22VP10 is a 24-pin PLD superset with improved output logic macrocell functionality.
The GA22V10 is a 24-pin PLD superset with output logic macrocells. It is pin and function compatible with all industry-standard 22V10s.
The GA23S8 is a 20-pin PAL-based sequencer with output logic macrocells and 6 buried registers.
The GA23SV8 is a 20-pin PLD-based superset of 32 common 20-pin PLDs, offering 8 full function output macrocells and 6 internal buried registers.
All of Gazelle's PLDs are differentiated by their full pin and functional compatibility and a 2x to 4x speed enhancement over existing silicon devices. This advantage results from our proprietary TTL-Compatible Gallium Arsenide circuit design techniques.

The GA23S8 is Gazelle's third gallium arsenide (GaAs)-based product. Its GaAs construction allows it to operate at more than four times the speed of equivalent silicon-based chips. The chip is easy to use because of 25 internal patent-pending circuit techniques that make its inputs and outputs 100% TTL compatible. Figure 1-64 shows the logic diagram of the GA23S8.

The new device has 6 buried registers, 8 output logic registers, and 124 logical product terms—all in a 20-pin package. When using the 6 buried registers for internal feedback, the device can run at clock rates of 165 MHz compared to 40 MHz for equivalent silicon-based chips.

The fast internal feedback clock rate is particularly useful for generating high-precision control signals with 6 ns resolution (useful in applications such as generating variable-length programmable clocks, or for system or video timing generation).

This type of speed is also important for the design of circuits that need to make fast sequential decisions. Such circuits are often a bottleneck to higher-system performance in workstations and computers, including clock generators, pipelined bus controllers, DRAM controllers, and cache controllers.

Using external feedback through its 8 output logic registers, the GA23S8 can clock at 95 MHz compared to 33 MHz in the equivalent silicon devices. In fact, the external clock rate of the GA23S8 is faster than any other silicon TTL-compatible PLD, including much simpler devices such as the 16L8 and 16R8.

The 95 MHz clock frequency makes the GA23S8 ideal support logic for the next-generation processors which operate at clock rates up to 40 MHz. Microprocessor support logic is required to operate at twice the processor's clock speed in order for the processor to operate at full speed. Because the GA23S8 runs at 95 MHz, it can be used with processors that operate with clock rates of

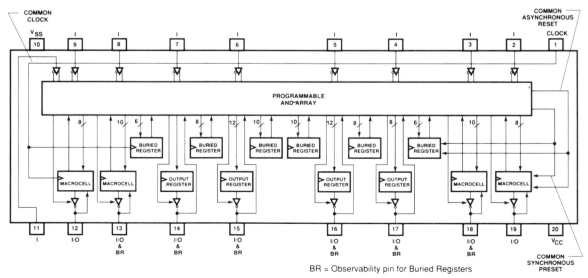

BR = Observability pin for Buried Registers

Fig. 1-64. Logic diagram of GA2358. Courtesy of Gazelle Microcircuits, Inc.

over 45 MHz. The fastest equivalent silicon device, which runs at 33 MHz, can support only 16 MHz processors.

In addition to its fast clock rates, the GA23S8 has a fast 7.5 ns propagation delay (tpd) that when considered with its 4 ns set-up time (ts) and 6.5 ns clock-to-out (tco) time means it is faster than discrete TTL logic. According to Gazelle, a single GA23S8 can typically replace 12 TTL random logic packages in a new design, while providing 20% greater speed.

The new Gazelle chip can be configured to be 100% pin and function-compatible with six different silicon PLDs, (16R8, 16R6, 16R4, and 16RP8, 16RP6, 16RP4) in addition to the 23S8. Thus, engineers can substitute the gallium arsenide GA23S8 in place of silicon PLDs that are system bottlenecks, and boost overall system performance.

On the applications side, according to Gazelle, prominent systems manufacturers have embraced GaAs for advanced products to be offered in the next five years. For example, the third-generation supercomputer from Cray Research, the Cray III, incorporates 58,000 GaAs logic devices. Moreover, Supercomputer Systems—a new venture formed in partnership with IBM—will produce yet another GaAs-based parallel-processing machine.

As far as processing is concerned, larger GaAs wafers are becoming available that will further bring costs in line with silicon. Notably, the trend by IC manufacturers to process single wafers at a time makes costs much less dependent on wafer area and much more dependent on throughput—an advantage for GaAs. On the horizon, thin GaAs layers grown on silicon will eliminate the slight difference in wafer costs.

Gazelle shares the development of processes with several leading foundries in engages in strategic relationships. As a result, it is poised to incorporate such advances as HEMT fabrication (high-electron-mobility transistors) as soon as they are proven.

Supercomputers and avionics spurred the development of digital GaAs ICs, but the advent of pure 5-V devices that can be substituted for standard silicon will benefit a broad range of applications. For example, desktop workstations for VLSI design could speed simulations—the major bottleneck in ASIC turn-around—by employing such logic without the need for noisy, expensive fans. Communications controllers based on GaAs circuits could substantially increase LAN bandwidth. High-resolution, color graphics systems could perform real-time animation. And, minicomputers could overshadow the processing power of a Cray I.

Ironically it was not the achievement of performance that confronted Gazelle, but reducing the speed of the GaAs gigahertz rates to speeds compatible with bipolar and CMOS ICs. Given this, from a speed point of view GaAs technology might find Emitter Coupled Logic (ECL) uncomfortable as a highly competitive foe. ECL devices can operate at speeds in excess of 500 MHz compared to GaAs 750 MHz to 1.5GHz. Trend isolation, poly-silicon base and emitter elements, and other developments have all contributed to the speeds. In addition, some improvements in the reduction of attendent ECL power levels are permitting high speeds at reasonable temperatures.

It is pointed out however that in electrical properties of GaAs has an advantage over ECL in this regard. The integration of more devices on a single IC for both GaAs and ECL technologies will improve propagation time by eliminating the delays a signal encounters as it is transmitted between ICs.

Silicon-based logic is approaching its limit in internal speed, and the latest performance improvements have been made by speeding up the rise and fall times of the TTL outputs. These extra-fast rise times, however, causes such problems as ground bounce, reflection, and cross talk. The GaAs ICs derive their speed from faster internal operation that is possible with the faster acting GaAs material yielding slower rise and fall times and consequently eliminating ground bounce and the like. Costwise, GaAs ICs are from two to three times the cost of comparable silicon ICs; however, the customer will receive in return two to three times the performance. These prices might drop in the future because fewer mask steps are required to fabricate GaAs ICs than silicon bipolar devices. As a result, more GaAs wafers can be processed per day. In addition, as the young industry matures, the investment in new foundries will be amortized and prices will continue to fall.

WHEN TO USE PLDS

The above gives an overview of the variety of PLDs as stated previously. Programmable logic devices provides designs that might be termed a middle-of-the-road option between the general purpose catalog logic devices and the semicustom and custom logic devices. Programmable logic devices incorporate the advantages of both technologies in many applications. How this is accomplished is subject of the following section.

Generally speaking, PLDs offer the best of standard and custom logic devices. Today's devices range from 200 to 1200 gates of varying complexity. Performance is high and propagation delays of 10 nanoseconds have been realized and clock rates around 40 Mhz are commonplace. The following discussion provides specific criteria that might guide the user in determining those applications wherein a PLD will offer superior performance over fixed function or custom or semicustom logic devices.

Design Flexibility

Circuit designers have in the past relied on catalog logic or custom SSI or MSI components. The implementation of the catalog logic frequently required chip counts where in many cases less than one-half or even one-fourth of the IC potential could be exploited. For example, an IC might contain four inverters while only one was required for the circuit as in the case of the 7404 IC. An IC may contain four NAND gates but a circuit might require only a single NAND gate (7412 TTL). In both cases, however, the total chip would be required to implement less than it was capable of providing although it consumed the space of a full IC on a printed circuit board. The PLD overcomes these constraints on the designer by permitting the designer to easily create a customized part for a specific application. Further design modifications and changes can easily be accommodated by reprogramming the PLD as opposed to relaying out a new board leading to a reduction in prototyping time of even weeks or months. The reduced design/prototyping time can be obtained because the PLD is customized to the design as opposed to the design time required to incorporate available fixed function devices or modify custom devices.

Board Space Reduction

A PLD device family can be used to replace up to 90% of the conventional TTL family. This high board efficiency utilization can be illustrated when it is considered that one of the designers of the VAX 11/730 minicomputer estimated that a single PLD replaced four 7400 series components in their design. Some of the newer PLDs can replace over ten of these 7400 series components. Thus the use of PLDs permits the designer to implement identical logic functions while providing more compact PC boards and reducing multicard systems to one card systems. These board saving approaches to product development can, in many cases, determine the difference between profit and loss for a company.

Also, the reduction of ICs leads to increased reliability. The number of connections between packages can be reduced increasing system reliability because bad connections are a common problem source and the last reliable part of a system.

Logic Design Security

A PLD's verification logic can be made secure from copiers or other unwanted intruders by blowing out a special *last link* or *security fuse*. Valuable data cannot then be copied or tampered with by unauthorized persons leading to a high degree of data integrity.

Reduced In-House Inventories

Frequently, it was necessary to maintain a large inventory of standard ICs for easy availability to the designer. These inventories are costly to maintain in terms of fund utilization for their purchase. Further, inventory space must be made available to store the standardized ICs. In addition, one or several persons must be hired to operate the "standardized IC store" by performing inventory status, ordering needed parts, negotiating for best prices, etc. Thus with PLDs, smaller inventories can be maintained and the above attendant inventory problems eliminated.

Competitive Speeds (Performance)

A PLD family can operate faster than or equal to the best bipolar transistor circuits. Various microcomputer systems can be made to handle high-speed data interfaces as an assistant to the microprocessor. Coupled with this, a designer can implement a PLD in such a way to improve performance. For example, consider when a logic function is implemented using several SSI/MSI packages. Propagation time can accumulate considerably for on and off clip buffers. If this same function, however, was implemented using a PLD, the average delay per logic gate is reduced because of the reduction using a PLD to a single pair of I/O buffers.

Cost

The cost savings realized from the utilization of PLDs in lieu of SSI and MSI components can cover a wide range depending on such factors as failure probabilities related to the types of devices under consideration (including the various types of PLDs as discussed earlier), quantity of boards manufactured, availability of parts, quantity discounts on parts, type of technology implemented, inventory levels, and the like. However, a PLD on the average should generally provide a greater cost savings than can be realized from the utilization of fixed-function devices and custom-integrated devices. For some applications and analyses, a ratio of 5:1 in favor of PLDs have been calculated.

This chapter has examined in detail the more popular PLD architectures that are currently available. The selection of the proper architecture to meet your design objectives should be coupled with other criteria such as erasability, speed, current requirements, technology (bipolar, CMOS) that are explored in more detail in Chapter 2.

2

PLD Technology Tradeoffs

Prior to 1985, almost all PLDs were manufactured using bipolar metal gate fuse technology. However, this technology posed several limitations on the circuit designer. Around 1985, CMOS EPROM technology was introduced for PLDs and, in 1986, CMOS EEPROM technology. This chapter summarizes the basic PLD technology tradeoffs and highlights the advantages and disadvantages of bipolar (Transistor to Transistor Logic (TTL) and Emitter Coupled Logic (ECL)), Complimentary Metal Oxide Semiconductor (CMOS) technology, Electrically Erasable PLDs, and Ultraviolet Erasable PLDs.

BIPOLAR FUSED-BASED PLDs

Bipolar technology, which employs bipolar transistors, is usually divided into Transistor to Transistor Logic (TTL) and Emitter Coupler Logic (ECL). TTL developed by Texas Instruments is perhaps the most wisely used type of technology in use today owing to its extremely low cost and flexibility. Its wide acceptance has given rise to the manufacturing of very large quantities of electronics parts leading directly to a reduction in cost. TTL circuits are basically an improved version of Diode Transistor Logic (DTL) yielding higher speeds than could be realized in DTL technology.

TTL Technology

Several variations and modifications of the basic TTL technology provide improved performance, higher switching speeds, and lower power consumption. The so-called low and high versions are basically the same except in low power TTL technology resistor values can be approximately ten times higher than in standard TTL logic. This results in power consumption of less than one-tenth of that found in the standard TTL circuit. However, the low power TTL is significantly slower in operation, reducing the propagation delay to those to four times that of standard TTL circuit.

On the other hand, the high power version TTL employs resistor values significantly lower than that found in standard TTL circuitry in an attempt to improve propagation delay performance. In some traditional cases, a Darlington transistor is employed to increase the base drive to the output transistor to increase its turn on time. Thus in TTL circuitry, power consumption and propagation delay are inversely related, that is, higher power levels are required to reduce propagation delay and must be traded against each other depending on the specific application.

Schottky TTL circuitry utilizes Schottky diodes to prevent the transistors from saturating, which usually results in increased speed at very little increase in power consumption. The advantage of the Schottky diode is that it does not have the standard PN junction, but is more of a metal semiconductor device. One of the elements called the *anode* is usually metal (mostly aluminum) while the cathode is n-type semiconductor material. No storage charge is associated with a Schottky diode.

The PAL devices offered by Texas Instruments (TI), combine the latest advanced low-power Schottky technology. Employing a process termed Implanted Advanced Composed Technology (IMPACT™), TI produces fast, dense, and low power products. The PLDs fabricated using TI's IMPACT yield dimensions of 2 microns while those fabricated using the IMPACT-X™ yield dimensions of 1.5 microns.

The PLDs manufactured by TI use a titanium-tungsten (TiW) fuse technology developed at TI in 1970 to improve programming reliability. Proven TiW construction essentially eliminates the tendency of a fuse to grow back by insulating it with a layer of titanium oxide.

The TI IMPACT 20-pin family includes 4 standard architectures available in any of 4 speed/power selections to achieve design requirements for flexibility, speed, and power conservation. The TI IMPACT 24-pin family includes 4 standard architectures available in 2 speed/power selections. The TIBPAL20XX-15 series PLDs offer a large number of inputs while maintaining a 15 ns propagation delay. Lower power requirements can be satisfied by the half-power TIBPAL20XX-25 PLD series with a 25 ns propagation delay and low 100 mA I_{cc}.

The TIBPAL22V10A and TIBPAL22VP10-20 are designed to implement those functions exceeding the architectural limits of simpler PLDs. These products provide superior flexibility and high speed. While the 22V10 has become a standard of its own, the TIBPAL22VP10-20 (now available from TI) offers a 20% improvement in speed.

Consider the TIBPAL16L8-12, TIBPAL16R4-12, TIBPAL16R-12, TIBPAL16R8-12, TIBPAL16L8-15, TIBPAL16R4-15, TIBPAL16R6-15, TIBPAL16R8-15 High-Performance IMPACT PAL circuits. High-performance operation yielding propagation delays of less than 12 ns are possible. They are functionally equivalent, to the PAL16L8B, PAL16R4B, PAL16R6B, and PAL16R8 are feature power-up clear on registered devices (all registered outputs are set low).

The TIBPAL20L8-15, TIBPAL20R4-15, TIBPAL20R6-15, TIBPAL20R8-15, TIBPAL20L8-20, TIBPAL20R4-20, TIBPAL20R6-20, TIBPAL20R8-20 High-Performance IMPACT PAL circuits feature f_{max} (without feedback) for the TIBPAL20R' C series is 45 MHz and TIBPAL20R' M series 41.5 MHz. They are functionally equivalent to the PAL20L8, PAL20R4, PAL20R6, and PAL20R8 with a reduced I_{cc} of 180 mA maximum.

The TIBPAL20L8-25C, TIBPAL20R4-25C, TIBPAL20R6-25C, TIBPAL20R8-25C, TIBPAL20L8-30M, TIBPAL20R4-30M, TIBPAL20R6-30M, and TIBPAL20R8-30M, low-power high-performance IMPACT PAL circuits feature low-power, high performance reduced I_{cc} of 105 mA max f_{max}, (TIBPAL20R'-25C Series): without feedback is 33 MHz min), with feedback is 25 MHz min, t_{pd} (TIBPAL20'-25C Series) is 25 ns Max.

They can serve as direct replacement for PAL20L8A, PAL20R4A, PAL20R6A, and PAL20R8A with at least 50% reduction in power. Their preload capability on output registers simplifies testing. They also feature power-up clear on registered devices.

The TIBPAL16L8, TIBPAL16R4, TIBPAL16R6, TIBPAL16R8, High-Performance IMPACT PAL circuits also feature high-performance operation with a propagation delay of 15 ns and f_{MAX} of 50 MHz. These circuits are functionally equivalent, but faster than PAL16L8A, PAL16R4A, PAL16R6A, and PAL16R8A and feature power-up clear on registered devices (all registered outputs are set low).

The TIBPAL16L8-10C, TIBPAL16R4-10C, TIBPAL16R6-10C, TIBPAL16R8-10C, TIBPAL16L8-12M, TIBPAL16R4-12M, TIBPAL16R6-12M, TIBPAL16R8-12M, High-Performance IMPACT PAL circuits also feature high-performance operation. For example:

F_{max} (w/o feedback)
    TIBPAL16R'-10C Series   62.5 MHz
    TIBPAL16R'-12M Series   56 MHz
f_{max} (with feedback)
    TIBPAL16R'-10C Series   55.5 MHz
    TIBPAL16R'-12M Series   48 MHz
Propagation Delay
    TIBPAL16L-10C Series   10 ns Max
    TIBPAL16L-12M Series   12 ns Max

They are considered functionally equivalent to existing 20-pin PALs and feature preload capability on output registers to simplify testing. Power-up clear on registered devices (all register outputs are set low, but voltage levels at the output pins remain high).

National Semiconductor offers a variety of PALs in six families:

20-Pin Small PAL Family
20-Pin Medium PAL Family
24-Pin Small PAL Family
24-Pin Exclusive-OR PAL Family
24-Pin Medium PAL Family
24-Pin Polarity PAL Family

All families utilize National Semiconductor's advanced oxide isolated Schottky TTL process and bipolar PROM fuse-link technology unless otherwise noted in this section.

The 20-pin Small PAL family contains nine popular PAL architectures. The devices in the Small PAL family draw only 90 mA maximum supply current for standard power versions, and as little as 45 mA for Series A2 as compared to 180 mA in the 20-pin Medium PAL devices. These devices offer speeds of 25 ns maximum propagation delay.

The 20-pin Medium PAL family contains four of the most popular PAL architectures used in industry. The Series-D devices are manufactured using National Semiconductor's isoplanar FAST-Z TTL process with highly reliable vertical-fuse programmable cells. Vertical fuses are implemented using National's Avalanche-Induced Migration (AIM) technology offering very high programming yields. This technology is an extension of National's FAST logic family. This family features power-up reset for registered outputs (Series D) and register preload facilitates device testing (Series B,D).

The 24-pin Small PAL family contains six popular PAL architectures. The devices in the Small PAL family draw only 100 mA maximum supply current as compared to 210 MA in the 24-pin Medium PAL devices. These devices offer speeds as fast as 25 ns maximum propagation delay.

The 24-pin exclusive-OR PAL family contains 4 industry-standard PAL architectures optimized for a specific class of applications. The PAL logic array has a total of 20 complementary inputs and 10 outputs generated by a single programmable AND-gate array with fixed OR-gate connections. Device outputs are either taken directly from the AND-OR functions (combinatorial) or passed through exclusive-OR gates and D-type flip-flops (registered). Registers allow the PAL device to implement sequential logic circuits. The exclusive-OR functions provide easy implementation of the "hold" operation used in counters and other state sequences. Tristate outputs facilitate busing and provide bidirectional I/O capability. The exclusive-OR PAL family offers a variety of combinatorial and registered output mixtures, as shown in Tables 1-1 and 1-2.

Series-A devices have power-up reset and register preload features available. On power-up, all registers are reset to simplify sequential circuit design and testing. Direct register preload is also provided to facilitate device testing. This family features propagation delay as fast as 30 ns (combinatorial).

The 24-pin Medium family contains 4 of the most popular PAL architectures with speeds as fast as 10 ns maximum propagation delay. These Series-D devices are manufactured using National Semiconductor's isoplanar FAST-Z TTL process with highly-reliable vertical-fuse programmable cells. Again featuring AIM technology, the PAL logic array has a total of 20 complementary input pairs and 8 outputs generated by a single programmable AND-gate array with fixed OR-gate connections. Device outputs are either taken directly from the AND-OR functions (combinatorial) or passed through D-type flip-flops (registered). Registers allow the PAL device to implement sequential logic circuits and as stated previously, tri state outputs facilitate busing and provide bidirectional I/O capability. The Medium PAL family offers a variety of combinatorial and registered output mixtures.

On power-up, Series D devices reset all registers to simplify sequential circuit design and testing and for Series B devices, the registers are set on power-up. For Series D and Series B devices, direct register preload is also provided to facilitate device testing.

The 24-pin Polarity Series B PAL allows the user to program individual outputs either active high or active low. This feature eliminates any possible need for inversion of signals outside the device.

Registers consist of D-type flip-flops that are loaded on the low-to-high transition of the clock. The registers power up with a high V_{OH} at the output pin, regardless of the polarity fuse. The family also features propagation delays as fast as 15 ns.

ECL Technology

What has come to be known as Emitter Coupled Logic (ECL) has led to some significant breakthroughs in the reduction of propagation delay. The use of saturated transistor switches (transistors that lend themselves to saturation) that carries with them the effects of discharge storage is the main cause of propagation delay in TTL circuitry. A saturated switching circuit cannot operate beyond a certain speed. As stated, Schottky diodes are normally employed to prevent the transistor from going into saturation. ECL circuitry is designed to reducing saturating in switching transistors. The ECL circuits perhaps offer more speed and related advantages than any other type of logic circuit where speed is the main concern in a digital system.

The speed advantages of ECL circuits over other forms of logic relate to their nonsaturation characteristics and very low voltage swings (normally less than 1 V). In addition, it has been found that the power dissipation of an ECL circuit is almost constant with respect to frequency. It is also less noisy. However, some very high-speed ECL circuits dissipate more power than other circuits although this situation is improving almost daily as ECL technology advances.

National Semiconductor offers a variety of ECL PALs. The Series-A ECL PAL devices are manufactured using National Semiconductor's advanced oxide-isolated process with titanium-tungsten fuse technology to provide high-speed user-programmable replacements for conventional ECL SSI/MSI logic with significant chip-count reduction (typically greater than 4:1).

The registered and latched ECL PAL family consists of six device architectures. A maximum propagation delay of 6 ns (input to output) characterizes the performance of this ECL PAL series.

The PAL transfer function is the familiar sum-of-products implemented with a single array of fusible links. The PAL device incorporates a programmable AND array driving a fixed OR array. The AND term logic matrix incorporates 16 complementary inputs and 64 product terms. The 64 product terms are grouped into 8 OR functions with 8 product terms each. All devices in this family are provided with output polarity fuses. These fuses permit the designer to configure each output independently to produce either a logic high (by leaving the fuse intact) or a logic low (by programming the fuse) when the equation defining that output is satisfied. In addition, the ECL PAL family offers these options:

- Output registers
- Output latches
- Dual (split) clocks
- ORed (common) clocks

Product terms with all fuses programmed assume a logical high state, while product terms connected to both the true and complement of any input assume a logical low state. All product terms in an unprogrammed part are logically low. All input and I/O pins have on-chip 50 K pull-down resistors. Registers consist of D-type flip-flops that are loaded in response to the low-to-high transition of the clock input(s). Latches are transparent while the enable inputs are low and hold data while the inputs are high.

Figure 2-1 shows the logic diagram of the PAL1016RC8/PAL10016RC8, while the logic diagram for PAL1016RC4/PAL10016RC4 is given in FIG. 2-2.

The PAL10/10016RM4A and PAL10/10016LM4A are also members of the National Semiconductor ECL PAL family. The ECL PAL Series-A is characterized by 4 ns maximum propagation delays (combinatorial input-to-output). The pinout, JEDEC fuse-map format, and programming algorithm of these devices are compatible with those of all prior ECL PAL products from National. Series-A ECL PAL devices among this family include the features:

t_{SU} = 3 ns min
t_{CLK} = 2 ns max
f_{MAX} = 200 MHz max (registered)
t_{PD} = 4 ns max (combinatorial)

The PAL 10/10012C4A is a member of the National Semiconductor ECL PAL family. Again the ECL PAL Series-A is characterized by 4 ns maximum propagation delays. The pinout, JEDEC fuse map format, and programming algorithm of these devices are compatible with those of all prior ECL PAL products from National.

Logic Diagram PAL1016RC8/PAL10016RC8

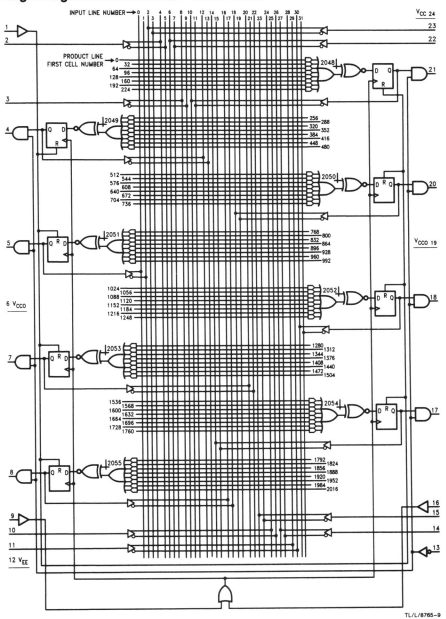

TL/L/8765–9

JEDEC logic array cell number = product line first cell number + input line number.

Fig. 2-1. Logic diagram of PAL1016RC8/PAL10016RC8. Courtesy of National Semiconductor Corporation.

Logic Diagram PAL1016RC4/PAL10016RC4

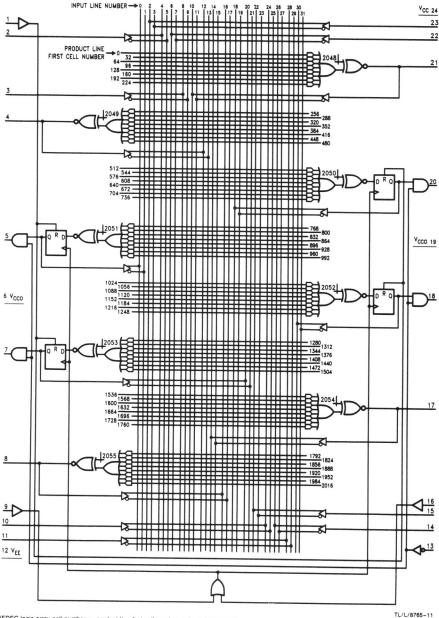

JEDEC logic array cell number = product line first cell number + input line number.

TL/L/8765-11

Fig. 2-2. Logic diagram of PAL1016RC4/PAL10016RC4. Courtesy of National Semiconductor Corporation.

The PAL 10/10012C4A logic array has a total of 12 complementary input pairs, 32 product terms, and 4 complementary output functions. Each output function is the OR-sum of 8 product terms. Each product term is satisfied when all array inputs which are connected to it (via intact fuses) are in the desired state. Complementary outputs eliminate the need for external inverters and allow for more convenient output OR-tying. They are also suitable for differential sensing for increased noise immunity. All input pins have 50 ks pull-down registers.

Figure 2-3 presents the logic diagram of the PAL1016RM4A/PAL-10016RM4A while FIG. 2-4 presents the logic diagram of the PAL1016LM4A/PAL10016LM4A.

The PAL1016P4A and PAL10016P4A are members of the National Seminconductor ECL PAL family. The PAL10/10016 P4A is a functional subset of the PAL10/10016P8 (6 ns t_{pd}) and is compatible in pinout, JEDEC map format, and programming algorithm.

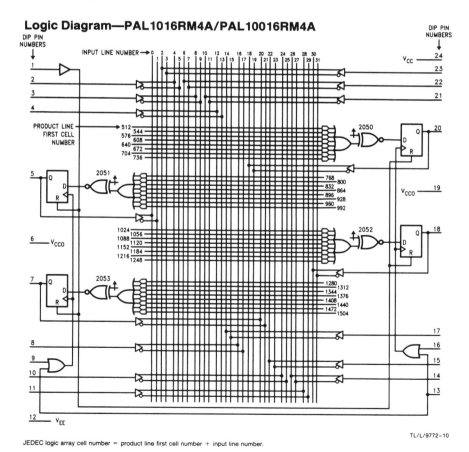

Logic Diagram—PAL1016RM4A/PAL10016RM4A

JEDEC logic array cell number = product line first cell number + input line number.

Fig. 2-3. Logic diagram of PAL1016RM4A/PAL10016RM4A. Courtesy of National Semiconductor Corporation.

Logic Diagram—PAL1016LM4A/PAL10016LM4A

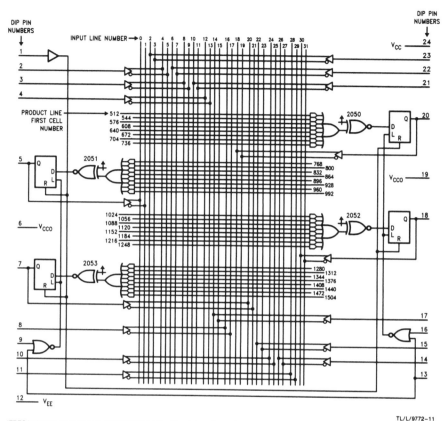

JEDEC logic array cell number = product line first cell number + input line number.

TL/L/9772–11

Fig. 2-4. Logic diagram of PAL1016LM4A/PAL10016LM4A. Courtesy of National Semiconductor Corporation.

The PAL transfer function is the familiar sum-of-products implemented with a single array of fusible links. The PAL device incorporates a programmable-AND array driving a fixed-OR array. The AND term logic matrix incorporates 16 complementary inputs and 32 product terms. The 32 product terms are grouped into 4 OR functions with 8 product terms each. All devices in this series are provided with output polarity fuses. These fuses permit the designer to configure each output independently to provide either a logic true (by leaving the fuse intact) or a logic false (by programming the fuse) when the equation defining that output is satisfied.

Product terms with all fuses programmed assume a logical high state, while product terms connected to both the true and complement of any input assume a logical low state. All product terms in an unprogrammed part are logically low.

Figure 2-5 shows the logic diagram of the PAL1016P4A/PAL10016P4A.

Logic Diagram PAL1016P4A/PAL10016P4A

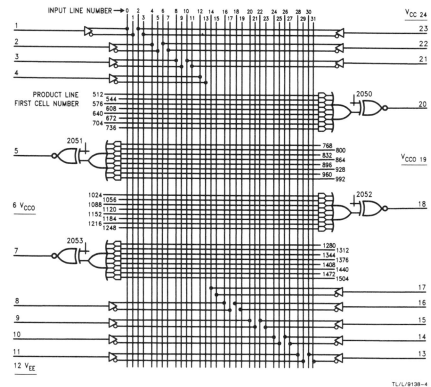

Fig. 2-5. Logic diagram of PAL1016P4A/PAL10016LP4A. Courtesy of National Semiconductor Corporation.

National also offers a family of Generic Array Logic (GAL) featuring the following architectures:

GAL16V8 Generic Array Logic
GAL20V8 Generic Array Logic
GAL16V8A Generic Array Logic
GAL20V8A Generic Array Logic
GAL16Z8 In-System reprogrammable (isp) Generic Array Logic

As with all field-programmable devices, the user of these devices provides the final manufacturing step. While major manufacturers of PAL devices undergo extensive testing when they are manufactured, their logic function can be fully tested only after they have been programmed to the user's pattern.

To ensure that the programmed PAL devices will operate properly in your system, National Semiconductor (along with most manufacturers of PAL devices) strongly recommends that PAL devices be functionally tested before they are installed in your system. Even though the number of post-programming functional failures is small, testing the logic function of the PAL devices before they reach system assembly will save board debugging and rework costs.

A variety of software tools and programming hardware is available to support the development of designs using PAL products. Software packages are discussed in Chapter 3, development systems in Chapter 4, and programmers in Chapter 5.

The main advantages of bipolar devices are high speed at low cost and high output drive current. A concern of bipolar technology relates to its high power consumption which is the result of the high temperatures at the internal junction points. The high amounts of heat might require special cooling appendages such as heat sinks or fans. Long term reliability of a semiconductor chip degrades proportionally with increasing junction temperatures following an exponential function described by the Arrhenius equation of kinetics of chemical reactions. The Arrhenius equation, which is a special case of the Van Hoff equation, assumes a failure rate proportional to EXP (Ea/kT) where Ea is the activation energy for the particular failure mechanism. The Arrhenius equation which governs the reaction rate of physical and chemical processes states that the reaction rate increases with temperature. The equation is:

$R = AC_{-Ea/kT}$, where

R = reaction rate

A = Frequency factor constant

Ea = Activation Energy (eV)

k = Boltzmann's constant

$(8.63 \times 10_{-5} \text{ eV/}°K)$

T = Absolute temperature (°Kelvin) at the site of the reaction

Reliability in this regard may be thought of as a measurement of how well an initially sound device will perform over time to its specified characteristics. Historically, semiconductor failures have primarily occurred during the early life phase of operation. After this initial phase, a low failure rate can be expected until the wearout phase is eventually reached. A large contributor to infant mortality (early life failures) in bipolar devices is operator variability in the manufacturing process. To minimize this problem, manufacturers employ the use of automated equipment to critical stages of semiconductor production and package assembly.

Device fabrication materials, chip mounting materials, handling procedures, and leadframe construction all affect device reliability. These and many other areas of product manufacturing are continuously investigated and refined. The manufacturers of PALs have in place of reliability testing programs that assure that the reliability of the programmable logic family meets established acceptable standards. A second concern related to bipolar PALs suggest that there are some problems that may be incurred in their integration into Analog systems.

There are also concerns that designs using PLDs require that the fuses be blown and because bipolar PLDs cannot be reprogrammed. In prototyping, several design iterations can increase the design cost significantly because each new design will require the use of a new part. In addition, if several parts have been programmed, and later a design error is uncovered, these programmed parts which might be stored in inventory must be discarded. A programmer PLD is tested by applying known values to its inputs and comparing the output to a known output map. Because bipolar fuses require that the fuses be blown one time, programmability suggests that an improperly programmed PLD must be discarded.

More specifically, in most conventional one-time-programmable TTL devices, programming is accomplished by running high current through tungsten alloy lateral fuse links, which in turn causes the tungsten to melt and break the connection to the transistor. This *lateral fuse* technique can in some cases create yield and test problems, such as partially tested fuses in which unmelted tungsten residue renders the device incapable of further programming. The burden of testing a programmer PLD is the customer's responsibility to ensure proper programming.

National Semiconductors has developed an *Avalanche Induced Migration* (AIM) technique that permits customer programming in steps. A relatively low initial level of current is applied, causing aluminum to heat and be diffused downward through the transistor junction to form connections without damaging the circuit. This *vertical fuse* can then be tested for programming integrity. If the desired connections are not fully formed, progressively higher levels of current can be applied to cause further diffusion of the aluminum. This iterative application of current and testing significantly improves programming yields without the risk of overstressing the circuitry. Even excessive aluminum migration only serves to enhance the programmed connection throughout the product's lifetime.

The vertical- use approach also permits more extensive manufacturer testing. Conventional devices include extra fuses in the array that are the only ones which can be tested for DC (voltage, current, power)/AC (frequency, propagation delay, rise and fall times) parameters; no testing can be performed on the fuses in the operational portion of the array. Devices programmed using the AIM technique permit testing of every cell for conductivity and programmability.

In addition, vertical-fuse devices require less space than lateral-fuse devices, which of course translates into higher densities and, thus, higher system speeds.

From the design perspective, the differences between lateral and vertical fuse techniques are totally transparent to the user because National's unique programming algorithm automatically compensates for the differences. Beginning with the equations that are put into the software through the JEDEC file that goes into the programmer, the design can be transported between the two techniques (vertical and lateral) to obtain the same result. This suggests that second sources can be designed for with no problem. National's algorithm is fully supported by all of the major programmer vendors, such as Data I/O to ensure industry-wide applicability.

National also produces EECMOS-based GAL devices, which offer dramatically improved programming and functional yields because they are instantly erasable and reprogrammable—with a minimum of up to 100 erase/write cycles guaranteed making them ideal for prototyping and for pattern changes or error recovery on the manufacturing floor.

Unlike conventional fuse-link TTL devices, which are tested on special test circuitry in the non-operational mode, GAL device AC/DC parameters and functionality are tested using the live circuitry that is actually used in the logic array. All programmable cells across the entire array can be tested in several different modes to check all worst-case patterns. In addition to a yes/no test for cell programmability, margin testing can determine the quality of programming achievable in any given cell. All inputs, product terms, and logic paths can be tested. As a result, the user is guaranteed 100% programming and functional yields.

The CMOS process, as discussed later in this section, also offers attractive speed/power advantages. Combining the EECMOS with the GALs architecture permits GAL devices to operate at bipolar speed and output drive levels while consuming less than half the power.

For maximum design flexibility, National's unique GAL architecture incorporates 8 Output Logic Macrocells (OLMCs) that enable the designer to configure outputs according to the specific application requirements. A single 20- or 24-pin device can emulate all common PAL architectures with full function, fuse map, and parametric compatibility.

ELECTRICALLY ERASABLE LOGIC

PEELs are manufactured using advanced EECMOS technology. This technology requires only about $1/8$ to $1/10$ of the power that is normally required with bipolar PLDs. In addition, this technology permits a device to operate a level less than 5 V, thus facilitating their use with analog circuits. The lower power consumption leads to lower operating temperatures and, of course, removal of the requirements for heat sinks and fans.

A PEEL device can be tested 100% at the factory for programmability, functionality, and parametric performance. All programmable bits can be checked as well as all AC and DC logic functions. While a bipolar PLD can be tested in a limited way for a specific application, a PEEL device can be tested independently for a specific application. These capabilities in some cases relate to a PEEL device resulting in reduced prototyping and production time. It normally requires 20 ns to erase a PEEL device compared with 20 minutes of exposure to UV light to erase an EPROM CMOS PLD. The added expense of a window in the chip is removed also because PEELs are electrically erased. PEEL devices are automatically erased by the PEEL programmer. Further, it is almost impossible to erase a PEEL device accidentally because their erasure requires special super voltages (16 V) and specific waveforms that are virtually impossible to duplicate unintentionally.

An EPROM cell is much smaller than bipolar fuse links, leading to high density on a PLD. In addition, the lower power requirements permit higher quantity of PEELs to be integrated on a PC board than bipolar PLDs do.

As discussed in Chapter 1, PLDs has a security bit that locks the designs from unwanted intrusion or copying. For bipolar devices, once the fuse is blown, it is very visible on the die permitting the logic fuse map to be reversed and made available to the unwanted intruder. On the other hand, EECMOS uses a floating gate to hold a charge that cannot be as easily seen as detected. Several PEELs have a signature word that permits a user to program an ID code that can be read after the security bit is set. This capability has found usefulness in inventory control procedures.

The two concerns related to the reliability of the EECMOS process in a PLD application are Endurance (P/E or Program/Erase Cycles) and Data Retention, that is, the time that the EECELL will hold its charge.

For PEEL reprogrammability, Fowler-Nordheim tunneling techniques are employed to trap charges onto a floating gate through a thin oxide insulator. The trapped charges remain after power has been removed allowing nonvolatility of programmed data. The charges can be removed by electrically erasing the device. Once fully erased, it can then be reprogrammed into a new configuration.

The PEEL according to its manufacturer is designed for programming endurance of up to 1000 complete erase/reprogram cycles with a data retention of 10 years—when used within the specified operating temperature range. This means that the PEEL can be reprogrammed up to 1000 times without degrading device operations and, similar to other nonvolatile memory technologies, the data last programmed will remain valid for 10 years.

GALs, manufactured by Lattice Semiconductors, also employs electrically erasable CMOS programmable logic technology. These devices are 100% bipolar compatible and provide a 24 mA output drive. A typical t_{pd} would be in 17 ns range. They are 100% programmable and reprogrammable. The outputs can be defined to be active high, active low, synchronous, or asynchronous.

COMPLEMENTARY METAL OXIDE SEMICONDUCTOR (CMOS) PROGRAMMABLE LOGIC (CPL)

Complementary Metal Oxide Semiconductor (CMOS) technology employs insulated-gate field effect transistors (IGFETs or MOSFETs) and appears to offer the ideal characteristics for logic circuits—low power dissipation, low propagation delay, controlled rise and fall time, and low noise immunity. Although CMOS circuits make use of the enhancement mode MOSFET, the use of both P and N channel types are combined. This combination gives rise to the term Complementary MOS (CMOS).

A typical CMOS gate dissipates less than 10 nanowatts of power and this small amount is due primarily to the flow of small leakage currents. Actually, the power dissipation that takes place in the gate is during switching. The actual amount of power dissipation depends on such tradeoff factors as power supply voltage, frequency of operation, output load, and input rise time. Today at 1 MHz, power dissipation is still less than 10 milliwatts.

The propagation delays through CMOS circuits are short in duration. For TTL and ECL circuits designed specifically for speed, CMOS circuits might be somewhat slower in some cases. Depending upon power supply voltage, the delay through a typical CMOS gate is less than 25 nanoseconds.

The rise and fall times of the voltage levels from CMOS circuits can be 20 to 50% more than the propagation delay. If the rise and fall times are displayed on an oscilloscope, they might appear more ramp-like than a step function. Lastly, the noise immunity is approximately 50% of the full logic voltage swing which makes this circuit as immune to noise as any other circuit.

The CMOS circuit operates from a positive supply voltage in the 3 to 18 volt range. Low power consumption is one of the most important features of CMOS technology. With most of the power dissipating only during device switching, it is important to describe the power dissipation in terms that reflect its dependency on operating frequency.

A standard power dissipation model includes the device's quiescent current (I_Q), the device's internal "power dissipation" capacitance (C_{PD}), the external load capacitance (C_L), and the output buffer capacitance (C_O):

$$P_D = V_{CC}I_Q + C_{PD}V_{CC}^2f + (C_L + C_O)V_{DS}^2f$$

The quiescent power is determined by the static current. The switching power consumption is determined by the internal power dissipation capacitance and by the operating frequency (f). The power consumed by driving the external load depends on the external load itself, the output buffer capacitance, the operating frequency (f), and the output low-to-high voltage swing (V_{DS}).

The internal power capacitance as well as the static supply current vary from one CPL type to another. Moreover, they depend on the specific code that is programmed into the device. The typical I_Q for CPL20 and CPL24 is 25 mA, and the typical C_{PD} is 45 pF. The load capacitance plays an even more important role in determining the power consumption of a CPL device. Because 8 outputs might toggle, each consisting of typically 10 pF, and each driving a 50 pF load, up to 2.4 mA per MHz can add to the device's static supply current.

The graph in FIG. 2-6 illustrates CPL power consumption as a function of operating frequency in comparison with bipolar PAL power consumption. All unused inputs are assumed to be tied to ground or V_{CC}, all active inputs are driven rail-to-rail, and the duty cycle is 50%. Measurements have shown that while the duty cycle does not greatly affect the CPL power consumption, up to 20% more power is consumed by the input buffers when the input voltage swings between .08 V and 2.0 V. Quarter power GALs operate cool at typically 30 mA.

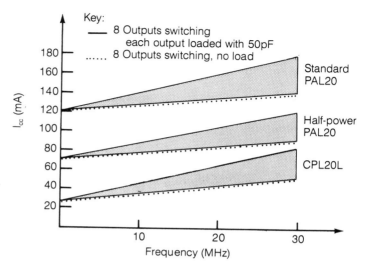

Fig. 2-6. CPL and PAL comparisons as a function of frequency. Courtesy of Samsung Semiconductor Corporation.

In circuits fabricated using CMOS technology, a parasitic four-layer SCR structure appears between V_{CC} and ground. This parasitic structure can short V_{CC} to ground when voltages greater than V_{CC} are applied to an input or an output pin. The phenomenon is called *latch-up* and can result in a damaged device. When a device is in latch-up mode, the power supply must be shut off to release the device back to normal operating mode.

The parasitic SCR structure in CMOS is illustrated in the simplified cross-section of an inverter shown in FIG. 2-7. Figure 2-8 shows a schematic representation of the same structure. When EA is raised above V_{CC}, current is injected from the emitter of QA and is swept to its collector. This current will increase the voltage at the gate of QB. Once above 0.78 V, it will turn QB on. QB will feed current back into RA and once a 0.7 V voltage drop appears across RA, QA will turn on and inject more current into RB. Once both transistors are on and enough current is provided to sustain the SCR, it will stay on even after EA and EB return to within the rail voltages.

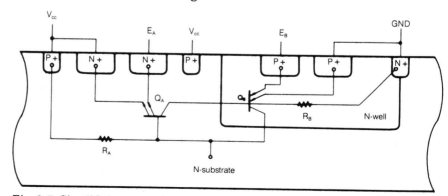

Fig. 2-7. Simplified cross-section of a CMOS inverter. Courtesy of Samsung Semiconductor Corporation.

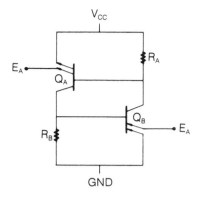

Fig. 2-8. CMOS SCR structure. Courtesy of Samsung Semiconductor Corporation.

Because low RA and RB resistance values reduce the gain of QA and QB, Samsung Semiconductors CPL devices are designed to have low RA and RB. In addition, large diodes are connected between each signal pin and the supply, to shut out latch-up trigger currents.

When a P-channel MOS transistor is used as a pull-up transistor on the output driver of an IC, another parasitic transistor is formed that worsens the latch-up problem. The CPL devices use N-channel pull-up transistors that maintain TTL compatibility and improve latch-up protection.

A substrate bias generator provides important additional latch-up protection in CPL devices. It keeps the substrate at approximately -3 V below ground level. The parasitic diode at an input pin will not turn on unless the voltage applied to that pin is more negative than -3 V. The substrate bias also eliminates the substrate currents due to undershoot, thereby providing higher input noise tolerance.

GAL devices are designed with an on-board charge pump to negatively bias the substrate. The negative bias is of sufficient magnitude to prevent input undershoots from causing the circuitry to latch. Additionally, outputs are designed with N-channel pull-ups instead of the traditional P-channel pull-ups to eliminate any possibility of SCR-induced latching.

Samsung Semiconductor's CPL devices are designed to withstand currents typically well above the specified minimum of 200 mA at 7 V, V_{CC} and 125°C. This parameter is measured on a static basis (see FIG. 2-9).

ESD protection is accomplished by preventing a high voltage from reaching the internal transistors of the integrated circuit. The circuit of each input pin includes a thick-oxide transistor, a thin-oxide transistor, and the line resistance, Rp, between the transistors (see FIG. 2-10). The thick-oxide transistor turns on when a large positive voltage is applied to the input pin. When the voltage arriving at the thin-oxide transistor exceeds 13 V, the transistor turns on and protects the internal circuitry by discharging the current to ground. This current is then limited by the line resistance, Rp. A high negative voltage applied to the input pin is similarly discharged by the network of the substrate diodes that start conducting when the applied negative voltage is below the substrate level. The ESD protection incorporated in the output structure is shown in FIG. 2-11.

Fig. 2-9. Test setup for measuring DC latch-up. Courtesy of Samsung Semiconductor Corporation.

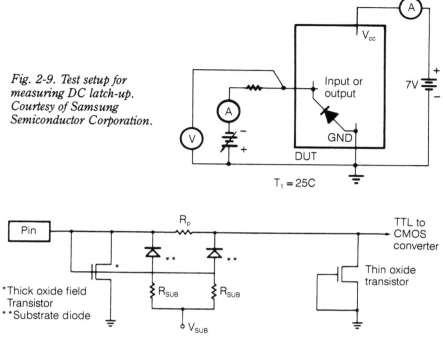

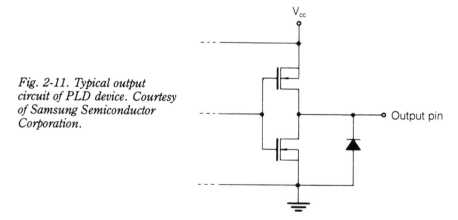

Fig. 2-10. Input protection circuit. Courtesy of Samsung Semiconductor Corporation.

Fig. 2-11. Typical output circuit of PLD device. Courtesy of Samsung Semiconductor Corporation.

CMOS technology appears to provide improved supply current requirements and input output propagation delay performance (see FIG. 2-12).

The performance and flexibility provided by a PEEL device is primarily due to CMOS EPROM technology offering low power, high speed, and nonvolatile reprogrammability. Utilizing this technology along with special design techniques, the PEEL maintains the low power characteristics of CMOS while achieving the speeds of standard bipolar PLDs. For instance, the maximum

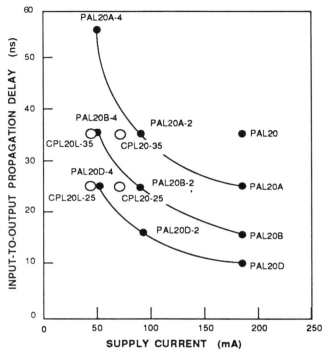

Fig. 2-12. CPL and PAL comparisons. Courtesy of Samsung Semiconductor Corporation.

supply current required by a standard PAL device can range from 90 mA to as much as 240 mA depending on the vendor and the type of device. Although half and quarter power PALs are available, the improvement in power consumption is usually at the sacrifice of speed and cost. Comparable PEEL devices, however, offer a normal standby current requirement in the tens of milliamps, with the active supply current typically adding 0.71/MHz switching frequency. Additionally, the Z version PEEL devices offer a special low power mode for minimized standby current consumption.

Although implemented in EPROM technology, often associated with the in-system reprogrammable memory devices, the PEEL is programmed out-of-system via a PLD programmer. However, several other beneficial reasons for using EPROM technology include: enhanced factory testing allowing 100% programming and functional integrity, cost-effective windowless packaging and erase/reprogram time in seconds instead of approximately 20 minutes for EPROM PLDs.

CMOS PEEL device technology offers improved noise margins. This is because PEEL device outputs will swing "rail-to-rail" (approximately 0-5 V when driving other CMOS components. Bipolar PLDs and many other CMOS PLDs only offer TTL interface levels typically ranging from 0.4 V for V_{OL} and 3.8 V for V_{OL} levels. Because of lower power consumption, PEEL device operating temperatures are dramatically lower. For example, the junction to ambient operating temperature of a plastic 20-pin bipolar PAL can be as high as 127°C with an ambient of 70°C in still air,, whereas the operating temperature of a CMOS PEEL 18CV8 device in the same package and ambient environment is less than 80°C, a 47°C improvement. A few benefits of lower operating temperatures include the elimination of expensive cooling techniques such as large vented cases and noisy fans. More importantly, lower operating temperatures mean improved reliability. This is because MTBF (mean time between failure) formulas are directly related to operating temperatures of both integrated circuits as well as complete system designs. Thus, the lower the operating temperatures, the longer the period of time between potential failures.

ULTRAVIOLET ERASABLE CMOS

Until the invention of the first EPLD by Altera in 1984, the only technology used for programmable logic devices was bipolar and fuse-based. The active elements on these devices were constructed from traditional bipolar transistors (TTL) with arrays of fuses providing programmable interconnect structures (see FIG. 2-13). These fuse elements were constructed from a variety of exotic metal alloys and/or polysilicon structures, but all as stated previously (save National Semiconductors AIM technology) relied upon the physical destruction of the fuse by passing large currents through their small geometries to open connections.

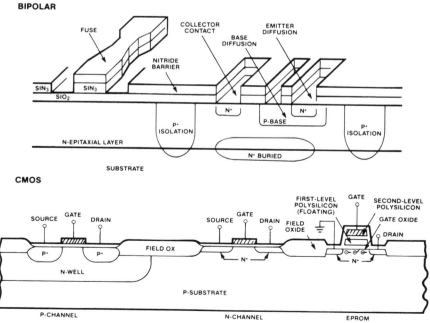

Fig. 2-13. Bipolar PLD and CMOS EPLD technology. Courtesy of Altera Corporation.

The power-hungry nature of bipolars severely limited integration levels. Altera replaced bipolar technology with CMOS and fuses with reprogrammable EPROM bits. These bits are much smaller in size, electrically programmable, and UV-erasable. They allow full factory testing, guaranteeing 100% programming yield at the customer site. CMOS technology, as stated, also provides low-power operation, allowing higher integration levels.

Figure 2-14 compares fuse and EPROM cell programming technology. The fuse destructively opens, while the EPROM cell operates via floating gate charge injection. The programming process consists of placing sufficient voltage (typically in excess of 12 V) on the drain of the transistor to create a strong electric field and energize electrons to jump from the drain region to the floating gate. Electrons are attracted to the floating gate and become trapped when the voltage is removed. If the gate remains at a low voltage during programming, electrons will not be attracted and the floating gate will remain uncharged. Trapped charge changes the threshold of the EPROM cell from a relatively low value with no charge present ("erased") to a higher value when programmed.

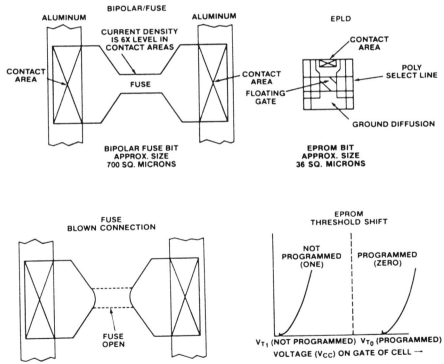

Fig. 2-14. PLD-programmable elements and programming technique. Courtesy of Altera Corporation.

Within the EPLD programmable array, a sense amplifier or comparator is placed at the end of each product-term line. By setting a reference voltage into it midway between the programmed and unprogrammed levels, the state of the

EPROM cells along the product term is sensed and used to select the desired logic function. Low threshold cells with a logical one placed on their select gates (associated input) will tend to pull the product term line down and cause the logic term to go to a zero. Transistors with high thresholds will not conduct even when their gates are at a logical one, and effectively represent a no-connect. This technology, pioneered with EPROM memory in the early 70s, provides reliable, testable programming and operation of Altera EPLDs. Altera devices currently use state-of-the-art 1.0 micron, CMOS EPROM technology, with work underway to move to submicron geometries. As the basic logic array is composed of N-channel EPROM transistors, device characteristics are optimized to maximize performance of the N-channel device. This approach minimizes overall input to output delays on the chip.

Referring back to FIG. 2-13 (a basic cross section of the cell technology), the gate oxide transistor is 200 angstroms thick and programmed cell threshold exceeds 6 V. Basic logic cell size is 24 square microns.

The CMOS push-pull output stages used on Altera EPLDs provide good AC and DC load driving capability in a system environment. Io and Ioh specs for general-purpose devices are guaranteed at 4 mA or 8 mA (depending on the device), adequate levels for all but system bus driving applications. New custom peripheral devices such as the EPB1400 (BUSTER) and EPB2001/2002 (Micro Channel Adapter Chip Set) are designed to drive the system bus directly, providing full 24 mA drive capability. AC output characteristics for Altera EPLDs are typically specified with 50 pF output loads. Additional output capacitive loading effects the device output delay. The timing parameter used is Tpd (input-output combinatorial delay). Incremental delay per picofarad of capacitance is typically 0.1 ns or less at room temperature.

A typical programming cycle for Altera EPLDs is shown in FIG. 2-15. The procedure is:

1. Raise input select lines for a given row of logic bits to a high Vpp voltage (12.5 V nominally).
2. Place either 0 or 12.75 V on associated product term or column lines.
3. Programming algorithm is a sequence of 1 ms pulses separated by program verify cycles.
4. Program pulse width controlled by a Vhh (super-high input level) signal applied to one of the device pins.
5. Once a byte has been verified to program correctly, "overprogram" pulses are applied to doubly ensure device programming.

The programming operation is done 8-bits at a time. Either Altera-supplied or other reviewed PLD programming hardware can be used. Altera devices also feature a security (verify-protect) bit that can be programmed to inhibit any verification or interrogation of the device's contents. This can be done as the final stage in the programming process to ensure device code security.

To ensure reliable operation in the user's system, substantial factory testing is performed on all devices prior to shipment. Foremost among these tests

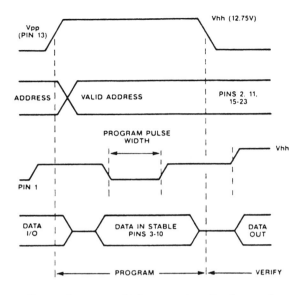

Fig. 2-15. Typical programming cycle. Courtesy of Altera Corporation.

are cell margin tests which guarantee the in-service retention of EPROM bit programming. Cell margin testing is a means to determine the amount of charge trapped on the floating gate structure.

Charge loss results from electrons leaking from the floating gate structure over time and results in a net reduction in programmed cell threshold. Charge gain results from an accumulation of charge on the floating gate, usually as a result of electric fields caused by operation of the device. Charge loss and charge gain mechanisms could affect program retention. To avoid such problems, Altera's reliability evaluation has included burn-in of devices at temperatures of up to 250°C for periods of a week or more. As a point of reference, this corresponds to well over 100,000 years of operation at 70°C.

Figure 2-16 illustrates the concept of program margin. As mentioned previously, EPROM arrays depend upon cell threshold shifts for correct operation.

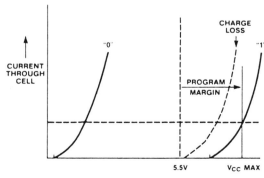

Fig. 2-16. The concept of program margin. Courtesy of Altera Corporation.

Zero and one I-V characteristics for the EPROM cell are shown. Program margin is a measure of the spread between actual device threshold and minimum required device threshold for correct operation.

To detect cell margin, Altera devices are subjected to special test modes that allow the external control of EPROM bit gate voltages. By varying this voltage, a measure of cell margin can be obtained. This can accurately monitor cell charge and retention.

Due to the fundamental structure of CMOS devices, parasitic bipolar transistors are present in the device structure. Typically, the base-emitter and base-collector junctions of these transistors are not forward biased and as a result the transistors are not turned-on. Figure 2-17 shows a cross-section of a CMOS wafer with the primary parasitic transistors indicated. By connecting the p-type substrate to the most negative voltage available on-chip (V_{cc}), all junctions should in theory remain reverse-biased. However, two factors can alter this ideal state.

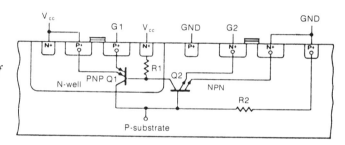

Fig. 2-17. Cross-section of a CMOS wafer with the parasitic transistors indicated. Courtesy of Altera Corporation.

Source of latch-up

As shown in the diagram, besides parasitic transistors, parasitic resistors also occur in the CMOS structure. These resistors are of no concern as long as currents do not flow through the structure laterally. But if any of the associated diodes turn on for any reason, I-R drops can occur in the structure. The initial turn on of these diodes usually is the result of power-supply or I/O pin transients that exceed the limits of V_{ss} and V_{cc}. These transients can be induced by signal ringing and other inductive effects in the system.

The potential problem is that once parasitic structures begin to conduct, the effect is regenerative, reinforcing itself until potentially destructive currents flow. As previously discussed, this effect is called latch-up. Referring back to the diagram, as current flows through the parasitic transistor, the I-R drop through the resistor increases, further forward-biasing the base-emitter junction. The cycle continues until current is limited by drops in the primary current path. However, this current could be at such a level that internal circuitry is permanently damaged.

Altera components have been designed to eliminate the effects of latch-up inducing transients. Under reasonable system operating conditions, all devices are guaranteed to withstand input extremes between $V_{ss} - 1$ volt and $V_{cc} + 1$ volt and force currents of 100 mA or less through the device pins. To minimize the possibility of inducing latch-up, some general system design guidelines on sequencing of power and inputs to the device are recommended. For example, the normal application sequence of voltages to the device should be:

1. V_{ss} or GND
2. V_{cc} (+5V)
3. Inputs

When removing power from the device, the sequence should be executed in reverse: first remove or take inputs low, then remove or lower V_{cc}. Simultaneous application of inputs and V_{cc} to the device, as might occur as a power supply ramps during power-up, should be safe. Care should be taken to ensure inputs cannot rise faster than supply under extreme conditions.

In some applications, boards are "hot-socketed" in the field. To ensure under these conditions that latch-up inducing levels are not applied to the EPLD, the circuitry shown in FIG. 2-18 can be used. This normally would be required only if the EPLD has inputs tied directly to the edge connector. The diodes clamp the inputs at acceptable levels and the series resistor further limits the injection of current into the EPLD input and clamp diodes. The result is an interface giving maximum protection.

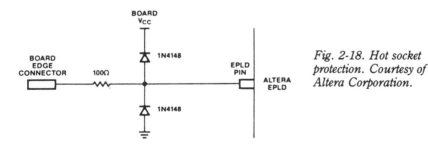

Fig. 2-18. Hot socket protection. Courtesy of Altera Corporation.

Electrostatic Discharge (ESD) can cause device failure when improper handling occurs. EPLD handling during the programming cycle increases exposure to potential static-induced failure. Voltages into the tens of kilovolts can be generated by the human body during normal activity. Wearing ground straps during device handling and grounding all surfaces that come in contact with components reduces the likelihood of damages.

Altera components employ special structures to reduce the effects of ESD at the pins. Figure 2-19 shows a representation of a typical input structure. Diode structures, as well as specialized field-effect transistors, shunt harmful voltages to ground before destructive currents will flow. Altera devices typically withstand ESD voltages in excess of 3 kV, and are thus safe under normal handling conditions.

Large switching currents can flow through supply and output pins during high-performance operation. If a 50 pF capacitor is charged from 0 to 5 V in 10 ns, a dynamic current of 25 mA will flow. If 24 outputs on an EPLD switch simultaneously, as might be the case with n EP900, the total transient current

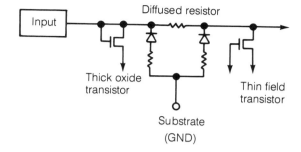

Fig. 2-19. EPLD input protection structure. Courtesy of Altera Corporation.

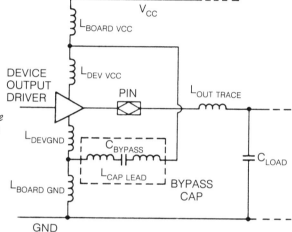

Fig. 2-20. Board level noise problem. Courtesy of Altera Corporation.

can exceed 600 mA! This can severely degrade V_{cc} supply voltage due to inductive effects in the device and system environment. Figure 2-20 shows the distribution of typical inductances that can contribute to the problem.

The key to controlling these inductive effects is to adequately decouple the V_{cc} supply to ground at each device by a suitable capacitor or combination of capacitors. This capacitor can then act as a reservoir of charge to supply the transient switching needs of the device. It is recommended that a 0.1 to 0.2 microfarad capacitor (depending on device, see the appropriate device data sheet) be connected from each V_{cc} pin to ground at the device. High quality capacitors with low internal and lead inductance should be used (monolithic ceramic or tantalum), and leads must be kept short to limit series inductance which degrades capacitor effectiveness. Careful decoupling of the power supply is just good design practice. Decoupling is particularly important in devices capable of large current drive, such as the EPB1400, a Buster device.

GALLIUM ARSENIDE (GaAs)

As stated in Chapter 1, GaAs has characteristics that make it very suitable for high-speed ICs, when compared with the previous devices that are usually manufactured using silicon. First, lower applied electric fields are possible with the higher electron mobility of GaAs transistor channels as compared with correspondingly doped silicon device channels. In addition, parasitic capacitances are normally less than silicon ICs owing to the fact that GaAs is a semi-insulating rather than semiconducting material. GaAs devices are capable of switching faster because of their drift velocity electric field relationship. Silicon has a monotonic rise of drift velocity versus the electric field and saturates at 6.5×10^6 cm/s, while GaAs is non-monotonic with a peak velocity of 2.2×10^7 cm/s. The benefits of the lower electric field of GaAs at maximum electron velocity results in lesser power dissipation than found in silicon for the same switching speeds. Because heat from the higher power devices can create problems at higher temperatures, GaAs might benefit those circuits that operate at very high speeds.

GaAs junction temperatures and device power are related approximately by the following relationship:

$$T_J = T_A + 10°C + (O_{SC} + O_{CA})P_D$$

where T_J = Maximum junction temperature (°C)
T_A = Maximum ambient temperature (°C)
P_D = Maximum device power dissipation (W)
O_{SC} = Die surface to case thermal resistance (°C/W) (determined by package design)
O_{CA} = Case to ambient thermal resistance (°C/W)(determined by board layout, etc.)

Comparisons are frequently made between bipolar ECL and GaAs. Bipolar ECL circuits are capable of operating in the 500 MHz range while GaAs are capable of operating at frequencies in the 750 MHz to 1.5 GHz range. Bipolar ECL devices contain up to 5000 gates while for GaAs between 500 to 2000 gates. When enhancement and depletion mode metal semiconductor field affect transistors (MESFETs) are used in GaAs at peak operating frequency, between 1-2.6 mw of power is dissipated per gate while for bipolar ECL between 1-3 mw per gate. From a cost standpoint, GaAs are three to six times as expensive as bipolar ECLs, more specifically bipolar ECLs can cost approximately $.05 per gate while GaAs cost approximately $.15 per gate (three times the ECL cost).

Lastly, GaAs ICs are radiation resistant unlike silicon based ICs primarily because there is no oxide or insulator between the gate and channel to charge up when ionizing radiation is present.

Reliability continues to improve in GaAs as continued research yields new knowledge and applications, one of the reliability inductors is the burn-in yield that is used to weed out infant mortality failures. The yield has increased from approximately 85% in 1985 to approximately 98% today. Early life (168-336 hours) failure after the infant failure have been removed are currently in the neighborhood of .05%.

GigaBit Logic Inc., subjects all ICs to a production burn-in screen at T = 150°C for periods varying from 24 to 168 hours depending on maturity and

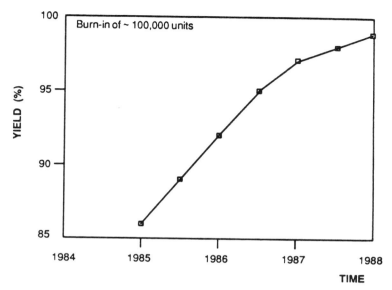

Fig. 2-21. Burn-in yield over a period of approximately three years. Courtesy of Giga-Bit Logic, Inc.

complexity. Figure 2-21 shows the burn-in yield over a period of approximately 3 years.

POINTS TO CONSIDER ABOUT PLD TECHNOLOGY

The intent of this chapter has been to provide a discussion of the various technology related tradeoff factors that would benefit the reader in selecting the appropriate PLD device for a specific circuit design. Bipolar PALs remain the best value and are in widespread use because of high speed at low cost, compatibility with Boolean equation sum of products form, architectural simplicity, user familiarity and the like.

As discussed, other technologies offer other advantages in terms of AC and DC characteristics as well as such considerations as erasibility and reliability.

I would like to point out that PLDs are becoming more and more complex as the future unfolds. Refer to Chapter 1 if you need to review several of the architectures discussed. However, complexity should not be taken as synonymous with"best." The appropriate PLD must be selected to best benefit the design. In many cases, members of the PAL family might meet the needs of a circuit at a cost significantly less than a more complex device that contains a great deal of unneeded features such as macrocells, buried registers and the like. On the other hand, these extra features might result in tremendous cost savings when circuits require flexibility by reducing the chip count because these features are already a part of the PLD design. Therefore, be careful not to undershoot and require a high chip count or overshoot and pay the penalty of unnecessary cost. Finally, consider testability as it relates to complexity. As a general rule, the more complex the PLD, the more formidable the task of testing the PLD.

As with all field programmable devices, the user provides the final manufacturing step. While PALs and other devices undergo extensive testing when they are manufactured, their logic function can be fully tested after they have been programmed.

As PLDs become more and more complex, new problems are emerging that the PLD user must address. Before the advent of the PLD, standard parts (ICs) were purchased from an IC vender and integrated onto a board with other standard parts. However, with PLDs and other Application-Specific Integrated Circuits (ASIC), the board of yesterday is contained within the ASIC today. To test a board of standard ICs presented problems. With the proliferation of ASICs, the testing of the board has become more complex as testing of the ASKs that comprise the board has become more complex. Thus the need of testing PLDs and ASICs has been accompanied by the need of test equipment capable of performing the necessary test in a time- and cost-saving manner due to increased competition.

The circuit designer of the ASIC and the vendor in today's environment must form a close partnership. If an ASIC does not perform as it was intended, the source of the problem must be identified as originating with the IC vendor or the circuit designer. This partnership grows out of the need to test the part quickly in top production.

The above gives rise to the need to quickly produce test programs, frequently within hours, that are free of bugs as debugging efforts will result in late deliveries and missed sales. Because the number of ASIC designs are increasing while large volume production remains low, learning curves are almost nonexistent as one would obtain with standard IC parts. Even further, the ASIC manufacturer only guarantees that the part is good, not that the design created by the circuit designer will work. Because the final burden of a properly functioning circuit is the responsibility of the design engineer, the design engineer must perform functional testing. The vendor, on the other hand, must ensure the part is free of defects by performing preload testing.

Functional testing (performed by the circuit designer) is usually performed by supplying several user-specified sets of vectors to the PLD under test. The vectors specify the expected output for the specified input. (The voltages applied are those required for the specific technology of the PLD, TTL, CMOS, etc.) The input vectors in many cases are created manually or with automatic test vector generation software.

Preload testing is done by PLD manufacturers and normally includes loading several arbitrary states into a register directly and recording its output. First, super voltages in the neighborhood of 10-15 V are applied to one or more pins and the data to be preloaded into the register applied to the other pins. Next, the supervoltage pins are reduced to normal operating voltage followed by a vector using normal voltages.

Several problems occur with preload testing. For example, if the PLD to be tested has been soldered on the circuit board, the supervoltages applied to the

PLD might damage other parts. In addition, the measurement of DC and AC parameters are very difficult to perform with preload vectors due to the fact that the supervoltages leave residual transients that must be allowed to settle. In this regard, the DC and AC measurements might not be true measurements but true measurements plus transient measurements.

Anvil ATG software (see FIG. 2-22) automatically generates high coverage functional test vectors for all types of PLDs, including PALs, FPLAs, FLGAs, FPLSs, and other architectures. These vectors are applied after programming, either on the programmer, on a device tester, or during in-circuit testing. Testing the PLDs individually prior to functional board test or system test results in large savings in testing, diagnosis, repair, and inventory costs.

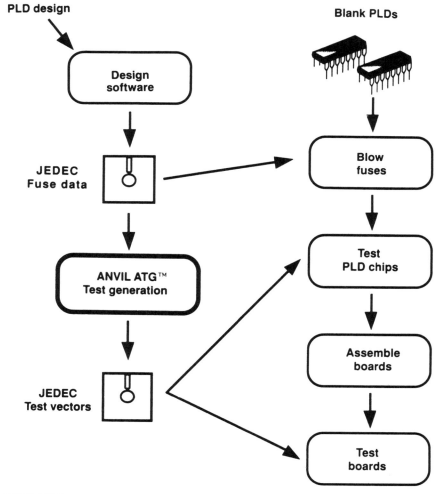

ANVIL ATG is a trademark of Anvil Software, Inc.

Fig. 2-22. Role of test generation software in modern electronics manufacturing. Courtesy of Anvil Software, Inc.

The software is composed of an event-driven time-based simulator, concurrent fault simulator, general purpose automatic test vector generator, a menu interface, and support programs. It is written in C and currently runs on PC/ST, PC/AT, and compatibles with 640K RAM and 4MB available disk space. Support for additional host computers is available.

ANVIL ATG software produces functional tests that operate the device as it will be used in the final application. No preload, "jam load," or other testing shortcut is used.

This software provides high fault coverage typically achieving 90-100% detection, even on highly sequential designs (such as state machines) and designs where feedback creates memory (as in a 16L8). Faults considered are:

Logic gates stuck-at-0 and stuck-at-1
Blown fuses faulted intact
Intact fuses faulted blown

Faults that are undetectable (due to redundancy or because they are in unused circuitry) are removed automatically so they do not obscure the true fault coverage. A typical 16R8 design has about 1200 detectable faults, while a typical 22V10 design has 3500 detectable faults.

Monitoring the effects of tester skew during simulation and masking out any output states that are not reliable and repeatable is possible with this software. In addition, any conflicts between the tester and chip are identified and fixed automatically. Any vectors provided by the user are checked for races, conflicts, and other problems, and are corrected automatically.

The software is operated through a simple menu and fill-in-form interface. The menu can be bypassed in order to run a series of jobs in batch mode without operator attention. An easy-to-read manual is provided with the software, both on paper and in machine-readable form so that extra copies can be printed by the user.

The ANVIL ATG software reads the fuse information from the JEDEC standard fuse file that all commercial design software produces and that all programming equipment reads. When the vectors have been generated, they are written back to the JEDEC file, again using the industry-standard formats.

Model Libraries

The ANVIL ATG S50 base product comes with a model library containing 5S commonly used parts:

16L8	16R4	16R6	16R8	22V10
20L8	20R4	20R6	20R8	20L10
20X10	20X8	20X4	20S10	20SR4
20SR8	16P8	16RP4	16RP6	16RP8
10H8	12H6	14H4	16H2	16C1
10L8	12L6	14L4	16L2	12L10

14L8	16L6	18L4	20L2	20C1
100	103	105	151	153
155	157	159	161	162
163	167	168	173	179
TII05	16V8	16V8A	20V8	20V8A

Other configurations of the base product are available. Some of the additional models are listed below (and sold separately):

20SR10 32VX10 20RA10 16V8 20V8 EP320 EP600
SIG405 ATMEL750 CYP33X Series EP900 EP1800

Some of these models may require additional RAM (beyond 640K).

Tester Support

Translators are available for the following testers:

Sentry GR1732 GR125 IMS GR227X Factron Teradyne L200
HP3065/3070 LMA323i/324i SCH300 Series

Call for information on these and other testers.

Because a PLD can be constrained by surrounding circuitry on the circuit board, ANVIL ATG software can be told which pins are tied high, low, together or are inaccessible, and generate vectors for an in-circuit tester accordingly.

The power-up state can be specified by the user as "unknown," "all registers low," or "all registers high."

Update Service

Updates during the first year are included with the product purchase. The update service includes bug fixes and enhancements to the software, documentation, and individual models plus telephone support. New models and major new software capability are not included in the update service—they are considered new products.

This chapter has provided a discussion of the various characteristics that the circuit designer should consider in selecting the proper PLD for the circuit under design. Both bipolar (TTL and ECL) and CMOS technologies were discussed as well as erasability technologies (electrical or ultraviolet). Gallium Arsenide technology features were also discussed. Lastly, testability was given brief treatment because the more complex the PLD the more difficult to test for operability.

In following chapters, PLD software is discussed to provide an overview of the various logic synthesis tools available for use by the circuit designer to make the task easier to accomplish.

3

Logic Synthesis and Software Tools

There has been a parallel growth in the development of software with the growth in complexity of integrated circuits. This growth has led to the concept of *logic synthesis*.

LOGIC SYNTHESIS

Figure 3-1 presents the refinement of a chart, originally developed by D. Gajaski and R. Kuhn[1] that might be helpful in understanding the concept. This chart is commonly referred to as the Y chart and is used as a model to identify the three domains of design specifications—behavioral, structural and physical.

The chart increases in abstraction as movement is made from the center to the outer edges of its three axes. The highest level of abstraction is found in the behavioral domain. Within this domain, no reference is made to the design in terms of the physical characteristics of the chip or layout of the board, but it abstractly identifies the specifications of the functional requirements of the design. These specifications can be given in the form of performance requirements or algorithms as high-level equations expressed with relational operators such as greater than or less than signs. The structural domain maps the functionality of the system (as described by the behavioral domain) into a set of structural components. Typically, at this level, the circuit designer might express the design in terms of the number and type of gates required and how the various elements of the circuit are interconnected. The physical domain relates to the geometrical representation of the design in terms of the layout of elements within a chip or board and the interconnections between them.

The Technology Research Group defines logic synthesis as "the automatic conversion of behavioral specifications into structural circuit descriptions."[2]

---

[1]D. Gajaski and R. Kuhn. "Guest Editors' Introduction: New VLSI Tools." *Computer*, Vol. 16, No. 12 pp. 11-14, December 1983.

[2]*The Technology Research Group Letter*, Vol. 2, No. 1, pp. 1-6, February 1987.

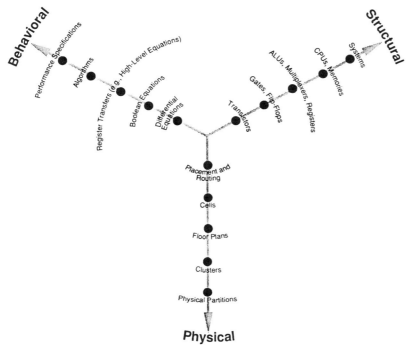

Fig. 3-1. The three domains of design requirements. Courtesy of Data I/O Corporation.

The structural descriptions are at the logic level of design representation, for example, the conversion of Boolean equations into flip-flops. The definition encompasses the functional block level of representations including the conversion of register transfer level (RTL) descriptions, state machines, high-level equations, and truth tables into ALUs, multiplexes, and registers.

In FIG. 3-2 concentric circles have been added to designate the five levels of design representation: architectural, algorithmic, functional block, logic, and circuit. The conversions from the behavioral to the structural domain are known as *synthesis*, while conversions from the structural to the physical domain are known as *compilation*. *Refinement* refers to the conversion of a more abstract design description into a more detailed representation. Logic synthesis tools can include compilation capabilities and refinement capabilities as well as optimizers to eliminate redundant circuitry and determine the best tradeoff between such factors as speed and size. The use of logic synthesis tools results in enhanced productivity, higher quality designs, fewer errors, lower chip costs, and technology flexibility. These tools facilitate the revisions of designs because the circuit designer is operating at a higher level of description than is possible with structural representations.

Logic synthesis tools initially were what can be considered partial tools, such as logic reduction algorithms that minimized circuit size by eliminating redundancies in the design or state machine synthesizers that converted behav-

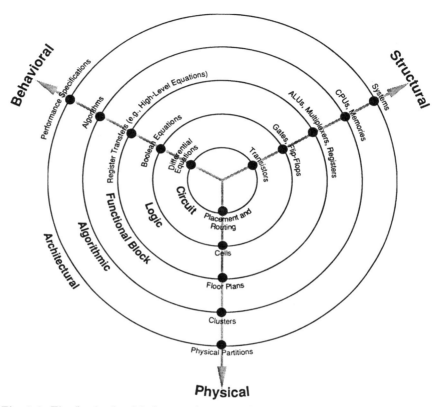

Fig. 3-2. The five levels of design requirements. Courtesy of Data I/O Corporation.

ioral representations of state machines to structural form. These tools performed only a small subset of the broad range of functions handled by today's tools. In addition, these early tools were not available in commercial form; they were either developed for in-house use by companies such as Bell Laboratories or else used for research purposes by universities such as Carnegie Mellon and the University of California at Berkeley.

Later work at Berkeley led to the development of the PRESTO and EXPRESSO logic reduction algorithms in the early 1980s. Strictly speaking, these algorithms are optimization tools; they minimize circuit size rather than converting behavioral descriptions to structural form. However, these reduction algorithms form the basis for the optimization routines used by many of today's tools and therefore deserve mention in any chronology of the origins of logic synthesis.

The first commercially available reduction algorithm appeared in the late 1970s and early 1980s. However, these first algorithms worked only with PLDs; they could not be used for any higher order ASICs, such as gate arrays, standard cells, or full custom chips. Because the higher order ASICs have large numbers of gates and an almost infinite number of architectural possibilities, it is much harder to write and process logic synthesis algorithms for them than for

PLDs, which have considerably fewer gates and only a small number of architectural variations.

The first of these early commercial products to reach the market was PALASM, introduced in the late 1970s by Monolithic Memories, Inc., (now part of Advanced Micro devices). PALASM converts PLD designs expressed in Boolean equations into fuse maps used for programming the devices.

Compared to the latest generation of logic tools, this early version of PALASM was relatively limited in its capabilities. Not only did it apply just to PLDs, but it applied just to one type of PLD: the PAL manufactured by Monolithic Memories, Inc. PALASM was also limited in that it accepted behavioral design descriptions only at the logic level (i.e., in Boolean equations) rather than at the functional block level. Finally, in its early form, PALASM did not include any optimization functions. Nevertheless, the early version of PALASM achieved broad success commercially and played a key role in generating widespread acceptance for the use of PLDs.

PALASM was followed several years later by third-party, vendor-independent logic synthesis tools for PLDs, such as ABEL from Data I/O. These tools were more sophisticated in that they allowed for higher-level behavioral descriptions (such as truth tables, state diagrams, and high-level equations) and could perform logic reduction as well as synthesis. However, these tools could not perform other types of design optimization available in today's logic synthesis tools, such as tailoring an optimization to favor speed over size. In addition, these tools were still limited to PLDs.

In the past few years, the greater complexity of chips has given rise to computer-aided manufacturing (CAM) tools that helped automate such functions as production testing and circuit board layout. These tools were followed by computer-aided design (CAD) and computer-aided engineering (CAE) tools which helped automate the process of describing and analyzing structural designs.

When performing a programmable logic design, a behavioral design description is first put into logic synthesis software which first partitions and analyzes the description to determine the nature of the functions and their interconnection. Then, using a series of rules for translating behavioral representations into structural representations, the software develops a plan for building the circuit and generates a structural description geared to the target technology.

Although all logic synthesis tools follow this general procedure, individual tools can differ significantly from one another. Some of the ways in which they differ include:

- *The sophistication of the input descriptions they accept.* Some tools, for instance, accept behavioral descriptions only at the logic level (i.e., Boolean equations); others accept descriptions at the functional block level as well.
- *The range of functions they understand.* For example, some tools work only with combinatorial logic, while others work with both combinatorial

and sequential logic. Similarly, some tools can be applied only to synchronous designs, while others work with both synchronous and asynchronous designs.

- *The way they translate behavior into structure.* Some tools apply rigid rules based on specific definitions of language constructs; others use more flexible approaches.
- *The number of different IC technologies they support.* Some tools support only PLDs, others support a range of user-configurable devices, and still others support high-end ASICs.
- *Whether they include optimization routines or not—and, if so, how effective these routines are.* For example, some tools can optimize only on a local basis; they can remove unnecessary gates from a particular function but cannot determine whether the function itself is unnecessary. Others can optimize designs on a global basis.
- *Whether they include partitioning routines or not.* Such routines are useful for fitting a large design into multiple smaller devices.

The steps listed below describe how the logic synthesis process works in the majority of today's products. Some products do not include such related capabilities as optimization and partitioning; however, these additional capabilities significantly enhance the usefulness of logic synthesis tools, resulting in better designs, greater engineering productivity, and reduced development time and costs.

Step 1: Design Entry

The first step in the logic synthesis process is to enter the design description in behavioral terms. Typically, logic synthesis tools provide the engineer with choices between several types of descriptions at the functional block level, such as high-level logic equations, truth tables, and state diagrams. Having a range of choices is helpful because different types of circuits are most easily described in different ways. Counters and multiplexers, for example, are most easily expressed in equations; display drivers and code converters in truth tables; and state machines and logic sequencers in state diagrams.

The more sophisticated tools also allow mixed-mode design entry, in which some elements are described in structural terms and others are described in behavioral terms. This mixed-mode capability is helpful because circuits that are basically data paths, such as memory arrays and data buses, are often easier to express in structural terms.

Step 2: Design Verification

This process takes place as soon as the design is entered to make sure that it performs the intended function. To do so, test vectors are generated that describe the inputs to the circuit and, if known, the expected outputs. The software then applies the test vectors to a behavioral model of the circuit, calculating the actual outputs that will result from each input.

By performing verification early in the development cycle, logic errors that are found can be corrected before they have a chance to affect later stages of the design process, thereby reducing total development time. If the functional verifier is both quick and interactive, it also makes it easy to experiment with various "what-if" scenarios, resulting in better, more creative designs.

Step 3: Optimization

Optimization capabilities are a useful addition to logic synthesis tools because they help ensure that the design meets the performance specifications. The more sophisticated optimizers allow the designer to specify the degree to which the design is to be optimized so that tradeoffs can be made between such factors as circuit speed and size. The optimization process can include such steps as:

- *Translation*, which transforms a design from an abstract description into a lower-level representation (e.g., from high-level equations to Boolean equations).
- *Logic reduction*, which increases the speed of the circuit and minimizes its size by eliminating any redundant terms. In addition, logic reduction creates circuits that are fully testable by making sure that there is only one path to each output.
- *Factoring*, which detects and extracts terms used more than once in a set of equations. By generating the terms only once and distributing them to multiple outputs in a multi-level configuration, factoring helps minimize space requirements.

Step 4: Implementation

Once the design has been entered, verified, and optimized, it is ready to be implemented into the target technology. This step has five parts: selecting the technology and device, partitioning the design, generating the output, documenting the design process, and verifying that the design as implemented meets all specifications.

Step 5: Technology and Device Selection

The first step is to choose the IC technology in which the design is to be implemented. For example, the designer might choose to implement the design into PLDs, PGAs, LCAs, gate arrays, standard cells, full-custom devices, or some combination of the above. It is also necessary to choose a specific architecture and vendor within the selected technology (although some engineers prefer to wait until after partitioning to make this decision). For PLDs, for example, typical architectural choices include PALs, FPLAs, EPLDs, PEELs, or CPLs.

Step 6: Partitioning the Design

Partitioning is necessary if the design is to be implemented in more than one device or technology. For example, it might be desired to build a PLD-based prototype of the design while waiting for a gate array to be manufactured or the bulk of the design can be implemented in a gate array but use fixed-function devices (TTL logic) for the interface "glue." Logic synthesis tools that include partitioning capabilities simplify the process considerably by performing much of the process automatically.

Step 7: Generating the Output

It is necessary to generate a structural description of the design in machine-readable form in the format appropriate to be selected IC technology. In the case of PLDs, for example, the output is formatted as a JEDEC Standard #3 fuse map; for gate arrays, a netlist in the format required by the gate array manufacturer is required.

All logic synthesis tools, by definition, are capable of generating structural output from behavioral input. However, individual tools differ considerably in the number of output formats they support. The greater the number of output formats, the more flexibility that is available not only in choosing the target technology and IC vendor, but also in transferring the design database to other systems and services (such as simulators, circuit board layout software, or wire-wrap services).

Step 8: Documenting the Design Process

Most logic synthesis tools automatically generate some form of documentation of the steps they perform. This documentation simplifies future design revisions by recording what was done at each step of the process. By generating the documentation automatically, logic synthesis tools enhance engineering productivity and ensure that the records will be there when you need them.

Step 9: Verifying the Implementation

The final step is to perform a complete verification of the design, including both a functional simulation and a timing analysis. This step reverifies the initial functional simulation, ensuring that no errors were introduced during optimization and implementation. It also verifies that the design will meet the timing specifications—a step that cannot be performed until a target technology has been selected.

Several software packages are currently available to the design engineer engaged in digital logic design. Among these packages are Data I/Os, ABEL, and GATES software packages, Signetics' AMAZE and SNAP, International's CMOS, Technology's PEEL, Intel's PLDS II, Logical Devices, CUPL. This chapter discusses various aspects of these software packages. Application examples that might demonstrate their capabilities are provided in Chapter 6.

FUTUREDESIGNER

FutureDesigner is a highly flexible design-entry tool that runs on a broad range of industry-standard hardware platforms, including IBM PC/XT systems and PC/AT systems and compatibles, 80386-based systems such as the COMPAQ DESKPRO 386, and Sun workstations. It is suitable for use with PLD, PGA, and LCA designs. Key benefits include mixed-mode design entry, quick functional verification, technology and vendor independence, powerful optimization routines, and implementation flexibility.

FutureDesigner combines two other Data I/O products: GATES, a logic synthesis tool for multiple-PLD designs, and DASH, an industry-standard schematic capture package to give the design engineer the capability for mixed-mode design entry, accepting both behavioral and structural descriptions. Upon entry, verification and optimization of the FutureDesigner automatically generates schematics for any modules that have been described behaviorally, merging them with the schematics for the portions of the design that were described structurally to create a complete schematic of the total design.

FutureDesigner's interactive design verifier provides quick functional verification to the designer early in the design process, giving immediate feedback on the design's ability to meet the functional specifications. The experimentation with different design alternatives is facilitated by the speed of the verification process.

FutureDesigner is both technology- and vendor-independent, permitting the design engineer to evaluate different design alternatives before making a commitment to a specific IC technology, move a design from one IC technology to another, and choose a vendor for the selected technology—or second-source ICs if the originally selected parts become unavailable.

FutureDesigner's optimization algorithms help the designer maximize the speed of design while minimizing space requirements through the use of two types of algorithms. First, FutureDesigner uses the Berkeley ESPRESSO logic reduction algorithm to remove any redundant circuitry in the design, reducing gate count by as much as 50% and circuit size by as much as 90%. FutureDesigner assigns whatever output polarity results in the lowest gate count, or the designer can assign the reduction level and output polarity manually. For any ''don't care'' values (i.e., output whose values don't affect the functioning of the circuit), FutureDesigner automatically assigns the value that results in the lowest gate count.

Secondly, FutureDesigner also uses its proprietary factoring algorithm to negotiate the optimum tradeoff between speed and space for a design. The sizes of gates available and the maximum number of logic levels to be used can both be specified so the design fits on the selected device and meets performance requirements. For example, if the design is to be implemented in traditional PLDs, a maximum of two logic levels would be specified, while for a gate array implementation, multiple logic levels would be specified.

FutureDesigner gives the design engineer a high degree of flexibility in implementing a design. A choice can be made from a broad range of user-configurable ASICs. If needed, a design can be partitioned among multiple devices.

To partition a design among multiple ICs, the designer specifies the outputs that are designed for each segment, and FutureDesigner automatically partitions the inputs. The design can be partitioned between several ICs of the same type (e.g., several PLDs) or a combination of different IC technologies (e.g., implementing part of the design in PLDs and part in gate arrays). By performing partitioning only after verification and optimization, FutureDesigner can reduce revision time significantly. FutureDesigner supports a wide range of user-configurable ASICs, including not only hundreds of different PLDs but also a variety of LCAs and PGAs that offer a high degree of flexibility in implementing a design. In addition to the symbol libraries that come with FutureDesigner, additional libraries can be purchased from individual device vendors or created personally by the designer. For PLD implementation, FutureDesigner generates JEDEC Standard #3 fuse maps; for LCAs and PGAs, it generates netlists with JEDEC Standard #12-3 macrocells, which will work with any manufacturer's devices. FutureDesigner's netlist output also allows an easy interface to most popular CAD systems, simulators, printed circuit board layout systems, and engineering service bureaus. FutureDesigner automatically generates a full set of documentation for analysis, archival, or manufacturing purposes, including complete connectivity reports and a list-of-materials report to help production facilities determine production costs and inventory needs. The product includes support for a variety of popular printers, with plotter support available as an option. For PLD implementations, FutureDesigner provides reverification at the device level at the end of the design process, allowing the designer to debug every fuse, node, and pin. For implementations using other ASICs, FutureDesigner outputs a netlist in formats accepted by industry-standard simulators.

GATES

GATES provides an interactive development environment for complex designs involving multiple PLDs. It runs on the same hardware platforms as FutureDesigner and includes many of the same capabilities. GATES is a key component of FutureDesigner with two main differences. First, GATES supports only PLDs—but it provides 100% vendor coverage for this ASIC technology. FutureDesigner supports LCAs and PGAs in addition to PLDs. FutureDesigner's support encompasses hundreds of different PLD architectures, including PALs, IFLs, FPLAs, EPLDs, and many other types of PLDs, both simple and complex. Secondly, GATES accepts only behavioral design descriptions rather than allowing a mix of behavioral and structural design descriptions. (FutureDesigner's ability to accept structural design input comes from DASH, its other key component.) Behavioral descriptions can be expressed as high-level equations, truth tables, state diagrams, or a combination of these forms. Because GATES supports only PLD technology, the only form of output it produces is a JEDEC Standard #3 fuse map, while FutureDesigner generates netlists with JEDEC Standard #12-3 for LCAs and PGAs.

GATES includes all the same verification, optimization, and partitioning capabilities as FutureDesigner and, like FutureDesigner, automatically generates its own documentation.

ABEL

ABEL is a logic synthesis tool for single-PLD designs. It runs on all the same hardware platforms as FutureDesigner and GATES, plus Apollo workstations and DEC VAX systems running either the UNIX or VMS operating system. Like FutureDesigner and GATES, ABEL is compatible with hundreds of different PLD architectures, including both simple and complex PLDs. ABEL accepts behavioral design descriptions in any combination of high-level equations, truth tables, or state diagrams. It then:

- Performs automatic logic reduction, using the Berkeley PRESTO logic-reduction algorithm, expressing the equations in the minimum number of logic terms.
- Converts the behavioral design description to structural form, producing a JEDEC Standard #3 fuse map.
- Creates a computer model of the PLD and simulates operation of the design, applying user-generated test vectors to verify that it will perform the intended function.
- Automatically generates documentation for each step in the design process.

The ABEL compiles logic designs for virtually any programmable logic device (PLD), including PAL's, PROMs, FPLAs, and PLEs, and permits the design to be expressed in any combination of truth tables, state diagrams, or Boolean equations. ABEL can provide an interface with Data I/O programmers.

DASH-ABEL permits the creation of designs using schematic capture and Data I/Os, FutureNet's DASH PC Schematic Capture System. Logic functions can be described by graphically arranging discrete or generic logic elements on a PC and automatically translating the design into programmable logic using ABEL. In ABEL, the design is optimized and translated into a logic programmer-readable syntax. While DASH and ABEL can function as stand-alone design tools, the DASH-ABEL interface combines the power of each for even greater design flexibility.

Developed by FutureNet, the DASH schematic designer package integrates the personal computer with graphics processing to create a personal computer workstation for board-level and chip-level system design. It virtually eliminates manual drafting by allowing the design engineer to create new schematics or change existing drawings directly on an IBM PC XT or AT.

The ABEL makes use of IF-THEN-ELSE and CASE statements to describe operations that depend on the state of other signals in a device. A set notation is used to group signals into sets for easier reference in the design. ABEL also features full arithmetic operators ($+$, $-$, $*$, $/$) and relational operators

$(>, <, > =, < =)$ in addition to standard logical operators such as AND, OR, and XOR. Macros and directives facilitate the description of more complex elements. Existing files can be incorporated into the file describing the design so that a library can be built of common design elements to use again and again.

Figure 3-3 shows the logic-design process and the approaches used by the ABEL. First the designer creates the ABEL source file required by the language processor which in turn generates the programmer-load file. The source file is written by the designer and contains a complete description of the logic design. The source file can be created manually by means of a text editor (or word processor) that generates ASCII files, or DASH/ABEL can be utilized to convert a DASH-generated schematic of the design to an ABEL source file.

The ABEL design language and language processor facilitates the design and test logic functions that are to be implemented with programmable logic devices. For example, a designer can design a three-input AND function with the inputs A, B, and C and the output Y using the following truth table:

Truth table for a 3-input AND gate

(A,B,C	Y)
[0,.X.,.X.]	0;
[.X.,0,.X.]	0;
[.X.,.X.,0]	0;
[1,1,1]	1;

The ".X."'s in the table indicate "don't-care" conditions. Note that the output Y is set to 1 only when all three inputs equal 1. The output Y could have also been specified in terms of simple Boolean operators and have achieved the same result. This is done here, where "&" is the logical AND operator:

Y = A & B & C;

Additionally, the language processor reduces a logic design to a near minimal form. The need for traditional methods such as Karnaugh maps and De Morgan's Theorem can be eliminated. Simulation can be performed after a logic design has been reduced and converted to a programmer-load file and the fuse map and test vectors used for simulation are the same as those that will be used to program and test the real device. If test vectors are specified in a source file, the programmer-load file created by the language processor contains these vectors in a form that can be used to test a programmed device with a logic programmer.

The ABEL language processor accepts the source file and performs various internal functions to produce a programmer-load file in the JEDEC format as well as the associated design documentation. The functions are listed below:

1. *Parse*—checks the syntax of the source file and flags and errors.
2. *Transform*—converts the logic description to an intermediate form.
3. *Reduce*—performs logic reduction.
4. *Fuse map*—creates the programmer-load file.

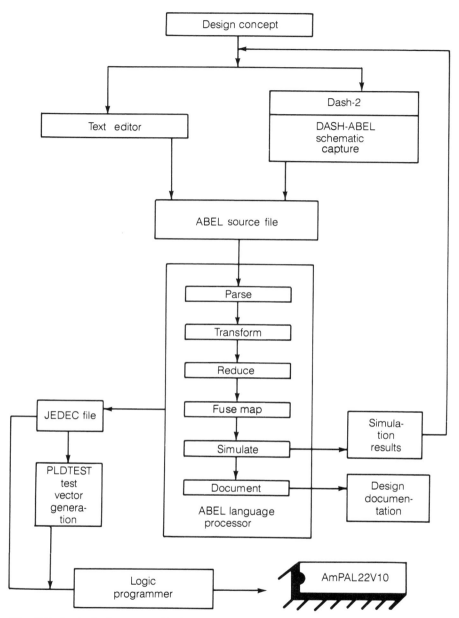

Fig. 3-3. Logic design steps with ABEL. Courtesy of Data I/O Corporation.

Now the programmer-load file can be downloaded to the logic programmer to program parts, or it can be first transmitted to PLD test, an automatic test vector generator.

    5. *Simulate*—tests the design of the part against the test vectors contained in the source file and reports any functional failure of the design.

The ABEL can now be used to translate the source file into a fuse map. After all circuit functions entered with DASH have been converted to Boolean equations, the language processor quickly performs the logic reduction and error-checking chores.

By using the test vectors that were created during the design phase, the ABEL can simulate operation and verify that the device will function properly before actual programming takes place. As a final step, it automatically creates documentation describing the design. This documentation includes a full list of the reduced equations, a record of test vectors, a fuse map, and a chip diagram showing the names of the input and output pins. The fuse maps and test vectors can now be loaded into the logic programmer.

6. *Document function*—generates a listing of the source file, a drawing of the logic device pin assignments, and a listing of the programmer-load file.

The standard programmer load file created by the language processor conforms to the JEDEC Standard #3 for data transfer to logic programmers.

ABEL presently runs on several computers and operating systems including the IBM AT/XT and MS-DOS compatibles. Other additional systems are available:

- IBM AT/XT and MS-DOS compatibles
- VAX/VMS
- VAX/Unix
- Sun
- Apollo/Mentor

The installation and utilization of ABEL is different for each type of system. To install ABEL specifically for a particular system, an installation guide is supplied with the ABEL package. In addition to the type of system in which it is to be employed, you need an editor or word processor to create ABEL source files. This is not included with the ABEL software package. This may be any editor of a designer's choice as long as it produces a standard ASCII file.

ALTERA A + PLUS PLD DEVELOPMENT SOFTWARE

Today, the most widely available source of computing power is the personal computer. By creating development tools that fit the personal computer environment, the three following criteria can be met: low cost, personal availability and access, and ease of use.

As in the area of component architecture, Altera also provides effective, flexible solutions to the CAD/CAE problems the system designer faces. Particularly in those areas which require extensive device-specific knowledge, Altera has developed an effective set of IBM PC- and PS/2-based CAD tools to handle the problems of design entry, design processing and device programming. This package, known as A + PLUS (Altera Programmable Logic User System), provides a powerful design support tool that matches the continually expanding capabilities of Altera programmable logic devices.

Within A + PLUS, the user can enter a design via high-level TTL macrofunctions or primitive gate symbols using graphic schematic captive, text-based netlist entries, state machine descriptions, or Boolean equations. Once the design is entered, Altera's fully automated integration process, called the Altera Design Processor (ADP), translates the design into an industry-standard (JEDEC) PLD programming file. The JEDEC file is used to directly program the target EPLD using Altera-supplied hardware or general-purpose third-party programmers.

Figure 3-4 shows an overview of Altera's Programmable Logic Development System. Data may be entered in the form of Boolean equations, state machine, and truth tables. Special features also available include LogiCaps and TTL macrofunctions.

LogiCaps

Digital logic designs that are originally conceived in the form of a logic or schematic diagram can be entered directly into the computer in the original schematic form, and the software will extract the equations. LogiCaps allows the user to draw the schematic on a computer screen. The LogiCaps library has been extended to include ADLIB to enable a user to design his own special macrofunctions for something like a 13-bit counter.

The schematic diagrams are drawn on the screen of a personal computer with the aid of a mouse. With a single command, a netlist file is then generated ready to be programmed into silicon. When combined with the Altera Programmable Logic User System (A + PLUS), LogiCaps provides a complete interactive EPLD development system. An engineer could start with a blank screen on a PC, then in minutes transform a circuit idea into a working, user-configured integrated circuit.

The most frequently used functions such as drawing and connecting of lines, moving and copying objects, and just getting around in the drawing can be performed by simple mouse motion or pressing a mouse button. Functions used less often are executed by pressing a single key, while those functions rarely used or requiring more data are selected from a nested command menu system. No command requires more than three key presses to execute unless a file name or some other text is needed.

Commands follow a straightforward intuitive format that eliminates the initial learning curve normally associated with software this powerful. Menus or prompts are always present indicating to the design engineer what to do next, and extensive on-line help information is available for every menu.

LogiCaps was designed with the What-You-See-Is-What-You-Get philosophy and there are no underlying data structure surprises. The internal data structure is fully represented by the visible drawing. A design engineer could easily become a proficient user within minutes.

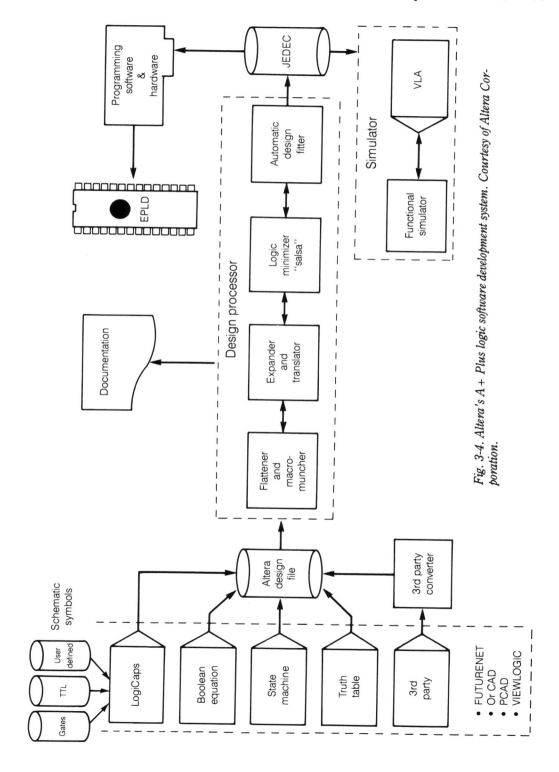

Fig. 3-4. Altera's A + Plus logic software development system. Courtesy of Altera Corporation.

What has been termed orthogonal rubberbanding (the process which permits symbols and areas to be moved, while the interconnection wires maintain 90 degree angles as they move to maintain connectivity of the schematic) is built into LogiCaps, permitting the design engineer to move symbols and areas of the drawing about while the software keeps the lines connected.

The mouse functions are context-driven; if a button is pressed with the cursor in a symbol, there is the obvious desire to do something with that symbol. If the cursor is on a line or on some text, there is the obvious desire to copy that line or text. Perhaps a design engineer would wish to draw a new line, move or copy an area, or make an interconnection dot. All of these things can be accomplished using the mouse to select in a natural manner.

Five line types and four character sets provide flexibility in schematic drawings. Complex symbol shapes are stored as library files for compactness and maximum flexibility. Areas of drawings can be saved and loaded from drawing files, permitting the user to build a library of standard modules that can later be combined in other applications. All of the function keys, in addition to having their preassigned functions, can be programmed to execute a user-defined sequence of keystrokes and/or mouse functions. These sequences can be as simple as executing one function or as complex as entering a 2000-gate design complete with documentation and generating the ADF file. Many features are provided to make the drawing entry task as quick as possible including a ''dual window capability'' that permits the user to view two independent regions of the drawing at once and jumping between them at the press of a key. The dual window capability also permits the designer to have simultaneous views at different zoom levels, the trees and leaves. This mode permits the designer to see the overall schematic and yet work in detail on any part of the design without having to zoom in and out or to view two different parts of the design and move back and forward between them. Single keystroke commands permit an immediate change of perspective of the design. Zoom in for detail; zoom out for an overview. Multiple levels provide useful intermediate views that can be used for wider, regional editing. Other features include quick jumps to previously-saved locations, a sophisticated reference grid system for easy alignment of objects in the drawing, and special cursor key modes (including panning across the drawing).

Drawing size can be set to the standard A, B, C, D, or E sizes, plus the maximum size of 90″ by 90″. Objects are positioned on a .10″ grid, providing 10 units per inch. Cursor coordinates are displayed as well as reference indices permitting the engineer to always know his location within the drawing.

LogiCaps produces an Altera Design File (ADF) netlist directly from the over 80 logic and I/O symbols to provide the basic building blocks for logic schematics. Familiar names like ''AND'' and ''XOR'' identify the logic symbols, and mnemonic symbols like ''RORF'' (Register Output, Register Feedback) define the EPLD I/O architecture configurations.

Frequently-used command sequences can be saved by the user as macro recordings and can be executed by a single keypress. This speeds design entry and permits customization of LogiCaps to suit the designer's own preferences.

Movement of an object to a new position can be performed as simple as positioning the cursor on the object and pressing a button. An outline of the object can then be moved to the new location where another press of a button will move the object there. A different button can be used for making copies of the object if that is desired.

Whole areas of a schematic can be moved, copied, erased, saved, or loaded. This makes construction of repetitive sections of a design quite practical. Through this technique a designer can build up his own library of sub-circuit functions that may be used in many different EPLD designs.

Sixty-two commands are arranged in a nested command menu structure for easy, consistent selection. The function and cursor keys and mouse commands add efficiency and speed to the Engineer/LogiCaps interface.

Design Capture

Boolean Equations. Boolean equation entry might in general be found attractive for low-density EPLDs. Any standard text editor can be used to type an ADF file containing Boolean equations. Equations may be entered as sums of product formats or product of sums formats and a mixture or both. Equations can be entered in minimal form or in the higher level form permitting a significant reduction in the size of the Boolean equation code and allowing the designer to define the logic in the most natural conceptual manner.

PLSME State Machine Entry. As is well known, the development of state machines by hand requires a large amount of tedious work. The advent of programmable logic, however, made it possible to implement very complicated state machines on a single chip. The logic array could be used to implement very demanding logic structures, while the on-chip registers could serve as state registers. In the past, to take advantage of programmable logic, the designer was required to write out all of the state equations and reduce them by hand and apply De Morgan's inversion to the resultant logic by hand. In the event that the design was incorrect or modified, this tedious time-consuming operation had to be repeated. If the design was incorrect or modified, the entire process had to be repeated.

Altera's Programmable Logic State Machine Entry (PLSME) when used in connection with A + PLUS development automatically transforms high-level state machine descriptions into device programming files. PLSME provides for state machine entry in addition to the traditional entry methods currently available to A + PLUS. Design information is entered using any standard (nondocument mode) text editor, and then processed by the state machine converter to a standard Altera design file format (ADF). This common intermediate format allows the linking of multiple state machines, schematic, Boolean equations, and design files to provide a rich development environment.

The syntax of state machine description is both easy to use and powerful. A *state machine* is defined by clock selection, state assignments coupled to state variables, and transition definition.

The state clock can be selected from any available clock on the device, including the dedicated synchronous clocks, and any asynchronous clock (i.e., signals created from logical signals with the EPLD). Multiple-state machines can be defined on one part, each with a different clock if so desired.

State assignments are defined in a tabular format by output variable only and are coupled to state registers by position in the table. The choice of register type is not required. Altera's design processor automatically selects the best register type to support the implementation's selections, thus freeing the design engineer from the selection of a specific register.

Definition of state transitions is accomplished with a simple IF-THEN-ELSE construct and transitions are defined to be mutually exclusive to remove any ambiguities about next state values. The power-on state is reset to an all low value that permits the designer to provide reliable operation at system start-up. Outputs that can be registered or combined can be associated with states in the state machine definition or external to it. If defined internal to the state machine, they can be unconditional, asserted on entry into a given state, or conditional, depending on present state and external input signals or expressions. The names associated with states can be used in logic equations outside the state machine definition, allowing easy interface to logic schematics.

Maintenance and modification of state machines is simple. High-level modification of the IF-THEN-ELSE statements allows redefinition of state transitions, and the inclusion or deletion of states can be performed with similar simplicity. Addition or deletion of additional state variables, outputs, or inputs is supported. The high-level descriptions are human readable to make the understanding of complex logical structures conceptually simple to support personnel to ease the maintenance of a complex design.

Because the syntax of truth table definition allows the high-level description of logic requirements without Boolean equations, truth table outputs can be used (as any Boolean statement can) as inputs to output primitives or logic.

The Boolean equations section allows the standard definition of intermediate values that can be accessed by the state machine. This allows a high-level description of otherwise discrete events and eases the readability of the state machine definition.

PLS LIB-TTL MacroFunctions

Altera has created the concept of *MacroFunctions*, which are high-level building blocks that allow the designer using LogiCaps to design at the TTL level.

Most macrofunctions are commonly used with SSI and MSI TTL parts which will aid the novice designer who is familiar with TTL functions. A few however, are specific to Altera and have been designed by EPLD design experts. They contain inner logic behavior to maximize EPLD speed and utilization and are particularly well-suited for logic design with Altera EPLD architecture.

The Altera MacroFunctions can be used with a variety of other macrofunctions and/or with Altera low-level logic primitives depending on the logic needed. They come in an easy-to-use symbol representation which includes such standards as inputs on the left, outputs on the right, and the name of the MacroFunction at the top. A typical MacroFunction symbol is shown in FIG. 3-5.

MacroFunctions are TTL compatible SSI and MSI circuits giving the circuit designer a high-level approach to EPLD design. MacroFunctions include input default values to unconnected inputs and "MacroMunching" to unused outputs. Altera's MacroFunction library consists of over 100 components.

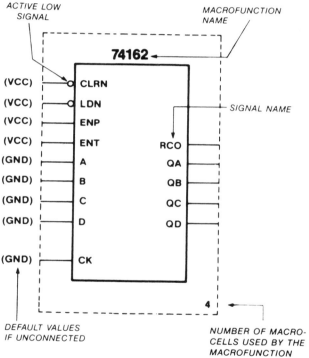

Fig. 3-5. *Typical macrofunction symbol. Courtesy of Altera Corporation.*

The number in the bottom right-hand corner of the MacroFunction symbol represents the maximum number of MacroCells that MacroFunction will use, which in turn is dictated by how many inputs and outputs are used. The inputs and outputs of the EPLD to be programmed are specified with Altera I/O design primitives.

The Altera design processor that comes with A + PLUS 4.5 has a built-in feature that automatically discards unused logic in the MacroFunction. This feature is appropriately called the "MacroMuncher." In FIG. 3-6, the MacroFunction uses up to 8 MacroCells if all of the inputs and outputs are connected. For this application, only half of the outputs are desired so only half of the Macro-Cells are needed. When this MacroFunction is put through the A + PLUS design processor, it only uses 4 MacroCells. All of the input pins are assigned default signal values so that they can be left unconnected when they are not needed. Similarly, any output pin can be left unconnected. All MacroFunctions come completely documented. This includes logic diagrams, function tables, and the associated default signal level. Table 3-1 shows the function table for the 74162.

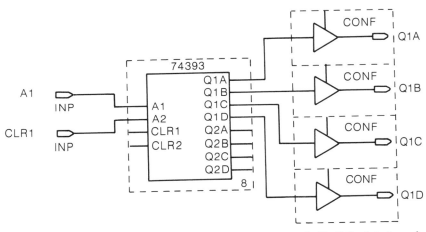

Fig. 3-6. The macrofunction will utilize up to eight macrocells if all the inputs and outputs are connected. Courtesy of Altera Corporation.

The MacroFunction library contains over 100 functions including the most commonly used TTL parts such as counters, decoders, encoders, shift registers, flip-flops, latches, multipliers, and the like. This library permits any TTL function not already in the library to be easily implemented using an existing part and some Altera low-level gate primitives. Table 3-2 shows the presently available MacroFunctions.

The following example shows the ease of designing with MacroFunctions and the efficiency of using EPLDs. In this example, design a chip that acts as a BCD counter to give the user the ability to choose one of four different counting speeds and have the outputs drive a seven-segment LED display. The basic strategy for the design is shown in FIG. 3-7.

By looking at the table of available MacroFunctions, you can see that the 7446 is a suitable seven-segment decoder, the 74162 is a BCD counter, the

Table 3-1. 74162 Function Table.

CK	LKN	CLRN	Inputs ENP	ENT	D	C	B	A	Outputs Q_D	Q_C	Q_B	Q_A	RCO
X	X	L	X	X	X	X	X	X	L	L	L	L	L
I	L	H	X	X	d	c	b	a	d	c	b	a	L
I	H	H	X	L	X	X	X	X	Q_D	Q_C	Q_B	Q_A	L
I	H	H	L	X	X	X	X	X	Q_D	Q_C	Q_B	Q_A	L
I	H	H	H	H	X	X	X	X		COUNT UP			L
I	H	H	H	H	X	X	X	X	H	L	L	H	H

H = High Level (steady state)
L = Low Level (steady state)
X = don't care (any input including transitions)
I = transition from low to high level
a,b,c,d = level of steady state input at inputs A,B,C,D

74153 is a 4-to-1 multiplexer, and that FREQDIV is an Altera-provided frequency divider. Everything that is required for this design is already available in the MacroFunction library.

To design the chip, the desired inputs and outputs are wired to Altera I/O design primitives, and the MacroFunctions are wired together just as the actual TTL chips would be wired. The actual design is shown in FIG. 3-8. The output primitive Y1 is connected to the output of the multiplexer to keep the number of P-terms under 8. Notice that the unused inputs and outputs of the MacroFunctions were left unconnected and how this helps alleviate design clutter.

Like all designs containing MacroFunctions, the MacroMuncher takes a bite out of this design by eating the unused part of the 74153 and the rest of the unused logic in the design. Also notice the ease of inverting the CLEAR input to the 74162 MacroFunction. This would require another whole chip if the design was being done with individual chips.

This entire design containing 5 TTL functions is implemented in an EP600 using the A + PLUS Design Processor. Hence, the entire design is completed. It takes less time than it would take to wire the individual chips together, and it comes in one package which eliminates the chance of wiring mistakes.

Figure 3-9 shows the current MacroFunction library. They are compatible with the LogiCaps schematic capture package and are supported by A + PLUS.

Design Processing

The A + PLUS design processor accepts the LogiCaps output file. As discussed previously, designs can be entered in a Boolean equation, state machine,

Table 3-2. Table of available macrofunctions.

TYPE	AVAILABLE
Adders	7480, 7482, 7483, 74183, 8FADD
Comparators	7485, 74158, 8MCOMP, 74518
Converters	74184, 74185
Counters	7483, 74160, 74161, 74162, 74163, 75190, 74160T, 74161T, 74162T, 74163T, 74190T, 74191T, 74192T, 74193T, 74393, 8COUNT, 16CUDSLR, UNICNT2, GRAY4
Decoder	7442, 7443, 7444, 7445, 7446, 7447, 7448, 7449, 74138, 74139, 75154, 7155, 74156
Flip-Flops	7471, 7472, 7473, 7474, 7475, 7476, 7478, 74173, 74174, 74175, 74273, 74374
Freq Divider	FREQDIV
Latches	7475, 7477, 74116, 74259, 74279, 74373, NANDLTCH, NORLTCH
Multipliers	74261, MULT2, MULT24, MULT4
Multiplexers	74147, 74148, 74151, 75153, 74157, 74158, 74298, 21MUX
Parity Generators	74180, 74280
Shift Registers	7491, 7494, 7496, 7499, 74164, 74165, 74166, 74178, 74179, 74194, 74198, 16CUDSLR, BARRELST, UNICNT2
SSI Functions	7400, 7402, 7404, 7408, 7410, 7411, 7420, 7421, 7427, 7430, 7432, 7486, INHB, CBUF
Storage Registers	7498, 74278
True/Comp Elements	7587
ALU	74181

or truth table format, thus not restricting the designer to just one entry format and permitting the designer to "mix or match" these entry methods and to submit multiple files to be compiled into a single EPLD. Once submitted, the design files are "flattened" into gate equivalent structures within an EPLD followed by a fitting algorithm that automatically performs logic placement and signal routing. This fitting the optimized design to the target EPLD is an extra bonus. If the target EPLD has not been specified, A + PLUS provides automatic EPLD part selection. The final output from the design processor is of course object code file (JEDEC file) used for device programming.

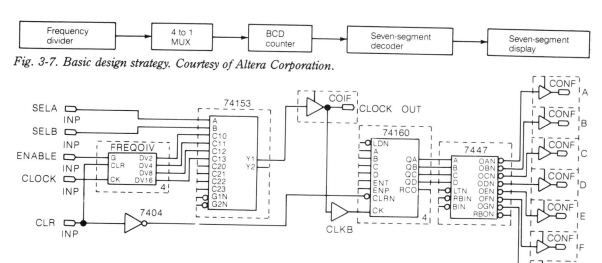

Fig. 3-7. *Basic design strategy. Courtesy of Altera Corporation.*

Fig. 3-8. *The actual design. Courtesy of Altera Corporation.*

A + PLUS Design Processor cuts the time it takes an engineer to compile a complex erasable programmable logic device (EPLD) design from an average of 30 minutes to under 90 seconds using an IBM AT or compatible. Table 3-3 shows Altera's software support products and corresponding EPLDs.

In addition to speed, efficiency has also been implemented with the A + PLUS. Minimizing and fitting algorithms allow the designer to pack more logic into all of the general purpose EPLDs manufactured by Altera or a second source (Intel).

Additionally, the software supports Altera's BUSTER device (an erasable programmable microprocessor peripheral) as well as the company's new high-speed, second generation, high-density general-purpose devices, the EP610, EP910, and EP1810.

The A + PLUS design processor lies at the heart of all Altera general-purpose EPLD development systems. The A + PLUS software accepts four different design entry formats: schematic capture, Boolean equations, truth table, or state machine input. These formats give the designer great flexibility. He can mix and match methods to best meet the needs of the overall circuit design. When required, the design entry format is converted to an Altera Design File (ADF), which is the common entry format for the A + PLUS software. The ADF is then submitted to the Altera Design Processor (ADP) which is comprised of a set of modules tied together to generate the industry standard JEDEC code used to program the EPLD. Documentation showing minimized logic and EPLD utilization is also produced by the design process. Once the JEDEC file is obtained, the user can functionally simulate the design. Finally, the user can program the specific EPLD with the LogicMap programming software and Altera programming hardware provided.

SHIFT REGISTERS

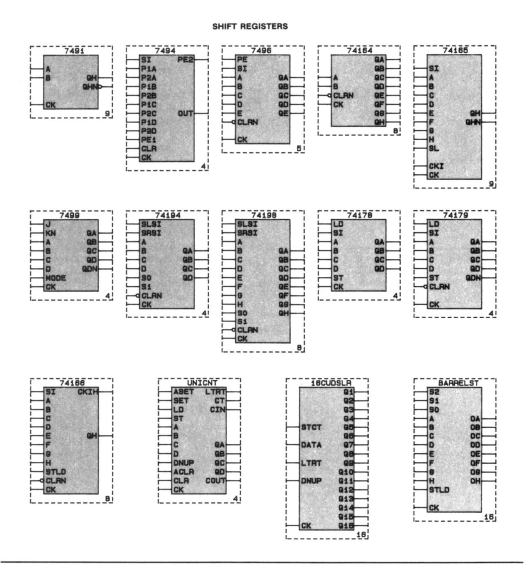

PARITY GENERATORS

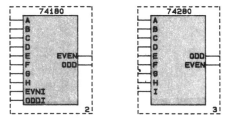

Fig. 3-9. Macrofunction library. Courtesy of Altera Corporation.

Fig. 3-9. Continued.

COUNTERS

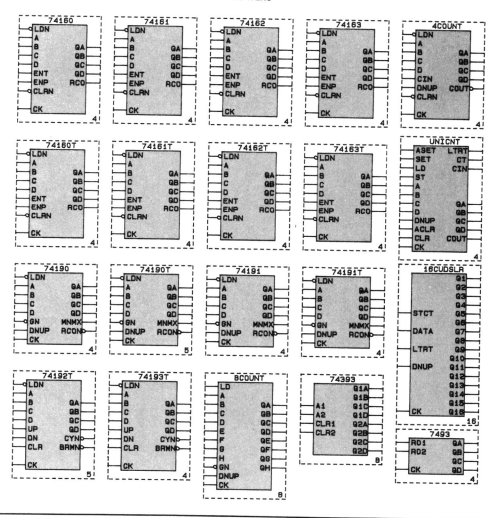

MULTIPLIERS

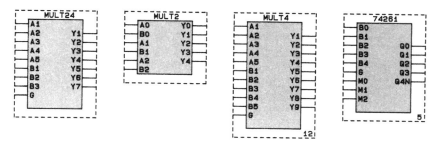

Fig. 3-9. Continued.

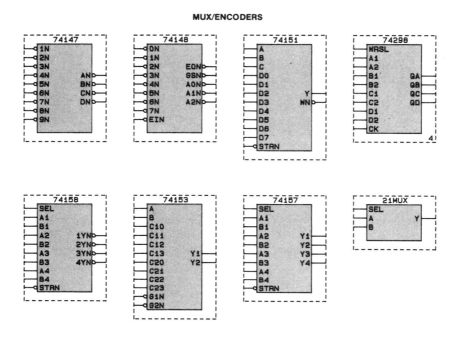

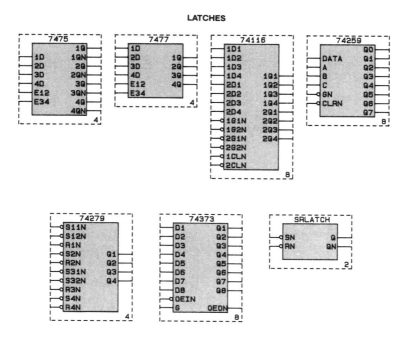

Fig. 3-9. Continued.

DECODERS/DEMULTIPLEXERS

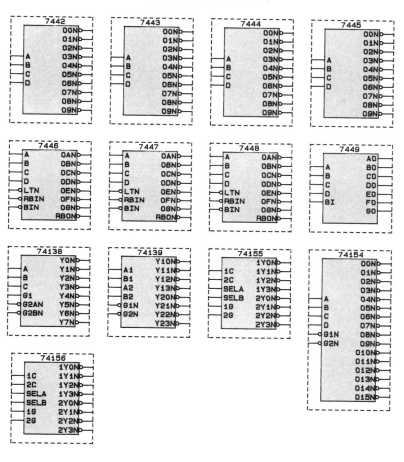

STORAGE REGISTERS   **CONVERTERS**

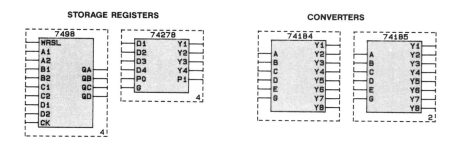

Fig. 3-9. Continued.

FLIP-FLOPS/REGISTERS

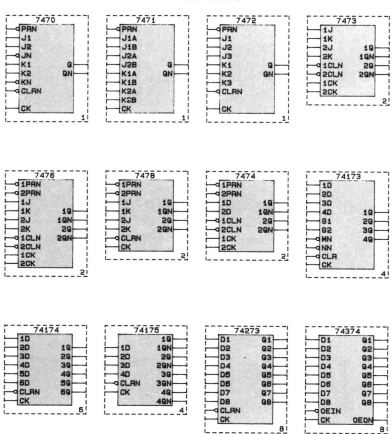

ADDERS

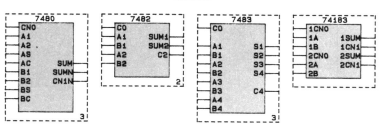

Fig. 3-9. Continued.

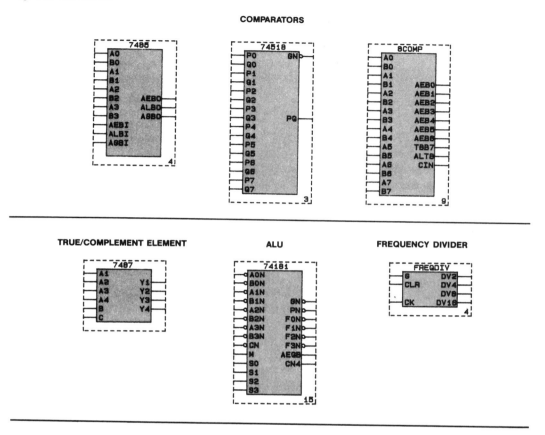

COMPARATORS

TRUE/COMPLEMENT ELEMENT   **ALU**   **FREQUENCY DIVIDER**

SSI FUNCTIONS

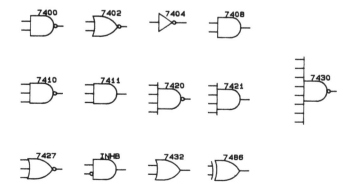

Note: Many of these SSI functions are identical to the primitive library elements. The SSI TTL part number equivalents are included for completeness.

Table 3-3. Altera software support tools.

PART	A + PLUS	SAM + PLUS	MAX + PLUS	
EP310, 320, 600, 610	X			(EPLDs)
EP900, 910, 1800	X			
EP1810, 1210, EPB1400	X			
EP512	X			
EPS448		X		(SEQUENCERS)
EPM5016, 5024, 5032			X	(EPLDs)
EPM5064, EPM5127, 5128			X	
5C031, 5C032, 5C060	X			(INTEL EPLDS)
5C090, 5C180, 5AC312	X			

The A + PLUS design processor accepts these four entry formats (even if they have been mixed and matched within a given design) and operates on them in a unique four-stage process.

The *Translator* converts the design into a sum of products Boolean expressions for implementation into a PLD. The *Design Minimizer* performs logic reduction using generalized consensus algorithms. De Morgan's Theorem is invoked automatically to generate expressions that require the fewest product terms. The *Design Fitter* automatically matches the logic capacity of the target EPLD to the requirements of the design engineer. This is analogous to the Automatic place and route capability in gate arrays design software and is essential for complex designs. The design fitter outputs a utilization report that shows how the logic was implemented. It also shows how much logic remains unused in the device, allowing the design engineer maximum capacity. The Design Fitter provides the industry standard JEDEC standard format for transferring device design information to an Altera or third-party programming unit. LogiCap provides the link between A + PLUS software and the Altera programming hardware. Through a series of hierarchical windows, the design engineer can review the completed design.

The design processor programming output file can also be input to the Altera software simulator called PLFSIM. By doing this, engineers can check their circuit design before committing to hardware. Or, alternatively, use it as a hardware debugging tool. The designer can simulate functional operation by applying selected test patterns and watching waveform responses on PC's screen.

In order to use PLFSM, three files are needed by the user: a JEDEC file, a vector file, and a command file. The JEDEC file is the design file created by the A + PLUS processor and contains all the logical information about the design. The vector file contains the logic values to be applied to the inputs and is created with a text editor. A command file tells PLFSIM what to do and when to do it. This instruction list can be created with a text editor.

A complete set of simulation commands permits the user to review and check critical logic within a design in a succinct manner. Users can specify commands to occur at particular events, such as during a given circuit condition or at an absolute simulation timestep. Modes can be forced to a chosen logic state to verify proper circuit behavior from any initial condition. And the input waveforms from the vector file can be superseded by another pattern at any point in time.

For debugging purposes, simulation breakpoints can be set to halt execution when a specified event occurs. This break command provides designers with the ability to detect illegal states. Once a break condition is met, a command sublist is activated to provide status information or to enter into a separate procedure. For example, a break point might signal an illegal state, display the current output waveform on the screen, enter a legal state, and continue with the simulation.

The commands can be entered interactively from the keyboard and can be logged into a text file for future use or can come from a precreated command file. A command file can be called up at any point in the simulation process, including from another command for example, a break command can execute a unique command file when a condition has been met.

PLFSIM is designed to allow flexible entry to input vectors. All input waveforms are defined in the vector file. Standard state table entry is allowed, as is pattern entry, for easy use of repetitious input waveforms. Legal input vectors include 1, 0, X and Z to allow complete simulation of the bidirectional architecture of the EPLD.

A set of inputs can be defined as a signal group that allows that group's input vector to be listed in hexadecimal, decimal, octal, or binary form. In addition, an input group can be given one of four predefined waveforms including binary count, grey code, rotating bit, and glitch detector.

During simulation, the user can change between multiple vector files to examine different aspects of the design as desired. Finally, simulation states from a given session can be saved and restored as initial conditions in a future session.

PLFSIM supports both waveform as well as tabular type outputs. The outputs formats are user-configured to show the logic states of input and output signals as well as buried nodes. The *simulation coverage* is calculated and included in the output file to indicate how thoroughly the design was exercised. Both output files can be shown on the screen or stored to a disk and printed for permanent documentation.

The state machine entry language found in SAM + PLUS, called ASMILE, is nearly identical to the input description found in PLSME.

AMAZE

The circuit diagram suitable for a small conventional PLD is significantly smaller and more complex than that required for larger more complex devices.

As PLDs continue toward increased complexity, software that permit the designer to take advantage of this increased sophistication is also moving forward. One software package that meets this need is Automatic Map and Zap Equation (AMAZE) developed by Signetics. Current developments are well on the way to making this system even more user-friendly. The PLD can be designed on either a mainframe or a personal computer. In addition to flexible input formats, AMAZE also provides full device documentation and functional simulation. Figure 3-10 shows a typical design process using AMAZE.

The AMAZE software package currently consists of five software modules:

- PLD SIM—PLD SIMulator
- BLAST—Boolean Logic and State Transfer
- PTP—PAL to PLD conversion
- DPI—Device Programmer Interface
- PTE—Program Table Editor

Other modules will be added as products developments require them.

PLD SIMulator Module

The AMAZE PLD SIMulator Module permits functional simulation of designs created from equations, program tables, or existing programmed devices, automatic test vector generation from standard or JEDEC PLD fuse map files, interactive keyboard entry or batch file input of test vectors. This module also detects illegal state machine transitions, flags affected p-terms, and has an on-line help screen.

BLAST Module

The Boolean Logic and State Transfer menu-driven software module checks design parameters and automatically compiles a program table from Boolean and state machine equations. TTL schematics generated by Futurenet-DASH by Data I/O are also accepted as input. Data from the program table is then used to produce a standard file. BLAST automatically partitions the state machine designs into specified devices and then deletes redundant terms during compilation.

Existing logic-sets can be modified that have been programmed into a device by overlaying new data on its unused gates.

This module has a user-friendly interactive pin list editor. It provides for Boolean equation or state vector entry and schematic entry (with external schematic capture package). The designer is capable of partitioning single designs into multiple PLDs, performing on-line error checking, and generating the standard PLD. The BLAST module supports all PLDs manufactured by Signetics and contains user-definable device files for support of PALs and other PLD devices.

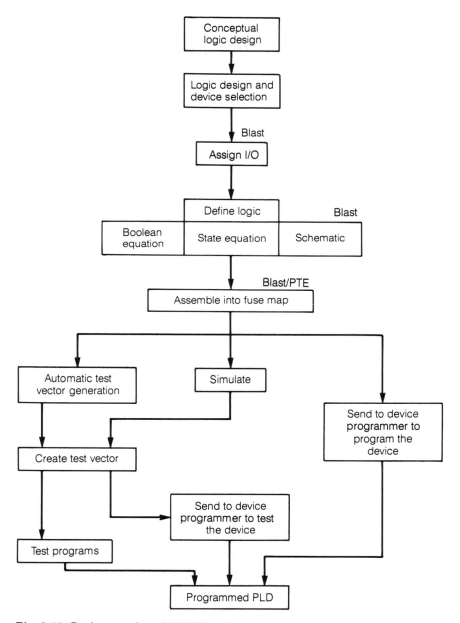

Fig. 3-10. Design overview of AMAZE. Courtesy of Signetics Corporation.

PTP Module

The PTP Module facilitates PAL to PLD translations of the various PAL circuits to the more flexible PLD circuits. This module has the capability to automatically upload the PAL pattern from a programmer, convert the pattern into a PLD pattern, and then download the PLD pattern into the programmer. After the PAL pattern and its corresponding PLD pattern are documented, the PLD pattern can be directed to other AMAZE modules. PTP can also translate the PAL fuse file in a HEXPLOT format.

This menu-driven module permits the fuse map conversion of 20- and 24-pin PALs to out pin and functional equivalent PLDs. An automatic assembler removes duplicated p-terms to provide efficient PLD mapping. Standard JEDEC fuse plot files or direct PAL master input files are accepted via a commercial PLD programmer. User-selectable RS-232 programmable interface parameters are provided as well as fuse map conversion documentation. The generated standard PLD fuse map files are compatible with other AMAZE modules.

DPI Module

This module supports both the standard JEDEC and Signetics High/Low fuse map file formats. An RS-232 interface to commercial PLD programmers is provided. Screen menus are provided for easy upload and download of fuse maps. The RS-232 parameters are user-selectable. Test vectors are automatically transferred to the programmer along with the fuse map file. The DPI module operates with standard PLD fuse map files.

PTE Module

The Program Table Entry (PTE) module is actually an interactive editor that permits the engineer to enter data into AMAZE in the form of Approved Program Tables. Each PLD data sheet includes the programmable format for the specified device. The PTE can also be used to document completed designs and to change logic functions that have been defined by the BLAST module. The PTE Module allows easy creation and editing of new and existing PLD designs. The PLD fuse map is represented in the high/low format in truth table form. An on-line editor provides automatic cursor control and prevents syntax errors and on-line help screen and print facility have been incorporated. The PTE module operates on standard PLD fuse map files.

AMAZE is supplied fully-documented and complete with the appropriate magnetic media.

To graphically enter the design, the engineer can use a schematic capture package from either FutureNet or CAD. The schematic-to-Boolean converter program in BLAST converts the schematic netlist file to Boolean equations and then to an AMAZE Standard Fuse File. A state machine design can be entered using state equation syntax, which is then compiled into the AMAZE Standard Fuse File. Or, Boolean equations can be written, with BLAST generating an AMAZE Standard Fuse File.

The designer enters the I/O labels for the PLD with an interactive pinlist editor. Before generating the fuse map file, BLAST performs syntax and consistency checking during compilation of the design input files. A superimposition compiler option lets the user modify previous designs programmed into a physical device. The modified design can often be superimposed on the existing device, thus making the PLD reprogrammable.

With the Program Table Editor (PTE), an interactive truth table editor, the design can be modified in the specific truth table format of an individual PLD. AMAZE then converts it to a Standard Fuse File. Each PLD has a different truth table format. The PTE automatically generates the appropriate table for the specific PLD that the user selects.

The PLD simulator (SIM) can be used to simulate a design after an AMAZE Standard Fuse File has been generated. The designer can interactively enter the vectors, or the simulator can read the inputs from a predefined vector file that the user has generated. Alternatively, an automatic test vector generator (ATVG) can be used to generate the test vectors.

During simulation, a log file stores the I/O values. The file can be used in conjunction with a commercial device programmer to test the actual device functionally.

After verifying that the logic functions properly, the designer uses the Device Programmer Interface (DPI), a module that creates a menu-driven link to a commercial programmer. DPI can download fuse map files in JEDEC format to a commercial programmer, down-load the simulator log file together with the fuse map file in JEDEC format to a commercial programmer that supports functional testing of PLDs, and receive a PLD pattern in JEDEC format from a commercial programmer. The uploaded pattern is converted from JEDEC format to an AMAZE Standard Fuse Map File format. It can then be used by the PTE for manipulation or by SIM for simulation.

Another module similar to DPI is the PAL-to-PLD (PTP) converter, which automatically converts PAL designs to Signetics' PLDs. By converting a PAL to a Signetics' PLD, the user can take advantage of the PLD architecture to pack more functions per chip.

Modular structure lets AMAZE easily adopt enhancements. Future releases of AMAZE will include support for Signetics' programmable macro logic family of devices: an event-driven simulator with timing outputs, a logic minimizer, a PML integrator to combine multiple PLDs into a single PML device, and a user-definable device database that enables designers to add any PAL or PLD not available in the current device database.

SNAP

Signetics/Phillips SNAP software has been designed to give a system designer the precise tools needed to successfully complete a PLD design. The initial offering is depicted in FIG. 3-11 in terms of the recommended sequence of operations to complete a Programmable Macro Logic (PML) design. Clearly, other sequences exist, but steps 1-9 are the most likely steps for the first user.

Step 1 in the process is design entry. This can be accomplished in a number of ways, but the most popular today is schematic capture. I assume you have some familiarity with the ORCAD/SDT-III package, but this is not the only one

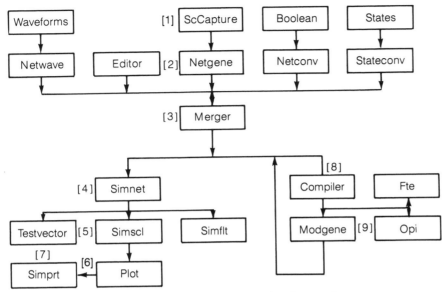

Fig. 3-11. SNAP software flow. Courtesy of Signetics Corporation.

planned for the future. Alternate methods of entry include Boolean equations, state equations, timing c, and manual netlist editing. The goal of Step 1 is to create a netlist description of a logic design that can be understood by the rest of SNAP.

Step 2 is essentially automatic in that netlist generation or conversion must all be in a consistent format.

Step 3 allows design pieces from different inputs to merge into a single netlist description. In theory, one section could be input by schematic capture, another by Boolean equation and another by state equation, etc. A composite netlist for all of these would be the output of MERGER.

Step 4 is the preferred next step—to verify the design by simulation. The bold designer could proceed to Step 8 and a final device, but if any problem occurs, he must return to Step 4 to debug. In SIMNET, a binary format of the design is generated for the logic and fault simulators. During this step, the original netlist is translated into simulator primitives. This is described in more detail in following sections.

Step 5, SIMSCL, reads the input vector (simuli description), loads the network into memory, and executes the logic/timing simulation. SIMFLT is an alternate simulation that gives a fault coverage assessment of the simulation. This tells the designer (in numbers) just how rigorous the simulation testing of the circuit is. This is discussed at length later.

Step 6, PLOT, allows a waveform display of selected nodes within the design so its creator may observe the circuits modeled behavior.

Step 7, SIMPRT, allows printout of the various simulation reports for documentation.

The designer should iterate through Steps 4-7 until satisfied that correct operation is occurring. Only if it is should the designer proceed to Step 8. Up to this point, there is no binding of the design to a specific Signetics part. In fact, the design could span multiple parts or be migrated from one PLD to another with only small effort.

Step 8 is the step where choice of the target part is made and a fuse table results. This can then be manually edited or programmed into a part as the designer chooses. However, one last action can be taken to help guarantee a successful final design. That action is post-compiled model generation.

Step 9 takes the resulting fuse map from the selected part and outputs a simulation model that reflects the precise models of the internal logic for the target PLD. Once this is done, Steps 5-7 can be repeated to verify one last time that the design works. If a problem arises, the designer can still edit the design to debug it. The final compilation yields a programmed part that meets the designer's simulated specifications.

Before starting, it is appropriate to make sure that the user's system is properly configured. SNAP should run on an IBM XT- or AT-compatible system with 640K of RAM and a hard disk. Assuming that you are knowledgeable in elementary PC jargon, you can proceed to load in the SNAP diskettes from a floppy drive to the hard drive.

The recommended file structure is as shown here:

```
                              C: \ (root)
        ┌──────────┬─────────────┼──────────┬─────────┐
     Other      SNAP     Schematic    Design    Other
     files                Capture      files    files
```

The schematic capture package currently supported is ORCAD/SDT. The user should proceed to make a directory for SNAP (MD \ SNAP) and proceed with a COPY A: *.*. Assuming the schematic capture package has been similarly loaded into its directory and configured for the system, the linkage can now be made between them.

Invoking SNAP. Once SNAP is copied into its directory and ORCAD/SDT is in place, the user simply types SNAP and presses Enter. Then the flow-chart SHELL is displayed. All future file linkage is keyed to the name of the initial design file used. To define the initial design file, strike F3 (from the first screen) and enter the design name at the prompt. When done, this is displayed on the screen for future reference. Type in the design name *without a file extension*. As you progress through the various phases of the SNAP execution shell, use the keyboard's function keys. Typically F1 displays a help window, and F2 executes the corresponding shell phase. Many intermediate design and error files are generated along the way and are discussed throughout this manual.

The SNAP shell expands with the key files generated off to the side of each block. Other utility files might be generated but have meaning only within the software development group. As a user becomes proficient with SNAP, he becomes aware of which files are generated at which module and can skip through the SNAP shell successfully and efficiently. If the user has a successful design in the file space, simply generating a floppy disk of it can be done by executing a COPY A: DESIGN*. to a previously formatted floppy diskette. When designing with SNAP, it might be useful to peruse the intermediate files with a test editor periodically. Figure 3-12 presents a SNAP design flow.

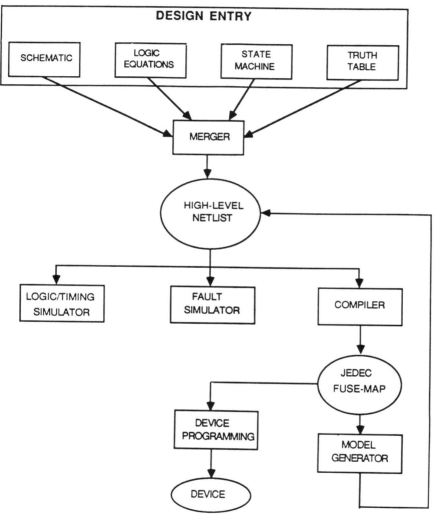

Fig. 3-12. SNAP design flow. Courtesy of Signetics Corporation.

THE COMPILER UNIVERSAL FOR PROGRAMMABLE LOGIC (CUPL)

CUPL was the first software CAD tool designed especially for the hardware designer for the support of all programmable logic devices (PLDs), including

PALs and PROMs. Figure 3-13 shows an overview of the CUPL design process. The goal of the CUPL language was chosen to make using programmable logic easier and faster than conventional TTL logic design.

CUPL supports products from every manufacturer of programmable logic. It has a PALASM-to-CUPL language translator that permits easy conversion from your previous PALASM designs to CUPL. It produces a standard JEDEC download file and is compatible with any logic programmer that uses JEDEC files.

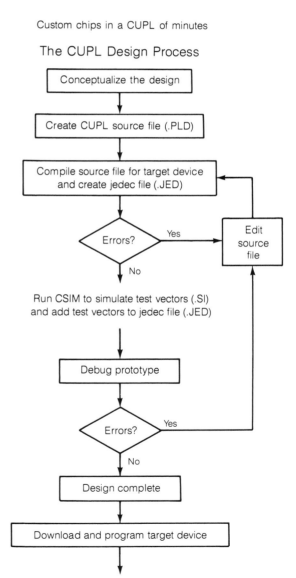

Custom chips in a CUPL of minutes

The CUPL Design Process

Fig. 3-13. The CUPL design flow. Courtesy of Logical Devices, Inc.

Data can be entered using the three conventional methods of equations, truth tables, or state machine syntax.

CUPL provides a template file which provides a standard "fill-in-the blanks" system that is uniform among all CUPL users. Also, CUPL allows for free-form comments so detailed explanations can be included in each part of the project. Error-checking capability is built in with detailed error messages.

With CSIM, the CUPL Simulator, logic can be simulated prior to the programming of an actual device. Simulation is valuable in debugging a system-level problem. Once the stimulus/response function table information has been entered into the simulator, CSIM verifies the associated test vectors. If desired, CSIM appends them to the JEDEC file for downloading to the logic programmer. The programmer verifies not only the fuse map, but also the functionality of the PLD, providing added confidence in the operation of the PLD. CUPL is designed for growth so as new PALs and other devices are introduced, the user will be kept current with updated device libraries and product enhancements.

CUPL pioneered high level, universal design software for PLDs. Today, CUPL continues to provide competitively the most powerful set of PLD tools available.

CUPL offers a variety of design expression formats, language flexibility, powerful logic minimization, De Morgan expansion and pre-processor capabilities, as well as simulation. All this while providing a variety of ways to process and transfer your data with surprisingly comprehensive support, even for the uninitiated user.

Design Expression Formats

State Machines. CUPL's state machine capability permits the circuit designer to describe his sequential PLD design using today's most advanced and highest level techniques. With one simple model, any state machine requirement can be handled. CUPL is the only popular PLD tool to properly handle both the Mealy and Moore models that many people use to categorize state machine design.

Truth Tables. The most elementary form of logic description, truth tables, occasionally offer the most convenient solution. This is especially true for custom decoders and code converters using truth tables.

Hi-Level Equations. CUPL was the first PLD language to go beyond the simple assembler/translators offered by many PLD manufacturers. First of all, parentheses can be used anywhere, and to any number of nested levels. CUPL's expression substitution capability can also be nested to any number of levels. It is highly useful for TTL schematic conversion and breaking large, complicated expressions into smaller, more understandable ones.

Language Flexibility

Bit Fields. CUPL permits the designer to group variables together, give the group a name, and thereafter treat the group as a single entity. For example,

FIELD ADDRESS = [ADR15...8]

causes ADDRESS to represent the address bus ADR15 through ADR8. Later, an equation that looks for the hexadecimal address range of B000 through CFFF can be written as follows using CUPL's range function.

Notice that the equation takes the description directly from the memory map. Designing at the level of your original thoughts is the essence of high-level design. For applications like this, hexadecimal is the number base used most often so CUPL defaults to hex unless you indicate octal, binary, or decimal.

Assertion Level Tracking. CUPL frees the designer from worrying about device architectures when designing with PLDs. Input and output signal assertion levels are specified in the pin declaration section of the logic description file. CUPL allows declarations for either active-hi or active-lo signals.

Logic equations can then be written without regard for voltages on the PLD pins. Changes in assertion levels need only be made in the pinlist, not in the logic equations. When necessary, CUPL automatically configures the proper fuses for programmable polarity devices.

Indexed Variables. Bits within an address or data bus are usually described by a symbolic name with an appended index number. The index number is always in decimal and indicates the relative significance of the bit. For instance, ADDR12 would be the 13th most significant bit of an address bus and DAT0 would be the least significant bit of a data bus.

Of all PLD design software, only CUPL understands indexed variables. This is useful in address decoding and state machine design. The most frequent use of indexed variables is the shorthand list notation. Without this feature, a typical address bus would be shown with each of its elements listed separately:

[ADR19, ADR18, ADR17, ADR16, ADR15, ADR14]

Through the use of indexed variables, the same list could be represented simply as:

[ADR 19...14].

Universal Support

JEDEC. CUPL produces the popular JEDEC format output file containing fuse programming and functional device testing information. This universal file allows CUPL to communicate with popular PROM and logic programmers including the original Data I/O 19/29 series and the newer ''configurable socket'' models available from a variety of other companies.

Devices. As the first universal language for PLDs, it is CUPL's charter to support popular devices from all manufacturers. To this end, CUPL was designed with a true database library containing device characteristics. This database is expandable for the future and today supports over 100 different device architectures from 15 PLD manufacturers including the latest CMOS EPLDs and EEPLDs.

Platforms. In addition to popular MS-DOS personal computers (including the IBM PC series with hard disk or high-capacity floppies and a minimum 512K of RAM), CUPL is available on a variety of popular UNIX-based workstations as well as the DEC VAX series running either UNIX or VMS.

PALASM Translator. Should you have an existing investment in PALASM format logic description files, CUPL's PALASM-to-CUPL translator (PTOC) converts them to a file with CUPL syntax. This saves time when you want to do further modifications on a PALASM file using CUPL's benefits or just want to put your files in a common format.

Comprehensive Documentation. CUPL both promotes and provides good documentation. CUPL's logic description template file eases design while encouraging comments and a structured information header. The documentation output file provides fuse map and/or expanded product term information as well as a chip diagram and a symbol table of all variables. An industry exclusive, the symbol table shows at a glance p-term usage and capacity, minimization, algorithm, and assertion levels for all variables.

Power Tools

Logic Minimization. CUPL is the only PLD design tool to offer you a choice of logic minimization algorithms. CUPL has Quick-Min and No-Min options. But instead of one full minimizer, you get three. Because logic minimization is not an exact science, different algorithms can provide different results in different applications. For maximum flexibility, any of the five minimization options can be assigned to different equations within a single PLD.

Option M0, the no-minimization option, can be used for outputs that require logic redundancy for applications such as reducing hazard conditions in asynchronous control lines.

The other options, M1 thru M4, are each tailored to take advantage of either system memory, compile time, or minimization completeness.

Preprocessor. CUPL's preprocessor, the first to be available for PLD design, provides string subsitution, file inclusion, and conditional compilation. These capabilities allow general-purpose logic descriptions, or modular portions of descriptions, to be developed and later customized for different applications.

Simulation. The CUPL simulator CSIM provides table-oriented simulation to help you verify the logic design or test vectors. Two exclusive features are proper handling of ''don't-care'' input and output states and the optional use of * in the output field to indicate that CSIM should generate the output value rather than verify a value you might supply. Message and Repeat Vector directives are included along with the ability to use hex values for representing fields of bits. The simulation input file is kept separate from the logic description file. This lets you run successive simulations without having to recompile each time.

When you negate an entire expression, CUPL automatically performs a De Morgan expansion for you. Lower level PLD tools require a manual expansion. For instance, without automatic De Morgan, the expression

!(A & B & C # D & E)

would have to be expanded manually to result in

!A&!D # !A&E # !B&!D # !B&!E # !C&!D # !C&!E

For more complex expressions, a large amount of time and memory is sometimes consumed. CUPL's Turbo-De Morgan algorithm, the fastest and most efficient in the industry, is most helpful where memory resources are limited. This is especially true for popular personal computers. A CUPL flow diagram is shown in FIG. 3-13.

PROGRAMMABLE LOGIC ANALYSIS BY NATIONAL (PLAN)

PLAN is the first architecture specific language for PLDs. With PLAN, a single language can be used to implement a design in any PLD manufactured by National. A specification for a PLD can be written without first determining the target device. In fact, PLAN selects the least complex PLD available to implement or design automatically. All this means that PLAN makes PLD circuit design faster than ever.

PLAN is easy to use, requires no complicated input/output procedures, and contains none of the input format constraints found in PALASM. It is designed to run on your IBM-compatible personal computer. Alternative operating systems will be accommodated in the future.

PLAN is table-driven to minimize maintenance. A table compiler allows new devices to be added in short order. The run-time is longer if new, unique architecture features are required.

Input to the assembler is device-independent. Source-file syntax provides for logic function description by a function-specific language. PLD attributes, device names, and pin assignments are required only as user options in the source file. Standard Boolean equation syntax and operators permit use of third-party minimizers, simulators, and vector generators.

The assembler is capable of fitting every conceivable user-defined functional requirement to the device. Every combination of macrocells and macrocell architectural configuration is accommodated by the software. This is accomplished with an embedded-table, configured-software model of each supported device.

Test vectors, created either manually or automatically, are correctly assimilated into a programming file that conforms completely to JEDEC Standard #3A and is acceptable by all device programming hardware. JED2BEQ, a JEDEC-file-to-assembler-input-file compiler, lets the user reverse engineer by placing any existing design into a National PLD. Complete error handling prevents invalid JEDEC maps from being generated.

In addition, PLAN provides full GAL support via a PAL-to-GAL translator, a high-speed map-to-map translator that produces a National assembler GAL-JEDEC file from any assembler JEDEC-formatted file.

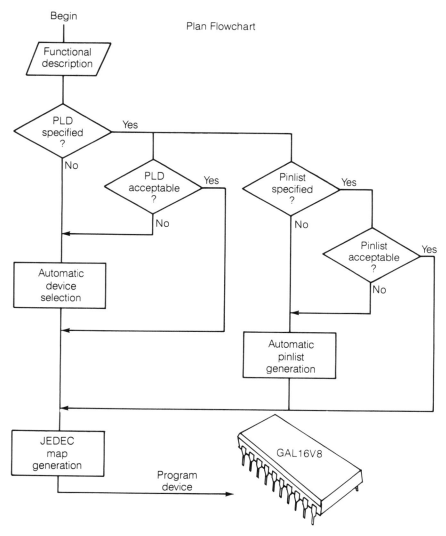

Fig. 3-14. Flowchart of PLAN software. Courtesy of National Semiconductors, Corporation.

The products and processes allow maximum flexibility in meeting the particular programming needs. If production considerations dictate that the user handle all programming, he can ship back PAL devices. Or, if the quality or schedule requires, the user can perform total programming and testing prior to shipment.

The National Masked Logic (NML) program, for example, was introduced to provide customers savings of 10-25% in large-volume applications of a given logic pattern. NML devices are mask-programmed and functionally tested in-house by National. Thus the user can simplify the production lines and save on programming costs as well. Any National programmable logic device can be ordered with the NML option. Each has the same data sheet specifications as its field-programmable counterpart.

Figure 3-14 shows a PLAN flowchart.

4

Development Systems

Several complete development systems provide all of the tools necessary for the design engineer's process of describing the specific design to programming and testing the PLD. The following summarizes the functions that a development should be capable of performing.

DESIGN DESCRIPTION

The description of PLD designs should be as easy and as natural as possible. The less translation that takes place between the way you conceive a design and the way you describe it, the less chance there is for error. PLD designs can be described by older methods such as marking Xs on a PLD schematic or using assembly-type languages or by new tools such as high-level design packages that support a wide range of devices that generally offer the most flexibility and are more natural expressions of a design.

Reduction

PLDs have a finite number of product terms that can be used up quickly by large or complex designs. Therefore, the design should be reduced so it uses as few product terms as possible. Logic reduction can be performed manually using Karnaugh maps and De Morgan's theorem, or automatically with logic reduction software. Automatic logic reduction is faster and less tedious than manual methods.

Simulation

A good logic simulator can make big differences in overall results with PLDs. A simulator can detect and report design errors before a device is programmed, thus saving the cost and time of misprogramming a device. If the simulator is fast and easy to use, it can also encourage designers to experiment with new designs or techniques, resulting in better solutions to design problems. Simulation is accomplished by applying sets of inputs to a design and checking the simulated outputs against expected results.

Fault Analysis and Test Vector Generation

When testability of programmed devices is a concern, fault analysis and automatic test vector generation are invaluable tools. The goal is to ensure that a programmed device can be adequately tested for correct operation. Fault analysis should pinpoint portions of a design that make a device untestable so the design can be corrected.

Once the device is determined to be testable, the tests that check its operation must be developed. Because test generation is a long, tedious process if done manually, automatic methods are preferred. Fast, automatic fault analysis and test generation encourage designers who might otherwise overlook this step to make sure a device can be fully tested.

Programming

The PLD programmer is the final link between a design concept and the PLD that implements that concept. Each different type of device—PALs, EPLAs, EPLSs, PROMs, EPROMs, EEPROMs—requires different programming techniques. Many different types of programmers exist on the market. Some program only one type of PLD or PROM. Other programmers offer comprehensive support for a wide variety of devices. Programmers should be accurate, easy-to-use, and fast.

Testing

Programmed devices should always be tested for correct operation. Testing is most easily accomplished if it is performed by the PLD programmer subsequent to programming. Errors reported by device testing routines should be clear and comprehensive.

Documentation

Design documentation should be performed throughout all the previous steps. Design documentation should include readable design descriptions, device pinouts, netlists (for larger systems), fault-analysis reports and any other information needed to document fully your design.

THE PERSONAL SILICON FOUNDRY (PSF)

The PSF is a comprehensive system to meet every requirement of the PLD development process. Developed by Data I/O and FutureNet, the Personal Silicon Foundry combines PC-based CAE and PLD design tools that are recognized industry leaders into one complete package.

A Personal Silicon Foundry (PSF) encompasses and optimizes every step of the design process—design description, reduction, simulation, fault analysis, test vector generation, programming, and testing. PLD designs can be entered using any combination of Boolean equations, truth tables, state diagrams, or schematics. Every process that can be automated is automated, and complete documentation is generated from start to finish.

The Personal Silicon Foundry frees designers to do what they do best—design—and relegates tedious mechanical tasks such as logic reduction and test vector generation to automated tools. The result is easy, efficient PLD design development with a complete process cycle often taking less than half a day.

The PSF by Data I/O is a specialized system of hardware and software tools surrounding an IBM XT or AT personal computer. The major components of a PSF are the personal computer, PLD design software, schematic design tools, and a PLD programmer. A complete PSF fits easily on a standard size desk and can be tailored to meet the needs of the modern design engineer.

The Personal Silicon Foundry is easily configured to meet a variety of needs. Each Personal Silicon Foundry comes standard with the design software, but beyond that the choices are decided by the circuit designer. In configuring a Data I/O PSF, consider these three questions:

1. What devices the circuit designer wants to program? (This determines the PLD programmer.)
2. Does the circuit designer wish to take advantage of schematic input capabilities?
3. Does the designer have an XT or AT personal computer?

For convenience, these questions and the possible answers have been organized in TABLE 4-1.

Table 4-1. PSF options available for various answers to the questions.

Question	Answer	PSF Option
What devices are wanted to program?	Popular PLDs	60A PLD programmer
	Most available PLDs	29B with LogicPak
	PROMS and most available PLDs	29B with LogicPak and UniPak 2B
What schematic design input capabilities?	Yes, enhanced color	DASH 3C
	Yes, monochrome	DASH 2
	No	—
Is a PC needed?	Yes, XT	XT System
	Yes, AT	AT System
	No	—

Fig. 4-1. Typical configuration of a Personal Silicon Foundry (PSF). Photograph courtesy of Data I/O Corporation.

This can be used to configure a Personal Silicon Foundry by answering each question and circling the appropriate answer. Then, look in the PSF option column to see which PSF options are needed.

The answers to each question configure a custom Personal Silicon Foundry. A typical PSF system is shown in FIG. 4-1.

To keep abreast of the ever-changing PLD market and to make sure the circuit designer has, Data I/O offers a wide range of PSF support and service, including programmer calibration and update services, software update services, complete service contracts, and technical support via telephone.

The Personal Silicon Foundry combines Data I/O's leadership in PLD support tools with FutureNet's expertise in PC-based CAE technology. Both Data I/O and FutureNet have set standards in their fields—for products and for customer support. Representatives are located worldwide to answer any questions you might have about the Personal Silicon Foundry or other Data I/O FutureNet products.

ALTERA'S DESIGN TOOLS

The Altera Corporation provides a full complement of design tools to support the design of EPLDs. Installed on an IBM XT, AT and PS/2, or compatible machine, these tools provide a fast, flexible, and easy to learn CAE development environment. They can be purchased as complete development systems or as individual software and hardware products.

EPLD designs can be entered in many convenient formats. These include schematic capture (basic gates and TTL MacroFunctions), Boolean equations, state machine, truth table, and microcode assembler entry. Design compilation performs logic minimization, automatic device fitting, and generation of programming data in the standard JEDEC format. Device fitting is the PLD equivalent to an automatic place and route capability. Fitting is done on a typical design in minutes. Design verification and device programming capabilities are also available. Altera development systems permit the use of many third-party software and hardware products via appropriate interface programs.

PLDVS (PERSONAL LOGIC DESIGN VERIFICATION SYSTEM)

The Altera PLDVS (Personal Logic Design Verification System) is a low-cost, general-purpose system for functional verification of TTL- or CMOS-compatible device prototypes such as gate array, standard cell, and programmable logic devices. It can be used for both production and engineering applications.

The system shown in FIG. 4-2 consists of two PC add-in boards, cables, DUT (Device Under Test) interface hardware, and the test program compiler. The add-in boards (the LP4 and the PLDV1) provide 5 individually programmable power supplies, I_{CC} measurement circuitry, 8 three-level drivers, and 128 independently configurable bidirectional test channels. Also, you get adapters for the MAX family of parts and a generic adapter that can be configured for generic devices.

The system can be used for very simple to very complex applications. First-time users can create simple test programs in minutes, while more

Fig. 4-2. The Personal Design Verification System (PLDVS). Photograph courtesy of Altera Corporation.

advanced users can develop highly complex test routines. The compiler combines high-level Pascal-like programming features with a powerful vector language. Fast compilation times of 200 instructions per second reduce debug time for both test programs and circuits. Test results can be stored, manipulated, and displayed from high-level software.

The compiler handles all hardware interactions. This allows the user to specify test requirements solely in terms of the device rather than in terms of the test hardware pin mapping. It also performs complex algorithms to facilitate the use of stored vectors, algorithmically generated vectors, and procedure-based vector parameter passing.

Simple test programs created with the PLDV compiler can be run independently. Larger and more complex test routines can be made by linking smaller independent modules together from within an executive shell routine written with Turbo Pascal.

The programming language has specific commands for applying test vectors to the DUT, comparing results, and masking data. The basic language elements allow simple vector sets to be written, compiled, and run in minutes. Unlike traditional test program languages, vector data can be integrated with Pascal constructs to create sophisticated and flexible algorithms.

The compiler provides additional instructions which include continuity checking, setting programmable voltages, measurement of I_{CC} and V_{CC}, and verification that the device being tested is correctly seated in its socket.

The PLDVS hardware provides 5 programmable power supplies and 128 configurable test channels. All of the data channels are double buffered, which allows data to be presented to the DUT after all channel states have been set. Thus, any number of DUT pins can be changed simultaneously. The CPU reads DUT output data by tristating the appropriate tester channels and reading the data through the PLDV System driver channels.

All tester channels drive CMOS and TTL levels and can read back any TTL-compatible logic levels. Data is driven to or read from the DUT at a rate dependent on the CPU and data transfers to the interface board. A 16 MHz 386 system can generate more than 50,000 vectors per second for 68-pin devices. For lower pin count devices, PLDVS can generate 200,000 vectors per second.

PLDVS has 4 positive and one negative programmable power supplies. PLDVS also has 8 three-level drivers to drive DUT pins which require a high-voltage (5-12 volts) in addition to normal logic level voltages. These are useful for entering test modes or for programming EPLDs and EPROMs. I_{CC} measurement circuitry that can measure supply currents from 50 mA to 500 mA is also provided.

The PLDV system can be integrated within Altera's MAX + PLUS development environment. The MAX + PLUS software provides a user-friendly, menu-driven environment for generating and simulating designs for the MAX family of EPLDs.

PLDVS has several advantages when used within the MAX + PLUS software. The PLDV system can be used for fast hardware simulations. It also can be used to program parts from the MAX family of devices. Test vectors can be applied to the programmed parts to verify that they are functional.

MAX + PLUS software includes a graphical waveform editor, a mouse-driven environment for editing and displaying waveforms. Hardware test results can be viewed as functional waveforms where nodes can be added, deleted, and grouped together into buses. Actual output waveforms can also be graphically compared with simulated outputs.

Input vectors are defined either in a simple test file format known as a vector file, or via waveform files created and edited in the waveform editor. Once the input vectors have been defined, they can be applied to the device continuously or with break conditions. PLDVS can be used entirely within the MAX-+ PLUS environment without any need to use the PLDV Compiler to aid MAX EPLD simulation and design verification.

The MAX + PLUS software can also be used to generate input test waveforms and display functional results for general purpose devices. The user simply defines the channel map and inputs stimuli for the device to be tested. MAX + PLUS applies the test vectors and displays the results in the waveform editor or in an ASCII table format. For more information on the MAX + PLUS software, see the PLDS-MAX datasheet.

The PLDVS has the capability to read and program EPLDs. It can also program MAX EPLDs and apply test vectors. Adapters are included for programming the EPM5128 and the EPM5032. PLDVS provides full continuity checked programming capability.

PLDVS includes the PLAD5032, a 28-pin DIP adapter socket for the EPM5032, and the PLAJ5128, a 68-pin J-lead adapter socket for the EPM5128. Also, a generic socket card (PLAG1 included) can be configured to support the specific device pinout.

PLCAD-SUPREME

The Altera PLCAD-SUPREME is a complete hardware and software solution that enables circuit designers to develop and implement custom logic circuits with Altera PLDs. The system contains A + Plus, Altera's programmable logic user software which allows a wide variety of design input methods that suit the particular logic design task. These include netlist, Boolean equation, optional schematic capture, and optional state machine design entries. Also included are a master programming unit, various adapters, and device samples. Figure 4-3 shows Altera's PLCAD-SUPREME/PS Development System with an IBM Model 50 PS/2 computer.

PLDS-SAM (PROGRAMMABLE
LOGIC DEVELOPMENT SYSTEM)

The Altera PLDS-SAM (Programmable Logic Development System) represents a complete software and hardware solution to implementing state

Fig. 4-3. PLCAD-Supreme/PS Development system displayed with an IBM Model 50 PS/2 computer. Photograph courtesy of Altera Corporation.

machine and microcoded applications into Altera's SAM family of function-specific EPLDs. PLDS-SAM is a comprehensive, easy to use system that encompasses design entry with SAM + PLUS, design debugging with SAMSIM, and device programming with the Altera programming hardware.

The SAM + PLUS processing software accepts two forms of design entry, state machine and assembly language, and automatically generates an industry standard JEDEC file. SAMSIM is an interactive functional simulator created specifically for verification of state machine and microcoded designs implemented in SAM EPLDs. The programming hardware consists of an Altera programming card, a master programming unit, and programming adapter for programming the SAM EPLDs.

For existing Altera PLDS or PLCAD users, PLSSAM (Programmable Logic Software) is available as a software enhancement to their current system.

MAX + PLUS DEVELOPMENT SYSTEM

The Altera MAX + PLUS Development System represents a complete hardware and software solution for implementing designs into Altera's MAX (Multiple Array Matrix) family of EPLDs. MAX + PLUS is a sophisticated Computer-Aided Design (CAD) system that includes design entry, design simulation, and device programming. Hosted on an IBM PC AT or compatible machine, MAX + PLUS gives the designer the tools to implement complex logic designs quickly and efficiently. A block diagram is shown in FIG. 4-4. Figure 4-5 shows the PLDs-MAX + PLUS development software and hardware for EMPXXX series devices.

Max + Plus design system

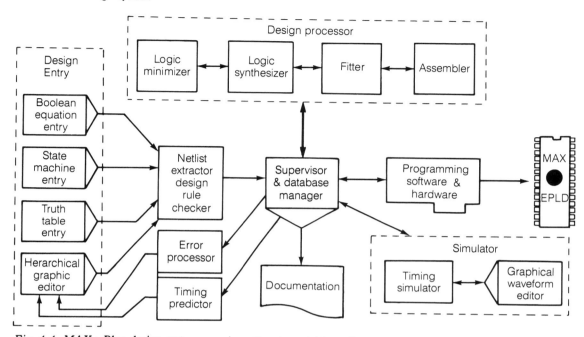

Fig. 4-4. MAX + Plus design system overview. Courtesy of Altera Corporation.

Fig. 4-5. PLDs-MAX: MAX + Plus development software and programming hardware for EMPXXXV Series devices. Photograph courtesy of Altera Corporation.

Designs are entered in MAX + PLUS using a hierarchical graphic editor. This editor has such features as multiple windows, multiple zoom levels, unlimited hierarchy levels, symbol editing, and a library of 7400 series devices in addition to basic SSI gate and register primitives. Also available is a timing calculator, in which the designer can pick two places in the schematic, and the software will display typical timing between those two points. Boolean equation, netlist, state machine, and truth table entry mechanisms can be used in conjunction with the graphic editor, giving added flexibility to the design environment.

In addition to a hierarchical design environment, MAX + PLUS has a sophisticated processing engine to exploit the MAX architecture. MAX + PLUS uses an advanced logic synthesizer and heuristic rules to process a design into a file for programming and/or simulation.

MAX + PLUS features a powerful event-driven simulator that displays typical timing results in an interactive waveform editor display. In this waveform editor, input vector waveforms can be directly modified and a new simulation run immediately.

PDS-1 PEEL DEVELOPMENT SYSTEM

The PDS-1 PEEL Development System is a powerful, yet low-cost, PC-based system for designing with PEEL devices. Key features include the APEEL Boolean-logic assembler and a PLD JEDEC-file translator that can automatically translate a wide variety of conventional PLD design files to PEEL programming files. Serving as a personal PLD workstation, the PDS-1 provides everything needed to implement logic designs from design entry to logic assembly/simulation to programming and testing of PEEL devices. With the APEEL Logic Assembler and PEEL device translator, verify and security operations and device logic testing are provided. Uniquely, this software gives the designer the ability to load the contents of PALs, EPLDs, and FPLAS devices for direct translation to PEEL devices. Programmers and development tool support for PEEL devices are also available from a variety of third-party manufacturers.

Basically, PEEL devices replace the one-time programmable metal fuse links of conventional PLDs with electrically erasable memory cells. Electrical reprogrammability adds convenience and cost savings in development because they can be reused instantly during prototyping.

The chart shown in FIG. 4-6 illustrates how the APEEL Logic Assembler of the JEDEC file translator can be used to create PEEL device designs.

APEEL Logic Assembler

The APEEL Logic Assembler can be used to create new or custom designs specifically for PEEL devices. Using the built-in text editor, APEEL logic equations and test vectors can be entered and saved as an APEEL input file.

Once entered and saved, APEEL can assemble the file, checking for syntax errors. If errors are found, APEEL interacts with the editor and directly specifies the location of the errors.

When the input file is successfully assembled, its logic functions can be simulated if user-defined test vectors were provided. If simulation errors are found, APEEL specifies the test vector where the error occurred. If no simulation errors are found, a PEEL JEDEC file can be created, or optionally, fault

Designing with ICT's PEEL development tools

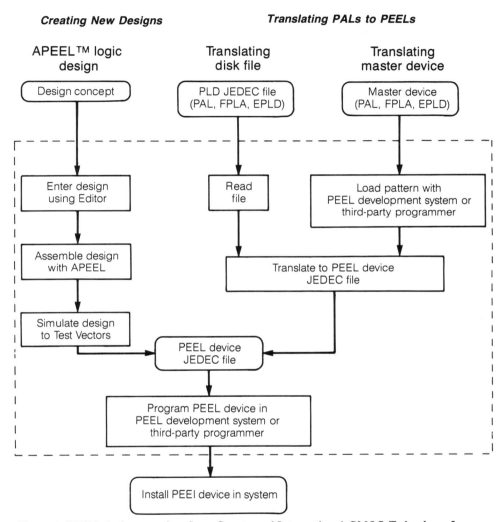

Fig. 4-6. PEEL design overview flow. Courtesy of International CMOS Technology, Inc.

grading (the means for measuring how well the test vectors for the APEEL file cover all possible logic conditions) can be performed. This is accomplished by exhaustively exercising the inputs of the simulated files to check for "stuck-at-1" and "stuck-at-0" fault conditions followed by a comparison of the vectors required. The final grading is provided as a percentage. The higher the percentage of coverage, the more likely the test vectors have tested all possible logic combinations. A very low percentage of APEEL file test vectors should require improvement. Because fault grading can be very time consuming, it is optional and is recommended only for design engineer with a requirement that would require its use.

When the design is successfully assembled, APEEL software translates the input file into a JEDEC fuse map, and converts the simulation vectors into JEDEC-formatted test vectors. The JEDEC file can then be downloaded to the PDS-1 programmer or a programmer from a third-party manufacturer for programming and testing a PEEL device.

APEEL source files can be created with any word processor or text editor that produces ASCII files. In addition, the APEEL software package sports a built-in word processor driven by familiar keyboard commands and convenient pull-down menus. The elements of an APEEL source file are shown in FIG. 4-7.

```
title 'title of design'

"  device declaration
                PEEL__device__number


"  pin and node assignments

                      name        pin     pin__#
                      name        node    node__#


equations
                name    =  expression
      enable    name    =  expression


test__vectors

(  input  input   ---->   output  output )
   input  input   ---->   output  output
   input  input   ---->   output  output
```

Fig. 4-7. Elements of an APEEL source file. Courtesy of International CMOS Technology, Inc.

In the figure, lines beginning with double quotes are comments and are ignored by the APEEL assembler. The expressions in bold type are key words that have special meaning to the APEEL assembler and must be included in the file. The expressions in italic are strings that you would replace with the appropriate pin name, logic expression, etc.

The elements of an APEEL source file are:

- Title—The title is optional and is used to describe the source file. The title is printed as a header when printing the JEDEC programming file. The title statement consists of the keyword ''title'' followed by the desired title of the design.
- Device declaration—The device declaration identifies the target device for the assembler. Use the ICT PEEL part number as the device identifier, e.g., PEEL 18CV8, or PEEL 173, etc.
- Pin and node assignments—This section defines the pins and nodes of the PEEL device with identifiers used in the source file.

- Equations—This section contains the Boolean equations that describe the logic design. Refer to the APEEL syntax section for details on the equations section of the source file.
- Test vectors—This section contains the optional user-defined test vectors. Test vectors can be used by the APEEL assembler's logic simulation function to verify the functionality of the logic design. The vectors are also used by the PEEL Development System to exercise the PEEL device after it has been programmed.

The PEEL device JEDEC file translator provides the means for quickly converting an existing conventional PLD design (PAL, EPLD, FPLA) instantly to a PEEL device design. Once the translation is complete, the PEEL device becomes a plug-in replacement for the original device with all the advantages of CMOS PEEL technology.

The translator works by simply reading the JEDEC file of the original PLD and converting it to new PEEL JEDEC file using the original file name with the JED extension modified to JEX. The JEX file can then be used to program a PEEL device.

Once a PEEL JEDEC file is created either by APEEL or the PEEL Device Translator, the PEEL device is ready for programming. This can be accomplished with a number of third-party PLD programmers or by using the ICT PEEL Development System (FIG. 4-8).

THE ıPLDS II

The Intel Programmable Logic Development System Version II is shown in FIG. 4-9 and block diagram in FIG. 4-10. All of the design entry methods—with the

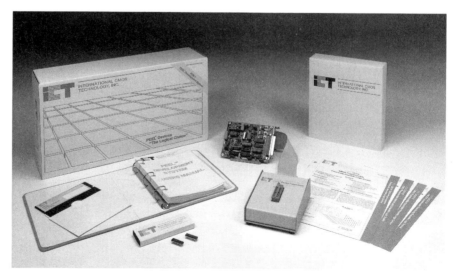

Fig. 4-8. PEEL development system. Courtesy of International CMOS Technology, Inc.

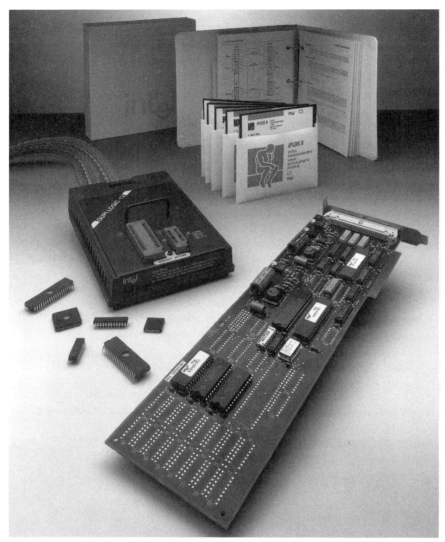

Fig. 4-9. The Intel Programmable Logic Development System II. Courtesy of Intel Corporation.

exception of graphic state machine entry—are supported by the iPLDS II software. iPLDS II supports netlist and Boolean equation entry using any standard text editor. State machine software and schematic capture libraries are also available from Intel as optional entry methods.

Depending on the entry format used, the design might require translation into Advanced Design File (ADF) format. Once the design is in ADF form, the Logic Optimizing Compiler expands any macros, minimizes all equations, and fits the design into a device-specific JEDEC design file. The JEDEC design file is programmed into the EPLD by the Logic Programmer Software using the

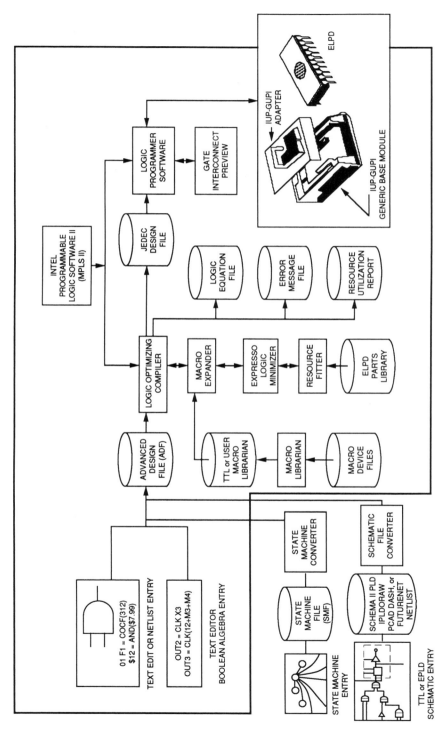

Fig. 4-10. Block diagram of IPLD Development System. Courtesy of Intel Corporation.

iUP-PC hardware. Thus, the circuit design is transformed into an operating EPLD on one workstation.

The Intel Programmable Logic Software II (iPLDS II) is composed of four functional modules: design entry, netlist conversion, file compilation, and device programming.

Design Entry

Design entry is typically accomplished by creating an ADF using an ASCII test editor or by using a schematic capture package.

Netlist Conversion

If schematic capture of state machine entry is used, the design must be converted into an ADF format. The optional SCHEMA II-PLD schematic capture package is a low-cost way to enter schematic designs. SCHEMA II-PLD supports EPLD primitives and TTL or user-defined macro symbols. It also outputs directly in ADF format. SCHEMA II-PLD contains the EPLD Manager, which provides a single-user interface to both SCHEMA II-PLD and iPLS II software.

The P-CAD and FutureNet systems can be used to capture EPLD symbols provided the EPLD libraries and ADF converters are used. State machine entry can be performed via the iSTATE software and a standard text editor.

File Compilation

File compilation is performed by the Logic Optimizing Compiler as shown in FIG. 4-11. The LOC accepts an ADF and converts it into an industry standard JEDEC file that is used to program the device. As a part of this process, the LOC expands TTL macros into equivalent EPLD logic, minimizes the logic

```
              Intel PRogrammable Logic Software II


LOC Menu

F1 HELP              ADF Minimization LEF-Analysis
F2 iPLS Menu         X CONTROL
F3 Input Format
F4 File Name(s)      *** INFO-LOC-Begin execution
F5 Minimization      *** INFO-LOC-4 macrofunctions resolved in XCONTROL
F6 Inversion Control *** INFO-LOC-ADF converted to LEF; XCONTROL
F7 LEF Analysis      *** INFO-LOC-Sum of Products (S.O.P. LEF produced
F8 Error File        *** INFO-LOC-LEF reduced
F9 Execute           *** INFO-LOC-LEF analyzed
                         *** INFO-LOC-Resource demand determined
                         *** INFO-LOC-Design fitting complete
                         *** INFO-LOC-JEDEC file output

                         LOC cycle successfully completed


Would you like to implement another design [Y/N]?\
```

Fig. 4-11. Intel Programmable Logic Software II. (menu screen).

equations using the Espresso algorithm, and maps the network and logic equations into a cell map for the selected device. The final output of the LOC is a JEDEC design file. The JEDEC design file describes the input design for the designated EPLD in JEDEC standard format.

For designs using the 5AC312 or 5AC324,iPLS II R2.0 utilizes proprietary algorithms to use efficiently the device resources. The improved Fitter in R2.0 optimizes fitting for all devices.

Device Programming

The programming hardware is controlled by the Logic Programmer Software. LPS takes the JEDEC file produced by the LOC and programs it into the device. LPS can also read a programmed device or verify that a device has been programmed correctly.

The Intel Universal Programmer for the Personal Computer (iUP-PC) is a versatile programming solution in a PC-based system. Installed in an IBM PC/XT, PC/AT, or compatible host, the iUP-PC emulates the performance of the stand-alone INTEL iUP-200A Universal Programmers. As such, it supports the iUP Generic Universal Programmer Interface (iUP-GUPI). With the appropriate socket adapters for the iUP-GUPI, the iUP-PC supports all Intel EPLDs. Future EPLDs will be supported by new GUPI adapters or adapter upgrades. Many other Intel devices—EPROMs, EEPROMs, and microcontrollers—are also supported by the GUPI. The iUP-PC is controlled by the LPS or the iPPS (Intel PROM Programmer Software). iPLDS II includes the iUP-PC, which contains the iPPS, PCPP programming card, interconnect cable, and the GUPI base. GUPI adapters are available separately.

iPLS II Software

The Intel Programmable Logic Software II (iPLS II) has many options and enhancements for implementing a logic design. iPLS II accommodates a wide variety of design input methods. Schematics, state machines, or Boolean equations can all be used provided the proper formats and converters are implemented as needed. No matter what method is chosen, the Logic Optimizing Compiler will minimize and fit the design during compilation. Finally, iPLS II contains the Logic Programmer Software which controls the iUP-PC programming hardware for all Intel EPLDs.

Design Input

The entire spectrum of design input methods is available to the logic designer in iPLDS II. Everything from TTL schematics to Boolean equations are accepted and processed by the LOC.

TTL Schematic Entry. SCHEMA II-PLD is an optional software package that allows EPLD design to be implemented with standard TTL functions. SCHEMA II-PLD contains a symbol library that includes common SSI/MSI

TTL symbols. SCHEMA II-PLD also outputs directly in ADF format. The TTL symbols appear in the ADF in the form of macro calls. During compilation, iPLS II automatically expands these calls from its TTL macro library. Thus, with SCHEMA II-PLD, conversion to EPLD logic primitives is performed automatically in a manner completely transparent to the user.

Only parts supported by the SCHEMA II-PLD TTL symbol library and the iPLS II TTL macro definition library can be used for RRL schematic entry. In most cases, this is not a limitation as the most common parts are included in both libraries. Parts not in the macro libraries can be created by the user and stored in proprietary user libraries. SCHEMA II-PLD also supports creating of user-defined macro symbols. The iPLS II Macro Librarian supports creation of iPLS II macro libraries.

Schematic Entry with Intel Symbol Library. If the user prefers designing with EPLD logic primitives but still wants to use schematic entry, SCHEMA II-PLD, in addition to supporting TTL schematic capture, also supports design using EPLD primitive symbols. Users can enter their design and have both a schematic drawing and an ADF version of the design. The logic symbols are loaded from the Intel library and connected in the usual manner. For quicker use of EPLD primitives, a second library, EPLDMAC.LIB is available for use. Optional symbol libraries are also available for PC-CAPS by P-CAD Corporation and DASH-2, -3, -4 by FutureNet (iSLIBPCAD, iSLIBFNET). The iSIMLIB optional library is available for simulating logic designs with P-CAD's PC-LOGS logic simulator.

Text Editor Entry. Designers who are familiar with the logic primitives and the Advanced Design File format can directly enter ADFs with a standard text editor. The bulk of the design entry can be accomplished using Boolean Equations obtained from a Karnaugh map or truth table. Hence, the need for conversion to gates is eliminated. This method of entry is useful for subcircuits that will be incorporated into larger designs.

State Machine Entry. In the past, state diagrams or flowcharts (ASM charts) were merely abstractions used to obtain the logic equations necessary to implement TTL designs. With the advent of the iPLS II state machine convertor (iSTATE), this is no longer the case. Using an IF-THEN-ELSE format, the designer can enter the state machine description without having to extract the logic and convert the equations into TTL components. The state-machine-to-Boolean-logic conversion is handled by the state machine convertor, provided the input file adheres to the specified State Machine File (SMF) format.

Summary of Optional Entry Requirements

TTL Schematic Capture:

1. TTL Macro Library
2. EPLD Custom Macro Library
3. SCHEMA II-PLD

PC-CAPS

1. Intel Library used to design logic circuit
2. Component List Output
3. PCAD convertor used in LOC (Library and Convertor contained in iSLIBPCAD)

DASH-2, -3, -4

1. Intel Library used to design logic circuit
2. Pinlist Output
3. FutureNet convertor used in LOC (Library and convertor contained in iSLIBPCAD)

State Machines

1. State Machine File (SMF) format used
2. Optional state machine convertor used in LOC (Convertor contained in iSTATE)

Logic File Compilation

Before programming the part, the designer must compile the input design file into a JEDEC standard file. This function is performed by the Logic Optimizing Compiler.

Logic Optimizing Compiler (LOC). Once the input file is in Advanced Design File (ADF) format, the LOC will compile it into a device-specific JEDEC design file. The first phase of this compilation is performed by the Macro Expander. The Macro Expander expands Intel or TTL macros into equivalent EPLD equations. The second phase is performed by the Espresso Minimizer. The Minimizer reduces all the logic equations to their simplest form using the Espresso II-MV algorithm. The final phase of compilation is performed by the Fitter. The Fitter creates a cell map of the minimized equations according to the resources available within the specified device.

Macro Expander. The input design file is initially passed through the Macro Expander. The Macro Expander searches the file for any non-EPLD network elements. If found, the Expander then searches the User Libraries and TTL Library for the unidentified element. Once the element is located, the design file element is replaced by the equivalent EPLD primitive implementation found in the library. Having the Expander search the User libraries allows the user to create his own macros. User macro files are created with a standard ASCII text editor and are stored in libraries by the iPLS II Macro Librarian.

Espresso Minimizer. The minimization in the LOC is performed by the Espresso II-MV Minimizer. Developed by the University of California at Berkeley, the Espresso II-MV algorithm is regarded by many as being the best minimization method available. Espresso II-MV uses De Morgan's and other logic theorems to reduce the equations to the least number of product terms possible. Because product terms are the key variable in the EPLD architecture, the Espresso II-MV Minimizer provides the simplest equations possible. As a result, the success rate for fitting large designs is dramatically increased.

Fitter. The Fitter examines the architecture of the specified device, then tries to map the minimized equations into the resources available. The Fitter automatically assigns pins unless pin assignments already specified in the design input file. The fitting sequence continues until a successful fit is accomplished or all possible implementations are exhausted. Release 2.0 of iPLS II includes a new, faster Fitter that supports PGA packages and the 5AC312, 5AC324, and 85C508. Also included in this new Fitter is the capability to allocate p-terms to adjacent macrocells for devices such as the 5AC312 and 5A324 that support p-term allocation.

Output Files.

JEDEC Design File. A properly designed circuit results in the desired file from the LOC—the JEDEC design file. The JEDEC design file is a device-tailored EPROM cell programming map expressed in JEDEC standard format.

Resource Utilization Report. The Resource Utilization Report gives an indepth view of what was used inside the EPLD. Items such as device pinout, macrocell usage, and feedback arrangements are all listed. Unused resources are also listed to aid the user in adding logic or merging EPLD designs.

Logic Equation File. The LEF file lists the logic equations after they have passed through the minimizer. It is these equations that are actually implemented in the final design.

Compiler Error File. If a logic circuit is incorrectly designed, messages are produced by the LOC denoting the errors. To assist the redesign, these errors are placed into the Compiler Error File for later reference.

File Merging. Once a design is successfully implemented, the LOC can merge it with other designs by simultaneously running the two ADFs. In this manner, LSI circuits can be broken into manageable chunks that can be implemented and tested individually. After each portion is completed, the subcircuits can be merged into one ADF to implement the total design.

Device Programming

After the design has been successfully entered, minimized and fitted, the designer programs his part using the JEDEC file produced by the LOC. Programming is accomplished by running the Logic Programming Software.

Logic Programmer Software. To program a device with the LPS, the user enters the file name and device to be programmed. The LPS checks if the device is blank, programs the device, then verifies that the device was programmed correctly. As a part of the Intel EPLD Programming Algorithm, each programmed cell is checked. Adding the complete device check after programming gives double verification that the part has been successfully programmed.

It is also possible to read a preprogrammed device and program other devices with the program read. The JEDEC Editor in LPS provides a hierarchical view of the device from the pin level, to the macrocell level, to the product term level. At the product term level, individual EPROM cells may be set or reset to connect or disconnect the logic equation inputs. If the user does not want an EPLD to be read, the security bit can be set when running the LPS. The security bit prevents a device from being examined after it has been programmed. This function is useful for protecting confidential designs.

iUP-PC Hardware. The Intel Universal Programmer for the Personal Computer consists of the PCPP programming card, 50-lead interconnect cable, GUPI base, and GUPI adapter. Together they form a system for programming most PROM-type Intel devices directly from the PC host.

PCPP. The Personal Computer Personal Programmer (PCPP) is the programmer interface card that fits into the IBM AT/XT or true compatible. It is capable of driving both the iUP-GUPI base and the iUP-FAST27K personality module. The PCPP emulates the performance of the Intel iUP-200A. The LPS or iPPS (Intel PROM Programmer Software) controls the PCPP, causing the programming card to generate the control signals for the GUPI base.

GUPI Base. The Generic Universal Programmer Interface (GUPI) is used for all programmable logic support. As all signal generation to devices is done by the GUPI, the programming waveforms are extremely reliable. Using the GUPI also allows upgrading for future devices with the simple addition of plug-in adapter. Future Intel EPLDs will be supported by the GUPI system.

5

PLD Programming Hardware

The programmer is the part of a PLD design operation that is responsible for programming the particular fuse pattern into the PLD device. Several PLD programmers from various companies are for the purpose of programming a PLD device. In general, programmers can be used as stand-alone units for some applications or connected to an IBM-compatible PC when it is desired to take advantage of some of the various software packages currently available as discussed in Chapter 3. Data I/O is the leader in the field of programmers serving approximately 70% of the market. While the design varies, programmers usually have the following features:

- A universal socket that can accept any PLD or an adapter to be used with PLDs that the socket cannot accept.
- An update service that normally contains the necessary information to process newly developed PLDs from all manufacturers.
- The ability to accept the download of a JEDEC standard file via an RS-232C input port.
- The ability to program and verify the security fuse.
- Support of the JEDEC-standard structured test vectors.
- The ability to accept a master device and program its pattern into unprogrammed parts from the same and different manufacturers.
- The ability to accept a JEDEC standard Programmable Logic Data Transfer Format (PLDTF) and program the PLD from the information contained on this file.

The copying of a programmed pattern typically involves setting up the programmer to copy the master device (such as installing the proper adapter if required) and entering a product code supplied by the manufacturer relative to the type of

PLD device to be programmed. Once the master device has been placed in the socket, the fuse pattern from the master device is read into the programmer's memory by pushing a read button or some sequence of buttons installed on the front panel of the programmer. Once the pattern has been accepted in the programmer's memory, a check sum usually appears on the programmer's display which the user can copy on paper for use in diagnosing any programming problems. The target device is installed next. The user executes the necessary push-button sequence to read the pattern stored in memory into the target device.

Programming a target device from a JEDEC file usually involves the use of an IBM-compatible PC. The JEDEC file is typically the output of a PC that has been used in creation of the file from a software design package as discussed in Chapter 3. The software can create the necessary test vectors to be applied to the device following the programming cycle. The programmer is connected to the IBM-compatible PC with an RS-232C cable. The necessary product code information is entered into the programmer by the keys located on the front panel of the programmer. Once the programmer is in the receive mode, a key sequence is executed on the PC and the file transmitted to the programmer and a check sum appears in the programmer's display. If this check sum is identical with the JEDEC file generated check sum, the transmission was successful. The file is typically read into the programmer's memory first and the target device programmed from the pattern contained in the programmer's memory.

DATA I/O UNIVERSAL PROGRAMMING
SYSTEM WITH LOGICPAK

Figure 5-1 shows the Universal Programming System from Data I/O. This system is capable of programming more than 1400 devices from CMOS to PROMs and vertical fuse bipolar PROMs, microcomptrollers, and of course PLDs. The system is designed and constructed around the concept of programming PAKs, permitting the design engineer to build as versatile a system as requirements dictate. The programming packs can also be replaced as new devices and technologies evolve. Of the Paks, the LogicPak is dedicated to PLDs, including IFLs, PLAs, 40-pin MegaPALs, 20- and 28-pin PLD devices in PLCC packages from several device manufacturers. A key feature of the 29B is its continuity testing capability wherein the LogicPak alerts the design engineer before programming begins if a socket has worn out or the PLD device has not been inserted in its socket properly. In addition, the LogicPak performs three selectable levels of device testing to ensure that programmed devices meet the design specification.

The 29B also accepts the unipak 2B which programs more than 1100 MOS, CMOS, and bipolar PROMs, EPROMs, EEPROMs and E-macros. A GangPak is also available which is capable of programming eight MOS or CMOS EPROMs or EEPROMs in one task operation.

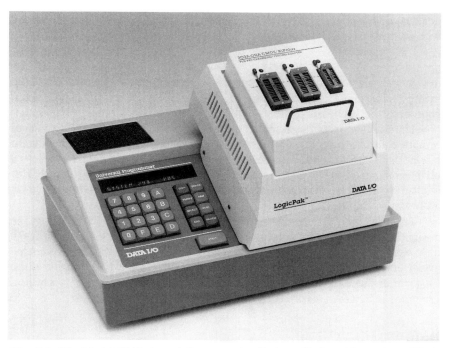

Fig. 5-1. The Model 29 Universal Programming System. Photograph courtesy of Data I/O Corporation.

Fig. 5-2. The Model 60A Logic Programmer. Photograph courtesy of Data I/O Corporation.

DATA I/O 60A LOGIC PROGRAMMER

The Data I/O 60A Logic Programmer shown in FIG. 5-2 uses various expansion adapters to program 20- and 24-pin PALs, 20- and 24-pin IFLs, and 28-pin IFLs. This programmer also supports a variety of EPROMs. When new devices are introduced, the 60A's device support capabilities can be expanded with user-installable software updates.

With a menu-driven interface, the 60A can be operated as a stand-alone programmer. An operating protocol using full-English commands guides the designer through all programmer functions. Device types are selected from the front panel by scrolling through a menu, or by entering Data I/O's family/pinout code from the keyboard.

The 60A supports two remote control protocols. With Data I/O's standard remote control protocol, the programmer can be operated from any host computer. Using the terminal remote control protocol, it can be controlled from a terminal attached to the programmer's RS232C serial port. Using the PROM-link interface and file management software, all functions can be controlled from an IBM-compatible PC.

Three levels of device testing ensure that programmed devices match the design specifications. An automatic array verification confirms that all fuses have been programmed correctly. An optional structured-vectors test compares actual device output with designer-specified results. Data I/O's unique Logic Fingerprint uses a signature analysis-based technique to compare newly programmed logic devices with correct master devices.

DATA I/O UNISITE 40

Figure 5-3 shows the Data I/O Unisite 40 which programs and tests any device of a given package type in a single site. A single socket DIP module sup-

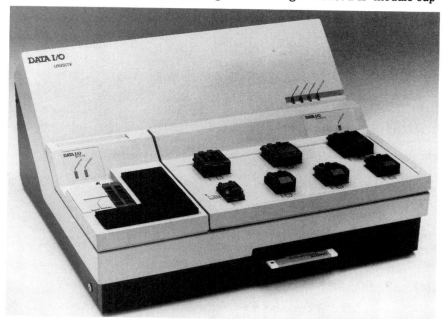

Fig. 5-3. The Unisite 40 Logic Programmer. Photograph courtesy of Data I/O Corp-oration.

ports devices up to 40 pins including PLDs, PROMs, IFLs, FPLAs, EPROMs, EEPROMs, and microcontrollers. The single module for surface mount packages includes six sockets for 29-, 28-, 32-, 44-, 52-, and 68-pin PLCCs and one socket that supports 20-, 22-, 24-, and 28-pin devices. The Unisite 40 includes prebuilt files for several popular devices. A "quick copy mode" permits the designer to program his device automatically in one test sequence. To support a specific device, the Unisite 40 reassigns pin functions as required and built in functional tests ensure that each pin driver is operating properly. This system automatically performs backwards device checks, continuity testing, and a blank check to ensure device integrity before programming.

With the Unisite 40, the downloading of separate data files or sections of files to program a set of devices is no longer required. Instead, an entire data file can be loaded into RAM (up to a maximum of 512K bytes on disk) in one operation. The data automatically splits according to work width into as many devices as required. Then the designer programs sequentially.

Data I/O's Smartport self-configurating serial interface reduces the need for special cabling to connect the Unisite 40 to a host computer. The Unisite 40 can support 41 I/O protocols and selectable data rates from 300 to 19,200 baud and can be used with most terminals by connecting the Unisite 40 between the terminal or personal computer and a host. A "transparent mode" allows them to communication directly.

Updates are available on 3½" diskettes. As new devices are introduced, Data I/O will provide a new master micro diskette. When the diskette is received, load it into the disk drive and the Unisite 40 is instantly updated. Updates can be ordered as required or received regularly through Data I/O update services.

LOGICAL DEVICES ALLPRO

Figure 5-4 shows the ALLPRO from Logical Devices. This programmer programs PALs, PLDs, GALs, EPLDs, PLAs, FPLAs, IFLs, PROMs, EEPROMs, and EPROMs. This programmer can interface an existing IBM PC AT or compatibles. The unit can also be purchased with an optional hardware/software package to allow direct connection to other PC-type computers through an RS-232 serial port. Custom interface software can be provided for mainframes such as VAX 11/7870 and Apollo. In the PC-based configuration, the user can purchase an additional interface card to improve portability; the interface card can be purchased with a serial port option to save a PC expansion slot.

This system is supported by PC-CAPs schematic entry software package that permits the user to input the requirements in graphics form. PC-CUPL is then used to translate design entry into a standard JEDEC file. The ALLPRO software can read the JEDEC output from any logic compiler. Once the programming of the device is completed, the user can apply the design test vectors for a functional test.

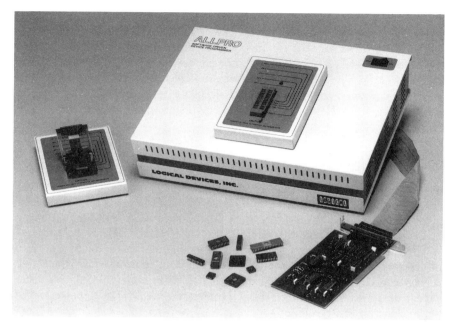

Fig. 5-4. The ALLPRO Logic Programmer. Photograph courtesy of Logical Devices, Inc.

The programmer can be configured to operate in stand-alone mode with the optional control unit. The control unit includes a 3½" 20K floppy drive, keyboard, full-screen LCD display, and serial RS-232 port.

KONTRON EPP-80

The EPP-80 from Kontron Electronics is shown in FIG. 5-5. This programmer is designed around the concept of personality modules. When inserted into the programmer, personality modules permit the design engineer to program devices and PAL devices. The integrated fuse logic module supports 20-pin to 28-pin programmable logic arrays from the Signetics Integrated Fuse Logic family (FPLA, FPLS, FPGA, FPRP). Different types of IFL chips are accommodated by means of low-cost plug-in identifiers. Fuse map data can be entered or dumped via the serial port in Signetics TWX format, or by interactively using a dumb terminal and the built-in line editor. The PAL programming module provides the capability to program PAL devices from several manufacturers. The Universal Programming module permits the user to program three different device technologies without socket adapters and identifiers, PALs, single voltage PROMs, and bipolar devices.

Fuse map data is entered via the serial port in industry-standard PAL assembler HEX format (MOD21) or in the JEDEC logic data transfer format (MOD 33). Fuse map data can also be output in these formats as well as in fuse-plot format. Fuse map conversion feature allows rapid transfer of logic functions

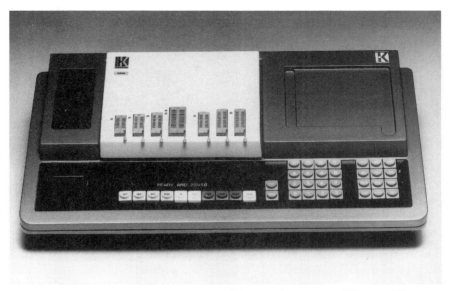

Fig. 5-5. The EPP-80 Logic Programmer. Photograph courtesy of Kontron Electronics, Inc.

from one PAL family to another. More powerful functions with regard to PAL handling are implemented in the UPM module.

The EPP-80 offers the possibility of installing two independent interfaces. An RS232C/20 mA current loop is standard and allows the basic version to have remote control of all functions via terminal or computer. Data communication is facilitated by a large number of ASCII, binary, or system-specific data transfer protocols. An integrated editor program with cursor control functions provides an ease of RAM-editing unknown before. The second interface can either be a Centronics-compatible parallel interface for printer-connection or a second RS232C/20 mA current loop interface for bidirectional data transfer.

SUNRISE Z-1000B UNIVERSAL PROGRAMMER

Figure 5-6 shows the Z-1000B Universal Programmer manufactured by Sunrise Electronics. The Z-1000B programs all logic families. The automatic logic programming sequence includes blank test, programming, fuse map verification, security fuse programming, and vector testing. It has a built-in logic mode fuse map editor and the JEDEC fuse map transfer format for easy interface to CUPL, ABEL, logic, and PALASM assemblers.

Every pin is individually driven and held to an accuracy of 1%. For devices with pin counts greater than 40, a simple pin-out adaptor plugs into two or more DIP ZIF sockets and terminates in the appropriate ZIF socket for the device being programmed.

The two RS-232 ports can function together in a transparent mode so that the programmer can be inserted between the programmer and your computer.

Fig. 5-6. The Z100B Universal Logic Programmer. Photograph courtesy of Sunrise Electronics, Inc.

The programmer can be controlled by a terminal or by a PC using the PC-PRO software included with each unit. In either the terminal control or stand-alone modes, the Z-1000B can accept or send data files in 8-, 16-, 32-bit words and fuse maps for every type of programmable logic device.

The Z-1000B supports functional test vectors and automatically exercises a programmable logic device when the test vectors are loaded from a JEDEC file.

INLAB MODEL 28 PROGRAMMER

The Model 28 Programmer by INLAB is shown in FIG. 5-7. The front panel of all Model 28 Programmers contains the operator controls and displays used during stand-alone operation. The controls and displays consist of a Zero Insertion Force (ZIF) socket, an LCD, and a set of control keys.

The ZIF socket provides the insertion point for PLDs, EPLDs, EEPLDs, PROMs, EPROMs, EEPROMs microprocessors or programmable devices being used. Device packages such as LCC, PLCC, and greater-than-28-pin DIPs are accommodated by use of adapters. Each pin is controlled through software, and can be set to 0-25 VDC in 200 mV increments. When this is combined with the ability of the Model 28 to control the current at any pin, from 0 to ± 1.5 amps, an exceptionally flexible programmer results.

The LCD display is used in stand-alone mode to prompt the operator and to show the current status of the Model 28. The display is conveniently divided into three areas. A status display shows whether the 32K byte buffer is full or

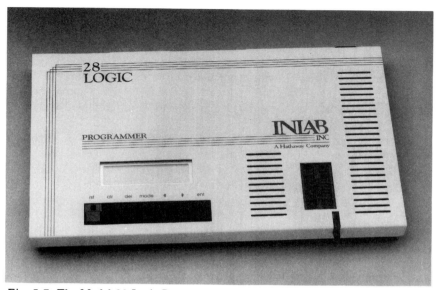

Fig. 5-7. The Model 28 Logic Programmer. Photograph courtesy of InLab, Inc.

empty, which mode the programmer is currently in, and which slot of the 8-slot menu is being displayed. The current device is the device the programmer expects to see in the ZIF socket. A prompt line requests the operator to perform the next operation in the selected sequence. Thus a great deal of information is made available to keep operation very simple and clear.

The control keys are labeled as to function. The **RST** (reset) button is a master system reset switch. The red LED in the RST key lights to show the operator that the unit is powered up. The **CLR** (clear) button clears the buffer memory of all data in preparation for new information. The **DEL** (delete) button clears a device from the menu, leaving a slot empty to allow selection of a different device. Note that while the menu only displays eight devices concurrently, the database in the Model 28 contains the algorithms for all currently supported programmable devices. The **MODE** button selects the operating mode including read, verify, program, test, or secure. The arrow buttons allow the operator to step through the various menus and options. The **ENTER** button is used to complete a command sequence or to direct the Programmer to begin an operation.

Two connectors along the back edge of the unit provide interface points for power and an RS232 serial data cable. These are polarized DB type connectors, ensuring that cables cannot be connected incorrectly.

DC power is supplied by a power source operating from 100, 110, 120, 220 or 240 VAC outlet. Power consumption is less than 12w while programming. As a result, the Model 28 Programmers are exceptionally cool running units, and require no fans.

The serial connector is a DB-25 female and provides connection to a standard RS232 serial data cable. All Model 28 Programmers can be interfaced with any dumb terminal or a host computer. Using the Model 28 in conjunction with a host computer or dumb terminal is a very common application. When used in this fashion, a series of external commands and operations become available to the user.

Combining the Model 28 with a computer provides a very powerful development tool. This allows the user to create and store files on a computer system and download to the programmer whenever a programmed device is required.

For the popular IBM-compatibles and the Apple Macintosh II, Inlab has developed a software communication package called ACE (Advanced Communications Environment). ACE provides a simple to use interface between the Model 28 and the serial port of the IBM or Macintosh computers via an RS232 cable. Using ACE, the Model 28 functions are available from the computer keyboard.

The Model 28 can be used with logic compilers that adhere to the JEDEC 3A standard. Files can be transported to and from a host system having data storage capability over the RS232 interface. Speed of transmission is selectable at baud rates of 300, 1200, 9600, or 19,200. When downloaded, the Model 28 immediately starts scanning the RS232 input for data. As characters are received, they are translated and loaded into the buffer. During an upload operation, the Model 28 begins to transmit the contents of the buffer immediately upon execution of the function. The buffer size is allocated based upon the device currently selected. The upload file format is determined by the device currently selected in the User Menu.

6

Application Examples

The examples outlined in this chapter range from direct applications to applications that are characterized by a great deal of sophistication. The examples cover the range of PLDs (PALs, EPLDs, PMLs and PEELS).

The first example is more of a manual solution to a four-bit binary decade counter in which Karnaugh map techniques are employed to reduce the original logic expression to its minimal form. Almost all software packages employ various proprietary algorithms that automatically perform the logic reduction process. The manual applications of Boolean algebra techniques and Karnaugh map techniques are no longer required when using today's logic synthesis software tools.

All systems provide for input in the form Boolean equations, state diagrams, and truth tables. Signetics' AMAZE and SNAP are designed to support some of their proprietary devices as is the case with Altera and Intel. Data I/O's FutureDesigner, GATES, and ABEL is not vendor-specific software and can support products from almost all manufacturers.

4-BIT BINARY DECADE COUNTER
Courtesy of Texas Instruments, Inc.

The object of this section is to generate a 4-bit binary counter that is fed by one of four clocks. Two lines are available for selecting the clocks, SEL1 and SEL0. Figure 6-1 shows the required input for the selection of the clocks. In addition, the counter should be able to switch from binary to decade count. This feature is controlled by an input called BD. When BD is high, the counter should count in binary. When low, the counter should count in decade.

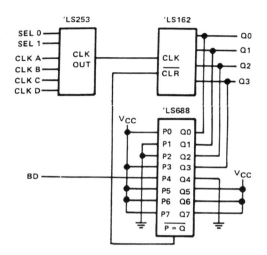

Fig. 6-1. Counter implementation with standard logic. Courtesy of Texas Instruments, Inc.

As can be seen, three MSI functions are required. The LSI62 is used to generate the four-bit counter while the clock selection is handled by the LS253. The LS6888 is an eight-bit comparator which is used for selecting either the binary or decade count. In this example, only five of the eight comparator inputs are used. Four are used for comparing the counter outputs, while the other is used for the BD input. The comparator is hard-wired to go low whenever the BD input is low and the counter output is 9. The $\overline{P = Q}$ output is then fed back to the synchronous clear input on the LS162. This resets the counter to zero whenever this condition occurs.

PAL Implementation

As stated before, the problem in programming a PAL is not in blowing the fuses, but rather what fuses need to be blown to generate a particular function. Fortunately, this problem has been greatly simplified by computer software. But before you examine these techniques, exploring the methods used in generating the logic equations might be beneficial. This will help develop an understanding and appreciation for these advanced software packages.

From digital logic theory, almost any type of logic can be implemented in either AND-OR-INVERT or AND-NOR form. This is the basic concept used in the PAL and FPLA. This allows classical techniques, such as Karnaugh maps, to be used in generating specific logic functions. The first function is the clock selector, but remember that the overall goal is to reduce this design example into one PAL.

PAL Selection

Before proceeding with the design for the clock selector, the first question that needs to be addressed is which PAL (and which output architecture) to use. Looking at the example, four flip-flops with feedback are required in the four-bit counter, plus input clock and clear lines. In addition, seven inputs plus two simple outputs are required in the clock selector and comparator. With this information, you can see that the TIBPAL16R4 (FIG. 6-2) will handle the application.

Clock Selector Details

The first step in determining the logic equation for the clock selector is to generate a function table with all the possible input combinations (see TABLE 6-1). From this table, the Karnaugh map can be generated as shown in FIG. 6-3. The minimized equation for CLKOUT comes directly from this (see p. 208).

It is important to notice that the equation derived from the Karnaugh map is stated in AND-OR notation. The selected PAL is implemented in AND-NOR logic. This means you either have to do De Morgan's theorem on the equation or solve the inverse of the Karnaugh map. Figure 6-4 shows the inverse of the Karnaugh map and the resulting equation. This equation can be easily implemented in the TIBPAL16R4.

4-Bit Binary Counter Details

The same basic procedure used in determining the equations for the clock selector is used in determining the equations for the 4-bit counter. The only difference is that now you are dealing with a present-state, next-state situation. This means a D-type flip-flop is required in actual circuit implementation. As before, the truth table is generated first (TABLE 6-2).

From the truth table, the equations for each output can be derived from the Karnaugh map (see FIG. 6-5). Note that the inverse of the truth table is being solved so that the equation will come out in AND-NOR logic form.

Binary/Decade Count Details

Recalling from the examples requirements that the counter should count in decade whenever the BD input is low, a truth table for this function is shown in TABLE 6-2. Because the counter is already designed to count in binary, this feature can simplify the design. The result needs to be a circuit whose output goes low whenever the BD input is equal to 9. This output can then be fed back to the CLR input of the counter so that it resets whenever the BD input is low.

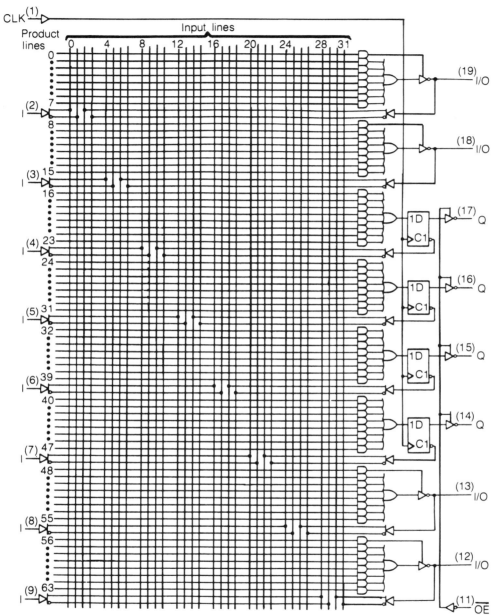

Fig. 6-2. TIBPAL16R4 logic diagram. Courtesy of Texas Instruments, Inc.

Whenever the BD input is high, the output of the circuit should be a high because the counter automatically counts in binary. Notice that $\overline{Q}$ shown in the truth table is the function desired.

Table 6-1. Function table for 4-bit
binary/decade counter. Courtesy of Texas Instruments, Inc.

SEL1	SEL0	CLKA	CLKB	CLKC	CLKD	CLKOUT	SEL1	SEL0	CLKA	CLKB	CLKC	CLKD	CLKOUT
0	0	0	0	0	0	0	1	0	0	0	0	0	0
0	0	0	0	0	1	0	1	0	0	0	0	1	0
0	0	0	0	1	0	0	1	0	0	0	1	0	1
0	0	0	0	1	1	0	1	0	0	0	1	1	1
0	0	0	1	0	0	0	1	0	0	1	0	0	0
0	0	0	1	0	1	0	1	0	0	1	0	1	0
0	0	0	1	1	0	0	1	0	0	1	1	0	1
0	0	0	1	1	1	0	1	0	0	1	1	1	1
0	0	1	0	0	0	1	1	0	1	0	0	0	0
0	0	1	0	0	1	1	1	0	1	0	0	1	0
0	0	1	0	1	0	1	1	0	1	0	1	0	1
0	0	1	0	1	1	1	1	0	1	0	1	1	1
0	0	1	1	0	0	1	1	0	1	1	0	0	0
0	0	1	1	0	1	1	1	0	1	1	0	1	0
0	0	1	1	1	0	1	1	0	1	1	1	0	1
0	0	1	1	1	1	1	1	0	1	1	1	1	1
0	1	0	0	0	0	0	1	1	0	0	0	0	0
0	1	0	0	0	1	0	1	1	0	0	0	1	1
0	1	0	0	1	0	0	1	1	0	0	1	0	0
0	1	0	0	1	1	0	1	1	0	0	1	1	1
0	1	0	1	0	0	1	1	1	0	1	0	0	0
0	1	0	1	0	1	1	1	1	0	1	0	1	1
0	1	0	1	1	0	1	1	1	0	1	1	0	0
0	1	0	1	1	1	1	1	1	0	1	1	1	1
0	1	1	0	0	0	0	1	1	1	0	0	0	0
0	1	1	0	0	1	0	1	1	1	0	0	1	1
0	1	1	0	1	0	0	1	1	1	0	1	0	0
0	1	1	0	1	1	0	1	1	1	0	1	1	1
0	1	1	1	0	0	1	1	1	1	1	0	0	0
0	1	1	1	0	1	1	1	1	1	1	0	1	1
0	1	1	1	1	0	1	1	1	1	1	1	0	0
0	1	1	1	1	1	1	1	1	1	1	1	1	1

In this particular example, a Karnaugh map is not required because the equation cannot be further simplified. The resulting equation is:

$$\overline{\text{BD OUT}} = \overline{\text{BDQ3Q2Q1Q0}}$$

Fuse Map Details

Now that the logic equations have been defined, the next step is to specify which fuses need to be blown. Before doing this, however, first label the input

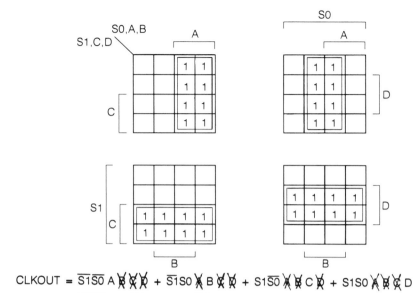

$$CLKOUT = \overline{S1}\,\overline{S0}\;A\;\cancel{B}\;\cancel{C}\;\cancel{D} + \overline{S1}S0\;\cancel{A}\;B\;\cancel{C}\;\cancel{D} + S1\overline{S0}\;\cancel{A}\;\cancel{B}\;C\;\cancel{D} + S1S0\;\cancel{A}\;\cancel{B}\;\cancel{C}\;D$$

$$CLKOUT = \overline{S1}\,\overline{S0}A + \overline{S1}S0B + S1\overline{S0}C + S1S0D$$

Fig. 6-3. Karnaugh map for CLKOUT. Courtesy of Texas Instruments, Inc.

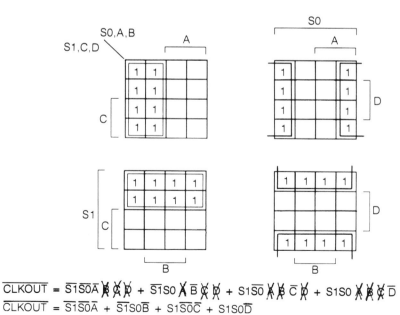

$$\overline{CLKOUT} = \overline{S1}\,\overline{S0}\,\overline{A}\;\cancel{B}\;\cancel{C}\;\cancel{D} + \overline{S1}S0\;\cancel{A}\;\overline{B}\;\cancel{C}\;\cancel{D} + S1\overline{S0}\;\cancel{A}\;\cancel{B}\;\overline{C}\;\cancel{D} + S1S0\;\cancel{A}\;\cancel{B}\;\cancel{C}\;\overline{D}$$

$$\overline{CLKOUT} = \overline{S1}\,\overline{S0}\,\overline{A} + \overline{S1}S0\overline{B} + S1\overline{S0}\,\overline{C} + S1S0\overline{D}$$

Fig. 6-4. Karnaugh map for $\overline{CLKOUT}$. Courtesy of Texas Instruments, Inc.

	PRESENT STATE				NEXT STATE			
CLR	Q3	Q2	Q1	Q0	Q3	Q2	Q1	Q0
0	X	X	X	X	0	0	0	0
1	0	0	0	0	0	0	0	1
1	0	0	0	1	0	0	1	0
1	0	0	1	0	0	0	1	1
1	0	0	1	1	0	1	0	0
1	0	1	0	0	0	1	0	1
1	0	1	0	1	0	1	1	0
1	0	1	1	0	0	1	1	1
1	0	1	1	1	1	0	0	0
1	1	0	0	0	1	0	0	1
1	1	0	0	1	1	0	1	0
1	1	0	1	0	1	0	1	1
1	1	0	1	1	1	1	0	0
1	1	1	0	0	1	1	0	1
1	1	1	0	1	1	1	1	0
1	1	1	1	0	1	1	1	1
1	1	1	1	1	0	0	0	0

Table 6-2. Truth table for 4-bit binary/decade counter. Courtesy of Texas Instruments, Inc.

and output pins on the TIBPAL16R4. By using FIG. 6-1 as a guide, make the following pin assignments in FIG. 6-6:

1	CLK	20	VCC
2	SEL0	19	CLKOUT
3	SEL 1	18	NC
4	CLKA	17	Q0
5	CLKB	16	Q1
6	CLKC	15	Q2
7	CLK	14	Q3
8	CLR	13	NC
9	BD	12	BD OUT
10	GND	11	OE

With this information defined, now insert the logic equations into the logic diagram as shown in FIG. 6-6 on p. 211. Figure 6-7 shows the associated fuse map. Screens 1 through 5 show an early version of Data I/O's software for this example. As seen from this example, Karnaugh mapping procedures were used to perform the necessary logic minimization function. With today's logic synthesis tools—including ABEL (as will be seen in the following two application examples)—it is not necessary to perform Karnaugh mapping or Boolean algebra

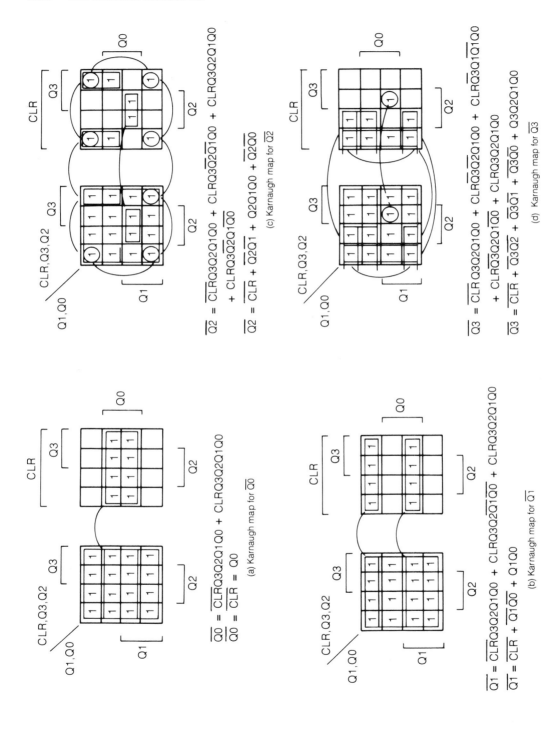

$\overline{Q0} = \overline{CLRQ3Q2Q1Q0} + CLRQ3Q2Q1Q0$
$Q0 = \overline{CLR} = Q0$

(a) Karnaugh map for $\overline{Q0}$

$\overline{Q1} = \overline{CLRQ3Q2Q1Q0} + CLRQ3Q2Q1\overline{Q0} + CLRQ3Q2Q1Q0$
$\overline{Q1} = \overline{CLR} + \overline{Q1Q0} + Q1Q0$

(b) Karnaugh map for $\overline{Q1}$

$\overline{Q2} = \overline{CLRQ3Q2Q1Q0} + CLRQ3\overline{Q2}Q1Q0 + CLRQ3Q2Q1Q0$
$\quad + CLR\overline{Q3Q2Q1Q0}$
$\overline{Q2} = \overline{CLR} + \overline{Q2}Q1Q0 + Q2Q1Q0$

(c) Karnaugh map for $\overline{Q2}$

$\overline{Q3} = \overline{CLR}Q3Q2Q1Q0 + CLR\overline{Q3}Q2Q1Q0 + CLR\overline{Q3}Q1\overline{Q1}Q0$
$\quad + CLR\overline{Q3}Q2Q1\overline{Q0} + CLRQ3Q2Q1Q0$
$\overline{Q3} = \overline{CLR} + \overline{Q3}Q2 + \overline{Q3Q1} + \overline{Q3}\overline{Q0} + Q3Q2Q1Q0$

(d) Karnaugh map for $\overline{Q3}$

Fig. 6-5. Karnaugh map $\overline{Q}_0$, $\overline{Q}_1$, $\overline{Q}_2$, and $\overline{Q}_3$. Courtesy of Texas Instruments, Inc.

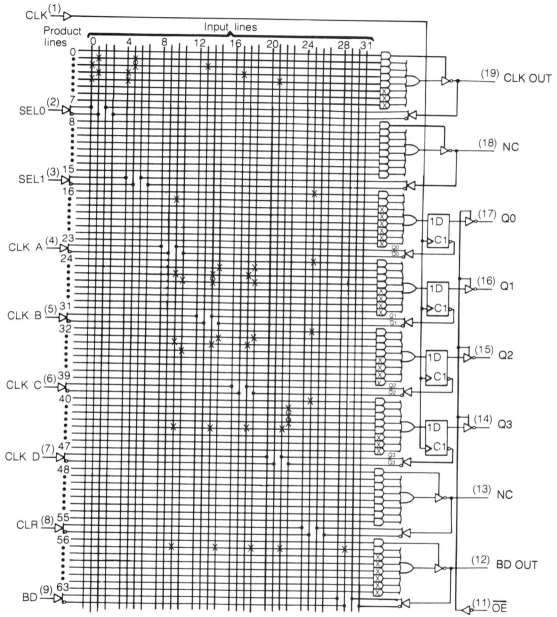

Fig. 6-6. Open and blown fuses for the implementation of a 4-bit binary decade counter.

operations to minimize logic functions. The logic synthesis tools of today have logic minimization algorithms built in as a part of the software package. This example was provided as a basis to indicate in the following application examples the modernization of today's tools.

```
0000  0000  0011  1111  1111  2222  2222  2233
0123  4567  8901  2345  6789  0123  4567  8901
/CLKOUT  =
----  ----  ----  ----  ----  ----  ----  ----   0 -
-X--  -X--  -X--  ----  ----  ----  ----  ----   1 -  /SEL1*/SEL0*/CLKA+
X---  -X--  ----  -X--  ----  ----  ----  ----   2 -  /SEL1*SEL0*/CLKB+
-X--  X---  ----  ----  -X--  ----  ----  ----   3 -  SEL1*/SEL0*/CLKC+
X---  X---  ----  ----  ----  -X--  ----  ----   4 -  SEL1*SEL0*/CLKD
XXXX  XXXX  XXXX  XXXX  XXXX  XXXX  XXXX  XXXX    5 -
XXXX  XXXX  XXXX  XXXX  XXXX  XXXX  XXXX  XXXX    6 -
XXXX  XXXX  XXXX  XXXX  XXXX  XXXX  XXXX  XXXX    7 -
               =
XXXX  XXXX  XXXX  XXXX  XXXX  XXXX  XXXX  XXXX    8 -
XXXX  XXXX  XXXX  XXXX  XXXX  XXXX  XXXX  XXXX    9 -
XXXX  XXXX  XXXX  XXXX  XXXX  XXXX  XXXX  XXXX   10 -
XXXX  XXXX  XXXX  XXXX  XXXX  XXXX  XXXX  XXXX   11 -
XXXX  XXXX  XXXX  XXXX  XXXX  XXXX  XXXX  XXXX   12 -
XXXX  XXXX  XXXX  XXXX  XXXX  XXXX  XXXX  XXXX   13 -
XXXX  XXXX  XXXX  XXXX  XXXX  XXXX  XXXX  XXXX   14 -
XXXX  XXXX  XXXX  XXXX  XXXX  XXXX  XXXX  XXXX   15 -
/Q0  =
----  ----  ----  ----  ----  ----  -X--  ----  16 -  /CLR+
----  ----  --X-  ----  ----  ----  ----  ----  17 -  Q0
XXXX  XXXX  XXXX  XXXX  XXXX  XXXX  XXXX  XXXX   18 -
XXXX  XXXX  XXXX  XXXX  XXXX  XXXX  XXXX  XXXX   19 -
XXXX  XXXX  XXXX  XXXX  XXXX  XXXX  XXXX  XXXX   20 -
XXXX  XXXX  XXXX  XXXX  XXXX  XXXX  XXXX  XXXX   21 -
XXXX  XXXX  XXXX  XXXX  XXXX  XXXX  XXXX  XXXX   22 -
XXXX  XXXX  XXXX  XXXX  XXXX  XXXX  XXXX  XXXX   23 -
/Q1  =
----  ----  ----  ----  ----  ----  -X--  ----  24 -  /CLR+
----  ----  ---X  ---X  ----  ----  ----  ----  25 -  /Q1*/Q0
----  ----  --X-  --X-  ----  ----  ----  ----  26 -  Q1*Q0
XXXX  XXXX  XXXX  XXXX  XXXX  XXXX  XXXX  XXXX   27 -
XXXX  XXXX  XXXX  XXXX  XXXX  XXXX  XXXX  XXXX   28 -
XXXX  XXXX  XXXX  XXXX  XXXX  XXXX  XXXX  XXXX   29 -
XXXX  XXXX  XXXX  XXXX  XXXX  XXXX  XXXX  XXXX   30 -
XXXX  XXXX  XXXX  XXXX  XXXX  XXXX  XXXX  XXXX   31 -
/Q2  =
----  ----  ----  ----  ----  ----  -X--  ----  32 -  /CLR+
----  ----  ----  ---X  ---X  ----  ----  ----  33 -  /Q2*/Q1
----  ----  --X-  --X-  --X-  ----  ----  ----  34 -  Q2*Q1*Q0
----  ----  ---X  ----  ---X  ----  ----  ----  35 -  /Q2*/Q0
XXXX  XXXX  XXXX  XXXX  XXXX  XXXX  XXXX  XXXX   36 -
XXXX  XXXX  XXXX  XXXX  XXXX  XXXX  XXXX  XXXX   37 -
XXXX  XXXX  XXXX  XXXX  XXXX  XXXX  XXXX  XXXX   38 -
XXXX  XXXX  XXXX  XXXX  XXXX  XXXX  XXXX  XXXX   39 -
/Q3  =
----  ----  ----  ----  ----  ----  -X--  ----  40 -  /CLR+
----  ----  ----  ----  ---X  ---X  ----  ----  41 -  /Q3*/Q2
----  ----  ----  ---X  ----  ---X  ----  ----  42 -  /Q3*Q1+
----  ----  ---X  ----  ----  ---X  ----  ----  43 -  /Q3*/Q0+
----  ----  --X-  --X-  --X-  --X-  ----  ----  44 -  Q3*Q2*Q1*Q0
XXXX  XXXX  XXXX  XXXX  XXXX  XXXX  XXXX  XXXX   45 -
XXXX  XXXX  XXXX  XXXX  XXXX  XXXX  XXXX  XXXX   46 -
XXXX  XXXX  XXXX  XXXX  XXXX  XXXX  XXXX  XXXX   47 -
               =
XXXX  XXXX  XXXX  XXXX  XXXX  XXXX  XXXX  XXXX   48 -
XXXX  XXXX  XXXX  XXXX  XXXX  XXXX  XXXX  XXXX   49 -
XXXX  XXXX  XXXX  XXXX  XXXX  XXXX  XXXX  XXXX   50 -
XXXX  XXXX  XXXX  XXXX  XXXX  XXXX  XXXX  XXXX   51 -
XXXX  XXXX  XXXX  XXXX  XXXX  XXXX  XXXX  XXXX   52 -
XXXX  XXXX  XXXX  XXXX  XXXX  XXXX  XXXX  XXXX   53 -
XXXX  XXXX  XXXX  XXXX  XXXX  XXXX  XXXX  XXXX   54 -
XXXX  XXXX  XXXX  XXXX  XXXX  XXXX  XXXX  XXXX   55 -
/BOOUT  =
----  ----  ----  ----  ----  ----  ----  ----  56 -
----  ----  --X-  ---X  ---X  --X-  ----  -X--  57 -  /B0*Q3*/Q2*/Q1*Q0
XXXX  XXXX  XXXX  XXXX  XXXX  XXXX  XXXX  XXXX   58 -
XXXX  XXXX  XXXX  XXXX  XXXX  XXXX  XXXX  XXXX   59 -
XXXX  XXXX  XXXX  XXXX  XXXX  XXXX  XXXX  XXXX   60 -
XXXX  XXXX  XXXX  XXXX  XXXX  XXXX  XXXX  XXXX   61 -
XXXX  XXXX  XXXX  XXXX  XXXX  XXXX  XXXX  XXXX   62 -
XXXX  XXXX  XXXX  XXXX  XXXX  XXXX  XXXX  XXXX   63 -
```

Fig. 6-7. Fuse map.

```
module BD COUNT
title 4-bit binary/decade counter
IC1  device P16RF':

" pin assignment and constant declarations
        CLK_IN SELO, SEL1.CLKA      pin 1,2,3,4:
CLKB.CLKC.CLKD           pin 5,6,7:
CLR,BD-IN.OE            pin 8,9,11:
BD_OUT.CLK_OUT           pin 12, 19:
Q3,Q2.QO             pin 14,13,16,17:
CL, L, H, X, Z    =    .C.,, 0, 1, .X., .Z.
OUTPUT         =    {03,02,Q1,Qo]


"counter states SO=^b0000;   S4=^b0100;   S8=^b1000;
S12=^b1100;
S1=^b0001;   S5=^b0101;   S9=^b1001;   S13=^b1101;
S2=^b0010;   S6=^b0110;   S10=^b1010;   S14=^b1110;
S3=^b0011;   S7=^b0111;   S11=^b1011;   SI5=^b1111;


equations
"   Clock selector
CLK_OUT = CLKA & SELO & SEL1 # CLKB &SEL1 &SEL0
#CLKC & SEL1 & SELO #CLKD & SEL1 & SELO
```

1/5

4-bit binary/decade counter, Screen 1.

```
"   count nine indicator for decade counting
BD_OUT = !('BD_IN & Q3 & 'Q2 & Q1 & QO):

STATE-DIAGRAM [Q3, Q2, Q1, Q0]
State   SQ:  IF CLR == 0 THEN SO ELSE S1:
State   S1:  IF CLR == 0 THEN SO ELSE S2:
State   S2:  IF CLR == 0 THEN SO ELSE S3:
State   S3:  IF CLR == 0 THEN SO ELSE S4:
State   S4:  IF CLR == 0 THEN SO ELSE S5:
State   S5:  IF CLR == 0 THEN SO ELSE S6: State   S6:  IF CLR == 0
THEN SO ELSE S7:
State   S7:  IF CLR == 0 THEN SO ELSE S8:
State   S8:  IF CLR == 0 THEN SO ELSE S9:
State   S9:  IF CLR == 0 THEN SO ELSE S10:
State   S10: IF CLR == 0 THEN SO ELSE S11:
State   S11: IF CLR == 0 THEN SO ELSE S12:
State   S12: IF CLR == 0 THEN SO ELSE S13:
State   S13: IF CLR == 0 THEN SO ELSE S14:
State   S14: IF CLR == 0 THEN SO ELSE S15:
State   S15: IF CLR == 0 THEN SO ELSE SO:

test-vectors        'clock selector'

([CLKA, CLKB, CLKC, CLKD, SEL1, SEL0] -> CLK_OUT [L  ,  X  ,
 X ,  X ,  L ,  L ] -> L:
```

2/5

4-bit binary/decade counter, Screen 2.

```
[H , X , X , X , L , L] -> H:
[X , L , X , X , L , H] -> L:
[X , H , X , X , L , H] -> H:
[X , X , L , X , H , L] -> L:
[X , X , H , X , H , L] -> H:
[X , X , X , L , H , H] -> L:
[X , X , X , H , H , H] -> H:
                    x text vectors  'counter'

([CLK_IN, QE, CLR, BD_IN] -> [OUTPUT, BD_OUT])
[ CK   L, L, X ] -> [SO,   H]:
[ CK   L, H, X ] -> [S1    H]:
[ CK   L, H, X ] -> [S2    H]:
[ CK   L, H, X ] -> [S3    H]:
[ CK   L, H, X ] -> [S4    H]:
[ CK   L, H, X ] -> [S5    H]:
[ CK   L, H, X ] -> [S6    H]:
[ CK   L, H, X ] -> [S7    H]:
[ CK   L, H, X ] -> [S8    H]:
[ CK   L, H, L ] -> [S9    L]:
[ CK   L, H, X ] -> [S10   H]:
[ CK   L, H, X ] -> [S11   H]:
[ CK   L, H, X ] -> [S12   H]:
[ CK   L, H, X ] -> [S13   H]:
                                          3/5
```

4-bit binary/decade counter, Screen 3.

```
[ CK   L, H, X ] -> [S14   H]:
[ CK   L, H, H ] -> [S15   H]:
[ CK   L, H, X ] -> [ S0   H]:
[ CK   H, X, X ] -> [ Z    H]:

END BD_COUNT
ABEL (tm) Version 1.OO - Document Generator 4-bit binary/decade
counter Equations for Module BD_COUNT Device IC1 .PA Reduced
Equations:

CLK_OUT = '((SEL1 SEL0 & !CLKD
#(SEL1 & !SEL0 & !CLKC
#(SEL1 & SEL0 & !CLKB
#!SEL1 & !SEL0 &  !CLKA)))): BD_OUT = !Q3 & !Q2 & !Q1 &!Q0 &
!BD_IN);
Q3 :=    !((Q3 & Q2 & Q1 & Q0
# (!Q3 & !Q2
# (!Q3 & !Q1
# (!Q3 $ !Q0
# !CLR1)))); Q2 := !((Q2 &Q1 &Q0 # (!Q2 & !Q1 # (!Q2 & !Q0 # !CLR))));
Q1 := !((Q1 & Q0 # (!Q1 & !Q0 # !CLR)));

Q0 := !((q0 # !CLR)); .PA Q2 := !((Q2 & Q1 # (!Q2 & Q1 # (!Q2 & !Q0 #
!CLR))));
                                          4/5
```

4-bit binary/decade counter, Screen 4.

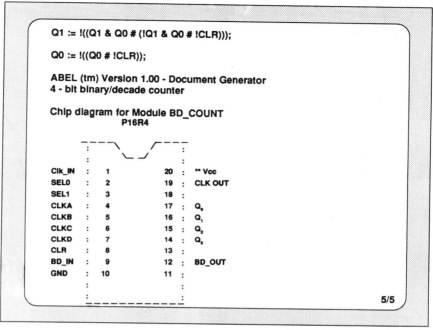

Q1 := !((Q1 & Q0 # (!Q1 & Q0 # !CLR)));

Q0 := !((Q0 # !CLR));

ABEL (tm) Version 1.00 - Document Generator
4 - bit binary/decade counter

Chip diagram for Module BD_COUNT
           P16R4

Clk_IN	:	1	20	:	** Vcc
SEL0	:	2	19	:	CLK OUT
SEL1	:	3	18	:	
CLKA	:	4	17	:	Q_0
CLKB	:	5	16	:	Q_1
CLKC	:	6	15	:	Q_2
CLKD	:	7	14	:	Q_3
CLR	:	8	13	:	
BD_IN	:	9	12	:	BD_OUT
GND	:	10	11	:	

5/5

Courtesy of Texas Instruments

4-bit binary/decade counter, Screen 5.

OCTAL COUNTER WITH SYNCHRONOUS CLEAR
Courtesy of Data I/O Corporation

In the following design example, you will see how to use both programmable logic devices and the associated design tools. Although the design is quite simple and uses only one PLD, the techniques are universal to all PLD designs. Once you have mastered the tools and methods of this simple design, you will be ready to tackle increasingly complex circuits with multiple PLDs.

The example shows you how to design an octal counter. The counter has three outputs, Q0, Q1, and Q2. These outputs are tristated by an 'OE' input. The counter is resettable by a synchronous clear input. The logic diagram is given in FIG. 6-8. A schematic and state diagram of the counter appear in FIG. 6-9.

Design Input

Counters are state machines, so you might decide to use ABEL's state machine notation. You could also use Data I/O's DASH, designing the counter in schematic form, but you would have to manually generate the logic schematic from the state diagram. ABEL's state machine notation saves you this tedious step. Schematic entry is more appropriate for a random logic ("glue" logic) circuit than a simple state machine.

ABEL source files are natural and easy to read. I separated the source file into sections to make the design process even clearer. The first section of the source file is called the declarations section (see Screen 1). It contains the preliminary information that ABEL needs to process the design. The declarations section of the source file follows. ABEL has added the line numbers to the source file as part of its compilation process.

Lines 1, 2, and 3 identify this design module as octal and provide comments to the ABEL file. A source file can have many modules, and each module can contain several PLD specifications. In this example, the design only has one module and one PLD.

Line 4 instructs ABEL to compile the state machine into a PAL16R4. You could change this line to read:

u3 device 'F8S2159';

which would compile the state machine into a PAL16R8. One of the most important features of ABEL is this ability to design a logic function, then choose the target PLD at will.

Lines 5 and 6 assign the signal names Clk, Clr, and so on to the actual pins on the PAL. This allows meaningful names in the source file instead of the PLD pin numbers.

Line 7 assigns the names Ck, X, and Z to the ABEL terms .C., .X., and .Z., which are internal representations of the clock, don't care, and tristate signals. Their use will become clearer when you examine the state machine notation.

Logic Diagram—PAL16R4

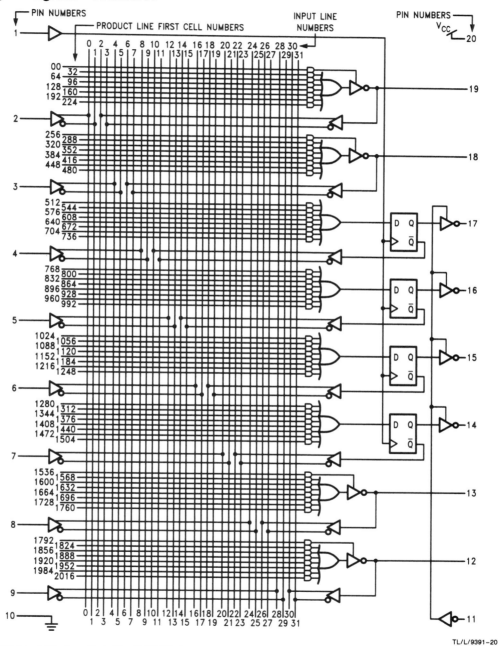

JEDEC Logic Array Cell Number = Product Line First Cell Number + Input Line Number

TL/L/9391–20

Fig. 6-8. PAL16R4 logic diagram. Courtesy of National Semiconductor Corporation.

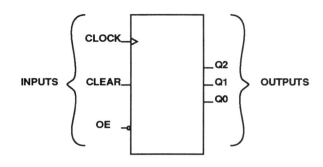

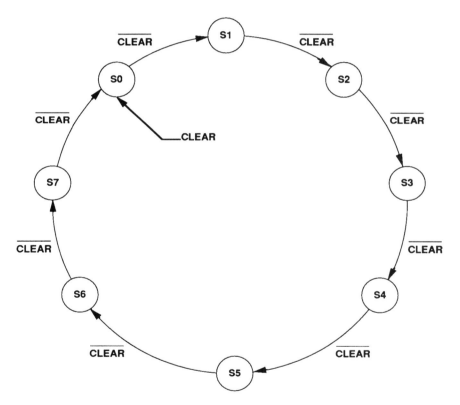

Fig. 6-9. Octal counter schematic and state diagram. Courtesy of DATA I/O Corporation.

Line 9 is a comment line; comment lines begin with the " symbol.

Lines 10 and 11 assign binary values to the eight states S0 through S7. You could assign decimal numbers instead of binary by changing to the following (shown for S0 only):

Sd0 = ^d0.

```
0001 :    module octal
0002 :    title octal counter with synchronous clear
0003 :    Data I/O Corporation
0004 :      u3           device      P16R4:
0005 :      Clk,Clr,DE   pin         1,2,11;
0006 :      Q2,Q1,Q0     pin            15,16,17;
0007 :      Ck,x,z       =           .C.,.x.,.z.;
0008 :
0009 :    Counter states
0010 :      S0 = ^b000; S2 = ^b010;  S4 = ^b100;  S6 = ^b110;
0011 :      S1 = ^b001; S3 = ^b011;  S5 = ^b101.  S7 = ^b111;
0012 :
0013 :    state diagram [Q2, Q1, Q0]
0014 :       State S0:    If !Clr then S1 else S0;
0015 :       State S1:    If !Clr then S2 else S0;
0016 :       State S2:    If !Clr then S3 else S0;
0017 :       State S3:    If !Clr then S4 else S0;
0018 :       State S4:    If !Clr then S5 else S0;
0019 :       State S5:    If !Clr then S6 else S0;
0020 :       State S6:    If !Clr then S7 else S0;
0021 :       State S7:    If !Clr then S0 else S0;

                                                          1/8
```

Octal counter with synchronous clear, Screen 1.

These binary numbers become the actual counter outputs that are assigned by ABEL to each of the seven states. In other words, for S4 the three outputs will be 1, 0, and 0 for Q2, Q1, and Q0, respectively.

Line 13 begins the state diagram. Lines 14 through 21 define the octal counter using a high level IF statement. Try reading line 15 as, "When in state S1, if Clr is low, go to state S2; otherwise go to state S0." The counter is explicitly defined using eight of these IF statements as shown in Screen 1.

Compare the state diagram printout with the state diagram of the counter in FIG. 6-8. The state diagram has been translated into words that can be processed by ABEL. Those of you who have programmed computers in the Pascal or C languages will recognize the IF-THEN-ELSE format. ABEL also supports other high-level statements such as CASE and unconditional GOTO.

You can use a more compact and elegant way to describe this counter design. If fact, you could use many different descriptions, all of which would generate the same counter from a blank PLD. Notice that the single line

Count: = (Count + 1) & !Clr

has replaced the nine-line state diagram section in the source file shown in Screen 2.

```
0001:    module octal
0002:    title octal counter with synchronous clear
0003:    Data I/O Corporation
0004:
0005:        u3         device        P116R4:
0006:
0007:        Clk, Clr, DE   pin        1,2,11;
0008:        Q2, Q1, Q0     pin       15,16, 17;
0009:
0010:        Ck,x,z, = .c., .x.,.z.;
0011:
0012:        Count  = [    Q2, Q1, Q0]
0013:
0014:    equations
0015:        Count := (Count +1) % !Clr;
0016:
                                                              2/8
```

Octal counter with synchronous clear, Screen 2.

Design Verification

Design verification is the process of double-checking a design by writing a set of design vectors to prove that the design performs exactly as intended. Design verification is performed entirely in software (ABEL or CADAT); it does not require you to test a programmed device.

Although verifying this simple counter design might seem trivial, it illustrates the process of verifying a larger PLD design. Design verification uses the ABEL simulator to exercise the PLD design in software. If the vectors are correct, then an error can be discovered in the design during the simulation phase. The test vector (design vector) section of the ABEL source file is shown in Screen 3.

As you have seen, an important part of the PLD design process is designing for testability. The octal counter already incorporates one design-for-testability feature—the ability to reset the state machine to a known reference condition—in this case, S0, the state to which Clear drives the counter.

The first line of the test vector section defines the format to be used in the vectors. Reading the symbol − > as "should generate the output" will help you to understand the vector format.

The first vector, line 24 clears the counter to state S0. The next eight vectors test the count mode. The final vector in line 33 tests the tristate mode. Again, this is a software simulation, not an actual device test.

```
0023:    test_vectors ([CLK,    DE, Clr ] -> [Q2,Q1,Q0])
0024:          [ CK,   0 , 1   ] -> SO;
0025:          [ CK,   0 , 0   ] -> S1;
0026:          [ CK,   0 , 0   ] -> S2;
0027:          [ CK,   0 , 0   ] -> S3;
0028:          [ CK,   0 , 0   ] -> S4;
0029:          [ CK,   0 , 0   ] -> S5;
0030:          [ CK,   0 , 0   ] -> S6;
0031:          [ CK,   0 , 0   ] -> S7;
0032:          [ CK,   0 , 0   ] -> S0;
0033:          [ CK,   1 , X   ] -> Z;
0034:
0035:    END OCTAL

                                                      3/8
```

Octal counter with synchronous clear, Screen 3.

Compiling the Design with ABEL

Now you have a complete source file for input to ABEL. For the example, I used an IBM Personal Computer XT on which the source file was edited and compiled. Execute ABEL by typing the following command (this is how the PC XT screen appears):

C > ABEL octal – r3

where octal is the file name for the octal counter source file.

ABEL contains a module that performs logic reduction on the Boolean equations it generates from the state machine description. Reduction level three (– r3), applies a reduction algorithm called PRESTO.

After successful compilation, ABEL generates the documentation in Screen 4 in addition to the JEDEC output file. Specifically Screen 4 of the documentation shows the state equations for the counter in ABEL's Boolean format. With high-level tools such as ABEL and DASH, designing PLDs using Boolean equations is becoming obsolete. Nonetheless, it is interesting to see the equations.

Screen 5 of the documentation shows a schematic diagram of the PAL with signal names assigned to the corresponding pin numbers.

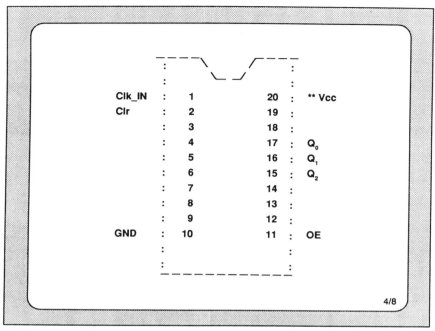

Octal counter with synchronous clear, Screen 4.

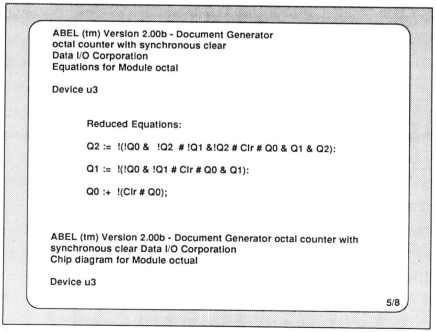

Octal counter with synchronous clear, Screen 5.

Using PLDtest

Ten design vectors verify the counter design. These vectors become the seed vectors for PLDtest. PLDtest is a tool for analyzing the testability of a design, called *fault grading,* and for automatically generating a set of test vectors. The complete set of vectors from PLDtest maximizes fault coverage during device testing of the finished PALs.

PLDtest uses a special intermediate file generated by ABEL (octal.out) as its input. PLDtest analyzes the design for testability by performing fault grading. PLDtest also automatically generates a set of vectors to test the programmed PALs. This set supplements the seed vectors and is appended to the JEDEC file by PLDtest. The report produced by PLDtest appears in Screens 6 through 8.

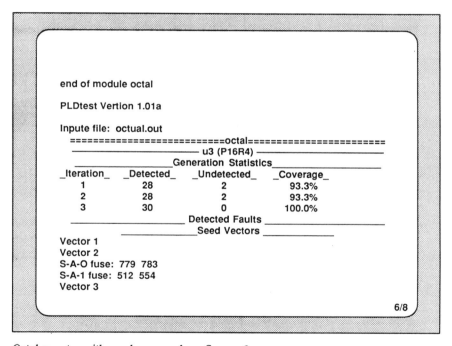

Octal counter with synchronous clear, Screen 6.

Notice that it took only three iterations of PLDtest's vector generation algorithm to test the PAL design to 100% fault coverage. PLDtest has reported which faults were detected by the design (seed) vectors and which faults were detected by the automatically generated vectors.

Programming and Testing

Figure 5-3 shows the Data I/O Unisite 40 together with the PC XT that I used for designing the counter. The Unisite 40 is an advanced device program-

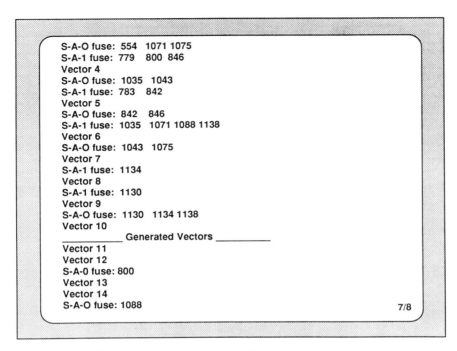

```
S-A-O fuse: 554   1071 1075
S-A-1 fuse: 779   800  846
Vector 4
S-A-O fuse: 1035  1043
S-A-1 fuse: 783   842
Vector 5
S-A-O fuse: 842   846
S-A-1 fuse: 1035  1071 1088 1138
Vector 6
S-A-O fuse: 1043  1075
Vector 7
S-A-1 fuse: 1134
Vector 8
S-A-1 fuse: 1130
Vector 9
S-A-O fuse: 1130  1134 1138
Vector 10
_____ Generated Vectors _____
Vector 11
Vector 12
S-A-0 fuse: 800
Vector 13
Vector 14
S-A-O fuse: 1088                          7/8
```

Octal counter with synchronous clear, Screen 7.

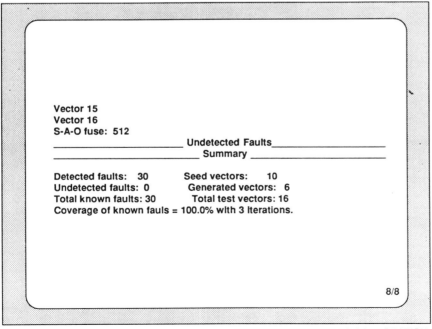

```
Vector 15
Vector 16
S-A-O fuse: 512
_____ Undetected Faults_____
_____ Summary _____

Detected faults:  30    Seed vectors:    10
Undetected faults: 0    Generated vectors:  6
Total known faults: 30   Total test vectors: 16
Coverage of known fauls = 100.0% with 3 iterations.

                                          8/8
```

COURTESY OF DATA I/O CORPORATION

Octal counter with synchronous clear, Screen 8.

mable/tester that can support virtually any type of programmable device in a single site.

Suppose you had PAL16R8s in stock, but not PAL16R4s. Simply edit the ABEL source file, changing line 4 to read:

    u3 device 'P16R8';

Then recompile the design with ABEL and produce a new set of test vectors with PLDtest. You now have a JEDEC file, called OCTAL.JED, that is ready to be downloaded to the Unisite 40 from the PC XT.

Using a terminal emulator such as Vterm, you can transfer the JEDEC file to the Unisite 40. Now that the file resides in the Unisite 40's RAM, you can proceed to program and test the first PAL.

TRAFFIC LIGHT CONTROLLER
Courtesy of Data I/O Corporation

This example introduces the use of ABEL with another type of PLD architecture, the Field-Programmable Logic Sequencer (FPLS) PLS167. The logic diagram is given in FIG. 6-10. The PLS167 is a Mealy-type programmable state machine that contains a programmable OR array as well as a programmable AND array (as found in the PAL type architectures). One advantage of using a device with both programmable OR and AND arrays is that common logic functions can be shared by different outputs in the device. Also, product terms can be divided up among the outputs as needed. In other words, you do not have a dedicated number of product terms for each output and ten products can be assigned to one output and while three product terms to another output.

This design is a traffic light controller and takes advantage of the ABEL state diagram syntax. Screen 1 shows a state graph for the traffic signal controller that shows the state transitions.

Begin this example with the required module statement and the optional flag statement. The "flag ' – r2" ' tells the ABEL compiler to use reduction level 2. ABEL has 5 different reduction levels, and level 2 is a global reduction using the PRESTO algorithm. Global reduction reduces the design and attempts to share product terms where possible. This takes advantage of the product term capabilities of the PLS167. Pin-by-pin reduction (– r3) would be another possible reduction option. This causes reduction for each pin to be performed individually rather than globally and is useful for devices that don't share product terms, such as a PAL 16R8.

The title statement as shown in Screen 2 is optional. TSC is the name of the JEDEC (programmer load file), and declare the device you will use.

Next, names are assigned to the pins and nodes to be used in the device as shown in Screen 2. *Nodes* are device internals that are accessible by the user. In the case of the PLS167, 6 buried registers are available to the user.

Constants can also be used in ABEL. The constants H and L are being assigned to 1 and 0 allowing H and L to be substituted whenever 1 or 0 is used. Ck and X are used in the test vectors for clocking and "don't care" values also shown in Screen 2.

The use of sets in ABEL is a powerful feature. The PLS167 uses SR flip-flops and both the SET and RESET terms are available to the user. Access to the SET term is done simply by writing an equation for the pin name. The RESET term is accessed by using the pin name with the extension .R added. An SR flip-flop has three legal conditions (00, 01, 10) and one illegal condition (11). Notice that what has been done here is to define two valid SR flip-flop conditions, "On = [1,0]" and "Off = [0,1]" and the value of these sets can now be assigned to the SET and RESET terms for the 6 output pins (pins 9 thru 15) used in the source file. By creating the two bit sets of Green A and B, Yellow A and B, Red A and B (which are the SET and RESET inputs to the SR flip-flops in the PLS167), you can assign the On/Off values to any of these SETs as seen in Screens 2 and 3.

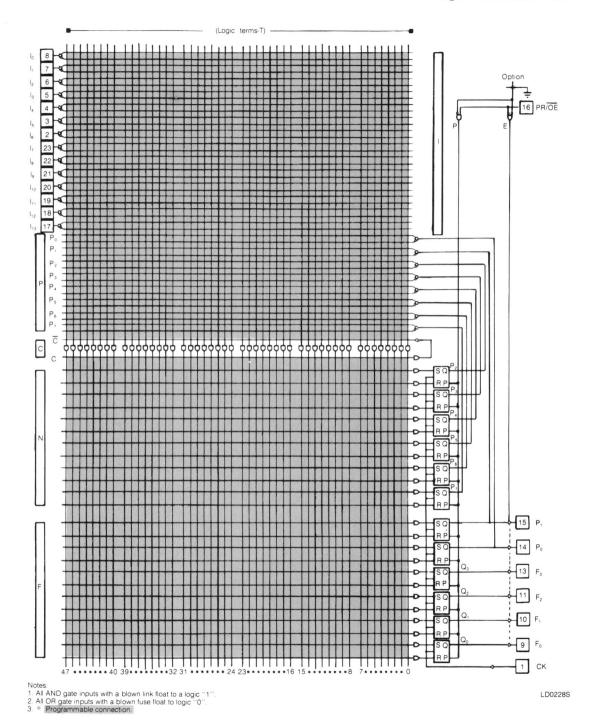

Fig. 6-10. FPLS logic diagram of PLS167. Courtesy of Signetics Corporation.

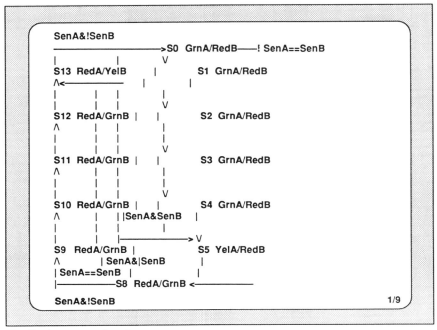

```
SenA&!SenB
————————————————————>S0  GrnA/RedB————! SenA==SenB
|         |          V
S13  RedA/YelB        |          S1  GrnA/RedB
Λ<—————————————       |          |
|      |   |     |    |          |
|      |   |     |    V
S12  RedA/GrnB |     |          S2  GrnA/RedB
Λ       |   |   |    |          |
|       |   |   |    |          |
|       |   |   |    V
S11  RedA/GrnB |     |          S3  GrnA/RedB
Λ       |   |   |    |          |
|       |   |   |    |          |
|       |   |   |    V
S10  RedA/GrnB |     |          S4  GrnA/RedB
Λ       |   | |SenA&SenB  |
|       |   |   |————————————>V
S9  RedA/GrnB |             S5  YelA/RedB
Λ       | SenA&|SenB          |
| SenA==SenB  |               |
|————————————S8  RedA/GrnB <————————————
SenA&!SenB                                    1/9
```

Traffic light controller, Screen 1.

```
module traffic    flag '-r2'
title 'Traffic Signal Controller
Data I/O Corp'

TSC   device 'F167';

Clk,SenA,SenB  pin  1, 8, 7;
PR        pin 16;        "Preset control
F3,F2,F1,F0    pin 13,11,10,9;
P1,P0      pin 15,14;

P7,P6,P5,P4    node 31,32,33,34; " Internal state counter

H,L,Ck,X = 1, 0, .C., .X.;

Count   = [P7,P6,P5,P4];

On    = [ 1,  0 ];
Off   = [ 0,  1 ];
GreenA = [P1,P1.R];
YellowA = [P0,P0.R];
                                              2/9
```

Traffic light controller, Screen 2.

```
RedA   = [F3,F3.R];
GreenB = [F2,F2.R];
YellowB = [F1,F1.R];
RedB   = [F0,F0.R];

equations

[F3.OE,F2.OE,F1.OE,F0.OE] = !0;
[F3.PR,F2.PR,F1.PR,F0.PR] = PR;
[P7.PR,P6.PR,P5.PR,P5.PR] = PR;
[P1.PR,P0.PR] = PR;

test_vectors

"  GreenA,YellowA,RedA,GreenB,YellowB,RedB
([Clk,PR,SenA,SenB] -> [Count, P1 , P0  , F3 , F2 ,  F1 , F0 ])
[ 1 , 1, 1 , 1 ] -> [ 15 ,  X  ,  X  , X , X ,   X  , X  ];
[ 1 , 0, 1 , 1 ] -> [ 15 ,  X  ,  X  , X , X ,   X  , X  ];
[ Ck, 0, 1 , 0 ] -> [  0  ,  H  ,  L  , L , L ,   L  , H  ];

test_vectors          " GreenA,YellowA, RedA,GreenB,YellowB,RedB

([Clk,PR,SenA,SenB] -> [Count, P1 , P0  , F3 , F2 ,  F1 , F0 ])
[ Ck, 0, 1 , 0 ] -> [  0  ,  H  ,  L  , L , L ,   L  , H  ];
                                                              3/9
```

Traffic light controller, Screen 3.

In the example, you need an equation section to define the output enable condition (set the output enables equal to !0, or always enabled, using .OE extensions), and define a PRESET term for all registers using the .PR extension. In this example, I map the PRESET to pin 16, defined as PR (see Screen 3).

The state_diagram is where the states, or the control sequence for the traffic lights, is defined using the state_diagram syntax and using CASE statements. We start out in state 0, and if it is the case that the sensor inputs for the two traffic lights are SenA equal to 1 and SenB equal to 0, then stay in state 0. If SenA is equal to 0 and SenB equal to 1, then go to state 4. If both SenA and SenB are equal, then go to state 1.

You can follow through, starting at state 0, and see how to transition for state to state using the CASE statement.

```
state_diagram Count

State ):        case    SenA &  !SenB : 0;
!SenA &         SenB    : 4;
(SenA = =       SenB)   : 1;
endcase;
State 1:                         goto 2;
State 2:                         goto 3;
State 3:                         goto 4;
```

Notice that when you are sent to state 4 (from state 1), you turn the green signal off on light A and turn yellow on. On the next clock, you are then forced to state 5 where YellowA is turned off, RedA is turned on, GreenB is also turned on, and RedB is turned off.

```
State 4:                GreenA   : = Off;
YellowA      : = On ;
goto 5;


RedB         : = On;
RedA         : = Off;
GreenA       : = On;
goto   0;


State 14:           goto 15;                    "Unused state


State 15:           GreenA      : = On;         "Power on initialize
state
YellowA      : = Off;
RedA         : = Off;
GreenB       : = Off;
YellowB      : = Off;
RedB         : = On ;
goto   0;
```

Test vectors are an important part of the design process. ABEL has a device level functional simulator that ensures the design is working as intended before committing it to silicon. When problems do occur, test vectors are a great aid in troubleshooting. Test vectors are also important because ABEL automatically adds them to the JEDEC file (programmer load file). These test vectors are then used by the device programmer to ensure the integrity of the device at the time of programming.

Inputs are listed on the left side of " – >" in the test vectors. You can change the inputs and the expected outputs to verify your design is working properly. Test vectors are shown at the bottom of Screen 3 and terminating in the middle of Screen 4.

Supplemental test vectors could also be added using Data I/O's PLDtest and PLDtest Plus. These products generate test vectors seeking 100% fault coverage for device testing. An important feature of PLDtest Plus is its ability to generate test vectors for nonpreloadable devices, test vectors that can be used by in-circuit testers as well as device programmers.

Screens 4 and 5 are a portion of the JEDEC file produced by ABEL. It contains the complete fuse map information for the device programmer. Notice the test vectors that were written for the design test at the source level are now included in the JEDEC file.

```
[ Ck, 0, 1 , 0 ] -> [ 0 , H , L ,L , L , L ,H ];
[ Ck, 0, 1 , 1 ] -> [ 1 , H , L ,L , L , L ,H ];
[ Ck, 0, 1 , 1 ] -> [ 2 , H , L ,L , L , L ,H ];
[ Ck, 0, 1 , 1 ] -> [ 3 , H , L ,L , L , L ,H ];
[ Ck, 0, 1 , 1 ] -> [ 4 , H , L ,L , L , L ,H ];
[ Ck, 0, 1 , 1 ] -> [ 5 , L , H ,L , L , L ,H ];
[ Ck, 0, 1 , 0 ] -> [ 8 , L , L ,H , H , L ,L ];
[ Ck, 0, 1 , 0 ] -> [12 , L , L ,H , H , L ,L ];
[ Ck, 0, 1 , 0 ] -> [13 , L , L ,H , L , H ,L ];
[ Ck, 0, 1 , 0 ] -> [ 0 , H , L ,L , L , L ,H ];
[ Ck, 0, 1 , 0 ] -> [ 0 , H , L ,L , L , L ,H ];
[ Ck, 0, 1 , 1 ] -> [ 1 , H , L ,L , L , L ,H ];
[ Ck, 0, 1 , 1 ] -> [ 2 , H , L ,L , L , L ,H ];
[ Ck, 0, 1 , 1 ] -> [ 3 , H , L ,L , L , L ,H ];

end traffic

ABEL(tm) 3.10 Data I/O Corp.  JEDEC file for: F167 V7.0
Created on: 13-Jan-89 01:32 PM
Traffic Signal Controller
Data I/O Corp*
QP24* QF3361* QV19*
L0000
11111111111111111111111111111111111111010110111111111111101111111111111
```

4/9

Traffic light controller, Screen 4.

```
11111111111111111111111111111111111111011101101111111111101111111111111
01101111111111111111111111111111111110101001111111111101111111111111111
11111111111111111111111111111111111110101101111111111100111111111111111
.
.
.
.
00000000000000000000000000000000000000000000000000000000000000000000000
00000000000000000000000000000000000000000000000000000000000000000000000
000000000000000000000000000000000000000000000000000000000000000000000000*
L3360
0*
V0001 1XXXXX11NNNNNNN1XXXXXXXN*
V0002 1XXXXX11NNNNNNN0XXXXXXXN*
V0003 CXXXXX01HLLNLLH0XXXXXXXN*
V0004 CXXXXX01HLLNLLH0XXXXXXXN*
V0005 CXXXXX01HLLNLLH0XXXXXXXN*
V0006 CXXXXX11HLLNLLH0XXXXXXXN*
V0007 CXXXXX11HLLNLLH0XXXXXXXN*
V0008 CXXXXX11HLLNLLH0XXXXXXXN*
V0009 CXXXXX11HLLNLLH0XXXXXXXN*
V0010 CXXXXX11HLLNLHL0XXXXXXXN*
V0011 CXXXXX01LLHNHLL0XXXXXXXN*
V0012 CXXXXX01LLHNHLL0XXXXXXXN*
```

5/9

Traffic light controller, Screen 5.

```
V0013 CXXXXX01LHLNHLL0XXXXXXXN*
V0014 CXXXXX01HLLNLLH0XXXXXXXN*
V0015 CXXXXX01HLLNLLH0XXXXXXXN*
V0016 CXXXXX11HLLNLLH0XXXXXXXN*
V0017 CXXXXX11HLLNLLH0XXXXXXXN*
V0018 CXXXXX11HLLNLLH0XXXXXXXN*
CA2CD*

- Reduced Equations:

_F3_E = (1);

_F3_PR = (PR);

P7 := (P5 & P6 & !P7 # P4 & P6 & !P7);

P6 := (!P4 & !P5 & !P6 & P7 & SenA & !SenB
# P4 & P5 & !P6
# !P4 & !P5 & !P6 & !P7 & !SenA & SenB);

P5 := (P4 & !P5 & !P6);

P4 := (!P4 & P5 # !P4 & SenA & SenB # !P4 & !SenA & !SenB # !P4 &
P6);
```

6/9

Traffic light controller, Screen 6.

```
_P7_R = (P4 & P6 & P7);

_P6_R = (P4 & P6 & P7 # P4 & !P5 & P6);

_P5_R = (P4 & P5 & !P6 # P4 & P5 & P7);

_P4_R = (P4 & P7 # P4 & !P5 # P4 & !P6);

P1 := (P4 & P6 & P7);

_P1_R := (!P4 & !P5 & P6 & !P7);

P0 := (!P4 & !P5 & P6 & !P7);

_P0_R := (P4 & P5 & P6 & P7 # P4 & !P5 & P6 & !P7);

F3 := (P4 & !P5 & P6 & !P7);

_F3_R := (P4 & P6 & P7);

F0 := (P4 & P6 & P7);

_F0_R := (P4 & !P5 & P6 & !P7);
```

7/9

Traffic light controller, Screen 7.

```
F2 := (P4 & !P5 & P6 & !P7);

_F2_R := (P4 & P5 & P6 & P7 # !P4 & !P5 & P6 & P7);

F1 := (!P4 & !P5 & P6 & P7);

_F1_R := (P4 & P6 & P7);


F167

      _____\   /_____
     |        \ /         |
     |         ‾‾          |
    Clk | 1              24 |
     |                     |
     | 2              23 |
     |                     |
     | 3              22 |
     |                     |
     | 4              21 |
     |                     |
     | 5              20 |

                                              8/9
```

Traffic light controller, Screen 8.

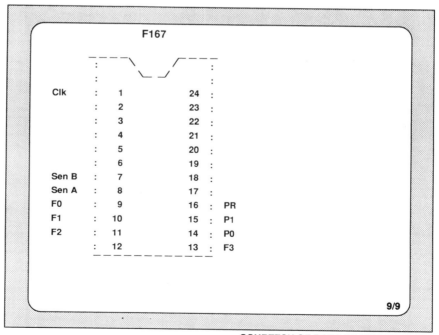

```
                    F167

          : ‾ ‾ ‾ \    / ‾ ‾ ‾ :
          :        \__/         :
    Clk   :    1           24  :
          :    2           23  :
          :    3           22  :
          :    4           21  :
          :    5           20  :
          :    6           19  :
    Sen B :    7           18  :
    Sen A :    8           17  :
    F0    :    9           16  :  PR
    F1    :   10           15  :  P1
    F2    :   11           14  :  P0
          :   12           13  :  F3
          ‾ ‾ ‾ ‾ ‾ ‾ ‾ ‾ ‾ ‾ ‾

                                              9/9
```

Traffic light controller, Screen 9.

ABEL converts all input methods—state diagrams, truth tables, high-level equations, or Boolean-level equations—to Boolean equations. The Boolean equations are then processed and reduced to minimal form for the device architecture state diagram language to equations for further processing. Screens 6 through 8 are what are known as the ''original equations'' in ABEL. The design engineer can see these equations in the ''DOCUMENT'' file that ABEL produces. The chip diagram for the traffic controller is shown in Screen 9.

3-BIT COUNTER

Courtesy of Logical Devices, Inc.

This design example is a state machine design for a 3-bit counter (or sequential circuit) that is intended to illustrate some aspects of the CUPL software. The counter will be implemented in a PAL16R4 whose logic diagram is given in FIG. 6-11. Figure 6-12 shows the state diagram. The three-state machine needs three registers, so select PAL16R4 as the target device. The source file is shown in Screens 1 and 2.

Keyword Field in line 20 is a bit field declaration statement which groups Q0, Q1, Q2 to a single name called counter. Lines 21-46 define the state machine. Keyword Present means the present state. For example, in line 22, "present 'b'000" means the present state is 000. The IF statement used in state machine syntax is similar to the CASE statement or the nested if structure in C language. Lines 22-45 also can be written in short form by using the $REPEAT macro command. Lines 22 through 26 of Screen 3 represent lines 22 through 45 shown in Screens 1 and 2. In Screen 3, lines 12 to the end represent a simulation input file for the counter design example. The header information is omitted. The value C is a positive edge-triggered clock for a CLOCK pin.

Simulation Waveform Output

CUPL 3.0 MS-DOS version provides a simulation waveform output that runs on video text mode, so it does not need any graphics support. The waveform output for the counter design example is shown in FIG. 6-13. The documentation output file and JEDEC download file is shown in Screens 4 through 9.

Logic Diagram—PAL16R4

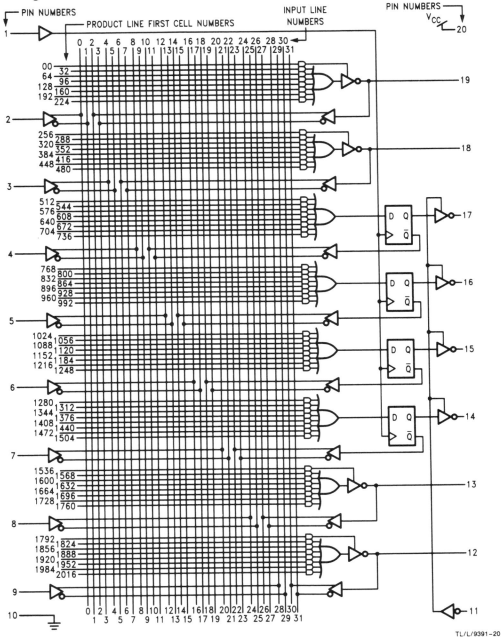

JEDEC Logic Array Cell Number = Product Line First Cell Number + Input Line Number

Fig. 6-11. PAL16R4 logic diagram. Courtesy of National Semiconductor Corporation.

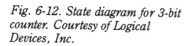

Fig. 6-12. State diagram for 3-bit counter. Courtesy of Logical Devices, Inc.

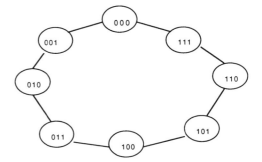

```
 1:     NAME  COUNTER3;
 2:     PARTNO        P002;
 3:     REVISION      01;
 4:     DATE          1-24-89;
 5:     DESIGNER      JEFF;
 6:     COMPANY       LOGICAL DEVICES;
 7:     ASSEMBLY      EXAMPLE;
 8:     LOCATION      U01;
 9:     DEVICE        P16R4;
10:     FORMAT        J;
11:
12:     /* input pins */
13:     Pin  1 = CLOCK;
14:     Pin  2 = ADVANCE;
15:     Pin  3 = RESET;

16:     /*     output pins */
17:     Pin  [17..15] = [Q2..0];
18:
19:     /* state machine design */
20:     Field   COUNTER = [Q2..0];
21:     sequence COUNTER {
22:     present 'b'000   if RESET  next 'b'000;
23:                      if !RESET & ADVANCE next 'b'001;      1/9
```

3-bit counter, Screen 1.

```
24:                    default  'b'000;
25:    present 'b'001  If RESET  next 'b'000;
26:                       If !RESET & ADVANCE next 'b'010;
27:                    default  'b'001;
28:    present 'b'010  If RESET  next 'b'000;
29:                       If !RESET & ADVANCE next 'b'011;
30:                    default  'b'010;
31:    present 'b'011  If RESET  next 'b'000;
32:                       If !RESET & ADVANCE next 'b'100;
33:                    default  'b'011;
34:    present 'b'100  If RESET  next 'b'000;
35:                       If !RESET & ADVANCE next 'b'101;
36:                    default  'b'100;
37:    present 'b'101  If RESET  next 'b'000;
38:                       if !RESET & ADVANCE next 'b'110;
39:                    default  'b'101;
40:    present 'b'110  if RESET  next 'b'000;
41:                       If !RESET & ADVANCE next 'b'111;
42:                    default  'b'110;
43:    present 'b'111  If RESET  next 'b'000;
44:                       If !RESET & ADVANCE next 'b'000;
45:                    default  'b'111;
46:    }
```

2/9

3-bit counter, Screen 2.

```
22:    $REPEAT i = [0..7]
23:    present 'b'{i}  If RESET next 'b'{0};
24:                       If !RESET & ADVANCE next 'b'{(i+1) % 8};
25:                    default  'b'{i};
26:    $REPEND


12:    ORDER: ADVANCE %2 RESET %2 CLOCK %2 Q2..0;
13:    VECTORS:
14:    0 1 C LLL
15:    1 0 C LLH
16:    1 0 C LHL
17:    1 0 C LHH
18:    1 0 C HLL
19:    1 0 C HLH
20:    1 0 C HHL
14:    1 0 C HHH
14:    1 0 C LLL
```

3/9

3-bit counter, Screen 3.

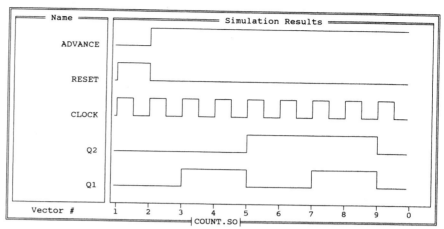

Fig. 6-13. Simulation results for. Courtesy of Logical Devices, Inc.

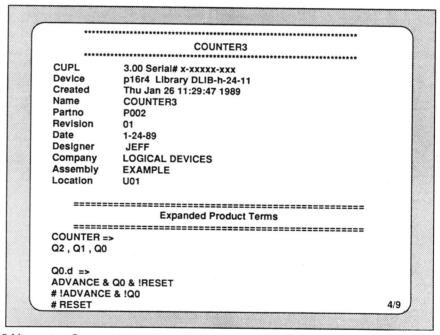

3-bit counter, Screen 4.

```
Q1.d =>
ADVANCE & Q0 & Q1 & !RESET
# RESET
# !ADVANCE & !Q1
# !Q0 & !Q1

Q2.d =>
ADVANCE & Q0 & Q1 & Q2 & !RESET
# RESET
# !ADVANCE & !Q2
# !Q1 & !Q2
# !Q0 & !Q2
```

```
===================================================
                    Symbol Table
===================================================
```

Pin Pol	Variable Name	Ext	Pin	Type	Pterms Used	Max Pterms	Min Level
	ADVANCE		2	V	-	-	-
	CLOCK		1	V	-	-	-
	COUNTER		0	F	-	-	-
	Q0		15	V	-	-	-
	Q0	d	15	X	3	8	1
	Q1		16	V	-	-	-
	Q1	d	16	X	4	8	1
	Q2		17	V	-	-	-
	Q2	d	17	X	5	8	1
	RESET		3	V	-	-	-

5/9

3-bit counter, Screen 5.

LEGEND	F	:	field	D	:	default variable
	M	:	extended node	N	:	node
	I	:	intermediate variable	T	:	function
	V	:	variable	X	:	extended variable
	U	:	undefined			

```
===================================================
                     Fuse Plot
===================================================
Pin #19
00000 xxxxxxxxxxxxxxxxxxxxxxxxxxxxxxxx
00032 xxxxxxxxxxxxxxxxxxxxxxxxxxxxxxxx
00064 xxxxxxxxxxxxxxxxxxxxxxxxxxxxxxxx
00096 xxxxxxxxxxxxxxxxxxxxxxxxxxxxxxxx
00128 xxxxxxxxxxxxxxxxxxxxxxxxxxxxxxxx
00160 xxxxxxxxxxxxxxxxxxxxxxxxxxxxxxxx
00192 xxxxxxxxxxxxxxxxxxxxxxxxxxxxxxxx
00224 xxxxxxxxxxxxxxxxxxxxxxxxxxxxxxxx
Pin #18
00256 xxxxxxxxxxxxxxxxxxxxxxxxxxxxxxxx
00288 xxxxxxxxxxxxxxxxxxxxxxxxxxxxxxxx
00320 xxxxxxxxxxxxxxxxxxxxxxxxxxxxxxxx
00352 xxxxxxxxxxxxxxxxxxxxxxxxxxxxxxxx
00384 xxxxxxxxxxxxxxxxxxxxxxxxxxxxxxxx
```

6/9

3-bit counter, Screen 6.

```
00416  xxxxxxxxxxxxxxxxxxxxxxxxxxxxxxxx
00448  xxxxxxxxxxxxxxxxxxxxxxxxxxxxxxxx
00480  xxxxxxxxxxxxxxxxxxxxxxxxxxxxxxxx
Pin #17
00512  x——x——x—x—x———————————
00544  ——x————————————————
00576  —x——————x——————————
00608  ————————x—x——————————
00640  ————————x———x————————
00672  xxxxxxxxxxxxxxxxxxxxxxxxxxxxxxxx
00704  xxxxxxxxxxxxxxxxxxxxxxxxxxxxxxxx
00736  xxxxxxxxxxxxxxxxxxxxxxxxxxxxxxxx
Pin #16
00768  x——x————————x—x——————
00800  —x——————————————————
00832  —x——————————x——————
00864  ————————————x—x—————
00896  xxxxxxxxxxxxxxxxxxxxxxxxxxxxxxxx
00928  xxxxxxxxxxxxxxxxxxxxxxxxxxxxxxxx
00960  xxxxxxxxxxxxxxxxxxxxxxxxxxxxxxxx
00992  xxxxxxxxxxxxxxxxxxxxxxxxxxxxxxxx
Pin #15
01024  x——x—————————x——————
01056  —x—————————————x—————
01088  ——x—————————————————
```

7/9

3-bit counter, Screen 7.

```
01120  xxxxxxxxxxxxxxxxxxxxxxxxxxxxxxxx
01152  xxxxxxxxxxxxxxxxxxxxxxxxxxxxxxxx
01184  xxxxxxxxxxxxxxxxxxxxxxxxxxxxxxxx
01216  xxxxxxxxxxxxxxxxxxxxxxxxxxxxxxxx
01248  xxxxxxxxxxxxxxxxxxxxxxxxxxxxxxxx
Pin #14
01280  xxxxxxxxxxxxxxxxxxxxxxxxxxxxxxxx
01312  xxxxxxxxxxxxxxxxxxxxxxxxxxxxxxxx
01344  xxxxxxxxxxxxxxxxxxxxxxxxxxxxxxxx
01376  xxxxxxxxxxxxxxxxxxxxxxxxxxxxxxxx
01408  xxxxxxxxxxxxxxxxxxxxxxxxxxxxxxxx
01440  xxxxxxxxxxxxxxxxxxxxxxxxxxxxxxxx
01472  xxxxxxxxxxxxxxxxxxxxxxxxxxxxxxxx
01504  xxxxxxxxxxxxxxxxxxxxxxxxxxxxxxxx
Pin #13
01536  xxxxxxxxxxxxxxxxxxxxxxxxxxxxxxxx
01568  xxxxxxxxxxxxxxxxxxxxxxxxxxxxxxxx
01600  xxxxxxxxxxxxxxxxxxxxxxxxxxxxxxxx
01632  xxxxxxxxxxxxxxxxxxxxxxxxxxxxxxxx
01664  xxxxxxxxxxxxxxxxxxxxxxxxxxxxxxxx
01696  xxxxxxxxxxxxxxxxxxxxxxxxxxxxxxxx
01728  xxxxxxxxxxxxxxxxxxxxxxxxxxxxxxxx
01760  xxxxxxxxxxxxxxxxxxxxxxxxxxxxxxxx
Pin #12
```

8/9

3-bit counter, Screen 8.

```
01792  xxxxxxxxxxxxxxxxxxxxxxxxxxxxxxxx
01824  xxxxxxxxxxxxxxxxxxxxxxxxxxxxxxxx
01856  xxxxxxxxxxxxxxxxxxxxxxxxxxxxxxxx
01888  xxxxxxxxxxxxxxxxxxxxxxxxxxxxxxxx
01920  xxxxxxxxxxxxxxxxxxxxxxxxxxxxxxxx
01952  xxxxxxxxxxxxxxxxxxxxxxxxxxxxxxxx
01984  xxxxxxxxxxxxxxxxxxxxxxxxxxxxxxxx
02016  xxxxxxxxxxxxxxxxxxxxxxxxxxxxxxxx

LEGEND   X : fuse not blown
- : fuse blown
=================================================================
                          Chip Diagram
=================================================================
                           COUNTER3
            CLOCK x---  1      20 ---x Vcc
          ADVANCE x---  2      19 ---x
            RESET x---  3      18 ---x
                  x---  4      17 ---x Q2
                  x---  5      16 ---x Q1
                  x---  6      15 ---x Q0
                  x---  7      14 ---x
                  x---  8      13 ---x
                  x---  9      12 ---x
              GND x---10      11 ---x            9/9
```

COURTESY OF LOGICAL DEVICES, INC.

3-bit counter, Screen 9.

3-TO-8 DECODER
Courtesy of Logical Devices, Inc.

The design example is to design a 3-to-8 decoder utilizing the CUPL software. It is a very simple PLD design and is implemented in a 16L8. The 16L8 logic diagram is shown in FIG. 6-14 and the circuit diagram in FIG. 6-15.

This is a combinatorial circuit. Many PLD devices fit this design, but for the example as stated I selected the 16L8, a small and very popular combinatorial PAL device. The first step in PLD design using CUPL is to create a CUPL source file. Any text editor (nondocument mode) can be used to create the source file.

CUPL both promotes and provides good documentation. CUPL's logic description template file eases source file creation while encouraging comments and a structured information header, shown in Screen 1.

The header section contains generic information about the design. The keyword DEVICE in line 9 is used to specify device name. The keyword FORMAT in line 10 is used to specify download output format which can be JEDEC (J), ASCII-HEX (H) and Signetics-HL output (I).

Following the header information are the pin declaration statements beginning at line 11 of Screen 1, and ending at the top of Screen 2 (line 24).

Lines 11 and 16 are comment lines. Lines 12-15 define the input pins. Each physical pin is associated with a variable name. Lines 17-24 define the output pins, and the exclamation point is used to define the output pin active low. CUPL automatically checks your design against the characteristics of the target device and will De Morganize your logic if necessary.

The next section in the source file is the logic equations section shown in lines 25-33 of Screen 2. CUPL offers a variety of design expression formats. In this example, Boolean equations are used. (''#'' is the OR operator, ''&'' is the AND operator, ''!'' is the negation operator and ''$'' is the EXCLUSIVE-OR operator.)

Line 25 is used for comments. Comments begin with /* and end with */ and can be placed anywhere in the source file. Lines 26-33 define the logic equations for output variables. These logical equations also can be written in short form by using the macro command $REPEAT, as shown in lines 25-28 of Screen 2.

Powerful Macro Capability

The $REPEAT keyword is a macro command in CUPL which performs the loop function just as the FOR statement in C language and the DO statement in FORTRAN. $REPEAT is one of several powerful macro commands that are available in CUPL beginning with version 3.0.

Design Verification

Design verification beginning in line 1 of Screen 2 in CUPL is the process of running a logic simulation program (CSIM) to verify your design before you program the chip. It creates a list of test vectors that are attached to the JEDEC

Logic Diagram—PAL16L8

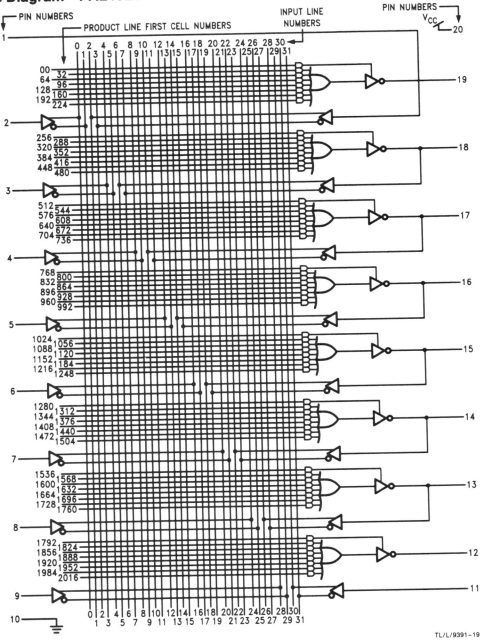

JEDEC Logic Array Cell Number = Product Line First Cell Number + Input Line Number

TL/L/9391–19

Fig. 6-14. Logic diagram. Courtesy of National Semiconductor Corporation.

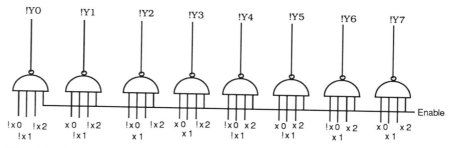

Fig. 6-15. 3-to-8 decoder. Courtesy of Logical Devices, Inc.

```
 1:    NAME DECODER;
 2:    PARTNO        P001;
 3:    REVISION      01;
 4:    DATE          1-24-89;
 5:    DESIGNER      JEFF;
 6:    COMPANY       LOGICAL DEVICES;
 7:    ASSEMBLY      EXAMPLE;
 8:    LOCATION      U01;
 9:    DEVICE        P16L8;
10:    FORMAT        J;

11:    /* input pins */
12:    Pin 1 = X0;
13:    Pin 2 = X1;
14:    Pin 3 = X2;
15:    Pin 4 = Enable;
16:    /* output pins */
17:    Pin 19 = !Y0;
18:    Pin 18 = !Y1;
19:    Pin 17 = !Y2;
20:    Pin 16 = !Y3;
21:    Pin 15 = !Y4;
22:    Pin 14 = !Y5;
23:    Pin 13 = !Y6;
                                              1/13
```

3-to-8 decoder, Screen 1.

file to allow functional testing. CSIM can run automatically after compilation, but because it is a separate program within CUPL, it can also run independently. The advantage of this is that you can run successive simulations without having to recompile your design each time. The simulation input file consists of three sections. The first section is the header section, which is the same as the CUPL source file header. The second section is the ORDER section which defines the variables you wish as indicated in lines 11 and 12 of Screen 3. ORDER in line 11 is a keyword. Line 12 defines the variables to be simulated. The %2 means leave 2 spaces between the previous variable and the next variable. The ! defines the active-low variable. The third section shown in Screen 3 line 13 is the test vectors section which defines the input value and the expected output value.

```
24:    Pin 12 = !Y7;
25:    /* Logic Equations */
26:    Y0 = !X0 & !X1 & !X2 & Enable;
27:    Y1 =  X0 & !X1 & !X2 & Enable;
28:    Y2 = !X0 &  X1 & !X2 & Enable;
29:    Y3 =  X0 &  X1 & !X2 & Enable;
30:    Y4 = !X0 & !X1 &  X2 & Enable;
31:    Y5 =  X0 & !X1 &  X2 & Enable;
32:    Y6 = !X0 &  X1 &  X2 & Enable;
33:    Y7 =  X0 &  X1 &  X2 & Enable;
25:    /* Logic Equations */
26:    $REPEAT I = [0..7]
27:         Y{i} = [X2,X1,X0]:{i} & Enable;
28:    $REPEND


1:     NAME DECODER;
2:     PARTNO        P001;
3:     REVISION      01;
4:     DATE          1-24-89;
5:     DESIGNER      JEFF;
6:     COMPANY       LOGICAL DEVICES;
7:     ASSEMBLY      EXAMPLE;
8:     LOCATION      U01;               2/13
```

3-to-8 decoder, Screen 2.

```
9:     DEVICE        P16L8;
10:    FORMAT        J;

11:    ORDER:
12:    X2..0, %2, Enable, %2, !Y0,!Y1,!Y2,!Y3,!Y4,!Y5,!Y6,!Y7;

13:    VECTORS:
14:    $MSG"    XXX E !!!!!!!!";
15:    $MSG"    210 N YYYYYYYY";
16:    $MSG"        A 01234567";

17:         000 0 HHHHHHHH
18:         001 0 HHHHHHHH
19:         000 1 LHHHHHHH
20:         001 1 HLHHHHHH
21:         010 1 HHLHHHHH
22:         011 1 HHHLHHHH
23:         100 1 HHHHLHHH
24:         101 1 HHHHHLHH
25:         110 1 HHHHHHLH
26:         111 1 HHHHHHHL


                                        3/13
```

3-to-8 decoder, Screen 3.

$MSG is a directive to place documentation messages or formatting information into the simulator output file. When you run CSIM, it reports any errors that exist. CSIM also writes the text vectors to the JEDEC file for functional testing.

Compiling the CUPL Source File

The CUPL compiler is run by typing CUPL, followed by various option flags and the name of the file:

CUPL −jsxfm4 DECODER

DECODER is the CUPL source file name, −jsxfm4 are option flags. The j flag generates a JEDEC download format, the s flag runs simulation after compiling, the x flag creates expanded product terms in the documentation file, the f flag creates a readable fuse map in the documentation file, and m4 (enhanced ESPRESSO) is one of four possible logic minimization algorithms you can choose to implement. After compilation, the three files created are the simulation output file (Screens 4 and 5), the documentation file (Screens 6 through 9), and the JEDEC download file (Screens 10 through 13).

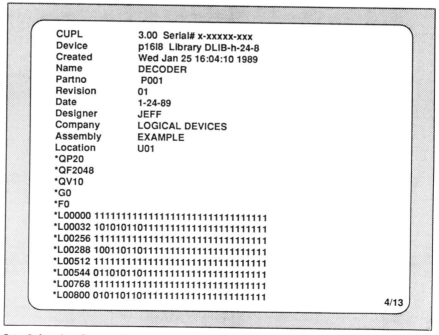

```
CUPL          3.00  Serial# x-xxxxx-xxx
Device        p16l8  Library DLIB-h-24-8
Created       Wed Jan 25 16:04:10 1989
Name          DECODER
Partno        P001
Revision      01
Date          1-24-89
Designer      JEFF
Company       LOGICAL DEVICES
Assembly      EXAMPLE
Location      U01
*QP20
*QF2048
*QV10
*G0
*F0
*L00000 11111111111111111111111111111111
*L00032 10101011011111111111111111111111
*L00256 11111111111111111111111111111111
*L00288 10011011011111111111111111111111
*L00512 11111111111111111111111111111111
*L00544 01101011011111111111111111111111
*L00768 11111111111111111111111111111111
*L00800 01011011011111111111111111111111
                                              4/13
```

3-to-8 decoder, Screen 4.

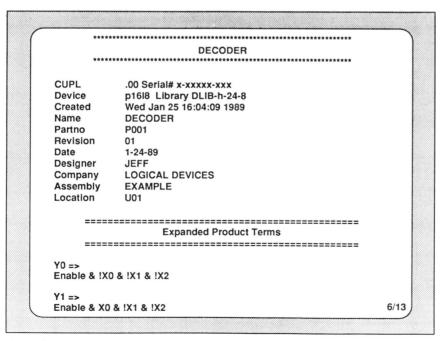

```
*L01024 111111111111111111111111111111111
*L01056 101001110111111111111111111111111
*L01280 111111111111111111111111111111111
*L01312 100101110111111111111111111111111
*L01536 111111111111111111111111111111111
*L01568 011001110111111111111111111111111
*L01792 111111111111111111111111111111111
*L01824 010101110111111111111111111111111
*C3EBC
*P 1 2 3 4 5 6 7 8 9 10 11 12 13 14 15 16 17 18 19 20
*V0001 0000XXXXXNXHHHHHHHHN
*V0002 1000XXXXXNXHHHHHHHHN
*V0003 0001XXXXXNXHHHHHHHLN
*V0004 1001XXXXXNXHHHHHHLHN
*V0005 0101XXXXXNXHHHHHLHHN
*V0006 1101XXXXXNXHHHHLHHHN
*V0007 0011XXXXXNXHHHLHHHHN
*V0008 1011XXXXXNXHHLHHHHHN
*V0009 0111XXXXXNXHLHHHHHHN
*V0010 1111XXXXXNXLHHHHHHHN
*20FB
                                              5/13
```

3-to-8 decoder, Screen 5.

```
*****************************************************************
                          DECODER
*****************************************************************

CUPL        .00 Serial# x-xxxxx-xxx
Device      p16l8  Library DLIB-h-24-8
Created     Wed Jan 25 16:04:09 1989
Name        DECODER
Partno      P001
Revision    01
Date        1-24-89
Designer    JEFF
Company     LOGICAL DEVICES
Assembly    EXAMPLE
Location    U01


     =================================================
                    Expanded Product Terms
     =================================================


Y0 =>
Enable & !X0 & !X1 & !X2

Y1 =>
Enable & X0 & !X1 & !X2                        6/13
```

3-to-8 decoder, Screen 6.

```
Y2 =>
Enable & !X0 & X1 & !X2

Y3 =>
Enable & X0 & X1 & !X2

Y4 =>
Enable & !X0 & !X1 & X2

Y5 =>
Enable & X0 & !X1 & X2

Y6 =>
Enable & !X0 & X1 & X2

Y7 =>
Enable & X0 & X1 & X2

Y0.oe =>
1

Y1.oe =>
1
```

7/13

3-to-8 decoder, Screen 7.

```
Y2.oe =>
1

Y3.oe =>
1

Y4.oe =>
1

Y5.oe =>
1

Y6.oe =>
1

Y7.oe =>
1


         ===========================================
                        Symbol Table
         ===========================================
Pin    VariablePterms  Max   Min
Pol     Name   Ext    Pin   Type   Used    Pterms   Level
 —     ————    —      —     ——     ———     ————     ——
```

8/13

3-to-8 decoder, Screen 8.

```
         Enable   4    V    -      -      -
           X0     1    V    -      -      -
           X1     2    V    -      -      -
           X2     3    V    -      -      -
            !    Y0   19    V      1      7      2
            !    Y1   18    V      1      7      2
            !    Y2   17    V      1      7      2
            !    Y3   16    V      1      7      2
            !    Y4   15    V      1      7      2
            !    Y5   14    V      1      7      2
            !    Y6   13    V      1      7      2
            !    Y7   12    V      1      7      2
           Y0    oe   19    D      1      1      0
           Y1    oe   18    D      1      1      0
           Y2    oe   17    D      1      1      0
           Y3    oe   16    D      1      1      0
           Y4    oe   15    D      1      1      0
           Y5    oe   14    D      1      1      0
           Y6    oe   13    D      1      1      0
           Y7    oe   12    D      1      1      0


 LEGEND   F  :  field                 D  :  default variable
          M  :  extended node         N  :  node
                                                          9/13
```

3-to-8 decoder, Screen 9.

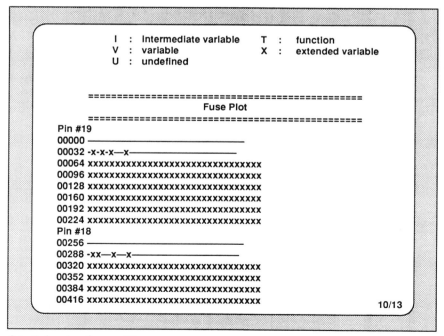

```
          I  :  intermediate variable   T  :  function
          V  :  variable                X  :  extended variable
          U  :  undefined



       ================================================
                          Fuse Plot
       ================================================
 Pin #19
 00000 ——————————————————————————————
 00032 -x-x-x—x—————————————————————
 00064 xxxxxxxxxxxxxxxxxxxxxxxxxxxxxxxx
 00096 xxxxxxxxxxxxxxxxxxxxxxxxxxxxxxxx
 00128 xxxxxxxxxxxxxxxxxxxxxxxxxxxxxxxx
 00160 xxxxxxxxxxxxxxxxxxxxxxxxxxxxxxxx
 00192 xxxxxxxxxxxxxxxxxxxxxxxxxxxxxxxx
 00224 xxxxxxxxxxxxxxxxxxxxxxxxxxxxxxxx
 Pin #18
 00256 ——————————————————————————————
 00288 -xx—x—x—————————————————————
 00320 xxxxxxxxxxxxxxxxxxxxxxxxxxxxxxxx
 00352 xxxxxxxxxxxxxxxxxxxxxxxxxxxxxxxx
 00384 xxxxxxxxxxxxxxxxxxxxxxxxxxxxxxxx
 00416 xxxxxxxxxxxxxxxxxxxxxxxxxxxxxxxx
                                             10/13
```

3-to-8 decoder, Screen 10.

```
00448 xxxxxxxxxxxxxxxxxxxxxxxxxxxxxx
00480 xxxxxxxxxxxxxxxxxxxxxxxxxxxxxx
Pin #17
00512 ————————————————————————
00544 x—x-x—x————————————————
00576 xxxxxxxxxxxxxxxxxxxxxxxxxxxxxx
00608 xxxxxxxxxxxxxxxxxxxxxxxxxxxxxx
00640 xxxxxxxxxxxxxxxxxxxxxxxxxxxxxx
00672 xxxxxxxxxxxxxxxxxxxxxxxxxxxxxx
00704 xxxxxxxxxxxxxxxxxxxxxxxxxxxxxx
00736 xxxxxxxxxxxxxxxxxxxxxxxxxxxxxx
Pin #16
00768 ————————————————————————
00800 x-x—x—x————————————————
00832 xxxxxxxxxxxxxxxxxxxxxxxxxxxxxx
00864 xxxxxxxxxxxxxxxxxxxxxxxxxxxxxx
00896 xxxxxxxxxxxxxxxxxxxxxxxxxxxxxx
00928 xxxxxxxxxxxxxxxxxxxxxxxxxxxxxx
00960 xxxxxxxxxxxxxxxxxxxxxxxxxxxxxx
00992 xxxxxxxxxxxxxxxxxxxxxxxxxxxxxx
Pin #15
01024 ————————————————————————
01056 -x-xx—x————————————————
01088 xxxxxxxxxxxxxxxxxxxxxxxxxxxxxx
                                    11/13
```

3-to-8 decoder, Screen 11.

```
01120 xxxxxxxxxxxxxxxxxxxxxxxxxxxxxx
01152 xxxxxxxxxxxxxxxxxxxxxxxxxxxxxx
01184 xxxxxxxxxxxxxxxxxxxxxxxxxxxxxx
01216 xxxxxxxxxxxxxxxxxxxxxxxxxxxxxx
01248 xxxxxxxxxxxxxxxxxxxxxxxxxxxxxx
Pin #14
01280 ————————————————————————
01312 -xx-x—x————————————————
01344 xxxxxxxxxxxxxxxxxxxxxxxxxxxxxx
01376 xxxxxxxxxxxxxxxxxxxxxxxxxxxxxx
01408 xxxxxxxxxxxxxxxxxxxxxxxxxxxxxx
01440 xxxxxxxxxxxxxxxxxxxxxxxxxxxxxx
01472 xxxxxxxxxxxxxxxxxxxxxxxxxxxxxx
01504 xxxxxxxxxxxxxxxxxxxxxxxxxxxxxx
Pin #13
01536 ————————————————————————
01568 x—xx—x————————————————
01600 xxxxxxxxxxxxxxxxxxxxxxxxxxxxxx
01632 xxxxxxxxxxxxxxxxxxxxxxxxxxxxxx
01664 xxxxxxxxxxxxxxxxxxxxxxxxxxxxxx
01696 xxxxxxxxxxxxxxxxxxxxxxxxxxxxxx
01728 xxxxxxxxxxxxxxxxxxxxxxxxxxxxxx
01760 xxxxxxxxxxxxxxxxxxxxxxxxxxxxxx
Pin #12
                                    12/13
```

3-to-8 decoder, Screen 12.

```
01792 ———————————————————————————
01824 x-x-x—x—————————————————————
01856 xxxxxxxxxxxxxxxxxxxxxxxxxxxxxxxx
01888 xxxxxxxxxxxxxxxxxxxxxxxxxxxxxxxx
01920 xxxxxxxxxxxxxxxxxxxxxxxxxxxxxxxx
01952 xxxxxxxxxxxxxxxxxxxxxxxxxxxxxxxx
01984 xxxxxxxxxxxxxxxxxxxxxxxxxxxxxxxx
02016 xxxxxxxxxxxxxxxxxxxxxxxxxxxxxxxx

LEGEND   X : fuse not blown
- : fuse blown

         =================================================
                          Chip Diagram
         =================================================

                          DECODER
              X0 x— 1          20 —x Vcc
              X1 x— 2          19 —x !Y0
              X2 x— 3          18 —x !Y1
          Enable x—4           17—x !Y2
                 x— 5          16 —x !Y3
                 x— 6          15 —x !Y4
                 x— 7          14 —x !Y5
                 x— 8          13 —x !Y6
                 x— 9          12 —x !Y7
             GND x— 10         11 —x            13/13
```

3-to-8 decoder, Screen 13.

CHANGE OF STATE PORT WITH INTERRUPT

Courtesy of International CMOS Technology, Inc.

This application uses the PEEL22CV10Z as an 8-bit input port for a microprocessor that can detect a change-of-state on its I(0-7) input pins. When detected, the INTR output is set for interrupting the microprocessor. The INTR output is also used to clock the PEEL device for latching the state change into the eight pseudo-buried registers. The registers can be read by the CPU on D0-D7 as listed in Screens 1 through 6. Once read, unless another change has occurred, the INTR is reset. The NEQ output provides a non-latched (not equal) output signal that can be used for the clock instead of the INTR pin. Doing this allows the last change to be saved instead of the first. The I(0-7) pins can also be directly read as a standard input port when addressed by A0. Figure 6-16 shows the system interface for V102PORT.APL while FIG. 6-17 shows a block diagram of internal functions of V102PORT.APL. Figure 6-18 shows the pinout for V102PORT.APL. The logic diagram is given in FIG. 6-19.

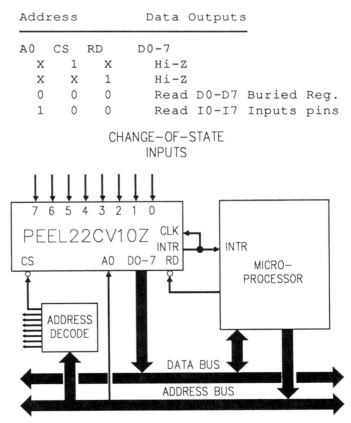

```
Address              Data Outputs
_____

A0  CS  RD    D0-7
    X   1   X     Hi-Z
    X   X   1     Hi-Z
    0   0   0     Read D0-D7 Buried Reg.
    1   0   0     Read I0-I7 Inputs pins
```

Fig. 6-16. System interface for V102PORT.APL. Courtesy of International CMOS Technology, Inc.

PEEL22CV10Z

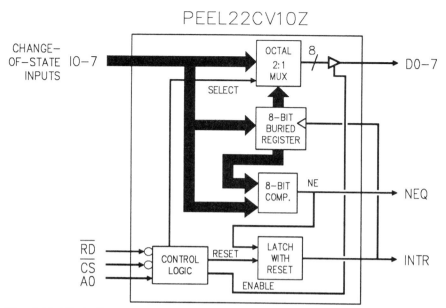

Fig. 6-17. Block diagram showing internal function of V102PORT.APL. Courtesy of International CMOS Technology, Inc.

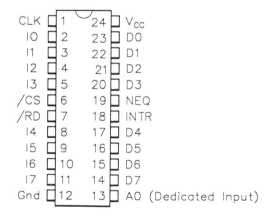

Fig. 6-18. Pinout for V102PORT.APL. Courtesy of International CMOS Technology, Inc.

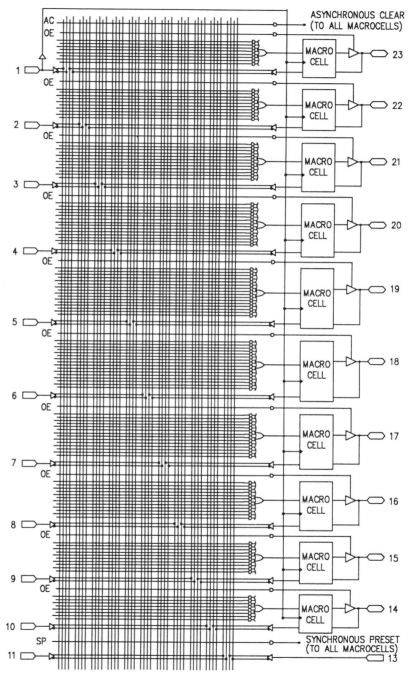

Fig. 6-19. PEEL22CV102 logic array diagram.

```
TITLE 'APEEL FILE:  PEEL22CV10Z CHANGE-OF-STATE INPUT PORT
WITH INTERRUPT DESIGNER:  Robin Jigour, ICT

PEEL22CV10Z    "The Key word 'ZERO_POWER' is omitted for non zero-
power mode.
"If zero-power is needed, this key word must be specified after "the part
number declaration but prior topin list definition

"PIN DEFINITIONS"

"Inputs"

CLK        pin 1      "Must be connected to pin 18, INTR"
I0         pin 2      "I0-I7 inputs can detect change of state"
I1         pin 3
I2         pin 4
I3         pin 5
!RD        pin 6
!CS        pin 7
I4         pin 8
I5         pin 9
I6         pin 10
I7         pin 11
A0         pin 13
                                                        1/6
```

Change of state input port with interrupt, Screen 1.

```
"Outputs"

D7     pin 14 = pos com feed_reg    "Pseudo buried registers.
D6     pin 15 = pos com feed_reg
D5     pin 16 = pos com feed_reg
D4     pin 17 = pos com feed_reg
INTR   pin 18 = pos com feed_or
NEQ    pin 19 = pos com feed_or
D3     pin 20 = pos com feed_reg
D2     pin 21 = pos com feed_reg
D1     pin 22 = pos com feed_reg
D0     pin 23 = pos com feed_reg

EQUATIONS

D0 = I0 & !CS #              "I0 to D0 register.
I0 & CS & !RD #             "I0 to D0 register.
D0 & CS & RD & !A0 #        "Read D0 register.
I0 & CS & RD & A0          "Read I0.
Enable D0 = CS & RD        "Enable onto data-bus.

D1 = I1 & !CS #              "I1 to D1 register.
I1 & CS & !RD #             "I1 to D1 register.
D1 & CS & RD & !A0 #        "Read D1 register.
                                                        2/6
```

Change of state input port with interrupt, Screen 2.

```
I1 & CS & RD & A0              "Read I1.
Enable D1 = CS & RD            "Enable onto data-bus.

D2 = I2 & !CS #                "I2 to D2 register.
I2 & CS & !RD #                "I2 to D2 register.
D2 & CS & RD & !A0 #           "Read D0 register.
I2 & CS & RD & A0              "Read I2.
Enable D2 = CS & RD            "Enable onto data-bus.

D3 = I3 & !CS #                "I3 to D3 register.
I3 & CS & !RD #                "I3 to D3 register.
D3 & CS & RD & !A0 #           "Read D3 register.
I3 & CS & RD & A0              "Read I3.
Enable D3 = CS & RD            "Enable onto data-bus.

D4 = I4 & !CS #                "I4 to D4 register.
I4 & CS & !RD #                "I4 to D4 register.
D4 & CS & RD & !A0 #           "Read D4 register.
I4 & CS & RD & A0              "Read I4.
Enable D4 = CS & RD            "Enable onto data-bus.

D5 = I5 & !CS #                "I1 to D5 register.
I5 & CS & !RD #                "I1 to D5 register.
```

3/6

Change of state input port with interrupt, Screen 3.

```
D5 & CS & RD & !A0 #           "Read D5 register.
I5 & CS & RD & A0              "Read I5.
Enable D5 = CS & RD            "Enable onto data-bus.

D6 = I6 & !CS #                "I6 to D6 register.
I6 & CS & !RD #                "I6 to D6 register.
D6 & CS & RD & !A0 #           "Read D6 register.
I6 & CS & RD & A0              "Read I6.
Enable D6 = CS & RD            "Enable onto data-bus.

D7 = I7 & !CS #                "I7 to D7 register.
I7 & CS & !RD #                "I7 to D7 register.
D7 & CS & RD & !A0 #           "Read D7 register.
I7 & CS & RD & A0              "Read I7.
Enable D7 = CS & RD            "Enable onto data-bus.

NEQ = I0 & !D0 # !I0 & D0 #    "Compare I0-7 with D0-7 registers.
I1 & !D1 # !I1 & D1 #          "NEQ=1 if I0-7 and D0-7 are not equal.
I2 & !D2 # !I2 & D2 #
I3 & !D3 # !I3 & D3 #
I4 & !D4 # !I4 & D4 #
I5 & !D5 # !I5 & D5 #
I6 & !D6 # !I6 & D6 #
I7 & !D7 # !I7 & D7
```

4/6

Change of state input port with interrupt, Screen 4.

```
INTR = NEQ  &  !CS  #      "Latch not-equal status for uP interrupt and
       NEQ  &  !RD  #      "PEEL clock. Clear interrupt when registers
       NEQ  &  A0   #      "are read and there are no more input state
       INTR &  !CS  #      "changes, that is, when NEQ, CS, RD and A0
       INTR &  !RD  #      "are all 0.
       INTR &  A0

(CLK I0 I1 I2 I3 I4 I5 I6 I7 A0 CS RD -> D0 D1 D2 D3 D4 D5 D6 D7 NEQ INTR)

0   0 0 0 0 0 0 0 0 X 0 X ->  Z Z Z Z Z Z Z Z   X   0
0   0 0 0 0 0 0 0 0 1 1 ->  X X X X X X X X   L   0
0   1 0 0 0 0 0 0 0 X 0 0 ->  Z Z Z Z Z Z Z Z   H   H
1   1 0 0 0 0 0 0 0 X 0 0 ->  Z Z Z Z Z Z Z Z   L   H
1   1 0 0 0 0 0 0 0 1 0 ->  Z Z Z Z Z Z Z Z   L   H
1   1 0 0 0 0 0 0 0 1 1 ->  H L L L L L L L   L   L
0   1 0 0 0 0 0 0 0 1 1 ->  H L L L L L L L   L   L
0   1 0 0 0 0 0 0 0 X 0 X ->  Z Z Z Z Z Z Z Z   L   L
0   0 0 0 0 0 0 0 0 X 0 0 ->  Z Z Z Z Z Z Z Z   H   H
1   0 0 0 0 0 0 0 0 X 0 0 ->  Z Z Z Z Z Z Z Z   L   H
1   0 0 0 0 0 0 0 0 1 0 ->  Z Z Z Z Z Z Z Z   L   H
1   0 0 0 0 0 0 0 0 1 1 ->  L L L L L L L L   L   L
0   0 0 0 0 0 0 0 0 X 0 X ->  Z Z Z Z Z Z Z Z   L   L
0   1 0 0 0 0 0 0 0 X 0 X ->  Z Z Z Z Z Z Z Z   H   H
1   1 0 0 0 0 0 0 0 X 0 X ->  Z Z Z Z Z Z Z Z   L   H
                                                        5/6
```

Change of state input port with interrupt, Screen 5.

```
1   1 1 1 1 1 1 1 1 X 0 0 ->  Z Z Z Z Z Z Z Z   H   H
1   1 1 1 1 1 1 1 1 0 1 0 ->  Z Z Z Z Z Z Z Z   H   H
1   1 1 1 1 1 1 1 1 0 1 1 ->  H L L L L L L L   H   L
0   1 1 1 1 1 1 1 1 X 0 0 ->  Z Z Z Z Z Z Z Z   H   H
1   1 1 1 1 1 1 1 1 0 1 0 ->  Z Z Z Z Z Z Z Z   L   H
1   1 1 1 1 1 1 1 1 0 1 1 ->  H H H H H H H H   L   L
0   1 1 1 1 1 1 1 1 X 0 X ->  Z Z Z Z Z Z Z Z   L   L
0   0 0 0 0 0 0 0 0 X 0 X ->  Z Z Z Z Z Z Z Z   H   H
1   0 0 0 0 0 0 0 0 X 0 X ->  Z Z Z Z Z Z Z Z   L   H
1   0 0 0 0 0 0 0 0 1 1 ->  L L L L L L L L   L   L
0   0 0 0 0 0 0 0 0 X 0 X ->  Z Z Z Z Z Z Z Z   L   L

(CLK I0 I1 I2 I3 I4 I5 I6 I7 A0 CS RD -> D0 D1 D2 D3 D4 D5 D6 D7 NEQ INTR)

0   1 0 1 0 1 0 1 0 X 0 X ->  Z Z Z Z Z Z Z Z   H   H
1   1 0 1 0 1 0 1 0 1 0 X ->  X X X X X X X X   L   H
1   1 0 1 0 1 0 1 0 1 1 ->  H L H L H L H L   L   H
1   0 1 0 1 0 1 0 1 1 0 X ->  Z Z Z Z Z Z Z Z   H   H
1   0 1 0 1 0 1 0 1 1 1 1 ->  L H L H L H L H   H   H
1   0 1 0 1 0 1 0 1 X 0 X ->  Z Z Z Z Z Z Z Z   H   H
1   0 1 0 1 0 1 0 1 0 1 1 ->  H L H L H L H L   H   L
0   0 1 0  0 1 0 1 X 0 X ->  Z Z Z Z Z Z Z Z   H   H
1   0 1 0 1 0 1 0 1 X 0 X ->  Z Z Z Z Z Z Z Z   L   H
1   0 1 0 1 0 1 0 1 0 1 1 ->  L H L H L H L H   L   L
0   0 1 0 1 0 1 0 1 0 0 X ->  Z Z Z Z Z Z Z Z   L   L
                                                        6/6
```

COURTESY OF INTERNATIONAL CMOS TECHNOLOGY, INC.

Change of state input port with interrupt, Screen 6.

8-TO-1 MULTIPLEXER

Courtesy of International CMOS Technology, Inc.

This application implements an 8-to-1 multiplexer that can be interfaced to a microprocessor bus. Any one of the 8 inputs (0-7) can be selectively routed to the output (OUT) by writing (/WR and /CS = 0) a 3-bit binary value to the data inputs (DI0-2). The value is stored into a 3-bit latch that controls the multiplexer selection. Because the latch utilizes internal asynchronous feedback (macro configuration #8), the value can also be enabled onto the data outputs (DOO-2). The DI and DO (0-2) pins should be tied together for write/read bus operation. The truth table for the mux is depicted via the test vectors. This application example was implemented using the APEEL PLD Development System. Screens 1 through 7 present the displays. The logic diagram is given in FIG. 6-20.

```
TITLE 'APEEL FILE:  PEEL18CV8 BUS PROGRAMMABLE 8 TO 1 MUX
DESIGNER:  Robin Jigour ICT
DATE:  9/13/87'


PEEL18CV8


"DESCRIPTION"
"                      PEEL18CV8


"       Bus Programmable 8 TO 1 Multiplexer
"
"             ___  ___
"              I    I
"       I0    ( 1   20 )  Vcc
"       I1    ( 2   19 ) - I5
"       I2    ( 3   18 ) - I6
"       I3    ( 4   17 ) - I7       ( - = output )
"       I4    ( 5   16 ) - OUT
"       DI0   ( 6   15 ) - DO0
"       DI1   ( 7   14 ) - DO1
"       DI2   ( 8   13 ) - DO2
"       /WR   ( 9   12 ) - /RD
"       Gnd   (10   11 ) - CS
"              I_____I
                                               1/7
```

Bus programmable 8-to-1 multiplexer, Screen 1.

```
EQUATIONS

"Clock Divider

SP  =  SET              "If SET = 1 set all CLK outputs high

CLK2  :=  !CLK2         "CLK divided by 2

CLK4  :=  !CLK4  &  CLK2  #      "CLK divided by 4
          CLK4  &  !CLK2

CLK8  :=  !CLK8  &  CLK4  &  CLK2  #    "CLK divided by 8
          CLK8  &  !CLK4  #
          CLK8  &  !CLK2

"Address Decoder (active low outputs)

SRAM  =  ( !A15 & !A14 & !A13 )

PORT  =  !( !A15 & !A14 & !A13 & !A12 & !A11 & !A10 & !A09 & !A08 )

UART  =  !( !A15 & A14 & !A13 & !A12 & A11 & !A10 & !A09 & A08 )

EEPROM = !( !A15 & A14 & !A13 & A12 & !A11 )

                                                          2/7
```

Bus programmable 8-to-1 multiplexer, Screen 2.

```
EPROM  =  !( !A15 )

( CLK  SET  ->  CLK8  CLK4  CLK2 )

C   1   ->    H     H     H
C   0   ->    L     L     L
C   0   ->    L     L     H
C   0   ->    L     H     L
C   0   ->    L     H     H
C   0   ->    H     H     L
C   0   ->    H     L     H
C   0   ->    H     H     L
C   0   ->    H     H     H
C   0   ->    L     L     L

( A15  A14  A13  A12  A11  A10  A09  A08  ->  EPROM  EEPROM  UART
PORT  SRAM)

0   0   0   X   X   X   X   X  ->   H      H     H    H   L
0   0   1   X   X   X   X   X  ->   H      H     H    H   H
0   1   0   0   0   0   0   0  ->   H      H     H    L   H
0   1   0   0   0   0   0   1  ->   H      H     L    H   H
0   1   0   1   0   X   X   X  ->   H      L     H    H   H
                                                          3/7
```

Bus programmable 8-to-1 multiplexer, Screen 3.

```
0   1   1   0   X   X   X   X  ->   H     H   H   H   H
1   X   X   X   X   X   X   X  ->   L     H   H   H   H

"PIN DEFINITIONS"

"Inputs"


I0              pin 1
I1              pin 2
I2              pin 3
I3              pin 4
I4              pin 5
DI0             pin 6
DI1             pin 7
DI2             pin 8
!WR             pin 9
!CS             pin 11
!RD             pin 12  =  pos com feed_pin   "use as inputs only
I7              pin 17  =  pos com feed_pin
I6              pin 18  =  pos com feed_pin
I5              pin 19  =  pos com feed_pin
.
                                                          4/7
```

Bus programmable 8-to-1 multiplexer, Screen 4.

```
"Outputs"

DO2     pin 13  =  pos com feed_or    "internal feedback
DO1     pin 14  =  pos com feed_or
DO0     pin 15  =  pos com feed_or
MOUT    pin 16  =  pos com feed_pin

EQUATIONS

D0  =       DI0 & WR & CS #    "set D0 latch from bus write
            DO0 & !WR #                "hold when not selected
            DO0 & !CS #
            DI0 & DO0 "prevent hazard"
            Enable DO0 = RD & CS        "Enable D0 output with bus read

D1  =       DI1 & WR & CS #    "set D1 latch from bus write
            DO1 & !WR #                "hold when not selected
            DO1 & !CS #
            DI1 & DO1 "prevent hazard"
            Enable DO1 = RD & CS        "Enable D1 output with bus read

D2  =       DI2 & WR & CS #    "set D2 latch from bus write
            DO2 & !WR #                "hold when not selected
                                                          5/7
```

Bus programmable 8-to-1 multiplexer, Screen 5.

```
                   DO2  & !CS  #
                   DI2  & DO2  "prevent hazard"
                   Enable DO2  =  RD  &  CS       "Enable D2 output with bus
                   read

     MOUT =    I0  &  !DO2  &  !DO1  &  !DO0  #    "Select I0 when D0-2 = 0
               I1  &  !DO2  &  !DO1  &   DO0  #    "Select I1 when D0-2 = 1
               I2  &  !DO2  &   DO1  &  !DO0  #    "Select I2 when D0-2 = 2
               I3  &  !DO2  &   DO1  &   DO0  #    "Select I3 when D0-2 = 3
               I4  &   DO2  &  !DO1  &  !DO0  #    "Select I4 when D0-2 = 4
               I5  &   DO2  &  !DO1  &   DO0  #    "Select I5 when D0-2 = 5
               I6  &   DO2  &   DO1  &  !DO0  #    "Select I6 when D0-2 = 6
               I7  &   DO2  &   DO1  &   DO0  #    "Select I7 when D0-2 = 7


     ( I0 I1 I2 I3 I4 I5 I6 I7  DI2 DI1 DI0  CS WR RD  ->  DO2 DO1 DO0 MOUT )

     1 0 0 0 0 0 0 0   0 0 0   1 1 1  ->   Z  Z  Z  H
     1 0 0 0 0 0 0 0   0 0 0   0 0 0  ->   Z  Z  Z  H
     0 0 0 0 0 0 0 0   X X X   0 0 0  ->   Z  Z  Z  L
     1 0 0 0 0 0 0 0   X X X   0 0 0  ->   L  L  L  H

                                                             6/7
```

Bus programmable 8-to-1 multiplexer, Screen 6.

```
     0 0 1 0 0 0 0 0   0 1 0   1 1 0  ->   Z  Z  Z  H
     0 0 1 0 0 0 0 0   0 1 0   0 0 0  ->   Z  Z  Z  H
     0 0 0 0 0 0 0 0   X X X   0 0 0  ->   Z  Z  Z  L
     0 0 1 0 0 0 0 0   X X X   1 0 1  ->   L  H  L  H

     0 0 0 0 0 1 0 0   1 0 1   1 1 0  ->   Z  Z  Z  H
     1 0 0 0 0 1 0 0   1 0 1   0 0 0  ->   Z  Z  Z  H
     0 0 0 0 0 0 0 0   X X X   0 0 0  ->   Z  Z  Z  L
     0 0 0 0 0 1 0 0   X X X   1 0 1  ->   H  L  H  H

     0 0 0 0 0 0 0 1   1 1 1   1 1 0  ->   Z  Z  Z  H
     0 0 0 0 0 0 0 1   1 1 1   0 0 0  ->   Z  Z  Z  H
     0 0 0 0 0 0 0 0   X X X   0 0 0  ->   Z  Z  Z  L
     0 0 0 0 0 0 0 1   X X X   1 0 1  ->   H  H  H  H






                                                             7/7
```

COURTESY OF INTERNATIONAL CMOS TECHNOLOGY, INC.

Bus programmable 8-to-1 multiplexer, Screen 7.

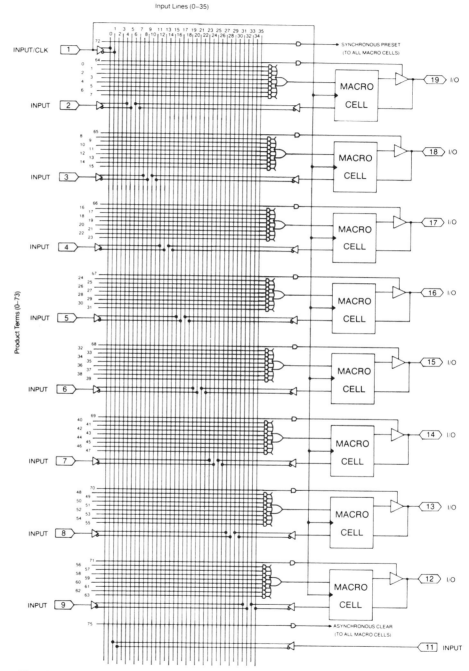

Fig. 6-20. PEEL 18CV8 logic diagram. Courtesy of International CMOS Technology, Inc.

EP1800 AS A BAR CODE DECODER
Courtesy of Altera Corporation

Bar code is a binary representation of data or program information. It has become an alternative to traditional forms of data entry. It compares well against optical character recognition for success on a first-time read. It is flexible and inexpensive and suits many applications where magnetic strip or other media would be impractical. Bar codes can come in many flavors; this application brief covers a vanilla version with some advanced features. The block diagram is given in FIG. 6-21.

Physical Specifications of Bar Code

Although many versions of bar code exist to support the variety of applications served, there is enough in common to treat a meaningful generic case. All bar codes have a header and tail sequence. They have a 0 and 1 character and a space character. The 0 and space character are the same width, while the 1 is twice that width. The header is a zero-zero combination, followed by a checksum byte. The tail is a one-zero byte. The number of bytes that can go between FIG. 6-22 are limited.

Bar Code Decoder Overview

The Bar Code Decoder consists of 5 different modules—a controller state machine, a sync counter, a byte counter, a shift register, and a microprocessor interface.

Sync Counter Specification. The sync counter serves to synchronize the reading of data. The width of the bar is timed and stored in a register. The counter is then down counted. When it reaches zero, it flags the state controller and reloads a latched count value. The count value should be half the max count value. This assures that the date is not read at the edge of the incoming data, but in the middle, providing greater noise immunity.

Byte Counter Specification. This is a glitch-free circuit that alerts the processor when 8 bits have been shifted in. Because it is a glitch-free counter, it has been implemented as gray code in a state machine format.

Shift Register Specification. The shift register loads in the synchronized data stream.

Macroprocessor Interface Specification. This consists of an open collector interrupt back to the processor for byte detection, and status bits for active read, direction, and header validity.

State Controller Specification. A state graph for the state controller is shown (FIG. 6-23). The algorithm is as follows:

- IDLE—the machine idles until a dark region is read by the input device (pen) at which time the sync counter is started.
- SYNC—the sync counter counts up while in this state. The machine stays in this state until reading the first light region. The count corresponds to the width of the first dark bar.

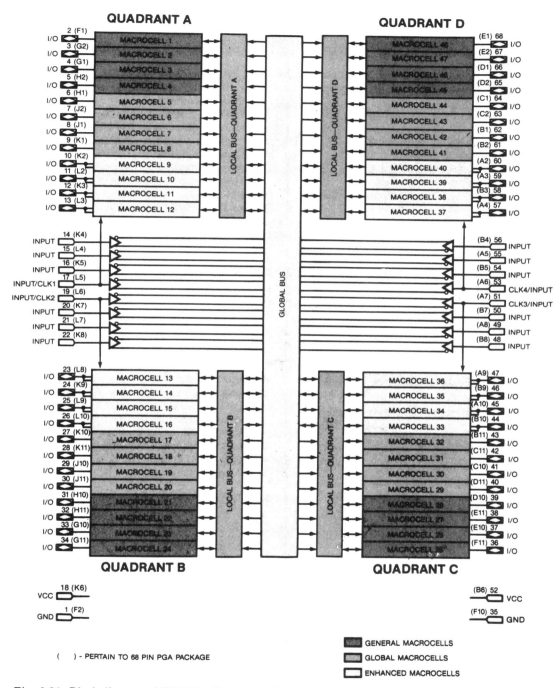

Fig. 6-21. Block diagram of EP1800. Courtesy of Altera Corporation.

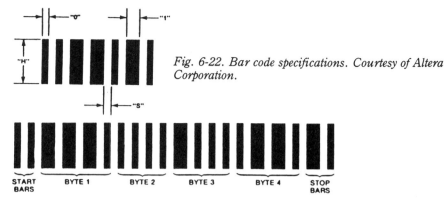

Fig. 6-22. Bar code specifications. Courtesy of Altera Corporation.

- LATCH—the machine latches the count value into a holding register. Hereafter, the sync count expires on every modulus of the latched count and cause the reading of the input stream.
- HDR1, HDR2, FWD, REV, ERR—the machine begins reading the rest of the header bits. Bear in mind that you get two different sequences depending if you read a 0-0 sequence or a 0-1 sequence. The 0-0 sequence is a forward read, while a 0-1 sequence is a backward read. If there are any improper reads, you will go to ERR. Direction status is latched dependent on either state FWD or REV. At the end of this, begin the reading of data and checksum bytes into the shift register.
- ACT1, ACT2, ACT3, ACT4—these are the active reading states. The ACT1-ACT3 loop indicates a zero was read. The ACT1-ACT2-ACT4 loop corresponds to the reading of a one. Reading is stopped when a long white space is read indicating the end of the bar code.

Implementation of the Bar Code Decoder

Figure 6-24 shows a LogiCaps schematic of the Bar Code Decoder. The sync counter is implemented by four MacroFunctions (8COUNT, 2 of 74157S, and the 74374) and terminal count circuitry comprised of logic and an NOCF primitive. The byte counter is implemented in state machine format in a file named GRAY3.SMF (Screen 1 and top of Screen 2). The shift register is implemented with MacroFunction 74164 and CONF output primitives. The microprocessor interface consists of a CONF configured as an open collector output and status flags implemented by SONF and RORF primitives. The state controller was implemented in a state machine file named BARCTL.SMF (Screens 2 through 5). The state machines are outlined on the schematic for documentation purposes only. The borders are not required for design processing.

Processing the Design

Design input is contained in three separate files with two different formats. LogiCaps generates the BAR.ADF file, whereas BARCTL.SMF and GRAY-3.SMF are state machine files. Linking all the design information is done in the

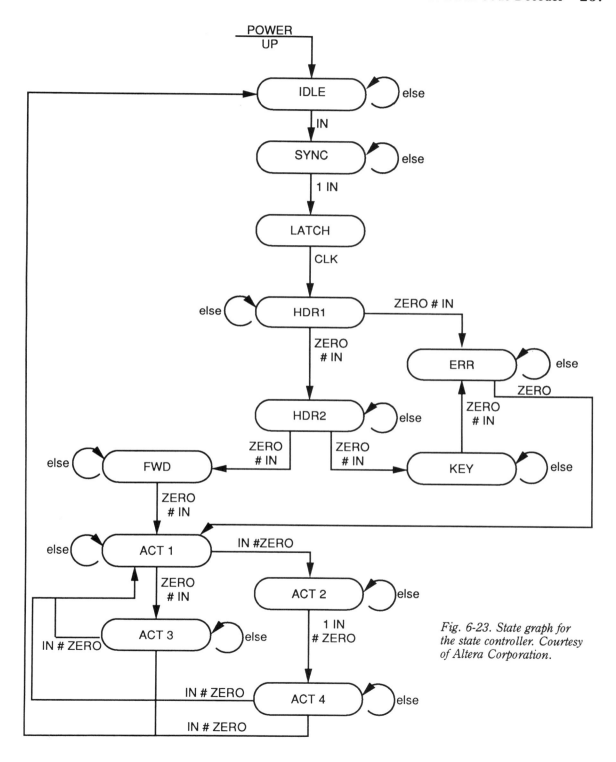

Fig. 6-23. State graph for the state controller. Courtesy of Altera Corporation.

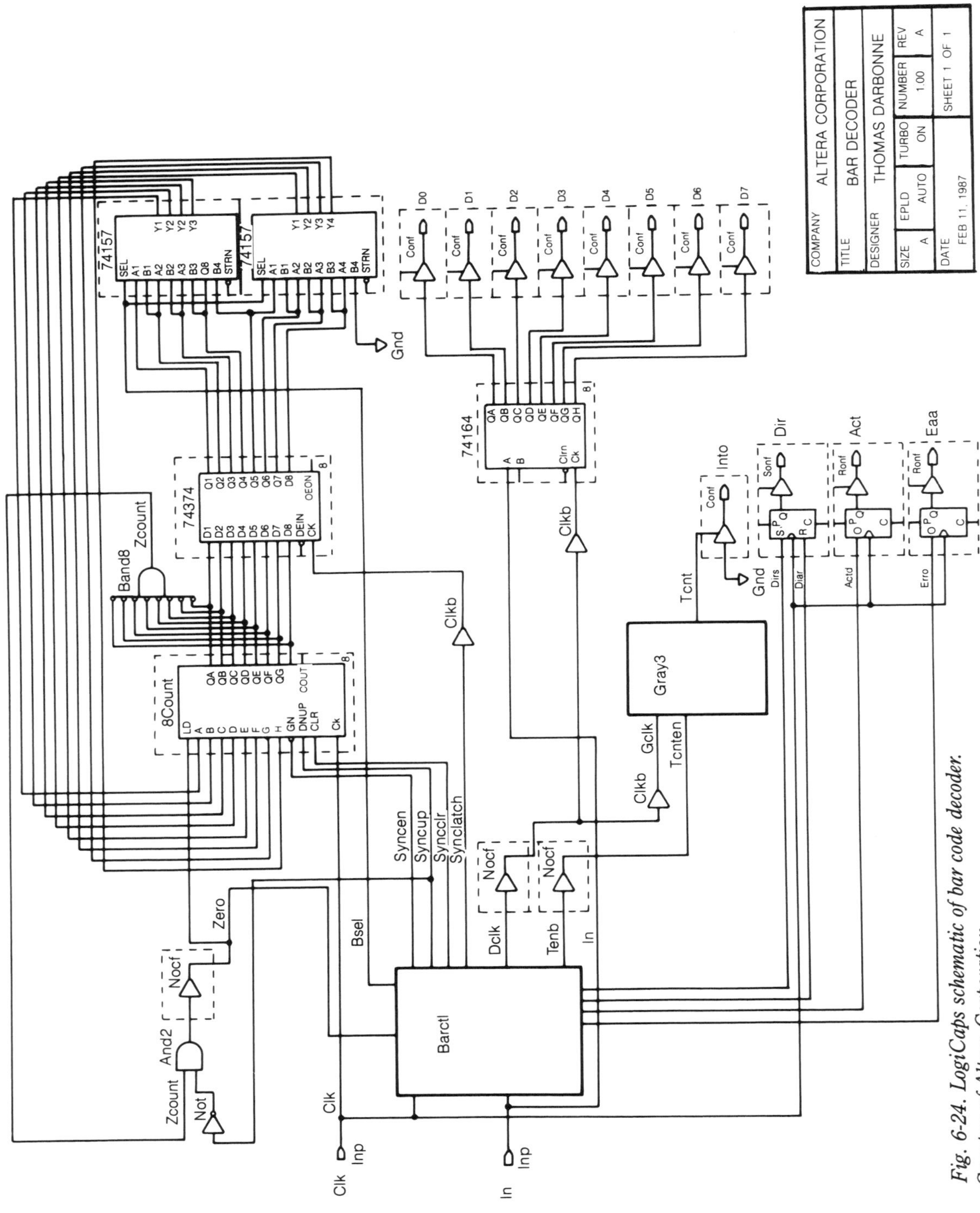

Fig. 6-24. LogiCaps schematic of bar code decoder. Courtesy of Altera Corporation.

```
% GRAY3 3 BIT GRAY COUNTER 5
PART: EP1800J
INPUTS:
OUTPUTS:
NETWORK:
EQUATIONS:
TCNT = TCNTEN*/G2*/G1*/G0;

MACHINE: GRAY3
CLOCK: GCLK
STATES: [ G2  G1  G0]
S0    [ 0   0   0]
S1    [ 0   0   0]
S2    [ 0   1   1]
S3    [ 0   1   0]
S4    [ 1   1   0]
S5    [ 1   1   1]
S6    [ 1   0   1]
S7    [ 1   0   0]

S0:  S1
S1:  S2
S2:  S3
```

1/5

EPB1800 as a bar code decoder, Screen 1.

```
S3:  S4
S4:  S5
S5:  S6
S6:  S7
S7:  S0

END$
% Bar Code Controller %
PART: EP1800J
INPUTS:
OUTPUTS:
NETWORK:
EQUATIONS:
    DIRS = FWD;
    DIRR = IDLE;
    ACTD = !IDLE;
    ERRD = ERR * !IDLE;
    SYNCCLR = IDLE * /IN;
    SYNCEN  = SYNC;
    SYNCEN  = IDLE;
    SYNCLATCH = LATCH;
    DCLK = ACT2 + ACT3;
    TENB = ACT2 + ACT3 + ACT4;
```

2/5

EPB1800 as a bar code decoder, Screen 2.

```
        BSEL = /LATCH;

    MACHINE: BARCTL
        CLOCK: CLK
        STATES: [ Q3  Q2  Q1  Q0]
        IDLE   [ 0   0   0   0]
        SYNC   [ 1   0   0   1]
        LATCH  [ 0   1   1   1]
        HDR1   [ 1   0   1   1]
        HDR2   [ 1   1   1   1]
        FWD    [ 0   1   0   1]
        REV    [ 0   1   1   0]
        ACT1   [ 0   1   0   0]
        ACT2   [ 1   1   0   0]
        ACT3   [ 0   0   1   0]
        ACT4   [ 0   0   1   1]
        ERR    [ 1   1   1   0]

    IDLE:
    IF  IN THEN SYNC
    SYNC:
    IF /IN THEN LATCH
    LATCH:
                                            3/5
```

EPB1800 as a bar code decoder, Screen 3.

```
    HDRL
    HDR1:
    IF IN*ZERO THEN HDR2
    IF /IN*ZERO THEN ERR
    HDR2:
    IF IN * ZERO THEN REV
    IF /IN * ZERO THEN ACT 1
    FWD:
    IF ZERO THEN ACT 1
    REV:
    IF IN * ZERO THEN ERR
    IF /IN * ZERO THEN ACT 1
    ACT1:
    IF IN * ZERO THEN ACT 2
    IF /IN * ZERO THEN ACT 3
    ACT2:
    IF IN * ZERO THEN ERR
    IF /IN * ZERO THEN ACT 4
    ACT3:
    IF IN * ZERO THEN ACT 1
    IF /IN * ZERO THEN IDLE
    ACT4:
    IF IN * ZERO THEN ACT 1
                                            4/5
```

EPB1800 as a bar code decoder, Screen 4.

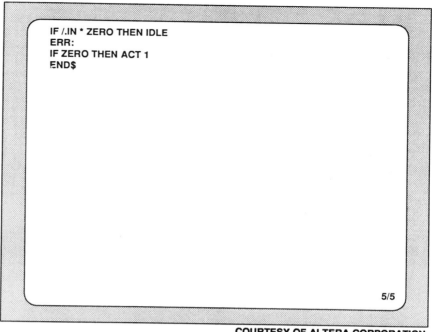

```
IF /.IN * ZERO THEN IDLE
ERR:
IF ZERO THEN ACT 1
END$
```

5/5

COURTESY OF ALTERA CORPORATION

EPB1800 as a bar code decoder, Screen 5.

Fig. 6-25. A + Plus Altera design processor menu. Courtesy of Altera Corporation.

FORMAT	: Adf
FILE NAME	: bar, barctl.smf, gray3.smf
NIN	: yes
INV CTL	: no
LEF ANAL	: yes

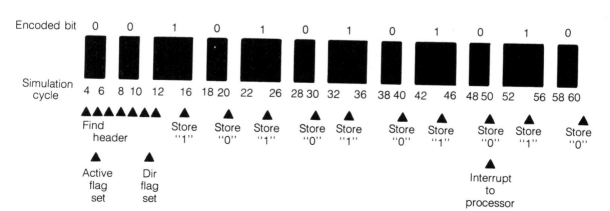

Fig. 6-26. Anticipated simulation data. Courtesy of Altera Corporation.

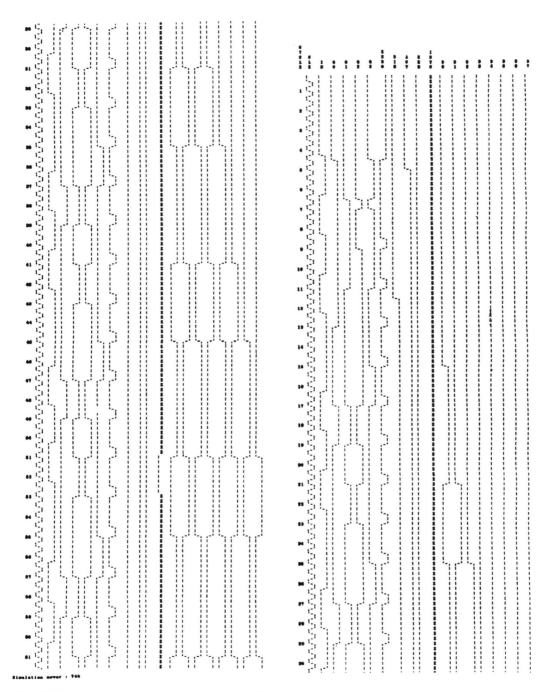

Fig. 6-27. Actual simulation data. Courtesy of Altera Corporation.

Altera Design Processor (ADP) section of the A + PLUS development software. This is done by answering all the prompts as shown in FIG. 6-25. The ADP automatically links the names between the various input files and creates an output file BAR.JED for device programming. Device utilization, given after processing, indicated that 38 of the 48 macrocells were used, 2 of the 7 inputs, and 36% of the available logic.

Simulation Verifies Operation before Programming a Device

Altera's PLFSIM simulated the device to assure proper operation. In this instance, a serial input stream corresponding to a valid bit stream is read by the design. It properly sequences through the states, latches the data, and interrupts a processor. The anticipated simulation data is shown in FIG. 6-26. The controller state machine is verified by comparing the Q0-Q3 outputs, and the state table values in Screen 3. The actual simulation run is shown in FIG. 6-27.

EPB1400 HIGH-PERFORMANCE PERIPHERAL DMA
Courtesy of Altera Corporation

A Direct Memory Access Controller (DMA) coordinates high-speed data transfer, typically between system memory and a peripheral subsystem or memory. DMA is used when faster data transfer rates are required than possible under processor control. For example, disk controller must upload or download buffered data from system memory synchronized with disk rotations at a fixed disk data rate. Graphics processors, which must directly update images stored within video memory in real time, also find DMA useful. High speed serial subsystems often require DMA to maintain communications link bit rates. This example focuses on a peripheral subsystem DMA Controller designed to transfer data between a peripheral device and buffer memory at data rates up to 30 Megawords/second.

Many different hardware DMA Controller implementations exist. Standard microprocessor peripheral DMA Controllers exist (e.g., Intel 8237), but might be unsuitable for speed, power consumption, or architectural reasons. The 8237 transfers data at 1.5 Mb/s and consumes 1.5 watts of power. If performance requirements are greater or specialized functions are required, you can design a DMA Controller with standard MSI TTL components (7400 series). This allows custom DMA protocols and higher performance, but MSI solutions have high power consumption and low integration density. The amount of PC board real estate consumed usually precludes this approach.

High-density programmable logic offers a better mix of performance, integration density, power consumption, and flexibility. This example illustrates a generic DMA Controller using the Altera EPB1400, a function-specific EPLD optimized for high-performance custom peripheral applications. Using the EPB1400, data transfer rates up to 30 MHz are possible between peripheral and memory with power consumption less than 600 mW.

Three major functional blocks of the DMA described here are the bus interface unit, DMA unit, and DMA control state machine. The block diagram is given in FIG. 6-28. The detailed implementation of each functional block is also presented. Finally, expected system performance is shown, together with critical timing considerations. The EPB1400 data sheet can be obtained from the Altera Corporation for details concerning device architecture and performance.

The DMA Process

Figure 6-29 shows a typical peripheral DMA controller application. The peripheral subsystem attaches to the main system address, data, and control buses. Within the peripheral subsystem is an MPU (microprocessor unit or microcontroller), buffer memory, DMA controller, and a peripheral. If an MPU is not present in the peripheral subsystem, the system CPU will provide buffer memory control and all other functions normally provided by the peripheral MPU. The DMA controller allows the peripheral to perform high speed data transfers by giving direct access to buffer memory. The DMA controller seizes

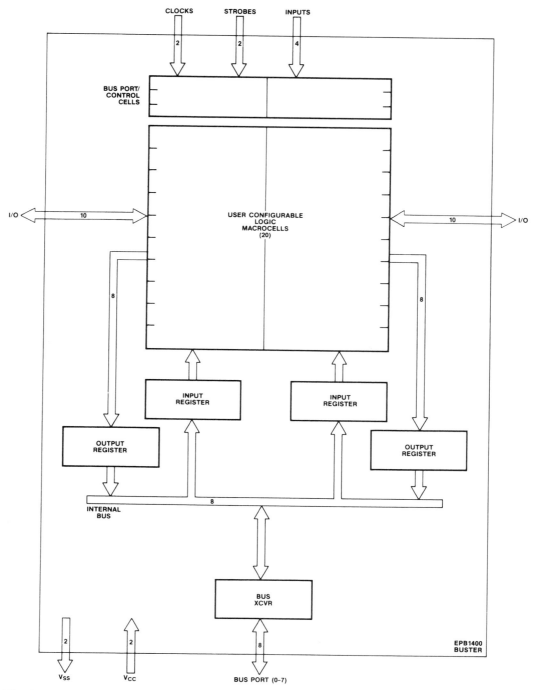

Fig. 6-28. Block diagram of EPB1400. Courtesy of Altera Corporation.

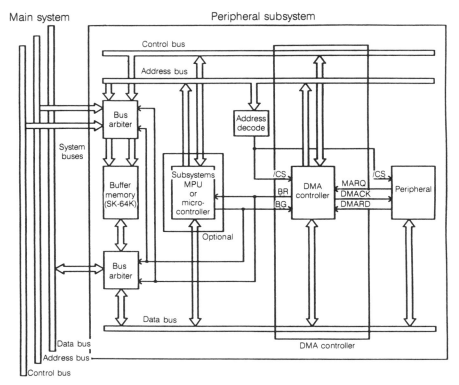

Fig. 6-29. System block diagram. Courtesy of Altera Corporation.

control of the MPU bus, performs the data transfer between the peripheral and buffer memory, and returns bus control to the MPU after each transfer is complete. Usually a high-performance, costly MPU is used in high-performance peripheral subsystems merely to support the buffer data rate. The dedicated, custom DMA using an EPB1400 can often eliminate the need for an MPU in this subsystem, or replace an expensive microprocessor with a low cost microcontroller.

The peripheral/DMA controller interface is implemented with a control handshake using the DMARQ (DMA request), DMACK (DMA acknowledge), and DMARD (DMA red) control signals (see FIG. 6-30). The peripheral generates DMARQ, indicating a requirement to either read or write to buffer memory. DMARD is a control signal sent from the peripheral and informs the DMA controller whether the DMA transfer is read or write to buffer memory. If DMARD is high, the current DMA cycle writes to memory. If the peripheral device does not provide a DMARD signal, one of the bits in the control register located in the bus interface unit can serve as DMARD. DMACK acknowledges DMARQ and informs the peripheral that bus control has been acquired from the MPU (or system CPU if an MPU is not present), and the DMA cycle can begin.

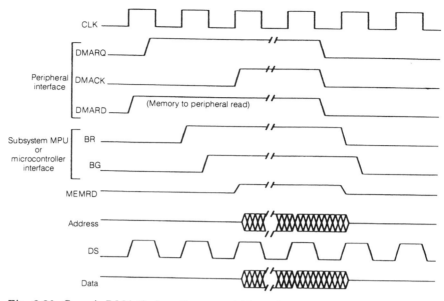

Fig. 6-30. Generic DMA timing. Courtesy of Altera Corporation.

To perform the DMA transfer, the peripheral places a new data word on the bus (write operation), or reads a data word off of the bus (read operation), on every subsequent clock cycle until all data words have been transferred.

The MPU/DMA controller interface uses a control handshake that coordinates the acquisition and eventual release of the bus. During the DMA cycle the DMA controller must acquire bus control from the MPU, provide the control for the data transfer, and restore control back to the MPU. The MPU/DMA controller interface (see FIG. 6-30) requires two signals to acquire bus control from the MPU: BR (Bus Request) and BG (Bus Grant). The DMA controller asserts BR high requesting bus control from the MPU. The MPU should release control of the buses by tristating its bus drivers and suspending bus operations. When the MPU is ready to relinquish control, it asserts BG high, indicating to the DMA controller that it has released control of the buses.

The DMA controller must drive the control and address buses to perform data transfer across the data bus. MEMRD (memory read) is control bus signal that indicates if a given transfer is read (MEMRD high) or write (MEMRD low). DS (Data Strobe) is another control bus signal, driven by the system clock signal (see FIG. 6-30) which strobes the data between the peripheral and memory during the DMA transfer. The DMA controller drives MEMRD with the same logic level as DMARD. The address bus is simultaneously driven by the DMA controller with the desired memory addresses. On every rising edge of DS, the DMA controller drives a new address and another word of data is transferred. When the transfer is complete, the DMA controller relinquishes bus control to the MPU.

Relinquishing bus control begins with the DMA controller negating the BR (Bus Request) signal, thus informing the MPU that it is finished with the bus. Simultaneously, the ADDRESS <0..10> and MEMRD signals are tristated. Control passes back to the MPU, which resumes execution from its previous state.

EPB1400-Based DMA Controller

Figure 6-31 shows the generic DMA Controller implemented using an EPB1400 and an external byte-wide address register with tristable outputs such as a 74LS374. The DMA controller supports a 16-bit address bus, although wider address buses are easily supported by adding external address registers. The external address register latches the upper 5 bits of the DMA transfer address, while the EPB1400 generates the low order 11 bits. The 11 bits allows DMA transfers of up to 2K words without processor intervention. The EPB1400 controls the external address register from its LDHIGH (load external address register) and ENHIGH (enable external address register) signals. LDHIGH enables the external address register to latch the upper byte of the address bus. ENHIGH enables the external address register to drive its contents onto the address bus.

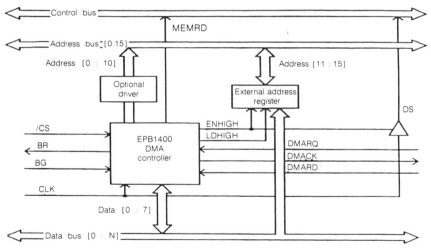

Fig. 6-31. DMA controller block diagram. Courtesy of Altera Corporation.

Figure 6-32 shows the functional block diagram of the EPB1400 used in the DMA controller. The EPB1400 contains the bus interface unit, the DMA unit, and the DMA control state machine.

Bus Interface Unit. Figure 6-33 details the contents of the EPB1400 bus interface unit showing the control registers, status registers, decoder, and transceiver. The microprocessor communicates with the bus interface unit to initialize and enable the EPB1400. Before initialization, the MPU must address the EPB1400 by driving /CS (Chip Select, active low) low. Then the MPU

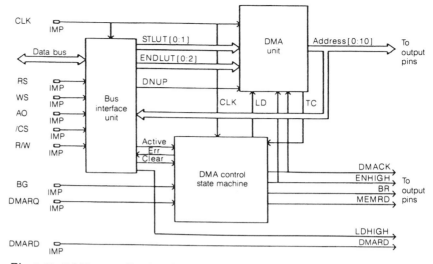

Fig. 6-32. DMA controller functional block diagram. Courtesy of Altera Corpora-tion.

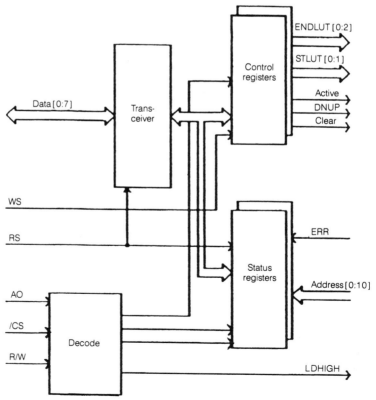

Fig. 6-33. DMA bus structure. Courtesy of Altera Corporation.

sends the EPB1400 two bytes. The first initialization byte writes to the control registers of the EPB1400, and the second writes to the external address register. The MPU relies on the address information contained in TABLE 6-3 to select among these registers.

Table 6-3. Bus interface address mapping.

RS	WS	CS	R/W	AO	Action
↑	x	0	1	0	Read status register 1
↑	x	0	1	1	Read status register 2
x	↑	0	0	0	Write control registers 1 & 2
x	x	0	0	1	Write high address bits (LDHIGH)

To write data to the EPB1400, the appropriate register must first be selected (see TABLE 6-3). The R/W (read/write) signal is driven low for a write cycle, indicating a data transfer from the MPU to the DMA controller. When the address bus matches the DMA controller address, the external address decoder (not shown) drives /CS low which enables the EPB1400 for the write operation. When the WS (Write Strobe) is driven high and the control registers selected, the data bus value is written into both EPB1400 control registers or the external address register.

The control registers are specific in Screen 1. Bit 0 is an enable/disable bit for the DMA controller function. If set, the EPB1400 responds to subsequent, DMA requests, otherwise the EBP1400 remains idle. Bits 1, 2, and 3 select the ending address from eight pre-programmed addresses. Bits 4 and 5 select the starting address from four pre-programmed values. Bit 6 determines whether the address is generated in ascending or descending order. Bit 7 resets an error condition set during DMA operation.

Two status registers in the EPB1400 (shown at the bottom of Screen 1 and terminating in Screen 2) allow the MPU to access the current address and error condition. Status register 1 contains the error condition bit (set if an error has occurred) for unused bits, and the counter value bits. Status register 2 contains the remaining counter value bits.

Detailed Bus Interface Unit. Figure 6-34 shows the detailed design of the bus interface unit. The transceiver function is implemented with a BUSX primitive, a dedicated byte-wide bus transceiver built into the EPB1400. The BUSX symbol is connected to two RBUSI input register primitives and two LBUSO output latch primitives, all of which are dedicated register functions built into the EPB1400. All five resources are connected together by an internal byte-wide bus. The RBUSI primitives implement the control registers while the LBUSO primitives implement the status registers. The low order data byte from the system data bus is connected to the BUSX transceiver, allowing the MPU to access the control and status registers. Access to the functions is dictated by the decoder circuitry included in FIG. 6-34, located below the BUSX primitive, and by the values of the dedicated RS and WS strobes.

Bit 0	ACTIVE	enable/disable DMA
Bit 1	ENDLUT [0]	irst bit of ending address select
Bit 2	ENDLUT [1]	second bit of ending address select
Bit 3	ENDLUT [2]	third bit of ending address select
Bit 4	STLUT [0]	first bit of starting addressselect
Bit 5	STLUT [1]	second bit of starting addressselect
Bit 6	DNUP	count up/down bit (1 = count up)
Bit 7	CLEAR	resets DMA State Machine

Bit 0	ACTIVE	enable/disable DMA
Bit 1	ENDLUT [0]	First bit of ending address select
Bit 2	ENDLUT [1]	second bit of ending address select
Bit 3	ENDLUT [2]	third bit of ending address select
Bit 4	STLUT [0]	first bit of starting addressselect
Bit 5	STLUT [1]	second bit of starting addressselect
Bit 6	DNUP	count up/down bit (1 = count up)
Bit 7	CLEAR	resets DMA State Machine

Status Register 1
Bit 0 ERR Current error condition
Bit 1 -Unused-

1/5

EPB1400 high performance peripheral DMA Controller, Screen 1.

Bit 2	-Unused-	
Bit 3	-Unused-	
Bit 4	-Unused-	
Bit 5	ADDRESS8	Address bit 8
Bit 6	ADDRESS9	Address bit 9
Bit 7	ADDRESS10	Address bit 10

Status Register 2
Bit 0	ADDRESS0	Address bit 0
Bit 1	ADDRESS1	Address bit 1
Bit 2	ADDRESS2	Address bit 2
Bit 3	ADDRESS3	Address bit 3
Bit 4	ADDRESS4	Address bit 4
Bit 5	ADDRESS5	Address bit 5
Bit 6	ADDRESS6	Address bit 6
Bit 7	ADDRESS7	Address bit 7

Address Select   Output Address
Preprogrammed 11 bit
STLUT [0]	STLUT [1]	Starting Address
0	0	starting address #1
0	1	starting address #2

2/5

EPB1400 high performance peripheral DMA Controller, Screen 2.

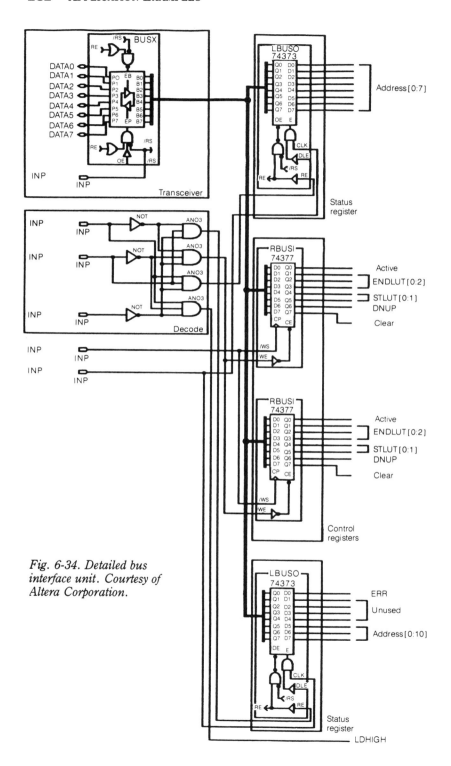

Fig. 6-34. Detailed bus interface unit. Courtesy of Altera Corporation.

DMA Unit. Figure 6-35 shows the architecture of the DMA Unit. This function puts the lower bit of the DMA transfer address on the address bus. The DMA control state machine provides control signals for the DMA unit. The number of addresses to generate is determined by the starting and ending address values as selected by the bus interface unit control registers. Because the starting and ending addresses are pre-programmed instead of read from the MPU, the DMA Controller is able to respond faster to a DMA request. This is very useful for fixed buffer applications, such as disk controllers and communications buffers. Refer to the DMA unit section for details on preprogrammed address implementation. The starting and ending addresses are provided by the ST_LUT (shown at the bottom of Screen 2 and top of Screen 3 respectively) and END_LUT (shown in Screen 3). STLITO [0] and STLUT [1] select one of the four preprogrammed 1-bit starting addresses in the ST_LUT. For example, if STLUT [0] = 0 and STLUT [1] = 1, then starting address #2 would be selected. ENDLUT[0], ENDLUT[1], and ENLUT[2] select one of eight preprogrammed 1-bit addresses in the END_LUT. The CLK signal is driven from the clock pin on the EPB1400 while ENHIGH and DMACK (functioning here as a count enable) come from the control state machine. Once the

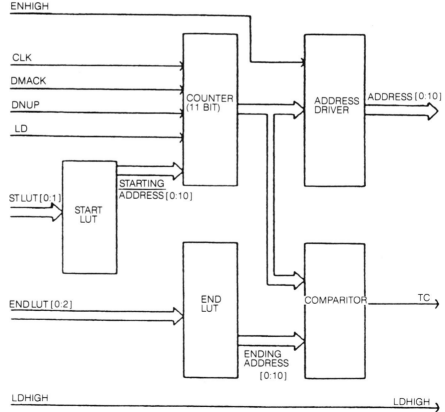

Fig. 6-35. DMA unit functional diagram. Courtesy of Altera Corporation.

1	0		starting address #3	
1	1		starting address #4	

Address Select		Output Address	
Preprogrammed 11 bit			
ENDLUT [0]	ENDLUT [0]	ENDLUT [0]	Ending Address
0	0	0	ending address #1
0	0	1	ending address #2
0	1	0	ending address #3
0	1	1	ending address #4
1	0	0	ending address #5
1	0	1	ending address #6
1	1	0	ending address #7
1	1	1	ending address #8

STATE	DMACK	BR	MEMRD	ERR	LD
INIT	0	0	0	0	0
IDLE	0	0	0	0	1
START	0	1	0	0	0
TRANSFER	1	1	1	0	0
ERROR	0	0	0	1	0

3/5

EPB1400 high performance peripheral DMA Controller, Screen 3.

DMACK and ENHIGH signals are driven high, the addresses are then generated by the counter and driven onto the address bus by the address driver. When the required addresses have been generated, the TC (terminal count) signal becomes active, signifying that the DMA transfer is complete.

Detailed DMA Unit. Figure 6-36 shows the detailed construction of the DMA unit. The counter is implemented with 8COUNT and 4COUNT Macro-Functions. Together, they form a loadable, 11-bit, up/down counter. The up/down control (DNUP) is directly connected to the DNUP control register bit from the bus interface unit. During normal operation the counter is disabled from counting by keeping the /GN input high. When the DMA cycle is initiated, /GN is brought low. This allows the counter to increment or decrement as determined by the value of DNUP on the rising edge of each system clock (CLK).

The value present on the 8COUNTs and 4COUNTs parallel load data input is loaded when the LD (Load) signal is high, and CLK has a rising edge. The value loaded into the counters depends on the starting lookup table ST_LUT (made up of the ST_LUT and ST_LUT4 blocks). The LUT is preprogrammed during the design of the DMA controller. Because all LUT values do not have to be uploaded each time the device is initialized, the initialization of the device is simplified. The lookup table approach works well for peripheral buffers, which usually have block-aligned start and end addresses.

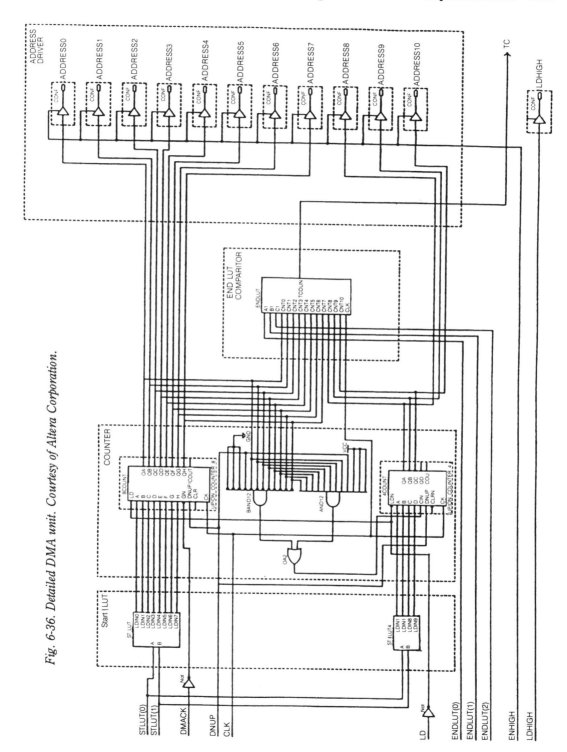

Fig. 6-36. Detailed DMA unit. Courtesy of Altera Corporation.

The address driver is implemented with 11 tristate primitives (CONF). The ENHIGH signal when driven high by the DMA Control State Machine enables the outputs onto the system address bus. The counters generate addresses, while the END_LUT determines the last address to be generated during the DMA cycle. TC (terminal count) goes high when the count value stored in the counter matches the desired ending address value minus 1.

DMA Control State Machine. Figure 6-37 details the EPB1400 control state machine used to coordinate the generation of DMA control signals for both the peripheral and MPU interfaces. The core of this block is a state machine synchronized to the system clock (CLK). The state machine output signals emulate the required control handshaking with the peripheral (DMARQ and DMACK) or with the MPU (BG, BR, MEMRD, ENHIGH). MPU generated initialization and command information is passed to the state machine by the bus interface unit ACTIVE and CLEAR control register bits. State machine error status information is passed back to the bus interface unit by the ERR signal.

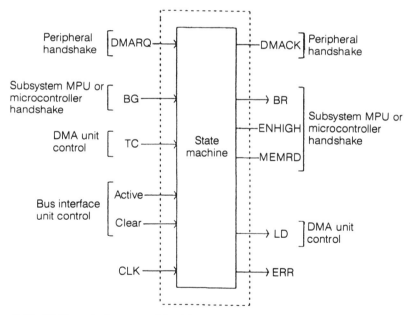

Fig. 6-37. DMA control state machine block diagram. Courtesy of Altera Corporation.

The remaining outputs control the DMA unit, loading the counter (LD), and enabling counter operation (DMACK). The input TC that comes from the DMA Unit, signifies when the specified number of bytes have been transferred using DMA.

A synchronous reset (CLEAR) signal allows the state machine to return to a known power-up site if a fatal error occurs. This signal is provided by the bus interface unit through the control registers and is controlled by the MPU.

Detailed Control State Machine. The control state machine is a synchronous state machine with 6 inputs (ACTIVE, CLK, CLEAR, CMARQ, TC, BG) and 5 state variables (DMACK, BR, MEMRD, ERR, LD). All 5 are used as outputs. One additional output, ENHIGH, is also generated by the state machine. The operation of the state machine is described in detail in the state diagram shown in FIG. 6-38. The state variable assignments are shown at the bottom of Screen 3.

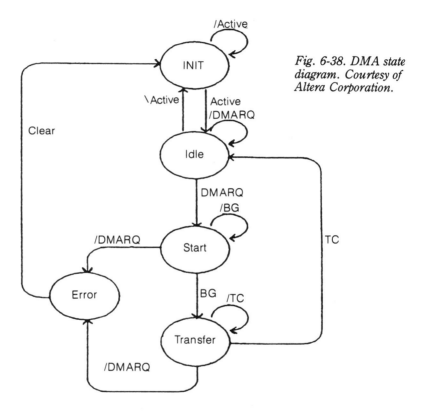

Fig. 6-38. DMA state diagram. Courtesy of Altera Corporation.

The control state machine powers up in the INIT state. If the MPU has set the ACTIVE bit in the control register allowing DMA transfers, the state machine proceeds to the IDLE state. The control state machine remains in IDLE until DMARQ is asserted by the peripheral. When DMARQ is received, the state machine proceeds to START and begins the DMA cycle.

BR, requesting bus control from the MPU, is asserted upon arriving at the START state. The state machine waits for BF, acknowledging bus control from the MPU, before proceeding to the TRANSFER state. In the TRANSFER state, DMACK and MEMRD are driven high. The DMA control state machine transfers all of the required words and jumps back to the IDLE state when TC is received from the DMA unit indicating the completion of the transfer.

An error condition can occur if DMARQ is driven low by the peripheral in the START or TRANSFER states indicating the peripheral has tried to start a new DMA cycle while unfinished with the current one. If this occurs, ERR is driven high and the machine freezes in the ERROR state until the CLEAR signal is asserted by the MPU clearing the error condition.

The state diagram shown in FIG. 6-38 is implemented by the state machine entry file shown in Screens 4 and 5. The state machine together with the bus interface unit and DMA unit schematics are then submitted to Altera's A + Plus Design processor, producing a programming file (JEDEC File) of the complete DMA controller.

Performance

Figure 6-39 shows the critical timing parameters for the DMA controller. The critical parameters are Tdkav (DMACK to first valid address) and Tavaz (the last address valid). Tavav (32ns) shows how quickly the EPB1400 can generate successive addresses, therefore determining the maximum clock rate (31.2 MHz) at which the DMA controller can operate.

The EPB1400 is a function-specific solution capable of implementing a DMA controller for peripheral interfaces. The EPB1400's mix of high-performance dedicated microprocessor interface functions and user-configurable programmable logic core allows the implementation of a customized bus interface

```
Parameter          EPB1400
TDKAV              15AS
TAVAZ              44AS
TAVAV              32AS
TCKAV              20AS


OPTIONS:   SECURITY-OFF
PART:      EP1800J
INPUTS:    TC, CLK, DMARQ, BG,
ACTIVE CLEAR
OUTPUTS:   ENHI, ERR, MEMRD,
DMACK, BR, LD

NETWORK:   ENHI - CONF (ENHIGH. )
EQUATIONS: ENHIGH - DMACK;

MACHINE: DMA - CONTROLLER
CLOCK: CLK
STATES:    [ DMACK  BR  MEMRD  ERR  LD ]
INIT    [ 0   0   0    0   0 ]
IDLE    [ 0   0   0    0   1 ]
START   [ 0   1   0    0   0 ]
                                          4/5
```

EPB1400 high performance peripheral DMA Controller, Screen 4.

```
TRANSFER  [ 1  1  1  0  0 ]
ERROR     [ 0  0  0  1  0 ]

INIT:    IF ACTIVE THEN IDLE
IDLE:    IF DMARQ THEN START
START:   IF BG THEN TRANSFER
IF /DMARQ THEN ERROR
TRANSFER:    IF TC THEN IDLE
IF /DMARQ THEN ERROR
ERROR:   IF CLEAR THEN INIT

END
```

5/5

EPB1400 high performance peripheral DMA Controller, Screen 5.

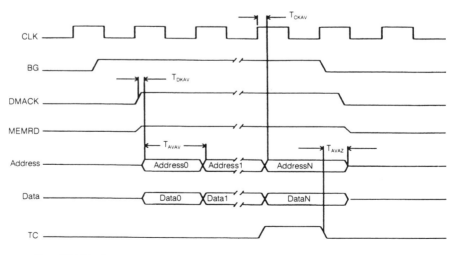

T_{DKAV} - DMACK to first address valid
T_{AVAZ} - Last address valid to bus tri-state
T_{AVAV} - Address valid to next address valid
T_{CKAV} - Clock to address valid

Fig. 6-39. Critical timing parameters. Courtesy of Altera Corporation.

unit, DMA unit, and DMA control state machine. The integration density, power, speed, and flexibility of the EPB1400 make it an excellent choice for a peripheral subsystem DMA controller. The DMA described here can transfer data at 30 Megawords/second. The design fits in a single EPB1400 device, requiring ½ square inches of board space and consuming only 600 mWatts.

The design files used to generate this EPB1400 DMA controller are available and can be downloaded using the Altera Bulletin Board Service. The detailed lookup table files (ST_LUT & END_LUT) are provided as well as all of the schematic and state machine design files. The following files comprise the entire EPB1400 DMA controller:

- DMA.SD
- ST_LUT.SD
- ST_LUT4.SD
- END_LUT.SD
- DMASM.SMF

68020 BUS ARBITER STATE MACHINE
Courtesy of Altera Corporation

This application example describes the ASMILE (Altera State Machine Input Language) state machine language syntax as used for entering designs into the SAM family of devices. Basic functionality and syntax are reviewed as well as the use of SAM internal resources. An application utilizing ASMILE input in the form of a 68020 Microprocessor Bus Arbiter is presented. This example provides illustrations of all basic concepts needed to execute a SAM design with ASMILE.

Refer to Altera's SAM EPS444/448 data sheet for details concerning device architecture and performance. A general knowledge of SAM device architecture is assumed as background for this example.

The SAM Solution

Altera's SAM (Stand-Alone Microsequencer) User-Configurable Sequencer Architecture provides a solution for high-performance control functions found in typical digital systems designed today. Figure 6-40 shows a SAM block diagram. Previously, two main approaches have been used in the design of high-performance state machine/control functions in digital systems—logic array-based sequencers and microcoded designs. Each approach has presented the designer with a set of benefits and drawbacks to be considered when deciding how to implement a specific application.

Logic array-based sequencers have been used for very fast state machines of low-to-medium complexity that required few outputs and relatively simple state flows or machine algorithms. Ability to perform multi-way control branching in a single clock cycle is a plus for this approach. Conventional registered PLDs are representative of this class. Product term count limitations, resulting

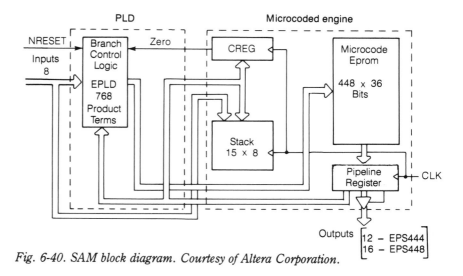

Fig. 6-40. SAM block diagram. Courtesy of Altera Corporation.

in the inability to generate complex output waveforms or state transitions, limits the utility of this approach when addressing larger control problems.

Microcoded approaches have been used for the implementation of complex control functions, requiring high control output counts. Until recently, however, the only mechanism for implementing this approach has been to glue together an assortment of bit-slice component building blocks. In addition, the approach also did not lend itself to rapid multi-way branching (a strength of logic arrays). Instead, it uses serial test-and-binary-branch mechanism.

An enhanced vehicle for state machine implementation really requires a marriage of these two architectures to obtain the high performance—multi-way branching based on real-time inputs characteristic of logic array-based sequencers, while having the ability to manage complex algorithms and generate high output counts characteristic of microcoded approaches. Altera's SAM family does exactly this.

SAM + PLUS System Overview

The versatility of the SAM architecture, and its applicability to both state machine and complex controller functions, has necessitated the need for multiple design input formats. Altera's SAM + PLUS PC-based Design Software allows the designer to enter a design in either a high-level state machine description using Altera's ASMILE language or in an efficient microcode assembler format known as ASM. A block diagram of this system is shown in FIG. 6-41. Given these options, the user can employ the design description most appropriate for the particular problem or with which he is most comfortable.

The SAM Design Processor (SDP) takes the input file, automatically minimizes the transition specification logic, and fits the resultant resource requests to the SAM architecture. A utilization report is generated to report total resources consumed, and unfittable requests, and assigned pinouts. Upon successful fitting, a standard JEDEC file is generated to allow programming of the device using a hardware programming card installed in the PC.

In addition, this JEDEC file, which represents the actual template of the specific application implemented, can be used as input to the SAMSIM (SAM SIMulator) program. This program provides functional simulation capability integrated into the total design environment. Hard-copy output of simulation

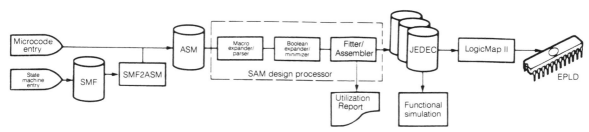

Fig. 6-41. SAM+Plus system diagram. Courtesy of Altera Corporation.

results can be obtained, as well as on-line logic analyzer viewing capability. The result is a design entry, compilation, and verification system that can be iterated rapidly until the desired functionality is obtained.

Sizing-Up a Potential SAM Design

The two broad categories of state machines are Mealy and Moore machines. A more in-depth discussion of the machines is provided in the logic tutorial of Appendix A. In the SAM architecture, the Moore machines can be directly implemented into a SAM component. SAM's outputs are a function of the currently addressed microcode location (state). Mealy machines specify outputs as functions of state and inputs. However, Mealy machines can frequently be converted to equivalent Moore machines. The general rule for this conversion is that for each transition into a state in the Mealy machine with a unique set of outputs, insert a state into the Moore machine with that output combination. Figure 6-42 illustrates this concept.

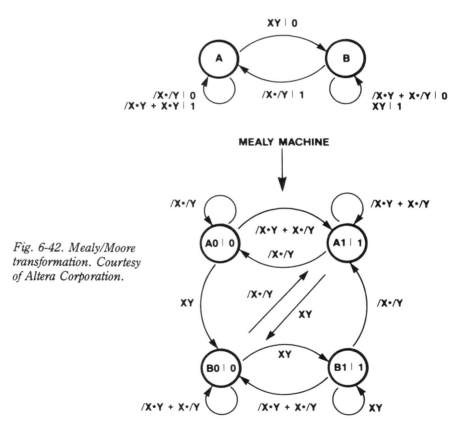

Fig. 6-42. Mealy/Moore transformation. Courtesy of Altera Corporation.

ASMILE supports the resources available on SAM for state machine design. Additional features, such as the stack and counter, are supported in the microassembler format that lends itself to their efficient use.

In order to determine whether a given application is suitable for SAM, a few brief guidelines derived from the device architecture and specifications are given:

- Operating frequency less than or equal to specified SAM device's Fmax.
- Synchronous Moore machine operation.
- Up to 8 state machine inputs (not including CLOCK or RESET).
- Up to 16 state machine outputs.
- Up to 64 multi-way (conditional) state branches.
- Transition expressions reducible to 4 product terms per IF-THEN expression.
- 192 or fewer unconditional state transitions.

An application that meets the above list of requirements will probably fit into a SAM device.

ASMILE Entry Overview

The basic format of a SAM ASMILE file consists of the following sections:

```
[Header]
 PART
 INPUTS
 OUTPUTS
[Equations]
 MACHINE
 CLOCK
 STATES
 Transition Specifications
 END$
```

Those sections surrounded by square brackets are optional and can be deleted if their use is not required in a given application.

ASMILE files can be constructed utilizing any standard text editor in non-document mode. Using an editor in document mode may inject spurious format control characters that will be called syntax errors by the ASMILE parser at compile time. Other than this constraint, input is essentially free-form and can be structured for readability and overall clarity.

The ASMILE file is case-sensitive so it is important to ensure that character case is maintained as text is entered. For example, the names RWB and rwb are not the same.

Comments can be inserted freely into the source code, delimited by leading and trailing percent signs, for example,

% This is a comment %

HEADER. The header contains user-specified identifier information. Typical information includes:

Designer's Name
Company
Date
Designer Number
Revision
SAM Part Number
Other Comments

PART. The PART section of the ASMILE file specifies the target SAM device the application is intended for.

INPUTS. The single INPUTS section of the ASMILE file defines all external inputs into the design, as well as any required user pin assignments. Pin assignments are optional and are assigned by SAM+PLUS if not specified. Pin assignments are specified by the format

input_name @ pin_number

OUTPUTS. The OUTPUTS section of the ASMILE file contains a list of all outputs from the design as well as any pin assignments. Pin assignment syntax is similar to input pin assignments.

EQUATIONS. The EQUATIONS section of the ASMILE file is available for the definition of intermediate equations to be used later in the design. Entry of transition specifications may be eased by defining intermediate variables initially, and then invoking them during the design. For example,

EventClk = I1*/I4 + I3*I6*/I7

might be defined in the EQUATIONS section, and then utilized later in an IF-THEN statement.

MACHINE. The format for the MACHINE declaration is

MACHINE: machine_name

The MACHINE section of the ASMILE file actually specifies the state machine's state, output, and transition definitions required from the SAM device. The three subsections to be included are Clock, States, and Transition Specifications.

Clock. The Clock subsection specifies the clock signal which will act as the synchronous clock source for the state machine and the resulting SAM device.

States. The STATES section specifies all states in the target machine, as well as outputs corresponding to these states. The general form of this statement, when used in a SAM design, is

STATES: [output_name_1...output_name_n]
state_name[output_value_list]

The output_names are a list of all SAM output names used in the design, separated by white space. Following this initial declaration, a list of all state_names appears, each followed by a binary string in brackets that specifies all output values to be provided when the machine is in that state. For example,

```
STATES:     [A B C D]
      S0    [0 0 0 0]
      S1    [0 1 1 0]
      S2    [1 0 0 0]
      S3    [0 0 0 1]
```

Specifies a machine with four outputs A through D. State S0 has all outputs low, S1 takes B and C to logic one, S2 has only output A high, etc.

Transition Specification. The form of the transition specifications in a SAM ASMILE design is

state_name : transition_specification

Every state in the machine must have a transition_specification which will specify successor states, either unconditionally

S0:   S2

or conditionally using IF-THEN statements.

The first state_name encountered in the transition specification section is defined as the initial state of the machine coming out of Reset. As such, it has special significance. Typically, this is defined as an inactive or passive machine state. Other transition specifications have no positional significance.

IF-THEN Statements. The SAM architecture implements in silicon the state transition specifications defined by a user in the chip's branch control logic block. This block allows, by its structure, the specification of up to 64 complex branching expressions in a single machine. (As noted above, up to 192 unconditional state transitions can be specified for a single SAM device.) Each IF-THEN expression can specify a direct branch from the current state to as many as four other successor states, based upon inputs to the SAM device. This is illustrated in FIG. 6-43.

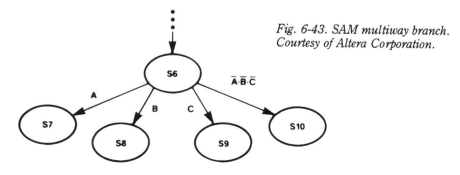

Fig. 6-43. SAM multiway branch. Courtesy of Altera Corporation.

SAM MULTI-WAY BRANCH

In specifying IF-THEN expressions, the order of the expression is important and can determine the machine flow. Transition specifications need not be mutually exclusive in such expressions. For example, the expression

S0:   IF I1*!2 + I5 THEN S1
      IF I5*!6 + I4/I3 THEN S2
      IF I4 THEN S3
      S4

might appear ambiguous under the condition that inputs I5 and I6 to the SAM device become true during S0. Is S1 or S2 the next state? At this point SAM's priority logic comes into play. Because the S1 transition is specified before the S2 in the design definition, it is the next state entered. Similarly, if I4/I3 becomes valid, S2 is the next state entered in preference over S3. This precedence-resolving capability is provided in the SAM silicon architecture which employs a hardware priority encoder in selecting the next state transition. This capability resolves conflicts and can be exploited in the design to prioritize transitions.

Default Transitions. One other benefit of this approach is the implicit default transition to be made. In the example above, S4 is the next state entered if S1, S2, and S3 are not selected by the appropriate conditions being true. This feature can reduce design effort and resource requirements substantially, because default transitions are frequently defined as the negation of non-default transitions. Such inverted expressions have a tendency to consume logic product terms or resources quickly. For example,

S0:   IF I1*!2 + I5*I7 + I0 THEN S1
      IF I3 + /I6*I4 THEN S2
      IF I2*I3*I4*I5*/I7 THEN S3
      S4

is a valid ASMILE SAM transition specification. If the notion of a default transition (S4) was not in the ASMILE syntax and had to be explicitly defined, you might have to specify the last transition as (unminimized)

IF/(I1*!2 + I5*I7 + I0) * /(I3 + /I6*I4) * /(I2*I3*I4*I5*/I7) THEN S4

Each expression (IF-THEN) can be a function of any of the eight SAM external inputs and can contain up to four product terms after logic minimization. For most designs, this should prove ample.

A tradeoff between number of branch destinations and product terms per destination can be made, as multiple IF-THEN expressions can point to the SAM destination. For example, the expression

S0:   IF (cond1) THEN S1
      IF (cond2) THEN S1
      IF (cond3) THEN S2
      S3

provides a three-way branch, with up to eight product terms available for the specification of transitions to state S1.

END$. Every SAM ASMILE source file must terminate with the END$ terminator.

SAM ASMILE Design Example

To illustrate SAM ASMILE input syntax in a real example, a 68020 Microprocessor Bus Arbiter state machine is examined. This machine, while not overly complex, illustrates most of the concepts of ASMILE entry.

Shown in FIG. 6-44 is a state machine diagram for the Bus Arbiter. The 68020-based system runs at 25 MHz, and therefore the Bus Arbiter machine must also run with a 40 ns clock period. The three signal lines on a 68020 bus that define the handshake required to arbitrate bus exchanges between multiple bus masters are request, grant, and acknowledge. The procedure of a bus master that desires access to the bus is illustrated in Screens 1 and 2 (68020 arbiter operation). The state labels S0-S6 designate correspondence between the operations shown and the state machine diagram.

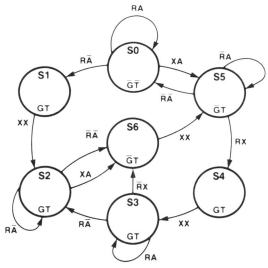

Fig. 6-44. Arbiter state flow. Courtesy of Altera Corporation.

R — BUS REQUEST INPUT
A — BUS GRANT ACKNOWLEDGE INPUT
G — BUS GRANT OUTPUT
T — THREE-STATE CONTROL TO BUS CONTROL LOGIC
X — DON'T CARE

Relating this sequence to the state diagram, S0 represents the normal or active state of the processor, S1 and S2 correspond to the grant phase, S5 and S6 the acknowledge phase, and S3 and S4 the rearbitration phase if requests are pending at the end of the current bus exchange.

The Design. The file shown in Screens 3 and 4 (68020 Bus Arbiter State Machine Input File—68020 ARB.SMF) is the actual ASMILE file generated for the machine from the state diagram. It conforms to the general file outline as described above. ASMILE source files are given the extension .SMF (for state

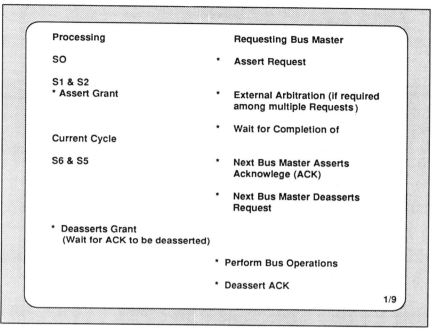

68020 bus arbiter state machine, Screen 1.

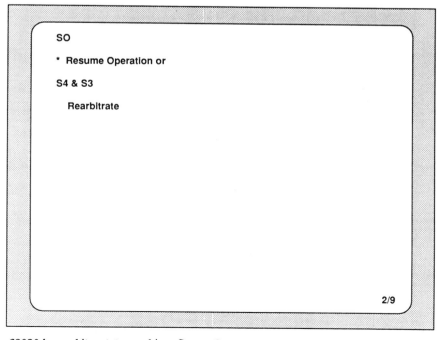

68020 bus arbiter state machine, Screen 2.

```
Stan Kopec
Altera Corp.
3/10/87
68020 Bus Arbiter for SAM
% This description uses IF...THEN Transition Specification %
PART: EPS444
% Pin Assignments (an Option) are made by the designer %
INPUTS: REQUESTS@1 ACK@2
OUTPUTS: GRANT @23  TRISTATE @22 0S0 0S1 0S2 0S3 0S4 0S5 0S6
MACHINE: BUSARBITER
CLOCK: CLK
% STATES gives the output value mapping %
STATES: [GRANT TRISTATE 0S0 0S1 0S2 0S3 0S4 0S5 0S6]

S0 [0 0 1 0 0 0 0 0 0]
S1 [1 1 0 1 0 0 0 0 0]
S2 [1 1 0 0 1 0 0 0 0]
S3 [1 1 0 0 0 1 0 0 0]
S4 [1 1 0 0 0 0 1 0 0]
S5 [0 1 0 0 0 0 0 1 0]
S6 [0 1 0 0 0 0 0 0 1]

% Transition Specifications follow %

S0:                                                    3/9
```

68020 bus arbiter state machine, Screen 3.

```
IF REQUEST*/ACK THEN S1
IF ACK THEN s5
SO

S1:
S2

S2:
IF /REQUEST*/ACK  +  ACK THEN S6
S2

S3:
IF /REQUEST THEN S6
IF REQUEST*/ACK THEN S2

S4:
S3

S5:
IF REQUEST THEN S4
IF /REQUEST*/ACK THEN S0

S6:
S5

END$                                                   4/9
```

68020 bus arbiter state machine, Screen 4.

machine file) when generated. In this case, the file would be 68020ARB.SMF. Note that in the OUTPUTS and STATES sections, output variables OS0-OS6 have been defined. Each variable is valid only during a unique state. As the design is simulated, these give an indication of which state the machine is at any given point in time.

To compile this design, the SAM+PLUS software is invoked, specifying that ASMILE (and not microassembler) input format is being used. Consult the SAM+PLUS User's Manual for a detailed description of the SAM+PLUS user interface and options. Compilation then proceeds automatically. Transition equations are automatically minimized. Object code is generated for the EPLD and EPROM blocks. As a result, a JEDEC programming file (.JED) is generated, as well as a utilization report file (.RPT) reporting the results of the compilation process. Functional simulation of the design can be performed using the .JED file as a design template as described below. The .JED file is not intended to be user-readable. The .RPT file contains valuable information such as design pin assignments and resource utilization. Screens 5 through 8 (68020 Bus Arbiter Design Report File—68020 ARB.RPT) shows key portions of this file. All ASMILE input is transformed into microassembler format before subsequent processing, and the equivalent microassembler code for the design is given in the .RPT file as well. More information on the interpretation of this code can be obtained from the references shown later in this section.

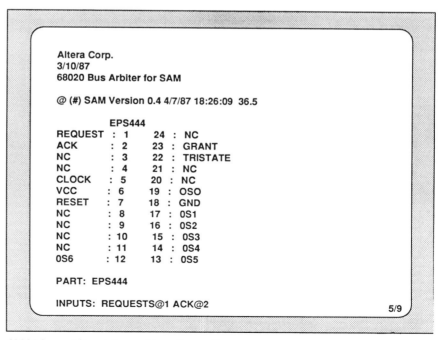

```
Altera Corp.
3/10/87
68020 Bus Arbiter for SAM

@ (#) SAM Version 0.4 4/7/87 18:26:09 36.5

               EPS444
REQUEST  :  1     24  :  NC
ACK      :  2     23  :  GRANT
NC       :  3     22  :  TRISTATE
NC       :  4     21  :  NC
CLOCK    :  5     20  :  NC
VCC      :  6     19  :  OSO
RESET    :  7     18  :  GND
NC       :  8     17  :  0S1
NC       :  9     16  :  0S2
NC       :  10    15  :  0S3
NC       :  11    14  :  0S4
0S6      :  12    13  :  0S5

PART: EPS444

INPUTS:  REQUESTS@1 ACK@2                   5/9
```

68020 bus arbiter state machine, Screen 5.

```
OUTPUTS:  GRANT @23,  TRISTATE @22, 0S0@19, 0S1@17, 0S2@16,
0S3@15,
0S4@14, 0S5  0S6@12

PINS:

DEFAULT: [000000000]

PROGRAM:

OD: [001000000] JUMP S0:
192D:
S0:  IF REQUEST * ACK' THEN
[110100000] JUMP S1;
ELSEIF ACK THEN
[010000010] JUMP S5;
ELSE
[001000000] JUMP S0;
1D:
S1:  [110010000] JUMP S2;
193D:

S2:  IF REQUEST' * ACK' +
                                                    6/9
```

68020 bus arbiter state machine, Screen 6.

```
ACK THEN
[010000001] JUMP S6;
ELSE
[110010000] JUMP S2;
194D:

S3:  IF REQUEST' THEN
[010000001] JUMP S6;
ELSEIF REQUEST * ACK' THEN
[110010000] JUMP S2;
ELSE
[110001000] JUMP S3;
2D:
S4:  [110001000] JUMP S3;
195D:
S5:  IF REQUEST THEN
[110000100] JUMP S4;
ELSEIF REQUEST' * ACK' THEN
[001000000] JUMP S0;
ELSE
[010000010] JUMP S5;
3D:
S6:  [010000010] JUMP S5;
                                                    7/9
```

68020 bus arbiter state machine, Screen 7.

```
END$

Statistical report:
Number of label definitions     :   8
Number of unconditional branches :   4
Number of conditional branches   :   4
Number of fatal errors          :   0
Number of warnings              :   0
Percent unconditional used       :   2.08%
Percent of conditional used      :   6.25%
```

8/9

68020 bus arbiter state machine, Screen 8.

Design Simulation. Integral to the SAM + PLUS design system is the SAMSIM functional simulator. Once a design has been successfully processed, the user can specify input stimulus in a variety of formats and observe the device response quickly and effectively using this unit-delay simulator. As mentioned before, SAMSIM supports both hard-copy and virtual logic analyzer output formats. Split-window, multiple zoom-levels, and delta time display are a few of the capabilities of this interactive display mode.

SAMSIM supports both interactive and command file input. Shown in Screen 9 (68020 Bus Arbiter DesignReport File—68020 ARB.RPT) is a simple input stimulus command file for the design. Typically command files are given the design name with the extension .CMD (for example, 68020ARB.CMD). The first line specifies the source design JEDEC file. The next two lines illustrate logic sequences for the two machine inputs. The PATTERN CREATE command allows the user to specify a sequence of input logic levels to be applied to the indicated node or nodes. The notation ( )*n means n clocks. Interactive display is invoked with the VIEW command.

Running the SAMSIM simulator with this command file produces the results shown in FIG. 6-45. The input stimulus to the SAM arbiter design and the resulting state machine operation is displayed on the screen.

The initial input stimulus applied to the SAM design shows a straightforward bus exchange between the 68020 and another bus master. This corresponds to the first REQUEST/GRANT/ACK sequence. Upon detecting a

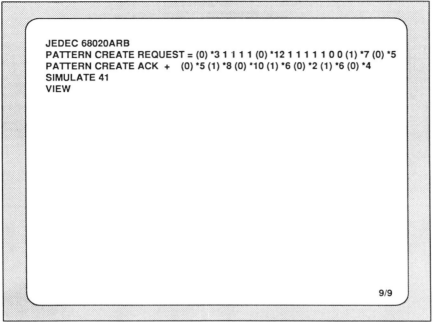

JEDEC 68020ARB
PATTERN CREATE REQUEST = (0) *3 1 1 1 1 (0) *12 1 1 1 1 1 0 0 (1) *7 (0) *5
PATTERN CREATE ACK +   (0) *5 (1) *8 (0) *10 (1) *6 (0) *2 (1) *6 (0) *4
SIMULATE 41
VIEW

9/9

COURTESY OF ALTERA CORPORATION

68020 bus arbiter state machine, Screen 9.

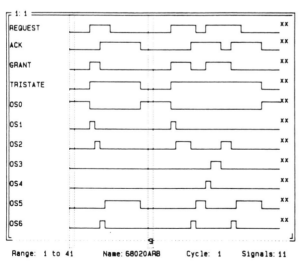

Range: 1 to 41   Name: 68020ARB   Cycle: 1   Signals: 11

Fig. 6-45. SAMSIM interactive output. Courtesy of Altera Corporation.

REQUEST, the 68020 asserts its TRISTATE line, and issues a GRANT pulse, allowing the new bus master to assume control. The alternate bus master asserts ACK when it detects the fact that the bus has been granted. When ACK finally drops, the 68020 knows it can resume control. The second such sequence involves not just a single initial REQUEST (bus master #1), but a second REQUEST from another bus master (#2) during the time bus master #1 has control. As a result, the 68020 must generate a new GRANT pulse (during S4-S2), and hand over bus control to bus master #2 when bus master #1 is finished (ACK is dropped). When bus master #2 is finished and no requests are pending, the 68020 retakes control of the bus (TRISTATE goes low).

State machine design is a straightforward process using the ASMILE input language in conjunction with the SAM device. When the design is debugged and complete, the SAM component can be programmed using PC-based hardware and software in seconds. Should design errors be detected after in-system test, a windowed SAM device can be erased, a design change compiled, and the device reprogrammed quickly.

9-BIT PARITY GENERATOR/CHECKER WITH 82S153/153A
Courtesy of Signetics Corporation

This application example presents the design of a parity generator using Signetics PLD, 82S153 or 82S153A, which enables the designers to customize their circuits in the form of "sum-of-products." The PLA architecture and the 10 bidirectional I/O's make it possible to implement the 9-bit parity generator/checker in one chip without any external wiring between pins. A logic diagram of the device is shown in FIG. 6-46, a block diagram in FIG. 6-47, a truth table in TABLE 6-4, and a pin list in FIG. 6-48.

The parity of an 8-bit word is generated by counting the number of 1s in the word. If the number is odd, the word had odd parity. Thus, a parity generator designed for even parity, for example, generates a zero if the parity is even, or a one if parity is odd. Conversely, an odd parity generator generates a zero if the parity of the word is odd, or a one if the parity is even. This bit is then connected to the word making it 9-bits long. When the word is used elsewhere, its parity can be checked for correctness.

Description

The most straightforward way of implementing the parity generator/checker is to take the 9-input truth table (8 inputs for the 8-bit word, and 1 input for cascading the previous state) and put it in a 256×4 PROM. Because there are 2^9 combinations and half of them are odd, the other half is even, the circuit takes 256 terms. An alternative is to divide the 9-bits into 3 groups of 3-bits as shown in TABLE 6-4. If the sum of the 3-bits is odd, then the intermediate output SU1, SU2, or SU3 equals 1. Otherwise it equals 0. The intermediate results are grouped together and SUM_o equals 0.

The circuit is implemented using AMAZE as shown in Screens 1 through 8. SU1 is an intermediate output for inputs I_0, I_1, and I_2. In the same manner, SU2 and SU# are intermediate outputs for I_3, I_4, I_5, I_6, I_7, and I_8. The design uses up 16 product terms and 5 control terms leaving 16 product terms and 4 bidirectional I/O's to implement other logic designs.

The design is tested by using the logic simulator provided by AMAZE. The input test vector is chosen to exhaustively test for all 8 input combinations at all 4 sections of the circuit.

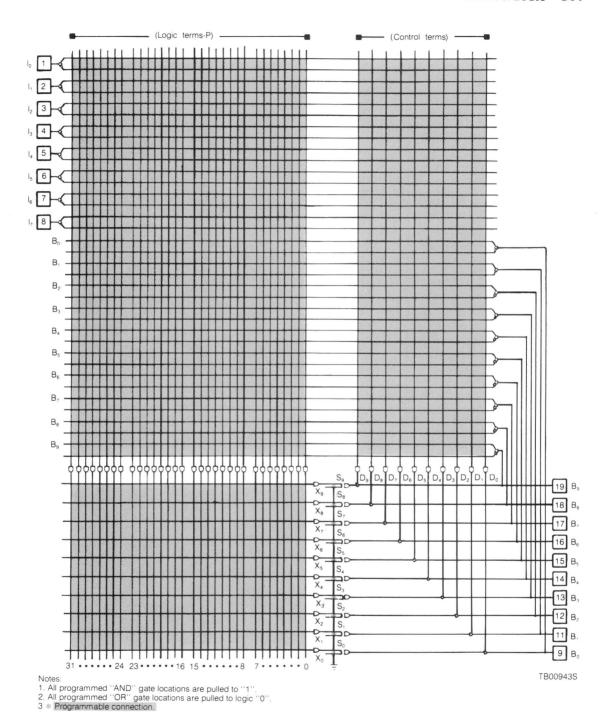

Notes:
1. All programmed "AND" gate locations are pulled to "1".
2. All programmed "OR" gate locations are pulled to logic "0".
3 ● Programmable connection.

TB00943S

Fig. 6-46. Logic diagram of PLS153. Courtesy of Signetics Corporation.

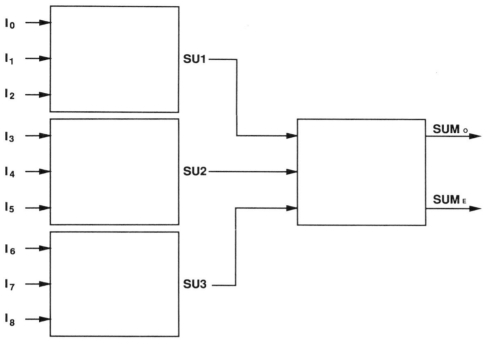

Fig. 6-47. Block diagram for 9-bit parity checker. Courtesy of Signetics Corporation.

Table 6-4. Truth table for 9-bit parity generator/checker.

I_0	I_1	I_2	SU1
0	0	0	0
0	0	1	1
0	1	1	0
0	1	0	1
1	0	1	0
1	0	0	1
1	1	0	0
1	1	1	1

I_3	I_4	I_5	SU2
0	0	0	0
0	1	1	0
0	0	1	1
0	1	0	1
1	0	1	0
1	1	0	0
1	0	0	1
1	1	1	1

I_6	I_7	I_8	SU3
0	0	0	0
0	1	1	0
1	0	1	0
1	1	0	0
0	0	1	1
0	1	0	1
1	0	0	1
1	1	1	1

SU1	SU2	SU3	SUM $_O$	SUM $_E$
0	0	0	0	1
0	0	1	1	0
0	1	0	1	0
0	1	1	0	1
1	0	0	1	0
1	0	1	0	1
1	1	0	0	1
1	1	1	1	0

***** **PARGEN** *****
P I N L I S T

LABEL	** FNC		** PIN	— — — —	PIN **	FNC	**	LABEL
10	** I		** 1 - :		: - 20 **	+5V	**	VCC
11	** I		** 2 - :		: - 19 **	/O	**	SUME
12	** I		** 3 - :		: - 18 **	O	**	SUMO
13	** I		** 4 - :	8	: - 17 **	B	**	N/C
14	** I		** 5 - :	2	: - 16 **	B	**	N/C
15	** I		** 6 - :	S	: - 15 **	B	**	N/C
16	** I		** 7 - :	1	: - 14 **	B	**	N/C
17	** I		** 8 - :	5	: - 13 **	O	**	SU3
18	** I		** 9 - :	3	: - 12 **	O	**	SU2
GND	** OV		** 10 - :	_ _ _ _	: - 11 **	O	**	SU1

Fig. 6-48. Pin list for 9-bit parity generator checker. Courtesy of Signetics Corporation.

```
******************* PARGEN *******************

@DEVICE TYPE
82S153
@DRAWING
***************************** PARITY GENERATOR/CHECKER
@REVISION
***************************** REV. -
@DATE
***************************** xx/xx/xxxx
@SYMBOL
***************************** FILE ID: PARGEN
@COMPANY
***************************** SIGNETICS
@NAME
@DESCRIPTION


****************************************************************
*                                           *
*   This circuit is a 9-bit parity generator/checker commonly used for
*
*   error detection in high speed data transmission/retrieval.  The odd
*
                                                            1/8
```

9-bit parity generator with 825153/153, Screen 1.

```
*    parity output (SUMO) is high when the sum of the data bits is odd.
*
*    Otherwise it is low.                              *
*    The even parity output (SUME) is high when the sum of the data bits
*
*    is even.  It is low otherwise.                         *
*                                                 *
*************************************************************************

@COMMON PRODUCT TERM
@I/O DIRECTION
"

*************************************************************************
*                                          *
*    SU1, SU2 and SU3 are outputs which are defined in the PIN LIST
and    *
*    therefore they don't need to be defined here again.        *
*                                          *
*************************************************************************

"
@OUTPUT POLARITY
"
                                                      2/8
```

9-bit parity generator with 825153/153, Screen 2.

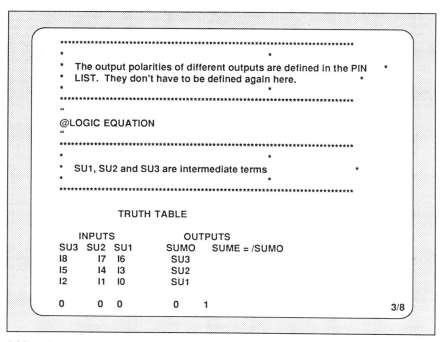

```
*************************************************************************
*                                          *
*    The output polarities of different outputs are defined in the PIN   *
*    LIST.  They don't have to be defined again here.           *
*                                          *
*************************************************************************
"
@LOGIC EQUATION
"
*************************************************************************
*                                          *
*    SU1, SU2 and SU3 are intermediate terms              *
*                                          *
*************************************************************************

            TRUTH TABLE

      INPUTS                  OUTPUTS
   SU3  SU2  SU1        SUMO    SUME = /SUMO
   I8    I7   I6         SU3
   I5    I4   I3         SU2
   I2    I1   I0         SU1

    0    0    0          0       1
                                                      3/8
```

9-bit parity generator with 825153/153, Screen 3.

```
0      0   1        1    0
0      1   0        1    0
0      1   1        0    1
1      0   0        1    0
1      0   1        0    1
1      1   0        0    1
1      1   1        1    0
```

SU1 = /I2 * /I1 * I0 + /I2 * I1 * /I0 +
I2 * /I1 * /I0 + I2 * I1 * I0 ;
SU2 = /I5 * /I4 * I3 + /I5 * I4 * /I3 +
I5 * /I4 * /I3 + I5 * I4 * I3 ;

SU3 = /I8 * /I7 * I6 + /I8 * I7 * /I6 +
I8 * /I7 * /I6 + I8 * I7 * I6 ;

SUMO = /SU1 * /SU2 * SU3 + /SU1 * SU2 * /SU3 +
SU1 * /SU2 * /SU3 + SU1 * SU2 * SU3 ;

SUME = /(/SU1 * /SU2 * SU3 + /SU1 * SU2 * /SU3 +
SU1 * /SU2 * /SU3 + SU1 * SU2 * SU3) ;

4/8

9-bit parity generator with 825153/153, Screen 4.

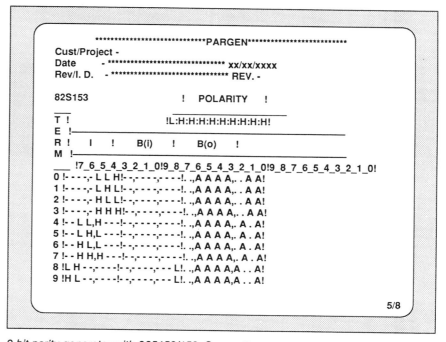

```
*****************************PARGEN*************************
Cust/Project -
Date      - *****************************  xx/xx/xxxx
Rev/I. D.  - *****************************  REV. -

82S153                     !   POLARITY    !
                          _____
T !                       !L:H:H:H:H:H:H:H:H!
E !——————————————————————————————————————————————————
R !     I    !    B(i)    !     B(o)     !
M !——————————————————————————————————————————————————
___  !7_6_5_4_3_2_1_0!9_8_7_6_5_4_3_2_1_0!9_8_7_6_5_4_3_2_1_0!
0 !----,- L L H!- -,- - - -,- - - -! .,A A A A,. . A A!
1 !----,- L H L!- -,- - - -,- - - -! .,A A A A,. . A A!
2 !----,- H L L!- -,- - - -,- - - -! .,A A A A,. . A A!
3 !----,- H H H!- -,- - - -,- - - -! .,A A A A,. . A A!
4 !- - L L,H - - -!- -,- - - -,- - - -! .,A A A A,. A . A!
5 !- - L H,L - - -!- -,- - - -,- - - -! .,A A A A,. A . A!
6 !- - H L,L - - -!- -,- - - -,- - - -! .,A A A A,. A . A!
7 !- - H H,H - - -!- -,- - - -,- - - -! .,A A A A,. A . A!
8 !L H - -,- - - -!- -,- - - -,- - - L!. .,A A A A,A . . A!
9 !H L - -,- - - -!- -,- - - -,- - - L!. .,A A A A,A . . A!

5/8
```

9-bit parity generator with 825153/153, Screen 5.

```
10 !L L - -,- - - -!- -,- - - -,- - - H!. .,A A A A,A . . A!
11 !H H - -,- - - -!- -,- - - -,- - - H!. .,A A A A,A . . A!
12 !- - - -,- - - -!- -,- - - -,H L L -!A A,A A A A,. . . A!
13 !- - - -,- - - -!- -,- - - -,L H L -!A A,A A A A,. . . A!
14 !- - - -,- - - -!- -,- - - -,L L H -!A A,A A A A,. . . A!
15 !- - - -,- - - -!- -,- - - -,H H H -!A A,A A A A,. . . A!
16 !0 0 0 0,0 0 0 0!0 0,0 0 0 0,0 0 0 0!A A,A A A A,A A A A!
17 !0 0 0 0,0 0 0 0!0 0,0 0 0 0,0 0 0 0!A A,A A A A,A A A A!
18 !0 0 0 0,0 0 0 0!0 0,0 0 0 0,0 0 0 0!A A,A A A A,A A A A!
19 !0 0 0 0,0 0 0 0!0 0,0 0 0 0,0 0 0 0!A A,A A A A,A A A A!
20 !0 0 0 0,0 0 0 0!0 0,0 0 0 0,0 0 0 0!A A,A A A A,A A A A!
21 !0 0 0 0,0 0 0 0!0 0,0 0 0 0,0 0 0 0!A A,A A A A,A A A A!
22 !0 0 0 0,0 0 0 0!0 0,0 0 0 0,0 0 0 0!A A,A A A A,A A A A!
23 !0 0 0 0,0 0 0 0!0 0,0 0 0 0,0 0 0 0!A A,A A A A,A A A A!
24 !0 0 0 0,0 0 0 0!0 0,0 0 0 0,0 0 0 0!A A,A A A A,A A A A!
25 !0 0 0 0,0 0 0 0!0 0,0 0 0 0,0 0 0 0!A A,A A A A,A A A A!
26 !0 0 0 0,0 0 0 0!0 0,0 0 0 0,0 0 0 0!A A,A A A A,A A A A!
27 !0 0 0 0,0 0 0 0!0 0,0 0 0 0,0 0 0 0!A A,A A A A,A A A A!
28 !0 0 0 0,0 0 0 0!0 0,0 0 0 0,0 0 0 0!A A,A A A A,A A A A!
29 !0 0 0 0,0 0 0 0!0 0,0 0 0 0,0 0 0 0!A A,A A A A,A A A A!
30 !0 0 0 0,0 0 0 0!0 0,0 0 0 0,0 0 0 0!A A,A A A A,A A A A!
31 !0 0 0 0,0 0 0 0!0 0,0 0 0 0,0 0 0 0!A A,A A A A,A A A A!

                                                    6/8
```

9-bit parity generator with 825153/153, Screen 6.

```
D9 !- - - -,- - - -!- -,- - - -,- - - -!          .
D8 !- - - -,- - - -!- -,- - - -,- - - -!          .
D7 !0 0 0 0,0 0 0 0!0 0,0 0 0 0,0 0 0 0!          .
D6 !0 0 0 0,0 0 0 0!0 0,0 0 0 0,0 0 0 0!          .
D5 !0 0 0 0,0 0 0 0!0 0,0 0 0 0,0 0 0 0!          .
D4 !0 0 0 0,0 0 0 0!0 0,0 0 0 0,0 0 0 0!          .
D3 !- - - -,- - - -!- -,- - - -,- - - -!          .
D2 !- - - -,- - - -!- -,- - - -,- - - -!          .
D1 !- - - -,- - - -!- -,- - - -,- - - -!          .
D0 !0 0 0 0,0 0 0 0!0 0,0 0 0 0,0 0 0 0!          .


I I I I I I I I S S N N N N S S S I S S N N N N S S S I
7 6 5 4 3 2 1 0 U U / / / / U U U B U U / / / / U U U B
M M C C C C 3 2 1   M M C C C C 3 2 1
E O               E O

"

*****************************************************
*  This is a test pattern for the 9-bit parity generator/checker  *
*  circuit.  The simulator will use this file as an input to      *
*  simulate the logical function.                      *
*****************************************************
                                                    7/8
```

9-bit parity generator with 825153/153, Screen 7.

```
"      SS          EXPECTED
"      UU   SSS     OUTPUTS
"IIIIIIII MMBBBBBUUUI     BBBBB
"76543210 EO76543218     98321
LLLLLLLL ////////H    "HLLLL
HLHHLHLL ////////L    "LHLLH
LHHLLHHL ////////H    "LHLHL
HHLHLLHL ////////L    "HLLHH
LLHLHHLH ////////H    "LHHLL
HLLHHLLH ////////L    "HLHLH
LHLLHLHH ////////L    "HLHHL
HHHHHHHH ////////H     "LHHHH
QUIT


82S153  A:pargen.STD
" This file is the result of logic simulation of the parity generator/
" checker circuit.  The inputs are read from input file PARGEN.TST
"

"  INPUTS <=B(I/O)=>   TRACE TERMS
" 76543210 9876543210
"
```

8/8

COURTESY OF SIGNETICS CORPORATION

9-bit parity generator with 825153/153, Screen 8.

HIGH-SPEED 12-BIT TRACKING ADC USING
FIELD-PROGRAMMABLE LOGIC SEQUENCERS
Courtesy of Signetics Corporation

The high-speed 12-bit tracking ADC described in this example is based on two logic sequencers type PLS179 from the bipolar Schottky Programmable Logic Device (PLD) Series-24 (24-pin DIL) family. These ICs are field-programmable by selective blowing of fusible Nichrome links and interconnected to form a 12-bit Successive Approximation Register (SAR), up/down counter, and biphase clock generator. Features of the PLS179 logic sequencer are:

- 45 product terms (32 logic terms, 13 control terms).
- 20 inputs (8 dedicated).
- 4 I/Os and 8 registered I/Os.
- typical propagation delay 25 ns (input to output).
- typical power dissipation 725 mW.
- maximum clock frequency 18 MHz.
- operating temperature range 0 to 75°C.
- encapsulated in 24-pin plastic DIL (PLS179N) or 28-pin PLCC (PLS179A).
- supported by Automated Map and Zap Equation (AMAZE) PLD design software which is free of charge to PLD users.

Operation Principles of the ADC

Figure 6-49 shows the logic diagram. The simplified block diagram in FIG. 6-50 illustrates the principle of operation of the ADC. When input ST is set low, the 12-bit SAR is initially loaded with its half full-scale value (2^{11} = 2048). It is then converted to analog form by a 12-bit DAC. An analog comparator senses whether the output level from the DAC is greater or less than the analog input level and causes the SAR to increment or decrement until parity is achieved by successive approximation. Output DONE is then set high. When output DONE is high, and as long as inputs ST and HOLD are high, a tracking mode of operation is available during which the SAR is converted into a 12-bit up/down counter by setting the TRACK input low. The up/down counter is incremented or decremented under control of the COMPARE inputs at the rate of one LSB per clock period to follow the analog input variations. The up/down counting can be halted at any time by setting the HOLD input low. The digital data output then remains constant indefinitely. This facility provides a very good sample-and-hold function because, unlike with analog sample-and-hold circuits using capacitor storage, the output level doesn't decay due to charge leakage.

Figure 6-51 shows a schematic diagram of the high-speed ADC. The starting for the initial successive approximation cycle are the TRACK and HOLD inputs set high and the ST input set low. On the rising edge of the first CLOCK 2 pulse after the ST input has been set low, the 12-bit SAR is loaded with its half full-scale value (2^{11} = binary 2048) and the DONE output is reset low (open

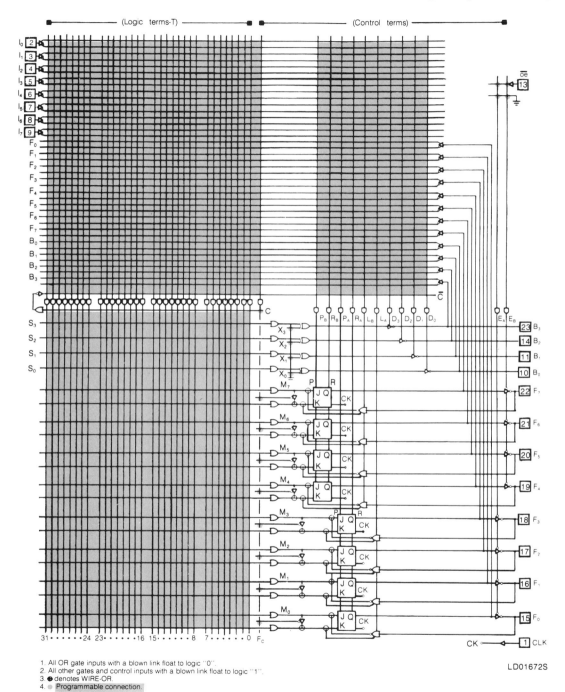

1. All OR gate inputs with a blown link float to logic "0".
2. All other gates and control inputs with a blown link float to logic "1".
3. ⊕ denotes WIRE-OR.
4. ● Programmable connection.

LD01672S

Fig. 6-49. FPLS logic diagram of PLS179. Courtesy of Signetics Corporation.

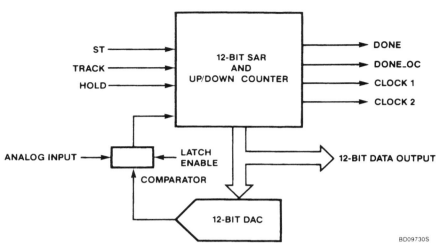

Fig. 6-50. Functional block diagram of high speed A/D converter. Courtesy of Signetics Corporation.

collector output DONE_OC high-impedance). The digital output from the SAR is in natural binary format (i.e., if all 12 bits are 0, the digital output value is zero; if all 12 bits are 1, the digital output value is $2^{12} - 1 = 4095$. As shown in FIG. 6-51, bits 0 to 4 are registered in PLS179 ADCB2, and bits 5 to 11 are registered in PLS179 ADCB1.

The digital output value from the SAR (initially binary 2048) is converted to analog form by the 12-bit DAC and compared with the analog input level by the SE/NE5105 comparator. The comparator output (high if the digital output value is greater than the analog input level, and low if it is less) is applied to the COMPARE input of both PLS179s. The output from the SE/NE5105 comparator is latched by CLOCK 1 to prevent violation of the set-up time due to changes of the analog input level whilst the SAR/counter is incrementing/decrementing. If an analog comparator without a latching facility is used instead of an SE/NE5105, an external latch must be used.

Figure 6-52 is a flowchart of the successive approximation algorithm for the SAR which can be summarized as follows. Figure 6-53 shows the timing diagram for Successive Approximation Cycle. If the digital output value from the ADC is greater than the analog input level (D > A), move the last bit in the SAR that was set to 1. Repeat this procedure until all 12 bits have been operated upon. Consequently, the last action in the successive approximation cycle is always to set the LSB in the SAR (bit 0) to 1.

At the rising edge of the CLOCK 2 pulse following the setting of the LSB in the SAR to 1, the initial successive approximation cycle is complete and output DONE is set high and open-collector output DONE_OC is set low. The states of these two outputs are latched until they are reset by setting the ST input low again to start another successive approximation cycle.

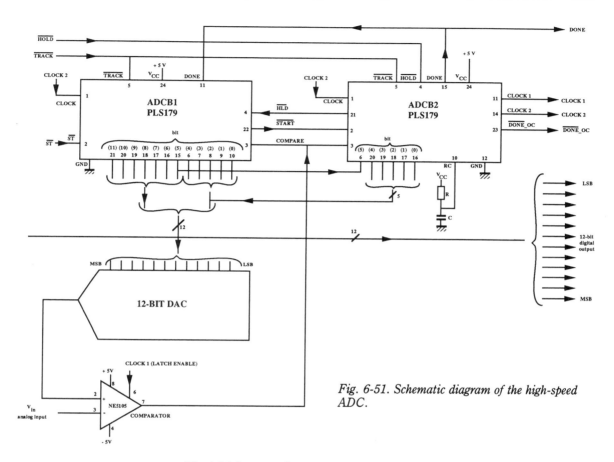

Fig. 6-51. Schematic diagram of the high-speed ADC.

The initial successive approximation cycle takes 13 periods of CLOCK 2 to complete. It is essential that the analog input level to the comparator remains constant during this period. If rapidly varying analog inputs are to be converted, it is necessary to incorporate an analog sample and hold circuit (controlled by output DONE) at the analog input to the ADC.

Up/Down Counter

When output DONE is high (successive approximation cycle complete) and input HOLD is high, input TRACK can be set low to convert the SAR into a 12-bit up/down counter consisting of 121 toggle flip-flops, each with two p-terms for directional control. The up/down counter can track variations of the level of the analog input signal at the rate of one LSB per CLOCK 2 period. The counting can be inhibited at any time by setting the HOLD input low. The digital output value from the ADC then remains constant indefinitely.

Input Latches

Because inputs ST and HOLD cannot be synchronized with CLOCK 2, they might possibly assume a metastable state if some precautions were not

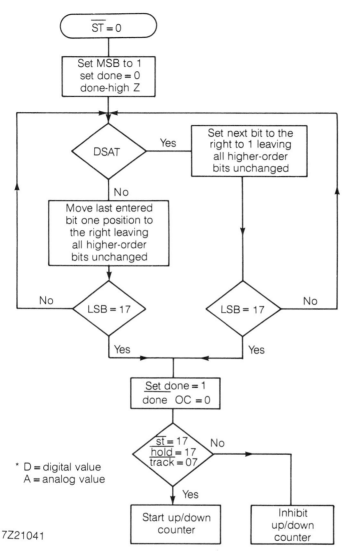

Fig. 6-52. Flowchart of successive approximation algorithm. Courtesy of Signetics Corporation.

taken. They are therefore each effectively latched by a flip-flop and two p-terms configured as a noninverting D flip-flop at output START and HDL respectively. Once latched, their logic states become effective at the rising edge of the next clock pulse.

Clock Generator

PLS179 ADCB2 generates biphase clock pulses (CLOCK 1 and CLOCK 2), the frequency of which is controlled by the RC network at pin RC. It is

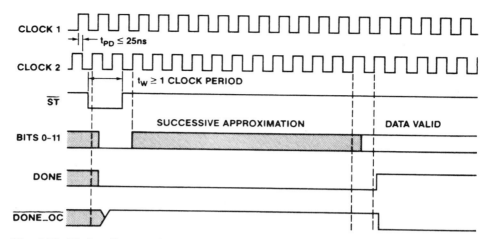

Fig. 6-53. Timing diagram of a successive approximation cycle. Courtesy of Signetics Corporation.

recommended that the value of the capacitor be made less than 1 nF. The actual RC time-constant for a particular frequency must be determined experimentally. The two clocks are basically anti-phase. CLOCK 2 controls the SAR and the up/down counter, CLOCK 1 controls the comparator latch. Figure 6-53 shows the timing diagram of a successive approximation cycle.

Comparator SE/NE5105

The high-speed, high-precision comparator SE/NE5105 has an input offset voltage of only 100 mV, an input offset current of 3 nA and a response time of 36 ns with 1, 2 mV or overdrive. It operates from a dual 5 V supply and incorporates an active-high output latch. It has a voltage gain of 88 db and is capable of driving 10 TTL loads.

Field Programming the PLS179s

The PLS179s are field-programmed using PLD programming software called Automated Map and Zap Equation (AMAZE) as shown in Screens 1 through 12. The SAR circuit is first designed as a state machine (in the file ADCS.SEE) and then, after pin assignments have been made, partitioned into two PLL179s. The up/down counter, input latches, biphase clock generator, and open-collector output DONE_OC are then implemented by using Boolean equations in the appropriate .BEE files (files ADCB.BEE and ADCB2.BEE) in AMAZE. These files are then assembled to produce fuse maps for programming the two PLS179s ADCB1.STD and ADCB2.STD (Screens 13 through 18).

```
@DEVICE SELECTION
ADCB1/PLS179
ADCB2/PLS179

@STATE VECTORS
[ /START, BIT11, BIT10, BIT9, BIT7, BIT6, BIT5, BIT4, BIT3, BIT2
BIT1, BIT0, DONE ]

INIT      = 0 —— —— —— - b;   "START CONVERSION PROCESS"
HALFSCALE = - 1000 0000 0000 0 b;   "SET SAR TO HALF SCALE"
ST2048    = 1 1000 0000 0000 0 b;   "PRESENT STATE = 2048 (HALF
SCALE)"
ST1024    = 1 -100 0000 0000 0 b;
ST512     = 1 —10 0000 0000 0 b;
ST256     = 1 —1 0000 0000 0 b;
ST128     = 1 —— 0000 0000 0 b;
ST64      = 1 —— -100 0000 0 b;
ST32      = 1 —— —10 0000 0 b;
ST16      = 1 —— —1 0000 0 b;
ST8       = 1 —— —— 0000 0 b;
ST4       = 1 —— —— -100 0 b;
ST2       = 1 —— —— —10 0 b;
ST1       = 1 —— —— —1 0 b;
                                          1/18
```

High-speed 12-bit tracking ADC using field programmable logic sequencers, Screen 1.

```
AD1024    = - -1— —— —— - b;   "ADD 1 BIT TO THE RIGHT"
AD512     = - —1- —— —— - b;
AD256     = - —1 —— —— - b;
AD128     = - —— 1— —— - b;
AD64      = - —— -1— —— - b;
AD32      = - —— —1- —— - b;
AD16      = - —— —1 —— - b;
AD8       = - —— —— 1— - b;
AD4       = - —— —— -1- - b;
AD2       = - —— —— —1- - b;
AD1       = - —— —— —1 - b;
END       = - —— —— —— 1 b;

SH1024    = - 01— —— —— - b;   "SHIFT ONE BIT TO THE RIGHT"
SH512     = - -01- —— —— - b;
SH256     = - —01 —— —— - b;
SH128     = - —0 1— —— - b;
SH64      = - —— 01— —— - b;
SH32      = - —— -01- —— - b;
SH16      = - —— —01 —— - b;
SH8       = - —— —0 1— - b;
SH4       = - —— —— 01— - b;
SH2       = - —— —— -01- - b;
                                          2/18
```

High-speed 12-bit tracking ADC using field programmable logic sequencers, Screen 2.

```
SH1    = - ——— ——— —01 - b;
SH0    = - ——— ——— —0 1 b;

@INPUT VECTORS
[ COMPARE ]
GREATER = 1 b ;  "IF DIGITAL OUTPUT IS GREATER THAN ANALOG
INPUT, ...."
LESS   = 0 b ;  "IF DIGITAL OUTPUT IS LESS THAN ANALOG INPUT,
...."

@OUTPUT VECTORS

@TRANSITIONS
WHILE [ INIT ]
IF [] THEN [ HALFSCALE ]  "INITIALIZE REGISTER TO HALF SCALE"
WHILE [ ST2048 ]
IF [ GREATER ] THEN [ SH1024 ]  "IF GREATER THAN, SHIFT 1 BIT"
IF [ LESS ] THEN [ AD1024 ]    "IF LESS THAN, ADD 1 BIT"
WHILE [ ST1024 ]
IF [ GREATER ] THEN [ SH512 ]
IF [ LESS ] THEN [ AD512 ]
WHILE [ ST512 ]
IF [ GREATER ] THEN [ SH256 ]
```

                                                                    3/18

High-speed 12-bit tracking ADC using field programmable logic sequencers, Screen 3.

```
IF [ LESS ] THEN [ AD256 ]
WHILE [ ST256 ]
IF [ GREATER ] THEN [ SH128 ]
IF [ LESS ] THEN [ AD128 ]
WHILE [ ST128 ]
IF [ GREATER ] THEN [ SH64 ]
IF [ LESS ] THEN [ AD64 ]
WHILE [ ST64 ]
IF [ GREATER ] THEN [ SH32 ]
IF [ LESS ] THEN [ AD32 ]
WHILE [ ST32 ]
IF [ GREATER ] THEN [ SH16 ]
IF [ LESS ] THEN [ AD16 ]
WHILE [ ST16 ]
IF [ GREATER ] THEN [ SH8 ]
IF [ LESS ] THEN [ AD8 ]
WHILE [ ST8 ]
IF [ GREATER ] THEN [ SH4 ]
IF [ LESS ] THEN [ AD4 ]
WHILE [ ST4 ]
IF [ GREATER ] THEN [ SH2 ]
IF [ LESS ] THEN [ AD2 ]
WHILE [ ST2 ]
```

                                                                    4/18

High-speed 12-bit tracking ADC using field programmable logic sequencers, Screen 4.

```
IF [ GREATER ] THEN [ SH1 ]
IF [ LESS ] THEN [ AD1 ]
WHILE [ ST1 ]
IF [ GREATER ] THEN [ SH0 ]
IF [ LESS ] THEN [ END ]


File Name  :  ADCB1
Date :
Time :
         ********************* P I N  L I S T ************************
```

LABEL	**	FNC	**	PIN	———	PIN	**	FNC	**	LABEL
CLOCK	**	CK	**	1-:		: -24	**	+5V	**	VCC
/ST	**	I	**	2-:		: 23	**	/B	**	N/C
COMPARE	**	I	**	3-:		: -22	**	0	**	/START
/HLD	**	I	**	4-:	P	: -21	**	0	**	BIT11
/TRACK	**	I	**	5-:	L	: -20	**	0	**	BIT10
BIT4	**	I	**	6-:	S	: -19	**	0	**	BIT9
BIT3	**	I	**	7-:	1	: -18	**	0	**	BIT8
BIT2	**	I	**	8-:	7	: -17	**	0	**	BIT7
BIT1	**	I	**	9-:	9	: -16	**	0	**	BIT6

```
                                                             5/18
```

High-speed 12-bit tracking ADC using field programmable logic sequencers, Screen 5.

BIT0	**	I	**	10-:		: -15	**	0	**	BIT5
DONE	**	I	**	11-:		: -14	**	/B	**	N/C
GND	**	OV	**	12-:		: -13	**	/OE	**	N/C

```
File Name  :  ADCB2
Date :
Time :
         ********************* P I N  L I S T ************************
```

LABEL	**	FNC	**PIN		———	PIN**	FNC	**	LABEL
CLOCK	**	CK	**	1-:		: -24 **	+5V	**	VCC
/START	**	I	**	2-:		: -23 **	/B	**	/DONE_OC
COMPARE	**	I	**	3-:		: -22 **	B	**	N/C
/HOLD	**	I	**	4-:	P	: -21 **	0	**	/HLD
/TRACK	**	I	**	5-:	L	: -20 **	0	**	BIT4
BIT5	**	I	**	6-:	S	: -19 **	0	**	BIT3
N/C	**	I	**	7-:	1	: -18 **	0	**	BIT2
N/C	**	I	**	8-:	7	: -17 **	0	**	BIT1
N/C	**	I	**	9-:	9	: -16 **	0	**	BIT0
RC	**	/B	**	10-:		: -15 **	0	**	DONE
CLOCK1	**	O	**	11-:		: -14 **	/0	**	CLOCK2
GND	**	OV	**	12-:		: -13 **	/OE	**	N/C

```
                                                             6/18
```

High-speed 12-bit tracking ADC using field programmable logic sequencers, Screen 6.

```
@DEVICE TYPE
PLS179
@DRAWING
@REVISION
@DATE
@SYMBOL
FILE NAME : ADCB1

@COMPANY
@NAME
@DESCRIPTION
@COMMON PRODUCT TERM
@COMPLEMENT ARRAY
@I/O DIRECTION
@OUTPUT POLARITY
@FLIP FLOP CONTROL
FC = 1 ;     "SET ALL FLIP FLOP TO BE J/K"

@OUTPUT ENABLE
@REGISTER LOAD
@ASYNCHRONOUS PRESET/RESET
@FLIP FLOP MODE
@LOGIC EQUATION
                                                            7/18
```

High-speed 12-bit tracking ADC using field programmable logic sequencers, Screen 7.

```
"NON-INVERTING INPUT LATCH: /START = /ST "
START : J = ST ;
K  = /ST ;
"UP/DOWN COUNTER ROUTINE"
/BIT5 : T = /START * TRACK * DONE * /HLD * COMPARE * /BIT0 * /BIT1 *
/BIT2 * /BIT3 * /BIT4 +
/START * TRACK * DONE * /HLD * /COMPARE * BIT0 * BIT1 *
BIT2 * BIT3 * BIT4 ;
/BIT6 : T = /START * TRACK * DONE * /HLD * COMPARE * /BIT0 * /BIT1 *
/BIT2 * /BIT3 * /BIT4 * /BIT5 +
/START * TRACK * DONE * /HLD * /COMPARE * BIT0 * BIT1 *
BIT2 * BIT3 * BIT4 * BIT5 ;
/BIT7 : T = /START * TRACK * DONE * /HLD * COMPARE *
/BIT0 * /BIT1 * /BIT2 * /BIT3 * /BIT4 * /BIT5 * /BIT6 +
/START * TRACK * DONE * /HLD * /COMPARE *
BIT0 * BIT1 * BIT2 * BIT3 * BIT4 * BIT5 * BIT6 ;
/BIT8 : T = /START * TRACK * DONE * /HLD * COMPARE * /BIT0 * /BIT1 *
/BIT2 * /BIT3 * /BIT4 * /BIT5 * /BIT6 * /BIT7 +
/START * TRACK * DONE * /HLD * /COMPARE * BIT0 * BIT1 *
BIT2 * BIT3 * BIT4 * BIT5 * BIT6 * BIT7 ;
/BIT9 : T = /START * TRACK * DONE * /HLD * COMPARE * /BIT0 * /BIT1 *
/BIT2 * /BIT3 * /BIT4 * /BIT5 * /BIT6 * /BIT7 * /BIT8 +
/START * TRACK * DONE * /HLD * /COMPARE * BIT0 * BIT1 *
                                                            8/18
```

High-speed 12-bit tracking ADC using field programmable logic sequencers, Screen 8.

```
BIT2 *  BIT3 *  BIT4 * BIT5 * BIT6 * BIT7 * BIT8 ;
/BIT10 :  T  = /START * TRACK * DONE * /HLD * COMPARE * /BIT0 * /
BIT1 *
/BIT2 * /BIT3 * /BIT4 * /BIT5 * /BIT6 * /BIT7 * /BIT8 *
/BIT9 +
/START * TRACK * DONE * /HLD * /COMPARE * BIT0 * BIT1 *
BIT2 *  BIT3 *  BIT4 * BIT5 * BIT6 * BIT7 * BIT8 * BIT9 ;

/BIT11 :  T  = /START * TRACK * DONE * /HLD * COMPARE * /BIT0 * /
BIT1 *
/BIT2 * /BIT3 * /BIT4 * /BIT5 * /BIT6 * /BIT7 * /BIT8 *
/BIT9 * /BIT10 +
/START * TRACK * DONE * /HLD * /COMPARE * BIT0 * BIT1 *
BIT2 *  BIT3 * BIT4 * BIT5 * BIT6 * BIT7 * BIT8 *
BIT9 * BIT10 ;
```

9/18

High-speed 12-bit tracking ADC using field programmable logic sequencers, Screen 9.

```
@DEVICE TYPE
PLS179
@DRAWING
@REVISION
@DATE
@SYMBOL
FILE NAME  :  ADCB2

@COMPANY
@NAME
@DESCRIPTION
@COMMON PRODUCT TERM
@COMPLEMENT ARRAY
@I/O DIRECTION
D0 = RC ;       "RC OSCILLATOR"
D3 = DONE ;     "ENABLE /DONE_OC TO OUTPUT A LOGIC LOW."
@OUTPUT POLARITY
@FLIP FLOP CONTROL
FC = 1 ;
@OUTPUT ENABLE
@REGISTER LOAD
@ASYNCHRONOUS PRESET/RESET
@FLIP FLOP MODE
"M0, M1, M2, M3, M4, M5 = 1 ;  SET F0 - F5 TO J/K FLIP FLOPS."
```

10/18

High-speed 12-bit tracking ADC using field programmable logic sequencers, Screen 10.

```
@LOGIC EQUATION
"NON-INVERTING INPUT LATCH:  /HLD = /HOLD "
HLD  : J = HOLD ;
K = /HOLD ;
"UP/DOWN COUNTER ROUTINE"
/BIT0 : T = /START * TRACK * DONE * /HLD ;
/BIT1 : T = /START * TRACK * DONE * /HLD *  COMPARE *  BIT0 +
/START * TRACK * DONE * /HLD *  COMPARE * /BIT0 ;
/BIT2 : T = /START * TRACK * DONE * /HLD * /COMPARE *  BIT0 * BIT1
+
/START * TRACK * DONE * /HLD *  COMPARE * /BIT0 * BIT1 ;
/BIT3 : T  = /START * TRACK * DONE * /HLD * /COMPARE *  BIT0 * BIT1
*
BIT2 +
/START * TRACK * DONE * /HLD *  COMPARE * /BIT0 * /BIT1 *
/BIT2 ;
/BIT4 : T = /START * TRACK * DONE * /HLD * /COMPARE *  BIT0 *
BIT1 *
BIT2 * BIT3 +
/START * TRACK * DONE * /HLD *  COMPARE * /BIT0 * /BIT1 *
/BIT2 * /BIT3 ;
/DONE_OC  = /( 1 ) ;

                                                              11/18
```

High-speed 12-bit tracking ADC using field programmable logic sequencers, Screen 11.

```
"RC OSCILLATOR"
RC        = /( 1 ) ;
CLOCK1    = RC ;
CLOCK2    = / ( CLOCK ) ;  "BUILT-IN DELAY OF 1 tPD"

                                                              12/18
```

High-speed 12-bit tracking ADC using field programmable logic sequencers, Screen 12.

```
                        FUSE MAP

PLS179              ! F/F TYPE   ! E(b)= !E(a) = !POLARTY!
                    !———————————!———!————!————!
T ! !               !A:A:A:A:A:A:A! 0   ! 0   !L:L:L:L!
E ! !———————————————————————————————————————————————
R ! !   I     ! B(I) !  Q(p)   !   Q(n)   ! B(o)  !
M !C!———————————————————————————————————————————————!
___!_!7_6_5_4_3_2_1_0!3_2_1_0!7_6_5_4_3_2_1_0!7_6_5_4_3_2_1_0!3_2_1_0!
0!A!- - - -,- - - L!- - - -!- - - -,- - - -!H - - -,- - - -!A A A A!
1!A!- - - -,- - - H!- - - -!- - - -,- - - -!L - - -,- - - -!A A A A!
2!A!L L L L,L L H -!- - H L!L - - -,- - - -!- - - -,- - - 0!A A A A!
3!A!H H H H,L H L -!- - H H!L - - -,- - - -!- - - -,- - - 0!A A A A!
4!A!L L L L,L H H -!- - H L!L - - -,- - - H!- - - -,- - 0 -!A A A A!
5!A!H H H H,L H L -!- - H H!L - - -,- - - L!- - - -,- 0 - -!A A A A!
6!A!L L L L,L H H -!- - H L!L - - -,- - H H!- - - -,- 0 - -!A A A A!
7!A!H H H H,L H L -!- - H H!L - - -,- - L L!- - - -,- 0 - -!A A A A!
8!A!L L L L,L H H -!- - H L!L - - -,- H H H!- - - -,0 - - -!A A A A!
9!A!H H H H,L H L -!- - H H!L - - -,- L L L!- - - -,0 - - -!A A A A!
10!A!L L L L,L H H -!- - H L!L - - -,H H H H!- - - 0,- - - -!A A A A!
11!A!H H H H,L H L -!- - H H!L - - -,L L L L!- - - 0,- - - -!A A A A!
12!A!L L L L,L H H -!- - H L!L - - H,H H H H!- - 0 -,- - - -!A A A A!
13!A!H H H H,L H L -!- - H H!L - - L,L L L L!- 0 -,- - - -!A A A A!
                                                        13/18
```

High-speed 12-bit tracking ADC using field programmable logic sequencers, Screen 13.

```
14!A!L L L L,L H H -!- - H L!L - H H,H H H H!- 0 - -,- - - -!A A A A!
15!A!H H H H,L H L -!- - H H!L - L L,L L L L!- 0 - -,- - - -!A A A A!
16!A!- - - -,- - - -!- - - -!H - - -,- - - -!- L H H,H H H H!A A A A!
17!A!L L L L,- - H -!- - L L!L L H H,H H H H!- H L -,- - - -!A A A A!
18!A!L L L L,- - L -!- - L L!L L H H,H H H H!- - L -,- - - -!A A A A!
19!A!L L L L,- - H -!- - L L!L - H,H H H H!- - - -,- - - -!A A A A!
20!A!L L L L,- - L -!- - L L!L - L H,H H H H!- - - L,- - - -!A A A A!
21!A!L L L L,- - H -!- - L L!L - - L,H H H H!- - - H,L - - -!A A A A!
22!A!L L L L,- - L -!- - L L!L - - L,H H H H!- - - -,L - - -!A A A A!
23!A!L L L L,- - H -!- - L L!L - - -,L H H H!- - - -,H L - -!A A A A!
24!A!L L L L,- - L -!- - L L!L - - -,L H H H!- - - -,- L - -!A A A A!
25!A!L L L L,- - H -!- - L L!L - - -,- L H H!- - - -,- H L -!A A A A!
26!A!L L L L,- - L -!- - L L!L - - -,- L H H!- - - -,- - L -!A A A A!
27!A!L L L L,- - H -!- - L L!L - - -,- L H!- - - -,- H L!A A A A!
28!A!L L L L,- - L -!- - L L!L - - -,- L H!- - - -,- - L!A A A A!
29!A!L L L L,- - H -!- - L L!L - - -,- - L!- - - -,- - H!A A A A!
30!0!0 0 0 0,0 0 0 0!0 0 0 0!0 0 0 0,0 0 0 0!0 0 0 0,0 0 0 0!A A A A!
31!0!0 0 0 0,0 0 0 0!0 0 0 0!0 0 0 0,0 0 0 0!0 0 0 0,0 0 0 0!A A A A!
Fc!A!- - - -,- - - -!- - - -!- - - -,- - - -!
Pb!.!0 0 0 0,0 0 0 0!0 0 0 0!0 0 0 0,0 0 0 0!                .
Rb!.!0 0 0 0,0 0 0 0!0 0 0 0!0 0 0 0,0 0 0 0!                .
Lb!.!0 0 0 0,0 0 0 0!0 0 0 0!0 0 0 0,0 0 0 0!                .
Pa!.!0 0 0 0,0 0 0 0!0 0 0 0!0 0 0 0,0 0 0 0!                .
                                                        14/18
```

High-speed 12-bit tracking ADC using field programmable logic sequencers, Screen 14.

```
Ra!.!0 0 0 0,0 0 0 0!0 0 0 0!0 0 0 0,0 0 0 0!          .
La!.!0 0 0 0,0 0 0 0!0 0 0 0!0 0 0 0,0 0 0 0!          .
D3!.!0 0 0 0,0 0 0 0!0 0 0 0!0 0 0 0,0 0 0 0!          .
D2!.!0 0 0 0,0 0 0 0!0 0 0 0!0 0 0 0,0 0 0 0!          .
D1!.!0 0 0 0,0 0 0 0!0 0 0 0!0 0 0 0,0 0 0 0!          .
D0!.!0 0 0 0,0 0 0 0!0 0 0 0!0 0 0 0,0 0 0 0!          .

B B B B / / C / N N D B / B B B B B B B / B B B B B B B N N D B
I I I I T H O S / / O I S I I I I I I I I S I I I I I I I / / O I
T T T T R L M T C C N T T T T T T T T T T T T T T T T C C N T
1 2 3 4 A D P   E O A 1 1 9 8 7 6 5 A 1 1 9 8 7 6 5   E O
C A        R 1 0        R 1 0
K R        T            T
E


                        FUSE MAP
PLS179              ! F/F TYPE   ! E(b)= !E(a) = !POLARTY!
___                 !————————!———!————!————!
T ! !               !A:A:A:A:A:A:A:A! 0  ! 0   !L:L:L:L!
E ! !———————————————————————————————————————————————————
___
R ! !    I    ! B(I) !   Q(p)   !   Q(n)   ! B(o)  !
M !C!————————————————————————————————————————————————————————!
                                                           15/18
```

High-speed 12-bit tracking ADC using field programmable logic sequencers, Screen 15.

```
___! !7_6_5_4_3_2_1_0!3_2_1_0!7_6_5_4_3_2_1_0!7_6_5_4_3_2_1_0!3_2_1_0!
0!A!- - -,- L - -!- - -!- - -,- - - -!0 H - -,- - -!. . . .!
1!A!- - -,- H - -!- - -!- - -,- - - -!0 L - -,- - -!. . . .!
2!A!- - -,L - - H!- - -!- L - -,- - - L!0 - -,- - 0 -!. . . .!
3!A!- - -,L - L H!- - - -!- L - -,- - L L!0 - - -,- 0 - -!. . . .!
4!A!- - -,L - H H!- - - -!- L - -,- - H L!0 - - -,- 0 - -!. . . .!
5!A!- - -,L - L H!- - - -!- L - -,- L L L!0 - - -,0 - - -!. . . .!
6!A!- - -,L - H H!- - - -!- L - -,- H H L!0 - - -,0 - - -!. . . .!
7!A!- - -,L - L H!- - - -!- L - -,L L L L!0 - - 0,- - - -!. . . .!
8!A!- - -,L - H H!- - - -!- L - -,H H H L!0 - - 0,- - - -!. . . .!
9!A!- - -,L - L H!- - - -!- L - L,L L L L!0 - 0 -,- - - -!. . . .!
10!A!- - -,L - H H!- - - -!- L - H,H H H L!0 - 0 -,- - - -!. . . .!
11!A!- - -,- - - -!- - - -!- - -,- - - -!0 - - -,- - - -!A . . .!
12!A!- - -,- - - -!- - H!- - -,- - - -!0 - -,- - -!. . A .!
13!A!- - -,- - - -!- - H -!- - -,- - - -!0 - -,- - -!. A . .!
14!A!- - -,- - - L!- - - -!- - -,- - - -!0 - H H,H H H H!. . . .!
15!A!- - H,- - H H!- - - -!- H H,H H H H!0 - L -,- - - -!. . . .!
16!A!- - H,- - L H!- - - -!- H H,H H H H!0 - L -,- - - -!. . . .!
17!A!- - -,- - H H!- - - -!- L H,H H H H!0 - H L,- - - -!. . . .!
18!A!- - -,- - L H!- - - -!- L H,H H H H!0 - - L,- - - -!. . . .!
19!A!- - -,- - H H!- - - -!- L,H H H H!0 - - H,L - - -!. . . .!
20!A!- - -,- - L H!- - - -!- - - L,H H H H!0 - - -,L - - -!. . . .!
21!A!- - -,- - H H!- - - -!- - -,L H H H!0 - - -,H L - -!. . . .!
                                                           16/18
```

High-speed 12-bit tracking ADC using field programmable logic sequencers, Screen 16.

```
22!A!- - -,- - L H!- - - -!- - -,L H H H!0 - - -,- L - -!. . . .!
23!A!- - -,- - H H!- - - -!- - -,- L H H!0 - - -,- H L -!. . . .!
24!A!- - -,- - L H!- - - -!- - -,- L H H!0 - - -,- - L -!. . . .!
25!A!- - -,- - H H!- - - -!- - -,- L H!0 - - -,- - H L!. . . .!
26!A!- - -,- - - H!- - - -!- - -,- - L H!0 - - -,- - - L!. . . .!
27!0!0 0 0 0,0 0 0 0!0 0 0 0!0 0 0 0,0 0 0 0!0 0 0 0,0 0 0 0!A A A A!
28!0!0 0 0 0,0 0 0 0!0 0 0 0!0 0 0 0,0 0 0 0!0 0 0 0,0 0 0 0!A A A A!
29!0!0 0 0 0,0 0 0 0!0 0 0 0!0 0 0 0,0 0 0 0!0 0 0 0,0 0 0 0!A A A A!
30!0!0 0 0 0,0 0 0 0!0 0 0 0!0 0 0 0,0 0 0 0!0 0 0 0,0 0 0 0!A A A A!
31!0!0 0 0 0,0 0 0 0!0 0 0 0!0 0 0 0,0 0 0 0!0 0 0 0,0 0 0 0!A A A A!
Fc!A!- - -,- - - -!- - - -!- - -,- - - -!
Pb!.!0 0 0 0,0 0 0 0!0 0 0 0!0 0 0 0,0 0 0 0!          .
Rb!.!0 0 0 0,0 0 0 0!0 0 0 0!0 0 0 0,0 0 0 0!          .
Lb!.!0 0 0 0,0 0 0 0!0 0 0 0!0 0 0 0,0 0 0 0!          .
Pa!.!0 0 0 0,0 0 0 0!0 0 0 0!0 0 0 0,0 0 0 0!          .
Ra!.!0 0 0 0,0 0 0 0!0 0 0 0!0 0 0 0,0 0 0 0!          .
La!.!0 0 0 0,0 0 0 0!0 0 0 0!0 0 0 0,0 0 0 0!          .
D3!-!- - -,- - - -!- - - -!- - -,- - - -!          .
D2!-!- - -,- - - -!- - - -!- - -,- - - -!          .
D1!-!- - -,- - - -!- - - -!- - -,- - - -!          .
D0!-!- - -,- - - -!- - - -!- - -,- - - -!          .

N B B B / / C / / C C R N / B B B B B D N / B B B B B D / C C R
                                                              17/18
```

High-speed 12-bit tracking ADC using field programmable logic sequencers, Screen 17.

```
/ / / I T H 0 S D L L C / H I I I I I 0 / H I I I I I 0 D L L C
C C C T R P M T 0 0 0 C L T T T T T M C L T T T T T N 0 0 0
5 A L P A N C C  D 4 3 2 1 0 E  D 4 3 2 1 0 E N C C
C D A R E K K                   E K K
K  R T _ 2 1                    _ 2 1
E  0                 0
C                    C
                                                              18/18
```

COURTESY OF SIGNETICS CORPORATION

High-speed 12-bit tracking ADC using field programmable logic sequencers, Screen 18.

16-BIT BINARY COUNTER
IMPLEMENTATION USING THE 5C060 EPLD
Courtesy of Intel Corporation

System designers often use programmable logic devices to implement counters. Use of PLA devices lets the user build customized counters to suit individual applications. In most cases such counters are not available as off-the-shelf SSI/MSI devices. In other applications, the PLA implementation allows the designer to squeeze the counter function along with other glue tasks into a single PLA, with the attendant higher integration benefits.

Use of traditional 20-pin and 24-pin PLAs, however, does not allow for the construction of large counters having greater than 10 significant bits. This is because these traditional PLAs have register and product term restrictions (even the larger bipolar PLAs have only 8 to 10 registers and less than 8 product terms per register). In contrast, the 5C060 24-pin erasable programmable logic device (EPLD) contains 16 registers that are programmable as D, T, SR, or JK types. These 16 programmable registers enable the construction of up/down counters with up to 16 significant bits.

This application example details the implementation of a 16-bit binary counter in the 5C060 EPLD. The design also demonstrates efficient counter construction utilizing toggle flip-flops (T-FF) that allows for minimum product term utilization. The macrocell architecture is given in FIG. 6-54.

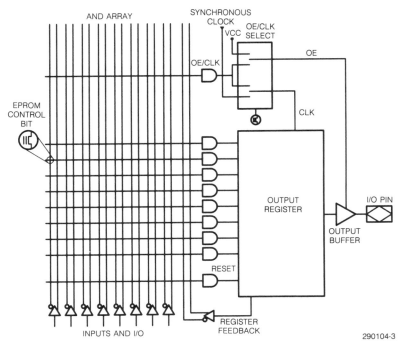

Fig. 6-54. Macrocell architecture of the 5C060. Courtesy of Intel Corporation.

Design Objective

The objective of the design is to implement a counter with the following features:

- 16-bit binary count.
- toggle flip-flops.
- asynchronous clear.
- RUN/$\overline{\text{STOP}}$ function.
- UP/$\overline{\text{DOWN}}$ function.

The function table is shown in TABLE 6-5.

Table 6-5. Function table for 16-bit binary counter.

RESET	UP/DOWN	RUN/STOP	Function
X	X	X	Inhibit Counting
0	0	1	Count Down
0	1	1	Count Up
1	X	X	Reset All Outputs to Low

Toggle Flip-Flop

Counters can be most effectively implemented in PLA architectures using toggle flip-flops. This is because counters constructed with D type flip-flops required an additional product term for every successive significant bit, whereas toggle flip-flop implementation requires only one product term per significant bit. Thus, the toggle flip-flop counter design is more miserly in product term consumption than the D register design. Because product term minimization is the key element to maximizing PLA utilization, the T-FF counter design is more efficient. The truth table for the toggle flip-flop is shown in TABLE 6-6.

T	Q(N)	Q(N + 1)
0	0	0
0	1	0
1	0	1
1	1	0

Table 6-6. Truth table for toggle flip-flop.

Solution

The 16-bit binary counter function was implemented in the 5C060 EPLD using the Intel Programmable Logic Development System (iPLDS). The Advanced Design File (ADF) is shown in computer Screens 1 and 2. The equations for the 16-bit binary counter with the RESET, UP/$\overline{\text{DOWN}}$ and RUN/$\overline{\text{STOP}}$ functions are shown in the EQUATIONS section of the Logic Equation

```
                         SCREEN PRINTS

     16-BIT BINARY COUNTER IMPLEMENTATION USING THE 5C060 EPLD

 LB Version 3.0, Baseline 17x, 9/26/85

 PART:   5C060

 INPUTS: RS, CLOCK, RESET

 OUTPUTS:     Q0, Q1, Q2, Q3, Q4, Q5, Q6, Q7, Q8, Q9, QA, QB, QC, QD,
              QE, QF

 NETWORK:
 Q0,Q0F = TOTF (Q0T,CLK,ICLR,GND,VCC)
 Q1,Q1F = TOTF (Q1T,CLK,ICLR,GND,VCC)
 Q2,Q2F = TOTF (Q2T,CLK,ICLR,GND,VCC)
 Q3,Q3F = TOTF (Q3T,CLK,ICLR,GND,VCC)
 Q4,Q4F = TOTF (Q4T,CLK,ICLR,GND,VCC)
 Q5,Q5F = TOTF (Q5T,CLK,ICLR,GND,VCC)
 Q6,Q6F = TOTF (Q6T,CLK,ICLR,GND,VCC)
 Q7,Q7F = TOTF (Q7T,CLK,ICLR,GND,VCC)
 Q8,Q8F = TOTF (Q8T,CLK,ICLR,GND,VCC)
 Q9,Q9F = TOTF (Q9T,CLK,ICLR,GND,VCC)
                                                              1/15
```

16-bit binary counter implementation using the 5C060, EPLD, Screen 1.

```
 QA,QAF = TOTF (QAT,CLK,ICLR,GND,VCC)
 QB,QBF = TOTF (QBT,CLK,ICLR,GND,VCC)
 QC,QCF = TOTF (QCT,CLK,ICLR,GND,VCC)
 QD,QDF = TOTF (QDT,CLK,ICLR,GND,VCC)
 QE,QEF = TOTF (QET,CLK,ICLR,GND,VCC)
 QF  = TONF (QFT,CLK,ICLR,GND,VCC)
 QOT = INP (RS)
 CLK = INP (CLOCK)
 ICLR = INP (RESET)
 Q1T = AND (QOF,QOT)
 Q2T = AND (Q1F,Q1T)
 Q3T = AND (Q2F,Q2T)
 Q4T = AND (Q3F,Q3T)
 Q5T = AND (Q4F,Q4T)
 Q6T = AND (Q5F,Q5T)
 Q7T = AND (Q6F,Q6T)
 Q8T = AND (Q7F,Q7T)
 Q9T = AND (Q8F,Q8T)
 QAT = AND (Q9F,Q9T)
 QBT = AND (QAF,QAT)
 QCT = AND (QBF,QBT)
 QDT = AND (QCF,QCT)
 QET = AND (QDF,QDT)
 QFT = AND (QEF,QET)
 END$                                                         2/15
```

16-bit binary counter implementation using the 5C060, EPLD, Screen 2.

File (LCF) of Screens 3 through 5. The pinout of the 5C060 with the implemented counter is shown in the RFP file (Utilization Report) Screens 6 through 15. This RFP file also shows, under the OUTPUTS section, that in each macrocell only one of 8 product terms is used. In contrast, the same 16-bit counter designed using D type flip-flops would have required more than 16 product terms for the significant bit.

```
                            SCREEN PRINTS

        16-BIT BINARY COUNTER IMPLEMENTATION USING THE 5C060 EPLD

        LB Version 3.0, Baseline 17x, 9/26/85

        PART:   5C060

        INPUTS:  RS, CLOCK, RESET

        OUTPUTS:      Q0, Q1, Q2, Q3, Q4, Q5, Q6, Q7, Q8, Q9, QA, QB, QC, QD,
                      QE, QF

        NETWORK:
        CLK  = INP (CLOCK)
        Q0T  = INPT (RS)
        ICLR = INP (RESET)
        Q0,Q0F  = TOTF (Q0T,CLK,ICLR,GND,VCC)
        Q1,Q1F  = TOTF (Q1T,CLK,ICLR,GND,VCC)
        Q2,Q2F  = TOTF (Q2T,CLK,ICLR,GND,VCC)
        Q3,Q3F  = TOTF (Q3T,CLK,ICLR,GND,VCC)
        Q4,Q4F  = TOTF (Q4T,CLK,ICLR,GND,VCC)
        Q5,Q5F  = TOTF (Q5T,CLK,ICLR,GND,VCC)
        Q6,Q6F  = TOTF (Q6T,CLK,ICLR,GND,VCC)
                                                            3/15
```

16-bit binary counter implementation using the 5C060, EPLD, Screen 3.

```
Q7,Q7F = TOTF (Q7T,CLK,ICLR,GND,VCC)
Q8,Q8F = TOTF (Q8T,CLK,ICLR,GND,VCC)
Q9,Q9F = TOTF (Q9T,CLK,ICLR,GND,VCC)
QA,QAF = TOTF (QAT,CLK,ICLR,GND,VCC)
QB,QBF = TOTF (QBT,CLK,ICLR,GND,VCC)
QC,QCF = TOTF (QCT,CLK,ICLR,GND,VCC)
QD,QDF = TOTF (QDT,CLK,ICLR,GND,VCC)
QE,QEF = TOTF (QET,CLK,ICLR,GND,VCC)
QF   = TONF (QFT,CLK,ICLR,GND,VCC)
```

EQUATIONS:

```
QFT =   QEF * QDF * QCF * QBF * QAF * Q9F * Q8F * Q7F * Q6F * Q5F * Q4F
        * Q3F * Q2F * Q1F * QOF * QOT;

QET =   QDF * QCF * QBF * QAF * Q9F * Q8F * Q7F * Q6F * Q5F * Q4F * Q3F
        * Q2F * Q1F * QOF * QOT;

QDT =   QCF * QBF * QAF * Q9F * Q8F * Q7F * Q6F * Q5F * Q4F * Q3F * Q2F
        * Q1F * QOF * QOT;

QCT =   QBF * QAF * Q9F * Q8F * Q7F * Q6F * Q5F * Q4F * Q3F * Q2F * Q1F
        * QOF * QOT;
```

4/15

16-bit binary counter implementation using the 5C060, EPLD, Screen 4.

```
QBT =   QAF * Q9F * Q8F * Q7F * Q6F * Q5F * Q4F * Q3F * Q2F * Q1F * QOF
        * QOT;

QAT =   Q9F * Q8F * Q7F * Q6F * Q5F * Q4F * Q3F * Q2F * Q1F * QOF * QOT;

Q9T =   Q8F * Q7F * Q6F * Q5F * Q4F * Q3F * Q2F * Q1F * QOF * QOT;

Q8T =   Q7F * Q6F * Q5F * Q4F * Q3F * Q2F * Q1F * QOF * QOT;

Q7T =   Q6F * Q5F * Q4F * Q3F * Q2F * Q1F * QOF * QOT;

Q6T =   Q5F * Q4F * Q3F * Q2F * Q1F * QOF * QOT;

Q5T =   Q4F * Q3F * Q2F * Q1F * QOF * QOT;

Q4T =   Q3F * Q2F * Q1F * QOF * QOT;

Q3T =   Q2F * Q1F * QOF * QOT;

Q2T =   Q1F * QOF * QOT;

Q1T =   QOF * QOT;
```

5/15

16-bit binary counter implementation using the 5C060, EPLD, Screen 5.

Logic Optimizing Compiler Utilization Report

**** Design implemented successfully

**** NOTE: Connect CLOCK to pins 1 and 13

5C060

```
    CLOCK   -I  1    24I  -   Vcc
    GND     -I  2    23I  -   RS
    Q8      -I  3    22I  -   Q0
    Q7      -I  4    21I  -   QF
    Q6      -I  5    20I  -   QE
    Q5      -I  6    19I  -   QD
    Q4      -I  7    18I  -   QC
    Q3      -I  8    17I  -   QB
    Q2      -I  9    16I  -   QA
    Q1      -I10    15I  -   Q9
    GND     -I11    14I  -   RESET
    GND     -I12    13I  -   CLOCK
    _____
```

INPUTS

6/15

16-bit binary counter implementation using the 5C060, EPLD, Screen 6.

Name Pin	Resource	MCell #PTerms	I	Feeds: MCells	OE
Clear (					
CLOCK1	INP	- - - -	-		
RESET14	INP	- - -	-	1	
			2		
			3		
			4		
			5		
			6		
			7		
			8		
			9		
			10		
			11		
			12		
			13		
			14		
			15		
			16		

7/15

16-bit binary counter implementation using the 5C060, EPLD, Screen 7.

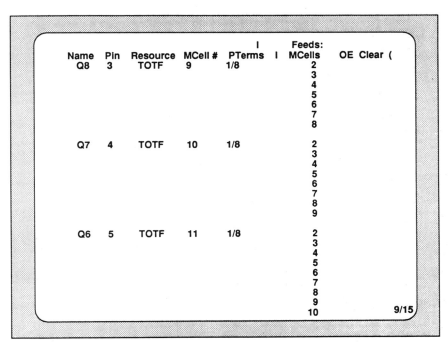

					Feeds:			
Name	Pin	Resource	MCell #	PTerms	I	MCells	OE	Clear (
RS	23	INP						
1								
						2		
						3		
						4		
						5		
						6		
						7		
						8		
						9		
						10		
						11		
						12		
						13		
						14		
						15		
						16		

OUTPUTS

8/15

16-bit binary counter implementation using the 5C060, EPLD, Screen 8.

					Feeds:		
Name	Pin	Resource	MCell #	PTerms	I	MCells	OE Clear (
Q8	3	TOTF	9	1/8		2	
						3	
						4	
						5	
						6	
						7	
						8	
Q7	4	TOTF	10	1/8		2	
						3	
						4	
						5	
						6	
						7	
						8	
						9	
Q6	5	TOTF	11	1/8		2	
						3	
						4	
						5	
						6	
						7	
						8	
						9	
						10	

9/15

16-bit binary counter implementation using the 5C060, EPLD, Screen 9.

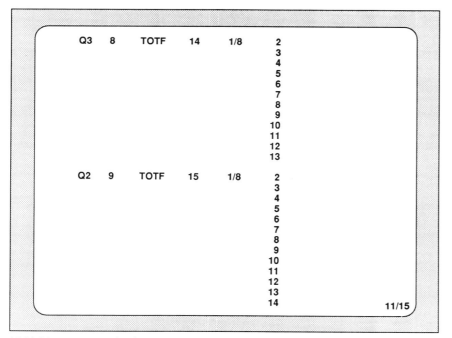

I Name	Feeds: Pin	Resource	MCell #	PTerms	I	MCells	OE	Clear (
Q5	6	TOTF	12	1/8	2			
					3			
					4			
					5			
					6			
					7			
					8			
					9			
					10			
					11			
Q4	7	TOTF	13	1/8	2			
					3			
					4			
					5			
					6			
					7			
					8			
					9			
					10			
					11			
					12			

10/15

16-bit binary counter implementation using the 5C060, EPLD, Screen 10.

Q3	8	TOTF	14	1/8	2			
					3			
					4			
					5			
					6			
					7			
					8			
					9			
					10			
					11			
					12			
					13			
Q2	9	TOTF	15	1/8	2			
					3			
					4			
					5			
					6			
					7			
					8			
					9			
					10			
					11			
					12			
					13			
					14			

11/15

16-bit binary counter implementation using the 5C060, EPLD, Screen 11.

Name	Pin	Resource	MCell #	I PTerms I	Feeds: MCells	OE Clear (
Q1	10	TOTF	16	1/8	2	
					3	
					4	
					5	
					6	
					7	
					8	
					9	
					10	
					11	
					12	
					13	
					14	
					15	
Q9	15	TOTF	8	1/8	2	
					3	
					4	
					5	
					6	
					7	12/15

16-bit binary counter implementation using the 5C060, EPLD, Screen 12.

Name	Pin	Resource	MCell #	PTerms	Feeds: MCells	
QA	16	TOTF	7	1/8	2	
					3	
					4	
					5	
					6	
QA	17	TOTF	7	1/8	2	
					3	
					4	
					5	
QA	18	TOTF	7	1/8	2	
					3	
					4	
QA	19	TOTF	4	1/8	2	
					3	
QA	20	TOTF	3	1/8	2	
QA	21	TOTF	2	1/8	-	13/15

16-bit binary counter implementation using the 5C060, EPLD, Screen 13.

Name	Pin	Resource	MCell #	PTerms	I	Feeds: MCells	OE	Clear (
Q0	22	TOTF	1	1/8		2		
						3		
						4		
						5		
						6		
						7		
						8		
						9		
						10		
						11		
						12		
						13		
						14		
						15		
						16		

UNUSED RESOURCES

14/15

16-bit binary counter implementation using the 5C060, EPLD, Screen 14.

Name	Pin	Resource	MCell #	PTerms
-	2	-	-	-
			3	
-	11	-	-	-

PART UTILIZATION

90%   Pins
100%   MacroCells
12%   Pterms

15/15

16-bit binary counter implementation using the 5C060, EPLD, Screen 15.

IMPLEMENTING A CMOS BUS
ARBITER/CONTROLLER IN THE 5C060 EPLD
Courtesy of Intel Corporation

This application example shows how to implement a CMOS Bus Arbiter/ Controller in an Intel 5C060 EPLD (Erasable Programmable Logic Device). The example includes a brief overview of a similar circuit implemented with typical PLA devices.

The bus priority resolution and arbitration scheme selected for the circuit is that used by the industry-standard Multibus I interface. Operation and timing for the Multibus I interface is well understood by most engineers and is described in readily available Intel publications. Thus, a description of the Multibus I interface is not included here. The bus arbiter/controller functions shown here support both serial and parallel priority resolution between bus masters. Timing is equivalent to Multibus I specifications. Electrical specifications for both the PLA and EPLD approaches vary from Multibus I standards. Neither of the two circuits discussed here provide the full current sink capability for all Multibus I signals. Because the EPLD implementation is designed for CMOS systems, however, this requirement is not relevant for the 5C060 implementation.

PLA Approach

The functional equivalent of a Multibus I arbiter/controller can be implemented in two 20-pin PLA-type devices as shown in FIG. 6-55 and FIG. 6-56 (Figure 6-55 shows the logic for the arbiter device. Figure 6-56 shows the logic for the controller and the connections to the arbiter.) Screen 1 shows the logic optimizing compiler main menu. Screen 2 shows the arbiter list file as an example of PLA-type files. Two different 20-pin PLA devices are required to implement the arbiter and controller functions, a 16R4-type device and a 16L8-type device.

Implementation of logic devices in PLA-type devices, such as those shown here, has proven to be quite beneficial. Development time and cost is much less than for custom silicon device designs. The two PLA-type devices take up less board space than a discrete TTL implementation of the same functions. In addition, the two raw devices can also be used for different functions in other products, thereby reducing inventory costs. As a result of these factors (and others), use of PLA-type devices has grown substantially in recent years.

With the increased density and flexibility of EPLD devices over typical PLA-type devices, even greater space, inventory, and cost savings can be obtained by using EPLDs. The following section shows an implementation of the same arbiter/controller functions in a single 24-pin 5C060 EPLD device.

5C060 Implementation

The equivalent functions for both the Multibus I arbiter and controller fit inside a single 5C060 EPLD device. The 5C060 device is available in a 24-pin 0 3"' DIP package. Figure 6-57 and 6-58 show logic diagrams for the arbiter and

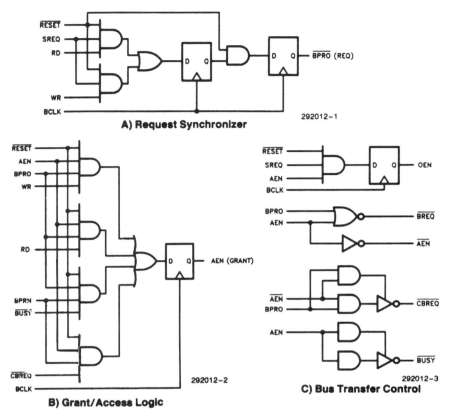

Fig. 6-55. *PLA approach to a bus arbiter. Courtesy of Intel Corporation.*

controller functions. When compared with the PLA implementation, some differences in the design are immediately apparent. These differences result from the characteristics of the EPLD macrocell or from corrections to the circuit used in FIGS. 6-55 and 6-56.

The major change resulting from the EPLD macrocell structure concerns the EPLD output buffers. Because output buffers from macrocells are noninverting (PLA-type devices typically contain inverting buffers), signals enter the buffers in the same logic orientation from which they are to appear at the output. The logic for the EPLD (shown in FIGS. 6-57 and 6-58) incorporates this change.

Some errors in the PLA-type implementation have also been corrected in the EPLD design. These changes are as follows:

- The $\overline{M/IO}$ input to the $\overline{MRDC}/$ and $\overline{MWTC}/$ gates is inverted. $\overline{M/IO}$ distinguishes between memory and I/O cycles. The PLA-type implementation does not use this signal properly; the PLA-type controller generates read or write commands to both memory and I/O at the same time, which can result in contention between memory and I/O during bus transfers.

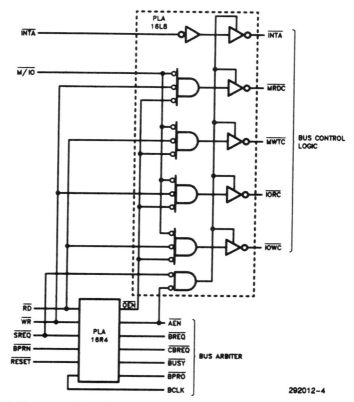

Fig. 6-56. Bus controller with arbiter connected. Courtesy of Intel Corporation.

- $\overline{\text{BPRO}}$/ is gated by $\overline{\text{BPRN}}$/ in the EPLD design. When using serial priority resolution, this allows the highest priority arbiter to prevent all other masters from controlling the bus. (In the PLA design, BPRO/ is enabled/ disabled only by a local request. Higher priority arbiters cannot disable all other arbiters. This can result in contention between bus masters. By gating $\overline{\text{BPRO}}$/ with $\overline{\text{BPRN}}$/ in the EPLD design, this source of bus contention is prevented.)

Screens 3, 4, and 5 show the iPLDS Network List File produced by the iPLDS software while Screens 6, 7, 8, and 9 show the iPLDS Report file. The report file contains a pinout diagram of the final programmed device and provides a resource usage map for the device.

Most of the input and output signals are self-explanatory to those familiar with Intel processors and the Multibus I interface. The $\overline{\text{SREQ}}$ input is the bus transfer request signal from the address decode logic. The $\overline{\text{BUSY}}$/ and $\overline{\text{CBREQ}}$/ outputs use the iPLDS 5C060 (Combinational-Output I/O-Feedback) primitive in the list file. The $\overline{\text{BUSY}}$/signal serves to illustrate this use of EPLD outputs.

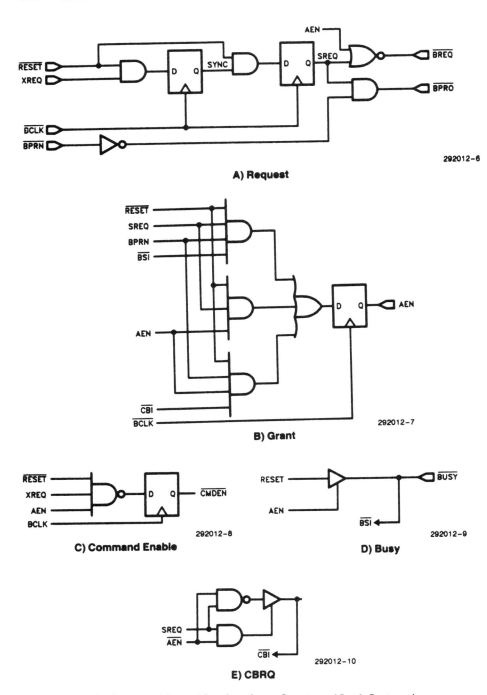

A) Request

292012-6

B) Grant

292012-7

C) Command Enable

292012-8

D) Busy

292012-9

E) CBRQ

292012-10

Fig. 6-57. Logic diagram of bus arbiter functions. Courtesy of Intel Corporation.

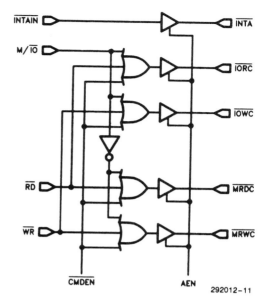

Fig. 6-58. Logic diagram of bus controller functions. Courtesy of Intel Corporation.

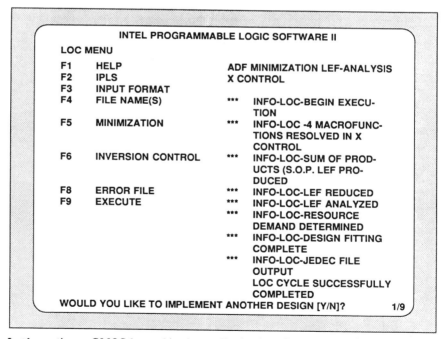

Implementing a CMOS bus arbiter/controller in the 5C060 EPLD, Screen 1.

```
PLA16R4                    PLA DESIGN FILE
ARB001                     D.E. ENGR. 1/1/85
MULTIBUS I ARBITER
SOME SYSTEM COMPANY
BCLK  /WR   /RD   /SREQ /RESET /BPRN  NC    NC    NC   GND
/E   /CBREQ /BUSY /SYNC /BPRO  /AEN   /OEN  /BREQ  NC
VCC

SYNC  :=  /RESET*SREQ*WR        +
/RESET*SREQ*RD

PBRO  :=  /RESET*SYNC

AEN   :=  /RESET* AEN*BPRO*WR    +
          /RESET* AEN*BPRO*RD    +
          /RESET*BPRO*BPRN*/BUSY   +
          /RESET* AEN*BPRN*/CBREQ

EN     :=  /RESET*SREQ*AEN

IF(BPRO*/AEN) CBREQ = BPRO*/AEN

IF(AEN)BUSY = AEN

BREQ = 'BPRO +
          AEN
                                              2/9
```

Implementing a CMOS bus arbiter/controller in the 5C060 EPLD, Screen 2.

```
DANIEL E. SMITH
INTEL CORPORATION
MARCH 27, 1986
VERSION 1.1
REV. A
5C060
CMOS BUS ARBITER/CONTROLLER

PART:      5C060
INPUTS:    BCLK, XREQ, RESET, BPRN, MIO, RD, WR, INTAIN
OUTPITS:   BPRO, AEN, BREQ, CBRQ, BUSY, INTA, MRDC, MWTC, IORC,
           IOWC


NETWORK:

BCLK      = INP  (BCLK)        %BUS CLOCK INPUT%
INTAIN    = INP  (INTAIN)      %INT. ACK. INPUT%
XREQ      = INP  (XREQ)        %SYSTEM REQUEST INPUT%
RESET     = INP  (RESET)       %RESET INPUT%
BPRN      = INP  (BPRN)        %BUS PRIORITY INPUT%
MIO       = INP  (MIO)         %MEMORY/IO INPUT%
RD        = INP  (RD)          %READ INPUT%
WR        = INP  (WR)          %WRITE INPUT%
                                              3/9
```

Implementing a CMOS bus arbiter/controller in the 5C060 EPLD, Screen 3.

```
BPRO          = CONF   (BPROc, VCC)           %BUS PRIORITY OUTPUT%
AEN, AEN      = RORF   (AENd, BCLK,           %ADDRESS ENABLE GRANT%
                        GND, GND, YCC)

BREQ          = CONF   (BREQc,VCC)            %BUS REQUEST%
CBRQ, CBI     = COIF   (CBRQc1, CBRQc2)       %CBRQ/ - - SIMULATED O.C.%
BUSY,BSI      = COIF   (BUSYc, AEN)           %BUSY/ - - SIMULATED O.C.%
INTA          = CONF   (INTAIN, AEN)          %INT. ACK. OUTPUT%
MRDC          = CONF   (MRDCc, AEN)           %MEMORY READ COMMAND%
MWTC          = CONF   (MWTCc,AEN)            %MEMORY WRITE COMMAND%
IORC          = CONF   (IORCc, AEN0           %I/O READ COMMAND%
IOWC          = CONF   (IOWCc, AEN0           %I/O WIRTE COMMAND%
SREQ          = NORF   (SREQd, BCLK,          %VALID BUS REQUEST%
                        GND, GND)

SYNC          = NORF   (SYNCd, BCLK,          %SYNCHRONIZED REQUEST%
                        GND, GND)

CMDEN         = NORF   (CMDENd,               %CMMAND ENALBLE%
                        BCLK, GND, GND)


EQUATIONS:

BPROc         = (SREQ * /BPRN);
AENd          = RESET * SREQ * /BPRN * BSI +
                RESET * SREQ * AEM +
```

4/9

Implementing a CMOS bus arbiter/controller in the 5C060 EPLD, Screen 4.

```
                 RESET * /BPRN * AEN*CBI;
BREQc       =   /(SREQ + AEN);
BUSYc       =   /RESET
CBRQc1      =   /(SREQ * /AEN);
CBRQc2      =   SREQ * /AEN
MRDCc       =   /MIO + RD + CMDEN;
MWTCc       =   /MIO + WR + CMDEN;
IORCc       =   MIO + RD + CMDEN;
IOWCc       =   MIO + WR + CMDEN;
SREQd       =   RESET * SYNC;
SYNCd       =   RESET * XREQ;
CMDENd      =   /(RESET * XREQ * AEN);



                     5C060

          BCLK  -: 1    24:- Vcc
           MIO  -: 2    23:- XREQ
      RESERVED  -: 3    22:- INTA
      RESERVED  -: 4    21:- IOWC
      RESERVED  -: 5    20:- IORC
           AEN  -: 6    19:- MWTC
          BPRO  -: 7    18:- MRDC
```

5/9

Implementing a CMOS bus arbiter/controller in the 5C060 EPLD, Screen 5.

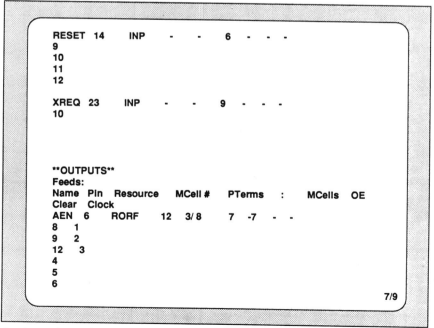

```
                INTAIN  -: 8     17:- BUSY
                   WR   -: 9     16:- CBRQ
                   RD   -:10     15:- BREQ
                 BPRN   -:11     14:- RESET
                  GND   -:12     13:- GND
                              _____

        **INPUTS**
        Feeds:
        Name Pin Resource   MCell #   PTerms   :   MCells   OE
        Clear  Clock
        BCLK  1    INP      -    -      -  -  -  - CLK1

        MIO  2     INP      -    -      2  -  -  -
        3
        4
        5

        INTAIN  8    INP    14   0/ 8   1  -  -  -
        WR   9       INP    15   0/ 8   2  -  -  -
        4

        RD  10       INP    16   0/ 8   3  -  -  -
        5

        BPRN  11     INP    -    -     12  -  -  -
        13                                          6/9
```

Implementing a CMOS bus arbiter/controller in the 5C060 EPLD, Screen 6.

```
        RESET  14    INP    -    -      6  -  -  -
        9
        10
        11
        12

        XREQ  23     INP    -    -      9  -  -  -
        10




        **OUTPUTS**
        Feeds:
        Name Pin Resource   MCell #   PTerms   :   MCells   OE
        Clear  Clock
        AEN   6    RORF     12   3/ 8   7  -7  -  -
        8    1
        9    2
        12   3
        4
        5
        6                                          7/9
```

Implementing a CMOS bus arbiter/controller in the 5C060 EPLD, Screen 7.

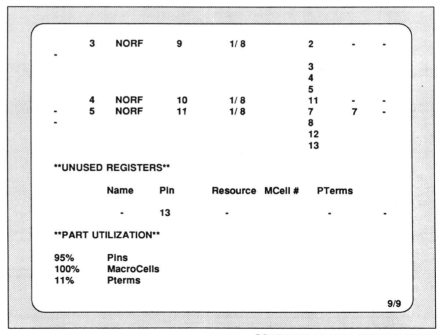

BPRO	7	CONF	13	1/8	-	-	-	-
BREQ	15	CONF	8	1/8	-	-	-	-
CBRQ	16	COIF	7	1/8	12	-	-	-
BUSY	17	COIF	6	1/8	12	-	-	-
MRBC	18	CONF	5	1/8	-	-	-	-
MWTC	19	CONF	4	1/8	-	-	-	-
IORC	20	CONF	3	1/8	-	-	-	-
IOWC	21	CONF	2	1/8	-	-	-	-
INTA	22	CONF	1	1/8	-	-	-	-

BURIED REGISTERS
Feeds:
Name Pin Resource MCell # PTerms : MCells OE
Clear Clock

8/9

Implementing a CMOS bus arbiter/controller in the 5C060 EPLD, Screen 8.

	3	NORF	9	1/8	2	-	-
-					3		
					4		
					5		
	4	NORF	10	1/8	11	-	-
-	5	NORF	11	1/8	7	7	-
-					8		
					12		
					13		

UNUSED REGISTERS

Name	Pin	Resource	MCell #	PTerms
-	13	-	-	-

PART UTILIZATION

95%	Pins
100%	MacroCells
11%	Pterms

9/9

Implementing a CMOS bus arbiter/controller in the 5C060 EPLD, Screen 9.

A pull-up resistor is used externally (i.e., on the backplane) to hold $\overline{\text{BUSY}}$/ high when no arbiter is in control of the bus. When the arbiter is granted control of the bus, $\overline{\text{AEN}}$ is clocked high, which enables the output of the $\overline{\text{BUSY}}$/ driver. Because the input to the $\overline{\text{BUSY}}$/driver is low during normal operation ($\overline{\text{RESET}}$/ inverted), the enabled driver pulls $\overline{\text{BUSY}}$/low to signal other arbiters that the bus, $\overline{\text{AEN}}$ goes low to disable the $\overline{\text{BUSY}}$/driver (three-state output). The pull-up resistor pulls $\overline{\text{BUSY}}$/high to signal other arbiters that the bus is free for use if needed.

Note that $\overline{\text{BUSY}}$/ is also routed into the bus grant logic as input $\overline{\text{BSI}}$. $\overline{\text{BSI}}$ prevents the arbiter from taking control of the bus (and driving $\overline{\text{BUSY}}$/low) when some other arbiter already has control of the bus. Thus only one arbiter can pull $\overline{\text{BUSY}}$/low at any one time.

The one difference between standard Multibus I logic levels and the EPLD implementation described here relates to the BCLK/ signal. Multibus I bus arbitration uses the negative-going edge of BCLK/ to synchronize events. All 5C060 flip-flops, however, clock on the positive-going edge of BCLK/. If all bus masters in the system use the same arbiter implementation, this poses no problem. Otherwise, an external inverter is required for the BCLK/input.

Comparison of PLA and EPLD Implementations

Both the PLA and EPLD implementations of the bus arbiter/controller result in a lower device count than a discrete logic circuit. Lower device count means less PC board space, fewer assembly steps, and fewer device interconnects. Both PLA and EPLD implementations are quicker and less expensive to develop than a custom gate array or dedicated silicon device.

In contrast to the PLA approach, however, the EPLD implementation requires only a single device, while the PLA approach requires two different devices. Thus the EPLD approach results in twice the cost savings (inventory and assembly) and half the programming activity to produce the device. Fewer device interconnects also means greater reliability. In addition, programmed EPLD devices can be erased and reprogrammed for a different application if needed, a feature not available with PLAs.

Overall, the greater flexibility and the incremental design, manufacturing, and cost advantages of EPLD devices make them ideal for many applications where PLA devices would otherwise be used.

7

Current and Future
Trends in PLD
Technology

Programmable logic devices which have traditionally been viewed as synonymous with the PROM, FPLA, and PAL have grown substantially in complexity and flexibility. While most PLDs are still based on the AND-OR architecture, several new devices have added features and new levels of sophistication.

I will now differentiate between what might be considered simple PLDs, moderately complex PLDs, and highly complex PLDs. Simple PLDs might comprise those sets of devices that have fixed combinatorial outputs, fixed registers, feedback paths, and synchronous clocking. Examples include the 16L2 and 16R6 as indicated with similar simple devices. Moderately complex PLDs include the industry standards 16V8, 22V10, and Altera EP320. These devices lend themselves to registered or combinatorial output selection and polarity preference. Highly complex PLDs are more application specific devices as opposed to general purpose devices. Such devices might contain programmable macrocells, hidden registers, sychronously clocked macrocells with a variety of flip-flop types, SR and JK, folded gate planes, synchronous and asynchronous state machine application capabilities. Signetics' PLS501 and PLS502 and Altera's EPB1400 can be considered highly complex PLDs.

Several highly complex PLDs are not designed around a Boolean sum-of-products form. Some consider that it was the sum-of-products form that suggested the initial possibility of PLD devices. As PLDs become more complex and application specific, logic synthesis tools must move forward to accommodate the new levels of complexity. Remember, a higher level of complexity is not synonymous with improvement in cases where simple or moderately complex PLDs can find more direct application.

The simple to moderately complex PLDs make up approximately 75–80% of today's market that can be programmed from a Boolean sum-of-products form. More complex PLDs might significantly reduce this percentage in the future.

Highly complex PLDs might contain an extensive amount of capability that might not be required for a specific application. Market-related factors, such as cost, technology preferences, and tradeoff factors as discussed in Chapter 2 should be considered in selecting the specific PLD type for the specific application. Bipolar PAL devices still maintain the edge of high speed at low cost.

There appears to be forward movement toward electrically erasable and CMOS devices. The PEEL device manufactured by International CMOS Technologies appears to be leading in this technology, having married the electrically erasable technology with the CMOS technology. These devices are capable of emulating several PALs currently on the market. They can be erased in 20 ns, hold a charge for 10 years without reprogramming, and be reprogrammed and erased 10,000 times. Gould also manufactures the PEEL device.

The Altera Corporation also employs CMOS technology in several application-specific devices. Several of their devices contain macrocells offering wider applications than can be normally found in PAL-like devices. Erase time for these devices requires approximately 20 minutes. The flexibility and capacity of the EPLDs manufactured by Altera approach the highest level of sophistication when compared with PAL type devices. For example, the Altera EP900 Erasable Programmable Logic Device can be used to implement over 900 equivalent gates of SSI and MSI logic, to accommodate up to 36 inputs and 24 outputs all within a 40-pin DIP or 44-pin J-leaded chip carrier. Each of the 24 macrocells contains a programmable AND, fixed OR PLA structure that yields 8 product terms for logic implementation and single product terms for output enable and asynchronous clear control functions. The Altera proprietary programmable I/O architecture allows the EP900 user to program output and feedback paths for both combinatorial or registered operation, active high or active low.

The EP900 input/output architecture provides each macrocell with over 50 programmable I/O configurations. Each I/O can be configured for combinatorial or registered output with programmable output polarity. Four different register types (D,T, JK,SR) can be implemented into every I/O without additional logic requirements. I/O feedback selection can also be programmed for registered or input (from the pin) feedback. Another characteristic of the EP900 I/O architecture is the ability to clock each internal register separately from asynchronous clock signals.

Consider the now MAX EPLD family of architecture. The EPM5000 series of MAX EPLDs has been designed as the first complete, high-performance CMOS logic building block family intended as a general-purpose, high-integration solution to a wide range of applications. Through exploiting the benefits of user-configurable technology and through multiple source licensing agreements on both development tools and silicon production, it is Altera's objective to establish MAX as the industry standard logic family of the 1990s.

The MAX architecture is an evolutionary development of the original EPLD structure and achieves both higher performance and more efficient use of logic resources. The powerful logic array structure, familiarity, and ease of use of PAL and EPLD devices are retained. Additional MAX architecture enhancements permit the integration of high-density combinatorial and register-intensive logic functions. The result is a flexible family of EPLDs that accommodate exact functional equivalents of hundreds of popular 7400 series elements.

These features are incorporated into the EPM5000 series of EPLDs from Altera. They comprise a consistent series of modular logic building blocks ranging from 20-pin dual-in-line packages to 68-pin and larger pin-grid array and surface mount packages. The integration density of these devices ranges from 2 or more PALs at the low end to 16 to 20 at the upper end. The latter is typically equivalent to 50 or more standard TTL packages.

At the top level, the MAX approach is based on the concept of a small, high-performance, flexible logic array module called a Logic Array Block (LAB). In the larger members of the MAX family, multiple LABs are linked together via a dedicated, programmable interconnect network called a Programmable Interconnect Array (PIA). The PIA allows any signal source to reach any destination on the chip without routing constraints. This structure allows many LABs to be interconnected to achieve large array density with the high performance of small arrays.

Smaller members of the MAX family with only a single LAB do not require a PIA. These include the EPM5016, EPM5024 and EPM5032. In these devices, all logic signal sources and destinations are fully interconnected directly on the device within the LAB.

The PIA acts as a programmable highway between all logic functions on the chip. Unlike masked or programmable gate arrays with routing channels, the PIA provides a crosspoint switch for logic communications. This eliminates routing bottlenecks and gives predictable uniform delays. Only a single, fixed array delay is incurred in the interconnection. Moreover, the delay is substantially less in magnitude than the macrocell delay. The variable and cumulative delays of gate arrays are eliminated.

The ability to interconnect all points ensures rapid, automatic completion of designs on low-cost, accessible, PC-based workstations. Typical MAX designs can be routed in minutes. High-density programmable gate array designs can take hours or days to complete. In many cases, they require significant manual intervention. Incremental, additive delays between various points can then result in debilitating skew and glitch problems requiring further, often multiple, iterations of the design.

Signetics continues to move forward with what it terms Programmable Macro Logic (PML). The company suggests that employing programmable AND-OR gate strings that permit implementing logic functions directly in sum-of-products form, as in current PLDs, often becomes a bottleneck that interferes with the efficient allocation of chip measures. PML is a novel architecture that breaks the AND-OR bottleneck by relying instead on a single NAND-gate array to implement SOP logic functions and to provide a central programmable interconnect site supporting a periphery of multi-level macros on a chip.

One way of relieving the burden placed on PLD architecture by the AND-OR gate string is to do away with it altogether, and replace it with a new programmable structure forged out of a new compromise on silicon between interconnect redundancy and ease of design and application. The approach adopted for PML is based on the fundamental equivalence between two-level AND-OR and NAND-NAND gate constructs in expressing combinatorial logic functions in SOP form.

Because programmable NAND-NAND logic chains can be formed by coupling identical NAND gates with programmable inputs, the NAND-array string can be implemented as a single global array with feedback. More complex functions can be implemented by programming multi-level logic loops through the array.

The PLHS501 provides up to 1300 equivalent gates in a 52-pin package. It employs third generation single NAND array architecture with NAND foldback paths and may be used for high-speed address decoding and bus interface applications.

In addition, Signetics produces several programmable logic sequencers (PLSs). The PLUS405 has a unique architecture that employs buried registers to store intermediate values. These PLSs make possible If-Then-Else states that can be found in advanced state machine design. Connecting any AND term to any OR term eliminates redundant state transition terms and JK or SR type registers optimize the logic used in generating state transistors.

For PAL type applications, Signetics offers the 12 ns PLUS173D PLA. The unique architecture of these devices eliminates "product-term depletion." All product terms (up to 48) can be shared among all individually controlled outputs.

The use of gallium arsenide instead of silicon can be anticipated in the future. Presently, Gazelle Microelectronics has given the industry standard 22V10 PLD a maximum clock frequency 90 MHz. It offers 12 dedicated inputs plus 10 I/O pins, each of which can be configured as a dedicated output or as bidirectional input/output. The only difference between this device and the standard 22V10 is that this device cannot be programmed by customers at their site. GaAs flip-flops today toggle at over 2 GHz. The 8-to-1 Multiplexer runs with 1-5 to 2 GHz clock frequencies. RAMs access data in 1 to 2 ns. Slow components can operate at clock rates of near 200 MHz. On the other hand, the drawbacks to GaAs must be balanced against these advantages. Compared to bipolar ECL components, they integrate less circuitry. Depending on specifications, they can cost more. However, GaAs does not appear to offer any advantages in terms of power dissipation per gate (1-3 mW for bipolar ECL versus 2-4 mW for GaAs).

Samsung Electronics offers a programmable logic device based on the basic PLA architecture but manufactured using CMOS technology. There might be less desirability for bipolar devices as the CMOS erasable devices continue to mature. However, cost must be considered where applicable because bipolar devices offer a significant cost advantage over other technologies. CMOS devices are advertised as direct replacements for the PAL 20 family. Some of the options offered include eight combinatorial outputs (16L8), eight registered outputs (16R8), and six combinatorial and two registered outputs (16R6).

Exel also produces an electrically erasable CMOS PLD CXL78C800 ERA-SIC with a propagation delay of 25 ns. Lattice also offers CMOS electrically-erasable PLDs such as the GAL16V8 and the GAL20V8. Both of these devices can emulate 20- and 24-pin PALs.

The Lattice E²CMOS GAL device combines a high-performance CMOS process with electrically-erasable floating gate technology. This programmable memory technology applied to array logic provides designers with reconfigurable logic and bipolar performance at significantly reduced power levels.

The 20-pin GAL 16V8 features 8 programmable Output Logic MacroCells (OLMCs) allowing each output to be configured by the user. Additionally, the GAL 16V8 is capable of emulating, in a functional/fuse map/parametric compatible device, all common 20-pin PAL device architectures.

The 24-pin GAL 20V8 also features 8 programmable Output Logic Macro-Cells (OLMCs) allowing each output to be configured by the user. Additionally, the GAL 20V8 is capable of emulating, in a functional/fuse map/parametric compatible device, all common 24-pin PAL devices architectures.

Programming for the 20-pin GAL 16V8 and the 24-pin GAL 20V8 is accomplished using readily available hardware and software tools. Lattice guarantees a minimum of 100 erase/write cycles and data retention exceeding 20 years.

Unique test circuitry and reprogrammable cells in GAL 16V8 and GAL 20V8 allow complete AC, DC, cell, and functionality testing during manufacture. Therefore, Lattice guarantees 100% field programmability and functionality of the GAL devices. In addition, electronic signature is available to provide positive device ID. A security circuit is built in to provide proprietary designs with copy protection.

Several devices that have been labeled ''application specific'' incorporate functions designed for specific applications and a user-configurable logic array. These devices permit shorter prototyping time as well as higher operating speeds.

PLX technology produces the PLX 448 programmable bus interface. The device is still very general-purpose in design, but the chip contains 48 mA and 24 mA drivers that are compatible with Multibus I and II standard bus specifications. The device is bidirectional, contains buried registers, and has combinatorial incircuit feedback.

In circuit programming, the technique of programming a PLD after it has been installed in the circuit board will replace gang programming in some areas and applications.

Texas Instruments manufactures a programmable address decoder (PA) that operates at a maximum propagation delay of 7 ns while maintaining current requirements at the 180 mA level.

In the area of logic synthesis, you can expect the next decade to produce products that are far more sophisticated than anything available today. The first step is to extend the current tools to provide support for more complex ASIC technologies, such as gate arrays, standard cells, and full custom chips. Such products are already starting to appear on the market, and you can expect to see more products and additional sophistication added over the next few years.

As the same time, logic synthesis tools will be extending the level of abstraction at which they can accept design descriptions. Current tools accept design descriptions at the functional block level. Future tools will be able to accept descriptions at the algorithmic—and even architectural—level. Initially, these advanced tools will be aimed at specific architectures in which the refinement process is relatively straightforward. (Data path structures and certain types of digital signal processors are good candidates for early tools of this type.) Later, high-level refinement capabilities will be extended to the full range of design architectures.

In the same time frame, still other advances will be creating a link between synthesis and compilation, leading to tools that will be able to generate placement and routing maps from behavioral design descriptions. As these capabilities are combined with those that extend the level of abstraction of behavioral descriptions, you will eventually see tools that can generate a fully laid-out ASIC design from an algorithmic or architectural description.

Finally, synthesis is extended from the ASIC level to the board—and even system—level. Initially, these board and system synthesis tools will be able to map high-level behavioral descriptions onto standard off-the-shelf parts. Eventually, as all of these advances are combined into universal synthesis-compilation tools, engineers will be able to describe a design in abstract behavioral terms, plug this description into an advanced synthesizer-compiler, and generate a physical layout for a complete chip, board, or system.

Appendix A

Logic Tutorial

The Decimal Number System
The Binary Number System
    Converting Decimal Numbers to Binary Numbers
    Converting Decimal Fractions to Binary Numbers
    Converting Binary Whole Numbers to Decimal Whole
        Numbers
    Converting Binary Fractions to Decimal Fraction Numbers
Binary Coding
The Octal System
    Converting Decimal Numbers to Octal Numbers
    Converting Octal Numbers
    Converting Binary Numbers to Octal Numbers
Hexadecimal System
Binary Coded Decimal
    Converting between Decimal Numbers and BCD Codes
    The BCD Gray Code
    Review of Other Codes
Computer Arithmetic
    Adding Positive Numbers
    Nine's Complement Subtraction
    One's Complement Subtraction
    Ten's Complement Subtraction
    Two's Complement Subtraction
    Representing Negative Numbers
    Negabinary Notation
    Adding Positive and Negative Numbers
    Adding Two Negative Numbers
    Adding BCD Numbers
Fixed and Floating Point Notation
Combinatorial Logic
    Logic Gates
    Boolean Algebra
    Karnaugh Maps
Sequential Circuits
    Flip-Flops
    Registers
    Counters

THE DECIMAL NUMBER SYSTEM

Familiarization with the principles of binary and octal arithmetic is essential to the understanding of digital computers. The binary system is represented by the radix two, the octal system by radix eight and decimal system by radix 10. It is instructional at this point to understand the meaning of the term *radix*. The radix of any number represents the number of symbols in that system. The radix therefore of the decimal system is 10 since the symbols 0, 1, 2, 3, 4, 5, 6. 7, 8, 9 comprise that system. Similarly the radix of the binary system is 2 because only two symbols (0 and 1) comprise that system. The symbols 0, 1, 2, 3, 4, 5, 6, 7 comprise the octal system.

There is great similarity in the meaning of the numbers in the decimal system and the meaning of binary numbers. Consider the number 1988. This number tells us that there are eight units, eight tens, nine hundreds and one thousands. This could be written as

$$1 \times 10^3 + 9 \times 10^2 + 8 \times 10^1 + 8 \times 10^0$$

Remember that any number or literal (letter) raised to the zero power equals 1. Thus

$$10^0 = 1$$

Each digit indicates the number of times a power of ten is taken, and the position of the digit indicates the power of ten. The 1×10^3 represents position of the 1; 9×10^2 represents the position of the 9. Both the digit and its position have a meaning.

The principle of positional value can best be understood by looking at an example. Consider the three numbers 701, 710, and 170. All three numbers contain the same symbols, and yet each number represents a different quantity. In the first number (701), the symbol 1 has an absolute value of one. In the second number (710), it has a value of ten. In the third number (170), it has a value of one hundred. The quantity that a number represents is determined not only by the symbols used, but also by the position of the symbols in the number.

The positional value principle is directly related to the base of a number system. In the decimal system, each position has a value 10 times greater than the position to its right. The position immediately to the left of the decimal point is called the units position; the next position to the left is the tens position; the next, the hundreds position, and so on. Moving to the left each position increases by a factor of 10.

Consider the number 1942. The 2 represents 2×1; the 4 represents 4×10; the 9 represents 9×10^2, and the 1 represents 1×10^3. In other words,

$$1942 = 1 \times 10^3 + 9 \times 10^2 + 4 \times 10^1 + 2 \times 10^0$$

Notice the principle used. The symbol in the units position (2) has its absolute value:

$$2 \times 10^0 = 2 \times 1 = 2$$

The next symbol (4) has its absolute value:

$4 \times 10^1 = 4 \times 10 = 40$

The next symbol (9) has its absolute value:

$9 \times 10^2 = 9 \times 100 = 900$

The final symbol (1) has its absolute value:

$1 \times 10^3 = 1 \times 1000 = 1000$

Thus

$1 \times 10^3 + 9 \times 10^2 + 4 \times 10^1 + 2 \times 10^0$
$1000 + 900 + 40 + 2$
1942

In positional notation, decimal fractions are expressed as negative powers of ten. For example,

$10^{-1} = .1$
$10^{-2} = .01$
$10^{-3} = .001$
$10^{-4} = .0001$
$10^{-5} = .00001$

Thus the number .824 could therefore be expressed as

$8 \times 10^{-1} + 2 \times 10^{-2} + 4 \times 10^{-3}$
$8 \times .1 + 2 \times .01 + 4 \times .001$
$.8 + .02 + .004 = .824$

THE BINARY NUMBER SYSTEM

While most computer arithmetic is today performed using specialized hand calculators, this section reviews the fundamentals related to the various operations required.

Converting Decimal Whole Numbers to Binary Numbers

The conversion of a decimal number to its binary equivalent is straightforward. Consider conversion of the number 27 to its binary equivalent. Figure A-1 illustrates this procedure. First write 27 and divide it by 2. Dividing 2 into 27 yields 13 with a remainder of 1. Write the 1 (the remainder) out to the right of the quotient 13, now divide 2 into 13 and write that quotient (6) beneath the 13 and the remainder to the right of 13.

Now divide 2 into 6, which results in a quotient of 3 with a remainder of zero. Write the 3 under the 6 and the 0 remainder to the right of 3. Next divide 2 into 3 which yields 1 and a remainder of 1. Write the quotient 1 under the 3 and the remainder 1 to the right of 1. Now divide 2 into 1, giving a quotient of 0 and a remainder of 1. Write the 0 under the 1 and the remainder 1 to the right of

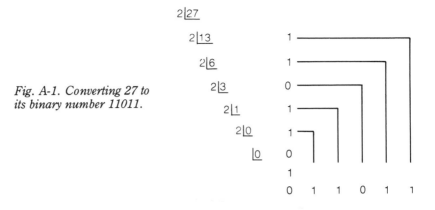

Fig. A-1. Converting 27 to its binary number 11011.

0. Lastly divide 2 into 0 which yields a quotient of 0 and a remainder of 0. Thus the binary equivalent of 27 yields:

011011

Note that the binary is written from *right* to *left* working from top to bottom. The same procedure can be used regardless of the size of the numbers. Figure A-2 converts 108 to binary numbers. First write the 108 as shown in FIG. A-2, then continually divide by 2 placing a 1 or 0 as the remainder after each division operation. First 108 divided by 2 gives 54 with 0 remainder. The 0 remainder is written to the right of the quotient 54. Next 2 divided into 54 yields 27 with remainder 0, the 0 remainder written to the right of the quotient. Now divide 2 into 27 which yields a quotient of 13 and remainder one. The 1 is written to the right of 13. Next divide 2 into 13 which gives the quotient 6 and 1 remainder which is written next to its quotient. The next division of 2 into 6 yields a quotient of 3 and 0 remainder followed by the division of 2 into 3 which gives a quotient of 1 and a remainder of 1. Now 2 divided into 1 gives a quotient of 0 and a remainder of 1 which is written next to the 0 quotient. Lastly 2 divided into 0 gives a quotient of 0 and remainder 0. Now writing the binary equivalent from left to right reading from bottom to top produces the binary equivalent of 108 to be 01101100.

Another system that can be used to convert decimal to binary numbers involves using a table as shown in FIG. A-3. This table gives the values of the powers of 2^0 through 2^{10}. If necessary, this table can be extended to any required value.

As an example, consider the value 18. To convert 18 to a binary number, first find the largest multiple of 2 that is smaller than 18. This number is 16 or 2^4. Because 16 is smaller than 18, a 1 is written as the first digit in the binary number. The quantity 16 + 8 is greater than 18, as is 16 + 4, so a 1 is not written as the second digit or third digit. The fourth digit will be 1 and yield 18.

Reviewing the numbers beneath the various powers of 2 as shown in FIG. A-4, it can be seen that each 2 indicates 1 time that particular power of 2. A 0 indicates not to use that power of 2 as shown for 2^3, 2^2, and 2^0.

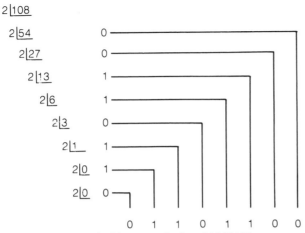

Fig. A-2. Converting 108 to its binary equivalent 01101100.

2^{10}	2^9	2^8	2^7	2^6	2^5	2^4	2^3	2^2	2^1	2^0
1024	512	256	128	64	32	16	8	4	2	1

Fig. A-3. Values of powers of 2.

2^{10}	2^9	2^8	2^7	2^6	2^5	2^4	2^3	2^2	2^1	2^0
1024	512	206	128	64	32	16	8	4	2	1
						1	0	0	1	0

1 X 16 + 1 X 2 = 16 + 2 = 18

Fig. A-4. Conversion of decimal 18 to its binary equivalent 10010.

Converting Decimal Fraction Numbers to Binary

Converting a decimal fraction to a binary fraction is a straightforward procedure. Consider the decimal .3125 as shown in FIG. A-5. First write down the number to be converted and multiply this number by 2. Thus, 2 times .3125 equals .6250 with no carry. Thus a zero is written in the column to the left. Next multiply the product .6250 by 2 to yield 1.2500. Because in this case a carry of 1 is obtained, a 1 is written in the column to the left. Now 2 times the decimal portion of the previous product (2 x .2500) yields .5000 and no carry.

```
                  .3125
                      2
 0        (0)     .6250
                      2
 1        (1)     .2500    Fig. A-5. Conversion of .3125 to its binary equivalent.
                      2
 0        (0)     .5000
                      2
 1        (0)     .0000
```

Thus a 0 is written in the column to the left. Next 2 times the decimal (.5000) yields 1.000. Noting a carry of 1, a 1 is written in the column to the left. Because the decimal portion has worked out to 0, the conversion is completed. Thus the binary equivalent of .3125 is binary .0101.

The previous example provided an exact binary equivalent because the final product ended as zero. However, this is not always possible. Consider converting the number .6 to its binary equivalent as shown in FIG. A-6.

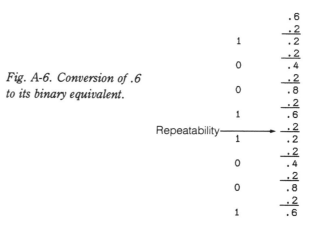

Fig. A-6. Conversion of .6 to its binary equivalent.

As in the previous example, .6 is multiplied by 2, with a carry of 0. As this procedure continues, the initial product (2 x .6 = 1.2) begins to repeat itself. At this point, regardless of how many times the multiplication operation is performed, the point wherein all decimal digits become 0 is never reached. This implies the number (.6 in the example) is not exactly convertible to a binary fractional equivalent.

It is necessary on some occasions to convert a decimal number that contains both whole numbers and a decimal part. When this situation arises it is necessary to convert the whole number part and the decimal part separately. After converting each part, the two parts (whole and decimal), are combined to give the complete binary number. Figure A-7 illustrates the conversion of 27.125 to binary.

Converting Binary Whole Numbers to Decimal Numbers

The conversion of a binary whole number to a decimal number can be performed easily by use of the table shown in FIG. A-3. As an example consider the conversion of the binary number 1101010 as shown in FIG. A-8. Placing a 1 under the second, fourth, sixth and seventh terms, and a 0 under the first, third and fifth term gives:

64 + 32 + 0 + 8 + 0 + 2 + 0 = 106

```
2 |27
    2 |13            1                              .125
       2 |6          1          0      (0)          .250
          2 |3       0          0      (0)          .500
             2 |1    1          1      (1)          .000
                2 |0 1                     .125  =  .001
                              thus 27.126 = 11011.001
                27 = 11011
```

Fig. A-7. Converting 27.125 to its binary equivalent.

2^7	2^6	2^5	2^4	2^3	2^2	2^1	2^0
128	64	32	16	8	4	2	1
1	1	0	1	0	1	0	

Fig. A-8. Conversion of 1101010 to decimal.

Converting Binary Fractions to Decimal Numbers

It is more difficult to convert a binary fraction to the equivalent decimal number than to convert a binary whole number to the equivalent decimal whole number. Figure A-9 provides a table that can be used to convert binary fractions beneath the equivalent columns starting at the left and working from the binary point to the right. For example, in FIG. A-10, the conversion of .01101 to a decimal is shown. Placing the binary digits below the appropriate columns the decimal equivalent is .625.

2^{-1}	2^{-2}	2^{-3}	2^{-4}	2^{-5}	2^{-6}	2^{-7}
.5	.25	.125	.0625	.03125	.015626	.00781

Fig. A-9. Table for converting binary fractions to decimal numbers.

2^{-1}	2^{-2}	2^{-3}	2^{-4}	2^{-5}	2^{-6}	2^{-7}
.5	.25	.125	.0625	.03125	.0156	.00781
0	1	1	0	1		

.25   +   .125   + .03125   =   .40625

Fig. A-10. Conversion of .01101 to its decimal equivalent.

The conversion of decimal .6 to a binary number gave a binary equivalent to eight decimal places (.10011001) as shown in FIG. A-6. The conversion back to a decimal number shown in FIG. A-11 yields .59375 which proves that .6 does not have an exact binary equivalent.

2^{-1}	2^{-2}	2^{-3}	2^{-4}	2^{-5}	2^{-6}	2^{-7}	2^{-8}
.5	.25	.125	.0625	.03125	.0156	.00781	.003906
1	0	0	1	1	0	0	1

$$.5 \quad + \quad .0625 \quad + \quad .03125 \quad + \quad .003906 \quad = \quad .59 \quad = \quad .6$$

Fig. A-11. Conversion of binary .10011001 to its decimal equivalent.

BINARY CODING

In the conversion between binary and decimal notation, the problem arises of determining how many bits are required to represent a certain decimal number. This relationship is expressed as:

Number of different states (a state may be thought of as a 0 or 1) $= 2^n$

The 2 is the radix 2 because of the binary system. Thus,

$2^4 = 2 \times 2 \times 2 \times 2 = 16$ states

These states are shown in TABLE A-1. It is emphasized that the highest decimal number represented is not equal to the the total number of states that can be represented. Thus a four-bit number can represent a maximum number of 15, instead of 16. The sixteenth number is zero. The maximum decimal number that can be represented by a given number of bits is computed by the expression

$2^n - 1$

Table A-1. Combinations of four binary digits.

	2^3	2^2	2^1	2^0
	D	C	B	A
0	0	0	0	0
1	0	0	0	1
2	0	0	1	0
3	0	0	1	1
4	0	1	0	0
5	0	1	0	1
6	0	1	1	0
7	0	1	1	1
8	1	0	0	0
9	1	0	0	1
10	1	0	1	0
11	1	0	1	1
12	1	1	0	0
13	1	1	0	1
14	1	1	1	0
15	1	1	1	1

As in the case of four bits, the number is $2^4 - 1 = 16 - 1 = 15$. Therefore, to calculate the number of bits needed to represent a given decimal number such as 230_{10}, the objective in determining the number of bits is to first determine the closest value (which is a function of 2^n) that exceeds the number to be represented. With an eight-bit binary number 256, 2^8 states can be represented or decimal numbers up to 255 which is the closest 2^n evaluation that exceeds 230.

As can be seen, the process of determining the number of bits needed to represent a given decimal number is a trial-and-error process that gives the closest value that exceeds the decimal number to be represented.

A second relation that can be used to calculate directly the number of bits needed to represent a decimal number is

$$n = 3.32 \log N$$

Where n is the minimum number of bits needed and N is the maximum decimal number or number of states to be represented. Using the previous example of 230_{10}:

$$n = 3.32 \log 230$$
$$n = 3.32 \times 2.36 = 7.6$$

Because a fractional part of a bit is not allowed, the number is rounded off to the next highest whole number or integer in this case 8.

THE OCTAL SYSTEM

The octal numbering system has a radix of eight and uses only the digits 0, 1, 2, 3, 4, 5, 6, and 7. Recall that the binary numbers indicate certain powers of 2 by their position. Similarly, the octal numbers indicate powers of 8. The procedures therefore for converting decimal numbers to octal and back to decimal are virtually the same as those used in converting back and forth between decimal and binary numbers.

Converting Decimals to Octal Numbers

The procedure used for converting from a decimal number is shown in FIG. A-12. For example to convert the decimal 486 to an octal number, the number 486 is written and divided by 8. The answer is 60 with a remainder of 6. The 60 is placed beneath the original number and the remainder of 6 off to the right.

```
8 | 486

  8   60          6
                          Fig. A-12. Decimal to octal conversion.
      8 | 7        4

        | 0        7


Decimal 359 = Octal 746
```

Now the 60 is divided by 8 to yield 7 and a remainder of 4. Dividing 7 by 8 gives 0 and a remainder of 7. The octal equivalent is obtained from the remainders; reading from the bottom to the top, the octal number is written 746.

Notice the similar procedure to the decimal/binary conversion. The only difference is that here you divide by 8 instead of 2. It is important to note that when dealing with numbers less than 8, the octal equivalent is the same as the binary equivalent for numbers written in the decimal system.

Converting from Octal Numbers to Decimal

The same approach is used in converting from an octal number back to a decimal as converting a binary number to a decimal number. As recalled, in the binary conversion, a table (FIG. A-3) was used indicating different powers of 2. In the octal conversion, a similar table is used based on the values of powers of 8 as shown in FIG. A-13.

	8^4	8^3	8^2	8^1	8^0
	4096	512	64	8	1

Fig. A-13. Powers of 8 based on octal-to-decimal conversion.

Consider the octal number 329 and its conversion to decimal. The procedure is to write the number 329 beneath the powers as shown in FIG. A-14. Note that because the number 329 is comprised of only three digits, only the first three powers of 8 are needed.

The procedure used in FIG. A-14 can be used to convert an octal number to a decimal number. Clearly, this procedure is similar to converting a binary number to a decimal. The only difference is that the respective values of the powers of 8 are multiplied by the respective digits that make up the octal number.

8^2	8^1	8^0
64	8	1
3	2	9

Fig. A-14. The conversion of octal 329 to decimal 217.

$$9 \times 1 = 9$$
$$2 \times 8 = 16$$
$$3 \times 64 = \underline{192}$$
$$217$$

Converting Octal Numbers to Binary Numbers

As discussed previously, the radix of the octal number is eight, requiring only the digits 0 through 7. In addition, it was stated that a three-bit binary number can represent a total of eight different states and numbers (0 through 7). TABLE A-2 shows all possible combinations of three bits and their respective number equivalents.

Octal or Decimal	2^2	2^1	2^0
0	0	0	0
1	0	0	1
2	0	1	0
3	0	1	1
4	1	0	0
5	1	0	1
6	1	1	0
7	1	1	1

Table A-2. Decimal-to-octal equivalents of three-bit binary numbers.

Because there are a total of eight different states, these binary numbers can also represent the eight octal numbers 0 through 7 as well as the decimal numbers. This important relationship permits octal numbers to be easily converted into binary numbers and binary numbers to be converted into octal numbers. For example, the octal number 3 is equal to 011_2, the same as 3 in decimal. Similarly, a binary 101 represents an octal 5 and decimal 5.

This relationship holds for larger octal numbers as well. For example, to convert 54_8 to binary, it is only necessary to substitute the equivalent three-bit binary number for each octal digit. Because 5 is the equivalent of 101_2 and 4 is the equivalent 100_2, 54_8 is equivalent to 101100_2.

For a larger number 475_8, the binary equivalent is 100111101_2.

Converting Binary Numbers to Octal Numbers

The relationship between octal and binary works well in reverse to the conversion of octal numbers to binary numbers. Consider 010101_2. To convert this number to octal, it is necessary to start at the binary point to the right of the binary number and mark off three-bit groups. Each three-bit group is then replaced with its octal equivalent. For example,

$$/010 \quad /100_2$$
$$\ \ 2 \qquad 4 \quad = 24_8$$

As proof that this procedure is correct convert 010100_2 to its decimal equivalent and 24_8 to its decimal equivalent.

Referring to FIG. A-3 and converting 010100_2 to its decimal equivalent yields:

2^5	2^4	2^3	2^2	2^1	2^0
32	16	8	4	2	1
0	1	0	1	0	0

$$0 + 16 + 0 + 4 + 0 + 0 = 20$$

Now referring to FIG. A-13 and converting 24_8 to its decimal equivalent yields:

```
   8²                      8¹                    8⁰            4 X 1  =   4
-----------------------------------------------------------
   64                      8                     1            2 X 8  =  16
-----------------------------------------------------------              20
   3                       2                     9
-----------------------------------------------------------
```

Because both 010100_2 and 24_8 convert to decimal 20, both numbers are equivalent.

There are situations wherein the binary number being converted is not a multiple of 3. For these types of situations, the necessary leading or trailing zeros are added to complete the three-bit group. In the conversion of 1100111011_2 to octal, the binary number is marked off in three-bit groups starting from the right:

1/100/111/011

Note that the left-most group must be completed with two leading zeros to yield:

0011/100/111/011
 1   4   7   3

The equivalent octal numbers are then substituted to yield 1473_8.

Binary fractions can be handled similarly. Consider converting

011101.111110_2

to octal. Again mark off the binary number in groups of three and replace each three-bit group by its octal equivalent:

011/101.111/110₂
 3   5 . 7   6

The binary and octal number relationship is quite useful in situations that require working with binary numbers that are comprised of large numbers of different states (bits). It is quite possible to lose track of the many ones and zeros that make up the binary number. However, by converting the binary number to its octal equivalent, a shorter number is obtained that can be easily remembered. For example, it is much easier to work with 1776 than 001 111 111 110.

Note then the octal number and binary number relationship facilitates the conversion between the binary and decimal systems. Although the conversion from binary to decimal and decimal to binary is direct, the process can be shortened by going through octal. For example, to convert

110111010110_2

to decimal, the weights of the positions where ones appear as in FIG. A-3 must be added. However by converting to octal first and then to decimal, the conversion is simplified. Consider again:

110111010110_2

First converting to octal yields:

110/111/010/110
 6   7   2   6 $= 6726_8$

Now converting 6276_8 to decimal yields

8^3	8^2	8^1		8^0
512	64	8		1
6	x	1	=	6
2	x	8	=	16
7	x	65	=	448
6	x	512	=	3072
				$\overline{3542}_{10}$

Now referring back to FIG. A-3 and converting 110111010110 to decimal yields:

2^{11}	2^{10}	2^9	2^8	2^7	2^6	2^5	2^4	2^3	2^2	2^1	2^0
1	1	0	1	1	1	0	1	0	1	1	0
2048	1024	0	256	128	64	0	16	0	4	2	0

2048 + 1024 + 0 + 256 + 128 + 64 + 0 + 16 + 0 + 4 + 2 + 0 = 3542

thus   binary 110111010110_2 = 3542_{10}
          octal 6726_8 = 3542_{10}

thus the conversion from binary to decimal and octal to decimal both convert to the same value (3542_{10}).

The binary to octal relationship is employed by many hardware designers especially where strings of on-off lights are a required display. The lights are normally marked off in groups of three to aid the technician in determining when the system under service is functioning properly. For example, a string of lights might be of the form 110111010110 where 1 indicates a light on and 0 indicates a light off, by conveniently marking this string of ones and zeros into groups of three

110/111/010/110
 6   7   2   6

the technician can easily remember that 6726 light configuration indicates the system is functioning properly.

THE HEXADECIMAL SYSTEM

The number system that is in wide use today is the hexadecimal number system. The radix of this system is 16, indicating there are sixteen different symbols used in representing numbers. The symbols are 0 through 9 and the six letters A through F. The hexadecimal system is related to the binary system in the same way as the binary and octal are related. Table A-3 shows this relationship. For example,

Hexadecimal		Binary	Decimal
DE	=	11011110	222
B9	=	10111001	185
66	=	01100110	102

		2^3	2^2	2^1	2^0
		D	C	B	A
0	0	0	0	0	0
1	1	0	0	0	1
2	2	0	0	1	0
3	3	0	0	1	1
4	4	0	1	0	0
5	5	0	1	0	1
6	6	0	1	1	0
7	7	0	1	1	1
8	8	1	0	0	0
9	9	1	0	0	1
10	A	1	0	1	0
11	B	1	0	1	1
12	C	1	1	0	0
13	D	1	1	0	1
14	E	1	1	1	0
15	F	1	1	1	1

Table A-3. Decimal, hexadecimal, and binary number relationships.

BINARY CODED DECIMAL (BCD) BASICS

Binary Coded Decimal (BCD) is a special binary code developed to facilitate communication between a user and machine (computer). The binary number system is better suited for computer operation while a user is more comfortable with the decimal system. The BCD system represents all ten decimal states 0 through 9 with various combinations of four binary digits. For example, the 8421 BCD code is shown in TABLE A-4. It is clear from this table that these four-bit numbers correspond to those in the binary or hexadecimal codes.

Decimal	BCD			
	8	4	2	1
0	0	0	0	0
1	0	0	0	1
2	0	0	1	0
3	0	0	1	1
4	0	1	0	0
5	0	1	0	1
6	0	1	1	0
7	0	1	1	1
8	1	0	0	0
9	1	0	0	1

Table A-4. 8421 binary coded decimal system.

The numbers at the top can be thought of as the weight of one bit in that particular column. Considering the 8421 code; by placing ones under the combination of numbers (8421), their sum yields the particular number under conversion. To convert to the 8421 code, a 1 should be placed under the numeral 8, not 4, 2, or 1. Because $4 + 2 + 1 = 7$, a 1 would be placed under the 4, 2, and 1 to yield 0111.

As stated previously, all BCD were developed for a specific reason, and all BCD codes have four bits per decimal digit.

Converting between Decimal Numbers and BCD Codes

To convert a decimal number into BCD notation, all that is required is that the four-bit code be substituted for each decimal digit. A space is usually left between each four-bit group to prevent one from confusing the BCD form with the pure binary form. For example 845_{10} written in BCD is 1000 0100 0101; pure binary converts to 1101001101. In BCD, it took 12 bits, four for each digit, while in pure binary it required only 10 bits. This is the main disadvantage of BCD, that is the requirement for more bits to represent a given number than would be required to represent that number in pure binary form. Because more bits are required in BCD notation, it is much less efficient than the pure binary form.

The BCD Gray Code

The BCD Gray Code is shown in TABLE A-5. This code is a non-weighted code and quite popular in that there is a change in only one bit from one code number to another, as in the change from 7_{10} (0111_2) to 8_{10} (1000_2). Note that all four bits changed in the pure binary code. Now compare this same change 7_{10} (0100) to 8_{10} (1100) wherein only one bit changed. Because of this feature, this

	D	C	B	A
0	0	0	0	0
1	0	0	0	1
2	0	0	1	1
3	0	0	1	0
4	0	1	1	0
5	0	1	1	1
6	0	1	0	1
7	0	1	0	0
8	1	1	0	0
9	1	1	0	1
10	1	1	1	1
11	1	1	1	0
12	1	0	1	0
13	1	0	1	1
14	1	0	0	1
15	1	0	0	0

Table A-5. Gray code.

code is known as the "error minimizing code" because ambiguity is substantially reduced in changing from one state to the next. This suggests that the implementation of the Gray Code in a digital circuit permits the circuit to operate at higher speeds due to the small number of bit changes required in the representation of numbers. The disadvantage, however, is that this code does not lend itself to arithmetic operations.

Review of Other Codes

Several other BCD Codes are in use, and each has its particular advantage. Table A-6 shows the 2421 code. The 2421 code is upon inspection a complement code that has found application in counting and various arithmetic functions. The 7421 code (TABLE A-7) is normally employed to conserve power in digital circuiting. For example, when lights are utilized, a 1 bit is represented with a light on and a 0 bit is represented by a light off. To conserve power, it would be desirable to have as few lights on as possible to represent a given number. This suggests that a minimum number of one bits must be used in code. Because the 7421 code requires a maximum of two one-bits to represent any decimal digit, power conservation is realized. The 7421 code is referred to as the minimum power code.

Decimal	2	4	2	1
0	0	0	0	0
1	0	0	0	1
2	0	0	1	0
3	0	0	1	1
4	0	1	0	0
5	1	0	1	1
6	1	1	0	0
7	1	1	0	1
8	1	1	1	0
9	1	1	1	1

Table A-6. The 2421 code.

Decimal	7	4	2	1
0	0	0	0	0
1	0	0	0	1
2	0	0	1	0
3	0	0	1	1
4	0	1	0	0
5	0	1	0	1
6	0	1	1	0
7	1	0	0	0
8	1	0	0	1
9	1	0	1	0

Table A-7. The 7421 code.

The 5421 BCD code shown in TABLE A-8 has found application in the design of decoding circuitry. By utilizing this code, it takes considerably less complete circuitry to decode the 5421 than any of the other codes.

Decimal	5	4	2	1
0	0	0	0	0
1	0	0	0	1
2	0	0	1	0
3	0	0	1	1
4	0	1	0	0
5	1	0	0	0
6	1	0	0	1
7	1	0	1	0
8	1	0	1	1
9	1	1	0	0

Table A-8. The 5421 code.

The Excess 3 Code (XS3) shown in TABLE A-9 is useful in performing BCD arithmetic. It is not a weighted code but the 8421 code with the number three greater than the given number. For example to obtain the Excess 3 Code, three is added to the decimal number that it is desired to convert and then the sum is converted to the 8421 equivalent. For example, the decimal numbers 8, 4, and 5 in Excess 3 Code are 1011, 0111, 1000 respectively.

Decimal				
0	0	0	1	1
1	0	1	0	0
2	0	1	0	1
3	0	1	1	0
4	0	1	1	1
5	1	0	0	0
6	1	0	0	1
7	1	0	1	0
8	1	0	1	1
9	1	1	0	0

Table A-9. Excess 3 code.

A modification of the BCD Gray Code can be made by shifting all numbers three positions, that is, 0_{10} = 0010, 1_{10} = 0110. This code is termed the Excess Three Gray code and is shown in TABLE A-10. It is clear from this table

Decimal				
0	0	0	1	0
1	0	1	1	0
2	0	1	1	1
3	0	1	0	1
4	0	1	0	0
5	1	1	0	0
6	1	1	0	1
7	1	1	1	1
8	1	1	1	0
9	1	0	1	0

Table A-10. Excess 3 gray.

that when the code cycles from 9_{10} to 0_{10} only one bit changes, thus retaining the fully cyclic nature of this code.

There is an almost infinite number of different code possibilities not limited to the ones discussed. The type of code employed impacts such considerations as power consumption, the optimum speed of operation, reliability, and circuit complexity as well as cost.

The 2-out-of-5 Code is shown in TABLE A-11. Close inspection of this code yields the feature that out of a total of five bits only two are binary 1 for any numbers, thus the name 2-out-of-5. This feature has found applications in facilitating error detection and decoding.

	7	4	2	1	0
0	1	1	0	0	0
1	0	0	0	1	1
2	0	0	1	0	1
3	0	0	1	1	0
4	0	1	0	0	1
5	0	1	0	1	0
6	0	1	1	0	0
7	1	0	0	0	1
8	1	0	0	1	0
9	1	0	1	0	0

Table A-11. The 2-out-of-5 code.

Similar to the 2-out-of-5 Code is the 2-out-of-7 Code shown in TABLE A-12. Because only 2 bits are binary 1 from a total of 7, it is referred to as a 2-out-of-7 code. This code also facilitates error detection and decoding.

	5	0	4	3	2	1	0
0	0	1	0	0	0	0	1
1	0	1	0	0	0	1	0
2	0	1	0	0	1	0	0
3	0	1	0	1	0	0	0
4	0	1	1	0	0	0	0
5	1	0	0	0	0	0	1
6	1	0	0	0	0	1	0
7	1	0	0	0	1	0	0
8	1	0	0	1	0	0	0
9	1	0	1	0	0	0	0

Table A-12. The 2-out-of-7 code.

The 1-out-of-10 Code shown in TABLE A-13 is comprised of 10 bits with the feature that only one bit changes out of ten states. The advantages of this relates to the fact that no decoding is necessary. On the other hand, it requires a great deal of electronic circuitry to implement which leads to other disadvantages such as propagation delay and high current requirements.

A code that has found application for counting is the Johnson Code shown in TABLE A-14. Close inspection of this code shows it to be cyclic in nature, easily

	0	1	2	3	4	5	6	7	8	9
0	1	0	0	0	0	0	0	0	0	0
1	0	1	0	0	0	0	0	0	0	0
2	0	0	1	0	0	0	0	0	0	0
3	0	0	0	1	0	0	0	0	0	0
4	0	0	0	0	1	0	0	0	0	0
5	0	0	0	0	0	1	0	0	0	0
6	0	0	0	0	0	0	1	0	0	0
7	0	0	0	0	0	0	0	1	0	0
8	0	0	0	0	0	0	0	0	1	0
9	0	0	0	0	0	0	0	0	0	1

Table A-13. The 1-out-of-10 code.

Decimal	E	D	C	B	A
0	0	0	0	0	0
1	0	0	0	0	1
2	0	0	0	1	1
3	0	0	1	1	1
4	0	1	1	1	1
5	1	1	1	1	1
6	1	1	1	1	0
7	1	1	1	0	0
8	1	1	0	0	0
9	1	0	0	0	0

Table A-14. The Johnson code.

decoded and normally requires minimal electronic circuitry. The code is comprised of five bits and one bit is shifted to the right for decimal digits 0 through 9. At decimal 0, the first 1 has not entered the code for shifting at decimal 1. The first 1 appears under A, at decimal 2 the 1 that was under the A column has been shifted to the B column; having been freed to the B column by the new 1 that has appeared under the A column has been completely shifted out of column E by decimal 6. This code is commonly referred to as the "walking code" or "creeping code." As stated previously there is an almost infinite number of codes. In the design of digital systems, selection of a proper code can result in many benefits related to hardware reductions, reduced propagation times, reduced power consumption—all which lead to lower cost.

COMPUTER ARITHMETIC

Binary numbers can be added and subtracted in basically the same way as decimal numbers. However, the computer normally performs only the addition of binary numbers. Subtraction is performed by "adding" the one's and two's complement (discussed in this section) to a number for which subtraction is to be performed. Multiplication is performed by "adding" the multiplicand as many times as determined by the multiplier and division is performed by "adding" the divisor until it equals or closely approximates the dividend.

Because a computer could perform all of the basic arithmetic operations through addition, circuitry in a computer's arithmetic section contained only an adder circuit eliminating the need for a subtraction, multiplication, and division circuits. Parallel processing today might show variations from this approach. This in turn simplified the computer's circuitry and reduced its cost. Basically, adders perform addition using the same approach that one would use in performing pencil and paper addition.

Adding Positive Numbers

In the binary system, addition is straightforward and based on the following rules:

$$0 + 0 = 1$$
$$0 + 1 = 1$$
$$1 + 0 = 1$$
$$1 + 1 = 10$$
$$1 + 1 + 1 = 11$$

Consider the addition of binary 1001 and binary 0010. Writing the two binary numbers as shown below:

```
1001        9
0010        2
----       --
1011       11
```

In the addition rules, 0 added to 1 equals 1. This rule can be applied to columns one, two, and four. Also the above rules state that 0 plus 0 equals 0, which can be applied to column three, yielding a sum of 1011.

Multiple carries are required in some situations. Consider the addition of binary 01001111 and binary 00010111. The two numbers are aligned, for addition as shown:

```
01001111        79
00010111        23
--------       ---
01100110       102
```

From the above rules note that

$$1 + 1 + 1 = 1$$

Beginning in the first column, 1 plus 1 equals 0 with a carry of 1 to column two. Thus, in column two, 1 plus 1 plus 1 equals 1 with a carry of 1 to column three, which results again in 1 plus 1 plus 1 with a carry to column four. Now column four can be added as 1 plus 1 which gives a 0 and a carry of 1 to column five where again 1 plus 1 gives a 0 and a carry of 1 to column six which can be added as 1 (the carry) plus 0 plus 0 to give a 1 as the sixth digit of the sum. The seventh digit of 1 results from 1 plus 0 and the eighth digit of 0 results from 0 plus 0. Thus the sum of the binary additions is

```
0110        0110
```

Nine's Complement Subtraction

The nine's complement of a decimal number that is the remainder is obtained when that number is subtracted from 9. For example the nine's complement of 4 is 5. In determining the nine's complement of a multidigit number, each digit must be subtracted from 9. For example, the nine's complement of 837_{10} is 162_{10} determined as follows:

$$\begin{array}{r} 999_{10} \\ -\,837_{10} \\ \hline 162_{10} \end{array}$$

Subtraction as stated previously is performed by a computer by employing the arithmetic operation of addition. From the above discussion, once the complement has been obtained, it is added to the *minuend* (the number from which you wish to subtract). As an example, consider the subtraction of 27 from 56. First, performing this operation manually, the answer of 29 is determined:

$$\begin{array}{r} 56_{10} \quad \text{(Minuend)} \\ -\,27_{10} \quad \text{(Subtrahend)} \\ \hline 29_{10} \end{array}$$

However, using nine's complement arithmetic, the first step is to find the nine's complement of 27 which is $99 - 27$ which equals 72. Next add the nine's complement to 56:

$$\begin{array}{r} 56_{10} \\ +\,72_{10} \\ \hline 128_{10} \end{array}$$

Next remove the leading one and add it to the least significant digit:

$$\begin{array}{r} 56_{10} \\ +\,72_{10} \\ \hline (1)\ 28 \\ +1 \\ \hline 29_{10} \end{array}$$

end around carry

the result (29) using the nine's complement method is the same as using the conventional method.

Consider subtracting 23 from 625. Performing subtraction the conventional way yields:

$$\begin{array}{r} 625_{10} \quad \text{(minuend)} \\ -\,23_{10} \quad \text{(subtrahend)} \\ \hline 602_{10} \end{array}$$

Now using the nine's complement method, the first step is to subtract 23 from 999. Note that 23 is not subtracted from just 99, but 999. It is the minuend that determines the quantity of nines from which to subtract the subtrahend. In reality the nine's complement was determined as follows:

$$999_{10} \quad \text{(minuend three digit number)}$$
$$-023_{10} \quad \text{(subtrahend three digit number)}$$
$$\overline{976_{10}} \quad \text{(nine's complement)}$$

Now add the nine's complement to the minuend of 625:

$$625_{10}$$
$$+976_{10}$$
$$\text{end around} \quad (1) \ \overline{601_{10}}$$
$$\text{carry} \qquad + \ \ 1$$
$$\overline{602_{10}}$$

Lastly, remove the leading one and add it to the least significant digit as shown.

One's Complement Subtraction

The above discussion of nine's complement arithmetic lays the foundation for the discussion of one's complement subtraction. A computer, of course, does not employ nine's complement arithmetic (because it is in the decimal system of radix 10) but one's complement arithmetic.

One's complement arithmetic is based on the same principle as nine's complement arithmetic. The one's complement is performed by subtracting the number to be subtracted from 1. The one's complement of 1 is 0 $(1-1=0)$ and the one's complement of 0 is 1 $(1-0=1)$.

This suggests that each bit is the complement of the other which leads to the following rule:

To find the one's complement of any binary number simply change all zeros to ones and all ones to zeros.

Thus the one's complement of 11001010 is 00110101.

Applying the same procedure for the subtraction of binary numbers using the one's complement of number consider the subtraction of 24_{10} from 73_{10}. Using the conventional method yields:

$$73_{10} \ = \ 01001001$$
$$- \ \ 24_{10} \ = \ 00011000$$
$$\overline{49_{10}} \ = \ 00110001$$

Now using the one's complement approach, which a binary adder circuit would be capable of performing, the first step would be to find the one's complement of 24_{10} (00011000_2). One's complement of 00011000_2 is 11100111_2 found by changing all ones to zeros and zeros to ones. Now add the one's complement to the minuend and perform the end around carry:

$$01001001_2$$
$$11100111_2$$
$$\text{end around} \quad (1) \ \overline{00110000_2}$$
$$\text{carry} \qquad \qquad 1$$
$$\overline{00110001_2} \qquad = \ 49_{10}$$

Thus the same result (49_{10}) was found as was determined by using the conventional method.

As a second example consider the subtraction of 00000100_2 from 00100000_2. First, the conventional method yields:

$$
\begin{array}{rcl}
32_{10} & = & 00100000 \\
-\quad 4_{10} & = & 00000100 \\
\hline
28_{10} & = & 00011100_2
\end{array}
$$

Now consider the one's complement approach.

First, find the one's complement of 4_{10} (00000100) by changing all ones to zeros and zeros to ones:

11111011_2

Now adding the one's complement to the minuend and performing the end around carry yields:

$$
\begin{array}{lcl}
 & & 00100000_2 \\
 & & 11111011_2 \\
\text{end around} & (1) & \overline{00011011_2} \\
\text{carry} & & \underline{\qquad\quad 1} \\
 & & 00011100_2
\end{array}
$$

Because 00011100_2 equals 28_{10}, the correct result was again using the one's complement approach.

Ten's Complement Subtraction

Subtraction by addition in the decimal number system can be accomplished also by an approach termed ten's complement. This procedure is somewhat similar to that of using the nine's complement. However, the need for an end around carry is eliminated.

The ten's complement of a decimal number is obtained by subtracting it from ten or a power of ten depending upon the size of the number. For example the ten's complement of 7 is 3 ($10 - 7 = 3$).

Subtraction is accomplished by the ten's complement approach by finding the ten's complement of the number to be subtracted and adding that number (ten's complement) to the minuend. The most significant digit (left-most digit) of the sum obtained is ignored, leaving the resulting number as the answer. No end around carry is required.

The rule, however, of the number of digits that make up the minuend must equal the number of digits that subtrahend still holds.

As an example of ten's complement subtraction consider the subtraction of 365_{10} from 17352_{10}. First using the conventional approach gives:

$$
\begin{array}{r}
17352_{10} \\
-\,00365_{10} \\
\hline
1687
\end{array}
$$

Now employing the ten's complement approach yields:

$$100000_{10}$$
$$00365_{10}$$
$$\overline{99635_{10}}$$

Now adding the ten's complement to the minuend yields:

$$17352_{10}$$
$$99635_{10}$$

Ignore leading   (1) $\overline{16987_{10}}$

gives 16987_{10}

Since the same answer (16987_{10}) was obtained using the conventional method as well as the ten's complement method, the results check.

The ten's complement is one greater than the nine's complement and when using the ten's complement in a problem, it is not necessary to perform the end around carry wherein the leading one is added to the least significant bit.

Two's Complement Subtraction

The preceding discussion lays the foundation for two's complement subtraction. The two's complement subtraction is equivalent to the ten's complement decimal subtraction. The two's complement of a number can be found by first finding the one's complement of a number and adding 1 to that number. For example,

Given original number of	11001101_2
one's complement	00110010_2
	$+1$
two's complement	00110011

Another procedure that can be used to find the two's complement of a number is to first look at the least significant bit (right-most bit) of the number to be the complement, and if that number is a 1, write a 1 for the least significant bit of the complement, and if the least significant bit is a 0 write a 0 for the least significant bit of the complement. This procedure is continued until a 1 has been recorded. At that point, a 1 is written in the complement. After the 1 bit is encountered, the remaining bits are complemented. Consider the following example:

1101101_2 original number
0010011_2 two's complement

To subtract binary numbers using the two's complement method, the first step is to find the two's complement of the subtrahend followed by the second step of adding the result to the minuend.

Consider for example the subtraction of 01100 from 10110

$$\begin{array}{ll} \text{subtrahend} & 01100 \\ \text{two's complement} & 10100 \end{array}$$

adding the two's complement to the minuend.

$$\begin{array}{r} 10110 \\ 10100 \\ \hline \text{Ignore} \quad (1) \quad 01010 \end{array}$$

As in the ten's complement operations, the most significant bit (left-most bit) is ignored and the above results can be verified by using the conventional approach:

$$\begin{array}{rcl} 10110_2 & = & 22_{10} \\ 01100_2 & = & 12_{10} \\ \hline 01010 & = & 10_{10} \end{array}$$

Because it is not required to perform the end around carry, circuitry can be implemented with less complex hardware than required with the one's complement approach leading to lower power consumption and propagation times.

As a final note, note that as in the nine's, ten's and one's complement method, if the answer to a problem in two's complement form is comprised of the same quantity of bits as the minuend and the subtrahend with no leading one bit to ignore, the answer is a negative number derived from the subtraction of a larger number from a smaller number. This indicates that the answer is already in complement form.

For example, consider the subtraction of 1101_2 (13_{10}) from 1011_2 (11_{10}) using the conventional method yields:

$$\begin{array}{r} 11_{10} \\ -13_{10} \\ \hline -2_{10} \end{array}$$

Using the two's complement approach the two's complement of the subtrahend is found to be:

0010

this yields:

$$\begin{array}{r} 1011 \\ 0010 \\ \hline (0) \quad 1110 \end{array}$$

The fact there is no leading 1 suggests the number is negative. When this situation occurs, it is necessary to take the two's complement of the result

$$\begin{array}{ll} 0001 & \text{one's complement} \\ 0010 & \text{two's complement} \\ & \text{(answer, but negative)} \end{array}$$

because -2_{10} equals -0010_2. The answer of -2 checks.

Representing Negative Numbers

Positive and negative numbers must be represented in a form that will permit circuitry to recognize the proper sign. For manual (hand) work as discussed previously, it is only necessary that the proper sign be placed in front of the number. However, a different approach must be used to represent plus and minus signs with computer hardware.

One approach to this problem suggests the use of one extra binary bit to represent the sign of the given number; a zero would be representing a positive number, and a one representing a negative number. This type of notation is known as *sign magnitude* representation of signed numbers. For example, using the sign bit notation the number 27_{10} would be written as 01010. The first bit indicates the sign of the number (27_{10}) to be positive and the remaining bits indicating the magnitude. A -15_{10} would be indicated as 11111_2.

Signed magnitude is simple and straightforward. However, its implementation in a computer system results in complex circuitry and consequently higher power and longer propagation times. These factors led to the consideration of other methods.

From the previous discussion, it was noted that the one's or two's complement of a number represented a convenient means of subtracting binary or decimal numbers. The subtraction of one number from another represents in effect the addition of a positive number (the minuend) to another positive number (the subtrahend). Therefore, many hold that the complement form represents a proven method of representing negative numbers.

The binary equivalent of 21_{10} is 10101. To express it as a negative number, it must be written in either one's or two's complement form:

$$-21_{10} = 01010 \text{ (one's complement form)}$$
$$-21_{10} = 01011 \text{ (two's complement form)}$$

The frequent problem of confusing the complement numbers with ordinary positive binary numbers has been overcome by adding an extra bit to indicate the sign as was indicated previously in representing numbers in sign magnitude form. A 0 bit indicates a positive number while a 1 bit designates a negative number. Thus the utilization of a sign bit with complement notation permits both positive and negative numbers to be easily represented in binary. Thus to convert a decimal number to a signed pure binary number, convert the decimal number to binary and add a single leading 0 to represent the positive sign.

Table A-15 presents a set of numbers represented in pure binary form, one's complement form, and two's complement form. This first bit is the sign bit. A 0 bit designates a positive number while a 1 bit designates a negative number. Thus to convert a decimal number to signed pure binary number, convert the decimal number to binary and add a single leading 0 to indicate the positive sign.

Now the complement forms indicate that the numbers are negative. For those numbers indicated under the one's complement column, inspection indicates that the 1 preceding each number indicates a negative value. Similarly, the

Table A-15. Representing positive and negative numbers.

| | | Negative | |
| | Pure | One's | Two's |
Decimal	Binary	Complement	Complement
8_{10}	01000_2	10111_2	11000_2
17_{10}	010001_2	101110_2	101111_2
84_{10}	01010100_2	10101011_2	10101100_2
225_{10}	011100001_2	100011110_2	100011111_2

two's complement column represents negative binary number equivalents of the decimal number in column 1.

When converting from complement form to decimal, there is no way to determine if the number is in one's or two's complement form. The design engineer must have this knowledge initially.

If you want to convert a one's complement to binary, by previous rules all 1s are changed to 0s and all 0s to 1s. For example,

11001 (one's complement)
00110 (binary)

with the original number in one's complement form and ignoring the sign bit, the remaining five-bit number can be converted to decimal for $(0 + 0 + 4 + 2 + 0 = 6_{10})$.

Given that the number was originally in complement form, it is clear that it was a negative number. Therefore, it is necessary to add a negative sign to the decimal number to obtain the correct result (-6_{10}).

Similarly however, if the original number was in two's complement form

110101_2	(two's complement form)
001010_2	(each bit complemented)
$\underline{\qquad 1}$	(one bit added to)
001011_2	least significant bit

convert this number to decimal

$$0 + 8 + 0 + 2 + 1 = -11_{10}$$

and add a negative sign because the initial sign bit was 1.

Negabinary

An interesting system that handles signs is a positional weighted system termed *Negabinary*. This system has a built-in technique for representing negative numbers without the requirement of a sign bit. Consider the negabinary number 1111_{-2} and 101_{-2}

$$
\begin{array}{ccccccc}
-2^6 & -2^5 & -2^4 & -2^3 & -2^2 & -2^1 & -2^0 \\
64 & -32 & 16 & -8 & 4 & -2 & 1 \\
& & & & 1 & 1 & 1 \\
& & & -8 \; + & 4 \; - & 2 \; + & 1 \; = \; -5 \\
& & & & 1 & 0 & 1 \\
& & & & 4 \; + & 0 \; + & 1 \; = \; +5
\end{array}
$$

Thus, it is possible to represent any decimal number, positive or negative utilizing the negabinary system. The advantage of this system is that a sign bit is not required. This yields a simplification of handling such a number.

Adding Positive and Negative Numbers

The addition of a positive number to a negative number should be viewed as subtracting one positive number from another positive number. However, the sign that is assigned to the answer is the sign of the larger number. The sign could be either positive or negative depending upon the size of the numbers involved in the calculation. For the addition of a positive and negative number, wherein the negative number is the larger and results in a negative answer, consider the following examples.

Consider $+27_{10}$ and -39_{10} two's complement negative numbers are used:

$$
\begin{array}{rcl}
+27_{10} & = & 00001\ 1011 \\
-39_{10} & = & 10010\ 0111 \\
\hline
-12_{10} & = & 10000\ 1100
\end{array}
$$

First the number $+27_{10}$ is converted to binary with the leading zero indicating a positive number. Similarly -39 was converted to binary with the leading one indicating it as negative. Next -39 was converted into two's complement form:

$$
\begin{array}{rcll}
+39_{10} & = & 00010\ 0111_2 & \\
-39_{10} & = & 11101\ 1000_2 & \text{(one's complement)} \\
& & \underline{\qquad\qquad 1} & \\
& & 11101\ 1001_2 & \text{(two's complement)}
\end{array}
$$

First this number was converted to one's complement form, then by adding one it was converted to two's complement form. Next the two's complement is added to the $+27_{10}$.

$$
\begin{array}{rcll}
+27_{10} & = & 00001\ 1011_2 & \text{Binary} \\
-39_{10} & = & 11101\ 1001_2 & \text{(two's complement)} \\
\hline
& & 11111\ 0100_2 &
\end{array}
$$

Notice that the sign bit is a one. This indicates that the answer is negative. However, to find the correct answer, it is necessary to find the two's complement of the answer:

$1\ 1111\ 0100_2$	answer	Note that the most significant
$0\ 0000\ 1011_2$	one's complement	bit (1) indicates the two's com-
$\underline{\qquad\qquad 1}$		plement answer will be nega-
$0\ 0000\ 1100_2$	$= 12_{10}$	tive.

The answer is a -12 recalling that the sign bit indicated the result is negative.

For the addition of a positive and negative number wherein the positive number is the larger and results in a positive answer, consider the following example,

$$
\begin{aligned}
+76_{10} &= 00010\ 1100_2 \\
-33_{10} &= 10010\ 0001_2 \\
\hline
+43
\end{aligned}
$$

first convert the $+76_{10}$ and -33_{10} to pure binary numbers. Next find the two's complement of -33_{10}:

-33	$1\ 0010\ 0001_2$	Pure binary
	$0\ 1101\ 1110_2$	(one's complement)
	$\underline{\qquad\qquad 1}$	(adding 1)
	$0\ 1101\ 1111_2$	(two's complement)

Notice that the sign bit is a zero indicating that the answer is positive. Now add the two's complement to $+76_{10}$:

$+76_{10}$	$=$	$00100\ 1100_2$	
-33_{10}	$=$	$\underline{01101\ 1111_2}$	(two's complement)
$+43_{10}$		$10010\ 1011_2$	

Note that in this problem the carry from the most significant bit position is added to the sign bit column. This gives the correct answer in sign and magnitude. However, remember this rule: If there is a carry from the most significant bit column, that carry must be ignored to obtain the correct answer.

Adding Two Negative Numbers

Consider the addition of a -21 and a -6. First find the two's complement of each number:

$+21_{10}$	$=$	$0\ 0001\ 0101_2$	Pure binary
-21_{10}	$=$	$1\ 1110\ 1010_2$	(one's complement)
		$\underline{\qquad\qquad 1}$	(adding 1)
-21_{10}		$1\ 1110\ 1011_2$	(two's complement)
$+\ 6_{10}$	$=$	$0\ 0000\ 0110$	Pure binary
	$=$	$1\ 1111\ 1000$	(one's complement)
		$\underline{\qquad\qquad 1}$	(adding 1)
$-\ 6_{10}$		$1\ 1111\ 1010$	(two's complement)

Next add the two's complement for each number.

-21_{10}		$1\ 1110\ 1011_2$
$-\ 6_{10}$		$\underline{1\ 1111\ 1010_2}$
	(1)	$1\ 1110\ 0101$

Ignoring the leading, 1, the sign bit indicates at this point that the answer will be negative.

Next, because the answer is in two's complement form, the following steps must be carried out to obtain the correct answer:

$1110\ 0101_2$ (two's complement)
$0001\ 1010_2$ (complement all bits)
         1   (adding 1)
$\overline{0001\ 1011_2}$ = 27

Recalling that the sign is negative from the above step, the answer is a -27.

BCD Addition

The addition of BCD numbers is similar to that of adding pure binary numbers. As recalled in BCD, each decimal digit is represented by a four-bit binary number and the most popular BCD form is the 8421 code wherein the numbers 0 through 9 are represented by the pure binary numbers in the 8421 weighted code form. Consider the addition of 6_{10} and 4_{10}:

$$
\begin{array}{rcl}
+6_{10} & = & 0110 \\
+4_{10} & = & \underline{0100} \\
+10_{10} & = & 1010
\end{array}
$$

The four-bit BCD numbers are added using the previously discussed binary rules. Note that the BCD numbers are added in binary. However, close examination indicates that the answer is equal to 10_{10}.

Recall that in BCD the answer in each digit of a decimal number must be represented by four bits. However 10_{10} in BCD is not 1010 but

    1/0
0001 0000
    or
00010000

In this regard, the answer determined by pure binary addition (1010) is correct for pure binary, but for BCD it is incorrect. However, the answer (1010) can be corrected to give the correct result in BCD form. To accomplish this the rule is quite straightforward. To convert a pure binary result that is greater than 9_{10} to a BCD result, add 6_{10} (0110_2) to the pure binary result:

$$
\begin{array}{rcl}
1010 & = & 10_{10} \\
\underline{0110} & = & 6_{10} \\
1\ 0000 & &
\end{array}
$$

or in BCD form:

0001/0000
  1   0

Adding the necessary zeros to this result provides the correct answer of 0001 0000.

It is noted that only the four least significant bits (0001) are used because each BCD digit contains exactly four bits. The one bit overflow was carried to the next position and the three leading zeros added to form a complete BCD number.

The need to correct the answer to BCD form can be understood more clearly when the pure binary forms and BCD forms are compared. With 4 digits, a total of 16 different arrangements can be represented. In pure binary the numbers 0 through 9 are used to represent the BCD numbers. Now because six of the four-bit combinations of the code are not used (10_{10} through 15_{10}), 6 must be added to correct the answer.

As a final example consider the addition of 95_{10} and 122_{10} in BCD form

$$
\begin{array}{rl}
95 = & 1001\ 0101 \\
\underline{122} = & \underline{0001\ 0010\ 0010} \\
217 &
\end{array}
$$

The first digit is 7_{10} ($5_{10} + 2_{10}$) which is less than 9_{10} so no correction is necessary. The next digit is 11_{10} ($9_{10} + 2_{10}$) which is greater than 9_{10} so it must be corrected:

$$
\begin{array}{rll}
& 1011 & = 11_{10} \\
& \underline{0110} & = 6_{10} \\
(1) & \overline{0001} & = 1
\end{array}
$$

Note that the addition of 6_{10} (0110) that is carried over to the next position yields:

$$
\begin{array}{lll}
0001 & & 1_{10} \\
\underline{0001} & & \underline{1_{10}} \\
0010 & \text{carry over from previous position} & 2_{10}
\end{array}
$$

thus

$$
\begin{array}{rl}
95 = & 1001\ 0101 \\
\underline{122} = & \underline{0001\ 0010\ 0010} \\
217 & 0001\ 1011\ 0111 \\
& \underline{0001\ 0110} \\
& \quad 2 \quad\ \ 1 \quad\ \ 7
\end{array}
$$

as explained above.

FIXED AND FLOATING POINT NOTATION

There are limits on the size of a number that can be handled by a computer which are a function of the hardware. If certain calculations contain numbers that exceed the maximum number of bits available, then it will be necessary for that number to be scaled to fit the registers in the computer. *Scaling* can be defined as the multiplication of a number by a *factor* (another number) that causes a reduction or increase in the size of the binary word available. It is incumbent upon the programmer to keep track of this scaling so as to correct the final answer. A multiplication operation might start with a small number of bits and give an answer that requires a large number of bits. Systems analysts have developed two methods to control these types of situations—fixed point notation and floating point notation.

Fixed point notation implies that a systems analyst fixes the point manually when the machine is programmed. If it is determined that the range of the numbers is quite large in magnitude, the upper and lower limits might exceed the registers that are available to accept the result. Some accuracy might be sacrificed by truncating some of the least significant bits.

Many times large and small numbers occur at the same time in a single problem producing situations that are very difficult to handle in a fixed point notation type of structure. To accommodate these types of situations, floating point notation was developed.

You can write a very large or small decimal number two ways. Four million can be written as 4,000,000 or as 4×10^6. Similarly, a very small number such as 00000000.326 can be written as 3.26×10^9. The primary purpose of these notational schemes is to keep track of the decimal point in a calculation because the number can be represented as a number between 1 and 10 and using a power of ten.

Essentially, this method is comparable to what is implemented in a circuit that employs floating point notation. Basically, the number operated on is broken down into two parts. The first part is a number between 0 and 1 and is termed the *mantissa*. The second part, called the *exponent*, is the power to which 2 (the base of the binary system) is raised. This second number locates and automatically keeps track of the binary point. The particular number that is represented is determined by multiplying the base raised to the exponent as given by the relationship

$$N = M \times 2^c$$

where M is the mantissa, C is the characteristic, and N is the number being represented. Consider:

.110 100

The first part of the number (.110) is the mantissa while the second part (101) is the exponent to which power the base (2) must be raised. To convert this into a decimal equivalent, you must perform a conventional binary-to-decimal conversion and substitute the numbers into the above formula as follows:

$$N = M \times 2^c$$
$$.110 = .375$$
$$101 = 5$$
$$N = .375 \times 2^5 = 12$$

The preceding sections have provided tutorial discussions of a variety of topics related to computer arithmetic operations. The following sections address combinatorial logic and sequential logic related mathematics and logic design.

COMBINATORIAL LOGIC

There are basically three types of logic circuits. First is a *combinatorial logic circuit* that can be defined as a digital logic system whose output at any given time is a function of the current inputs to the system. Second is a *sequential logic circuit* that can be defined as a digital logic block whose outputs are a function of the current inputs and previous inputs. Third are the *combinatorial-sequential circuits* combined into a single digital system.

In general, combinatorial logic is limited to the basic gates (AND, OR, XOR, NAND, NOR) while sequential logic usually refers to flip-flops (D, SR, T, JK), registers, and counters.

Logic Gates

The basic five logic gates and the AND gate, OR gate, XOR gate, NAND gate, and XOR gate. The discussion following summarizes the truth tables associated with these gates and concludes with a discussion of their respective relationships.

AND Gates. The AND electronic circuit has two or more inputs and a single output. The truth table for this gate with two inputs is shown in FIG. A-15. All of the inputs must be a binary 1 simultaneously to generate a binary 1 output. If any one of the inputs is a binary 0, the output C is binary 0.

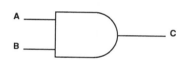

Conventional symbol as printed.

TRUTH TABLE

INPUTS		OUTPUT
A	B	C
0	0	0
0	1	0
1	0	0
1	1	1

Fig. A-15. The AND logic gate symbol and truth table.

OR Gate. The OR gate is an electronic circuit with two or more inputs and a single output. Its truth table is shown in FIG. A-16. This circuit generates a binary 1 at its output. It generates a binary 0 only if all of its inputs are binary 0.

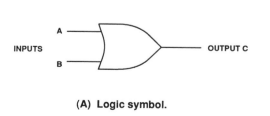

(A) Logic symbol.

TRUTH TABLE

INPUTS		OUTPUT
A	B	C
0	0	0
0	1	1
1	0	1
1	1	1

Fig. A-16. The OR gate logic symbol and truth table.

Any digital logic function can be designed using the AND or OR logic functions. However, it was soon discovered that the use of these gates resulted in limited speed and a rapid deterioration of the logic levels in shape and amplitude as they passed through several stages and levels of gates. Further, study capacities caused increased propagation times and rise and fall times of logic pulses. In addition, the absence of amplification caused the signal amplitude to be reduced as it passed through several levels of gating. It was discovered that by adding a transistor logic inverter to each diode gate as extra buffering, the above problems were reduced. This resulted in the development of the NAND (NOT AND) and NOR (NOT OR) gates.

NAND Date. A NAND gate is an electronic logic circuit with two or more inputs and a single output. The truth table and logic symbol for this gate is shown in FIG. A-17. Close inspection shows that a binary 0 can only be generated if all inputs are binary 1.

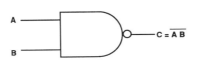

TRUTH TABLE

INPUTS		OUTPUT
A	B	C
0	0	1
0	1	1
1	0	1
1	1	0

Fig. A-17. The NAND gate logic symbol and truth table.

NOR Gate. A NOR gate is an electronic circuit with two or more inputs and a single output. The truth table and logic symbol for this gate is shown in FIG. A-18. An inspection of the truth table indicates that a binary 1 can be obtained only if all inputs are binary 0.

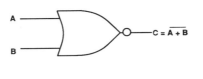

TRUTH TABLE

INPUTS		OUTPUT
A	B	C
0	0	1
0	1	0
1	0	0
1	1	0

Fig. A-18. The NOR gate logic symbol and truth table.

XOR Gate. Another type of gate that appears frequently in logic diagrams is the exclusive OR (XOR) gate. Similarly, this gate is a logic circuit with two or more inputs and a single output. Figure A-19 shows the truth table and symbols for this gate. Close inspection shows binary 0 as output if and only if all of its inputs are at the same binary state.

TRUTH TABLE

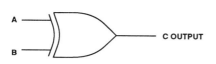

INPUTS		OUTPUT
A	B	C
0	0	0
0	1	1
1	0	1
1	1	0

Conventional Symbol.

Fig. A-19. The XOR logic symbol and truth table.

Buffers. Figure A-20 shows the truth table and the four basic buffers found in the logic diagram of digital circuitry. HI-Z refers to high impedance. The relationships between the AND/OR gates is shown in FIG. A-21.

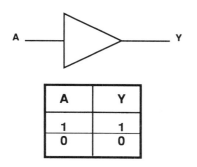

A	Y
1	1
0	0

(A) Noninverting buffer.

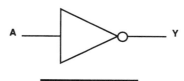

A	Y
1	0
0	1

(B) Inverting buffer.

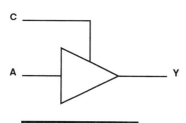

C	A	Y
1	0	0
1	1	1
0	X	HI-Z

NOTE:
C is the control input
X denotes "don't care"

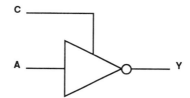

C	A	Y
1	0	1
1	1	0
0	X	HI-Z

NOTE:
C is the control input
X denotes "don't care"

Fig. A-20. Basic buffers and tristate buffers.

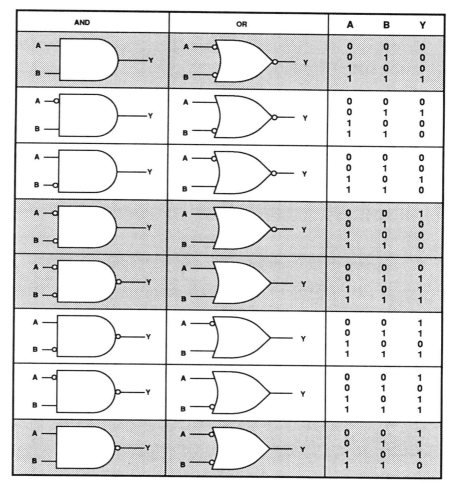

		A	B	Y
AND	OR	0	0	0
		0	1	0
		1	0	0
		1	1	1
		0	0	0
		0	1	1
		1	0	0
		1	1	0
		0	0	0
		0	1	0
		1	0	1
		1	1	0
		0	0	1
		0	1	0
		1	0	0
		1	1	0
		0	0	0
		0	1	1
		1	0	1
		1	1	1
		0	0	1
		0	1	1
		1	0	0
		1	1	1
		0	0	1
		0	1	0
		1	0	1
		1	1	1
		0	0	1
		0	1	1
		1	0	1
		1	1	0

▒ **De Morgan's Theorem Relationships**

Fig. A-21. The relationships between logic gates and truth tables.

Boolean Algebra

Boolean Algebra is comprised of a set of laws and techniques that can be used to express and manipulate logic equations. Essentially every Boolean expression can be expressed in the form of a logic circuit. The laws of Boolean algebra have found widespread application in the reduction of original Boolean equations into their minimal form consisting of the minimum number of gates used to perform a logic function. When a Boolean equation is derived from a truth table, its implementation normally requires several more gates than are required after the laws of Boolean algebra have been applied.

For example, a typical logic circuit might initially require seven gates to implement. However, if the Boolean equation can be reduced by applying the

Boolean Algebra laws, only three gates might be required. This leads to the advantage of cost savings related to a reduction in hardware (gates) cost. This section discusses the laws of Boolean Algebra followed by two examples of how these laws can be applied to reduce a Boolean expression to its minimal form. Table A-16 provides an algebraic summary of these laws.

Table A-16. Laws of Boolean algebra.

1. A(1) = A A(0) = 0	**Laws of Intersection**
2. A + 1 = 1 A + 0 = A	**Laws of Union**
3. A · A = A A + A = A	**Laws of Tautology**
4. A · $\overline{A}$ = 0 A + $\overline{A}$ = 1	**Laws of Complements**
5. A = $\overline{\overline{A}}$	**Law of the Double Negative**
6. AB = BA A + B = B + A	**Laws of Commutation**
7. A(B + C) = AB + AC (A + B) (A + C) = A + BC	**Laws of Distribution**
8. A(BC) = (AB)C = ABC A + (B + C) = (A + B) + C = A + B + C	**Laws of Association**

9. A(A + B) = A
    A($\overline{A}$ + B) = AB
    AB + $\overline{B}$ = A+ $\overline{B}$
    A$\overline{B}$ + B = A + B
	Laws of Absorption

Laws of Intersection. This law is specifically related to AND gates and is expressed as A(1) = A, A(0) = 0. For the first part of this law, it can be stated that when one of the inputs is a 1, the output is determined by the specific input represented by A. For a two-input AND gate, the relationship can be illustrated as in FIG. A-22. Clearly the input A can assume a binary 1 or binary 0.

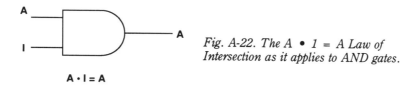

A · I = A

Fig. A-22. The A • 1 = A Law of Intersection as it applies to AND gates.

If a binary 1 is applied as the A input, the output is A (1 in this case). If a binary 0 is applied to the A input, the output is 0. Thus when a binary 1 is applied as one input, the output of the AND gate is the input applied to the A input. Note that these Laws of Intersection apply to AND gates with more than two inputs. This law states that the output is equal to the input multiplied by 1. For example, consider a three-input AND gate with inputs A and B and binary 1. The output is AB(1) = AB, that is, the ANDing of A and B. The second part of this law A(0) = 0 shown in FIG. A-23 also applies to multiple AND gates. When one of the inputs is a binary 0, the output is always 0, or the output is the input multiplied by 0 which always yields 0 as the output. This leads to the conclusion that the only time the output of an AND gate is a binary 1 is if all inputs are binary 1.

Fig. A-23. The A • O = O Law of Intersection as it applies to AND gates.

Laws of Union. While the Laws of Intersection apply to the AND gate, the Laws of Union apply to OR logic gates. The two parts to this law are A + 1 = 1 and A + 0 = A. The first part A + 1 = 1 implies that the output of an OR gate is always a binary 1 if a binary 1 is applied to one input and some logic signal to the other. Figure A-16 shows the OR gate truth table. An OR gate produces a binary 1 if one or more of its inputs are binary 1. Thus if one of the inputs to an OR gate is permanently applied as a binary 1, the output is always a binary 1 independent of the state of A input. This part of the Law of Union is shown in FIG. A-24.

Fig. A-24. The A + 1 = 1 Law of Union as its applies to OR gates.

The second part of this law (A + 0 = A) implies that the output is always logic A if the other inputs are binary 0. However, if input A is a binary 0, the output is a binary 0 because all inputs are binary 0 simultaneously. This part of the Law of Union is illustrated in FIG. A-25.

Fig. A-25. The A + O = A Law of Union as it applies to OR gates.

If more than one logic input signal is applied to an OR gate while a binary 1 is applied to one of the other inputs, the output is always at binary 1. However, if a binary 0 is applied to one input of a multiple input OR gate, the output is determined by the other inputs. It must be remembered that the binary 0 applied to one of the inputs has no effect on the output.

Laws of Tautology. Like the Laws of Intersection and Union, there are two parts to the Law of Tautology. These parts (A • A = A and A + A = A) both demonstrate the elimination of redundant terms in a Boolean expression. The first part (A • A = A) states that if the logic signal A is applied to two inputs of an AND gate the output is A. The second part similarly states the same fact for OR gates, that is, if logic signal A is applied to both inputs of an OR gate the output is A. Figure A-26 illustrates the first part of this law for AND gates while FIG. A-27 illustrates the second part of this law. Thus for an AND gate, if both inputs are binary 1, the output is binary 1, and if both inputs are binary 0, the output is binary 0.

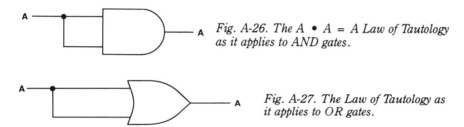

Fig. A-26. The A • A = A Law of Tautology as it applies to AND gates.

Fig. A-27. The Law of Tautology as it applies to OR gates.

Similarly for the OR gate, if both inputs are binary 1, the output is binary 1, and if both inputs are binary 0, the output is binary 0.

Generally the Laws of Tautology state that the output of an AND gate or OR gate equals the inputs when those inputs are the same logic level (both binary 1 or both binary 0).

Law of Complements. The two parts to the Law of Complements are; A • $\overline{A}$ = 0 and A + $\overline{A}$ = 1. The first part (A • $\overline{A}$ = 0) implies that if a signal A and its complement A are applied to two inputs of an AND gate, the output of that AND gate is always a binary 0. The second part of the law (A + $\overline{A}$ = 1) states that if a logic signal A and its complement is applied to an OR gate the output of that OR gate is binary 1. Figure A-28 illustrates the first part of the law while FIG. A-29 illustrates the second part of the law.

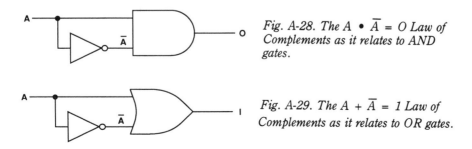

Fig. A-28. The A • $\overline{A}$ = 0 Law of Complements as it relates to AND gates.

Fig. A-29. The A + $\overline{A}$ = 1 Law of Complements as it relates to OR gates.

Law of Double Negative. This law states that each time a logic signal A is inverted, the complement can be generated by placing a bar over that letter as shown in FIG. A-30. Clearly two bars placed over a letter is equivalent to no bars over the letter because each bar effectively cancels the other.

Fig. A-30. The Law of Double Negatives.

Laws of Commutation. This law also has two versions AB = BA and A + B = B + A. This law states that the order is not important when the variables are written in a logic equation.

Laws of Distribution. This law states that when the variable A is multiplied by the variable B and C that are ORed together as

A (B + C)

the expression equals A times the first variable plus C times the second variable to yield:

AB + AC

Conversely, this expression can be simplified back to the original form:

A (B + C)

Similarly for the same three variables A, B, C,

(A + B) (A + C) = AA + AC + BA + BC

by the Law of Tautology AA = A leaving:

A(1 + C + B) + BC.

Further, by the Law of Union, (1 + C + B) equals 1, leaving A(1) = A and finally:

A + BC

Laws of Association. Generally the Laws of Association state that the parenthesis in a Boolean expression can be removed to assist in simplifying a logic expression:

(A + B) + C = A + (B + C) = A + B + C

Similarly

(A B)C = A(B C) = A B C

Law of Absorption. The two parts to this law can be used to reduce a logic expression to its simplest form. The first part states that

A(A + B) = A

First, by the Law of Distribution:

AA + AB = A

Since AA = A by the Law of Tautology, the expression leaves:

A + AB = A

Now factoring from using the Law of Distribution gives:

A(1 + B) = A

By the Laws of Union

(1 + B) = 1

leaving:

A(1) = A

Thus

A = A

by the Laws of Intersection.
The second part of this law states that:

$A(\overline{A} + B) = AB$

First applying the Law of Distribution:

$A\overline{A} + AB = AB.$

Now

$A\overline{A} = 0$

by the Law of Complements leaving

0 + AB = AB

or

AB = AB.

Figure A-31 shows the basic Boolean operators.

OPERATOR	SYMBOL
AND	.
OR	+
** NOT	/

ELEMENTARY BOOLEAN OPERATORS

Fig. A-31. Boolean operators.

** NOT also indicated by symbol " — " such as $\overline{X}$

De Morgan's Theorem

An important theorem without which it might be impossible to reduce a Boolean expression to its minimal form is De Morgan's Theorem. This important Theorem has two parts:

$$\overline{A + B} = \overline{A}\,\overline{B}$$
$$\overline{AB} = \overline{A} + \overline{B}$$

This theorem illustrates the connection between an OR expression to an AND expression. Its importance lies in its use in converting a logic expression from its AND form to its OR form and vice versa. For example,

$$\overline{AB + CD} = \overline{(AB)}\,\overline{(CD)}$$
$$\overline{B + \overline{C}} = \overline{B}C$$

De Morgan's Theorem is traditionally proven using truth tables. Table A-17 lists the possible combinations of the variables A and B, the terms $\overline{A}$, $\overline{B}$, $\overline{(A + B)}$ and $\overline{A}{\bullet}\overline{B}$. To prove that

$$\overline{A + B} = \overline{A}{\bullet}\overline{B}$$

note that the A + B column is the basic OR gate truth table outputs, as shown in FIG. A-16. The $\overline{A + B}$ column is obtained by complementing the A + B expression. The $\overline{A}$ and $\overline{B}$ columns were derived by complementing the A and B variable columns. The $\overline{A}{\bullet}\overline{B}$ column was derived by ANDing the $\overline{A}$ and $\overline{B}$ columns. Note that the $\overline{A}{\bullet}\overline{B}$ column follows the AND gate truth table shown in FIG. A-15.

A	B	$\overline{A}$	$\overline{B}$	A + B	$\overline{A + B}$	$\overline{A} \cdot \overline{B}$
0	0	1	1	0	1	1
0	1	1	0	1	0	0
1	0	0	1	1	0	0
1	1	0	0	1	0	0

Table A-17. Truth table for proof of De Morgan's $\overline{A + B} = \overline{A}{\bullet}\overline{B}$.

The results of these operations shows that the $\overline{A + B}$ column and the $\overline{A}{\bullet}B$ column are identical thus proving:

$$\overline{A + B} = \overline{A} \bullet \overline{B}$$

Now conversely to prove

$$\overline{A \bullet B} = \overline{A} + \overline{B}$$

Consider the truth table shown in TABLE A-18. Using the same procedure to develop the content of the different columns, note that the $\overline{A} + \overline{B}$ and the A $\bullet$ B are identical thus proving that:

$$\overline{A \bullet B} = \overline{A} + \overline{B}$$

Table A-18. Truth table for proof of De Morgan's $\overline{A + B} = \overline{A} \cdot \overline{B}$.

A	B	$\overline{A}$	$\overline{B}$	$\overline{A + B}$	$A \cdot B$	$\overline{A \cdot B}$
0	0	1	1	1	0	1
0	1	1	0	1	0	1
1	0	0	1	1	0	1
1	1	0	0	0	1	0

Consider the following expression that benefits from the application of De Morgan's Theorem:

$$Y = \overline{\overline{A}\,\overline{C}D} + \overline{ACD} + \overline{A + D}$$

Applying De Morgan's Theorem yields:

$$Y = A + C + \overline{D} + (\overline{A}\,\overline{C}\,\overline{D}) + \overline{A}\,\overline{D}$$

Applying the Laws of Commutation gives:

$$Y = A + \overline{A}\,\overline{C}\,\overline{D} + \overline{A}\,\overline{D} + C + \overline{D}$$

Next utilizing the Laws of Distribution:

$$Y = \overline{A}(1 + \overline{C}\,\overline{D} + \overline{D}) + \overline{C} + \overline{D}$$

Now applying the Laws of Union:

$$Y = \overline{A}(1) + \overline{C} + \overline{D}$$

Finally in minimal form after utilizing the Law of Intersection:

$$Y = \overline{A} + \overline{C} + \overline{D}.$$

Sum of Products (SOP) Form and Product of Sums (POS) Form.
Any logic expression can be reduced to a two-level form and expressed as either a Sum-of-Products (SOP) or Product-of-Sums (POS). A sum-of-products expression is a product term or several product terms logically added together, for example $A \cdot B + C \cdot D$. A product-of-sums expression is a term or several sum terms logically multiplied together such as $(A + B) \cdot (C + D)$.

Basically five types of terms are related to Boolean equations. These terms are:

- Product Term—A product term is a single variable or the logical product of several variables. The variable may or may not be complemented. For example $A \cdot B \cdot C$.

- Sum Term—A sum term is a single variable or the sum of several variables. The variables may or may not be complemented. For example $A + B$.

- Normal Term—A normal term is a product or sum term in which no variable appears more than once would be ABC or A + B + C.

- Minterm—A minterm is a product term containing every variable once and only once (either true or complemented).
- Maxterm—A maxterm is a sum term containing every variable once and only once (either true or complemented).

With the above discussion, consider the following two examples to demonstrate how Boolean Algebra laws can be applied to reduce a Boolean expression to its minimal form.

From Boolean Logic Expressions to Minimal Form. First using the Boolean algebra techniques discussed minimize

$$Y = AB\overline{C}D + ABC\overline{D} + B\overline{C}D + \overline{A}BC\overline{D}$$

The logic diagram is shown in FIG. A-32. First applying the Law of Commutation the function reduces to:

$$Y = AB\overline{C}D + B\overline{C}D + ABC\overline{D} + \overline{A}BC\overline{D}$$

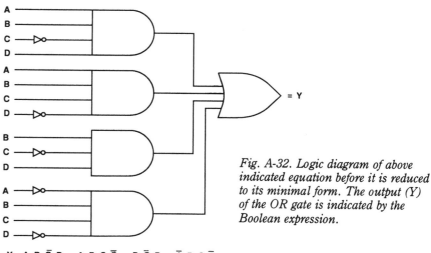

$$Y = A B \overline{C} D + A B C \overline{D} + B \overline{C} D + \overline{A} B C \overline{D}$$

Fig. A-32. Logic diagram of above indicated equation before it is reduced to its minimal form. The output (Y) of the OR gate is indicated by the Boolean expression.

Now applying the Laws of Distribution yields:

$$Y = B\overline{C}D(A+1) + BC\overline{D}(A + \overline{A})$$

Now following with Laws of Union and Complements produces:

$$Y = B\overline{C}D(1) + BC\overline{D}(1)$$

The Law of Intersection yields:

$$Y = B\overline{C}D + BC\overline{D}$$

and finally the Law of Distribution yields the original function in minimal form:

$$Y = B(\overline{C}D + C\overline{D})$$

The logic diagram in minimal form is shown in FIG. A-33. The original Boolean function required four AND gates and one OR gate. The final logic diagram shown in FIG. A-33 requires only two AND gates and one OR gate, a significant reduction in hardware.

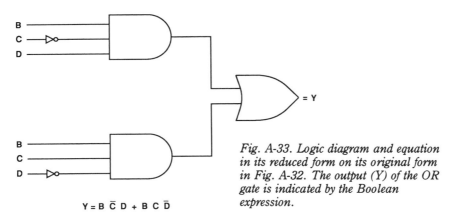

$$Y = B \bar{C} D + B C \bar{D}$$

Fig. A-33. Logic diagram and equation in its reduced form on its original form in Fig. A-32. The output (Y) of the OR gate is indicated by the Boolean expression.

Lastly, consider the procedure of beginning with a truth table, developing the Boolean equations, reducing the Boolean equation to its minimal form, and ending with the reduced logic diagram.

From Truth Table to Boolean Logic Expression to Logic Diagram. To obtain the Boolean expression from a truth table, consider the truth table given in TABLE A-19.

A	B	C	Y
0	0	0	0
0	0	1	0
0	1	1	0
0	1	0	0
1	1	0	1
1	1	1	1
0	1	0	1
1	0	0	0

Table A-19. Truth table for deviation of Boolean expression.

Inspection of this truth table implies that it is desired that Y equal binary 1 for the condition:

010, 110, and 111

and a binary 0 for all other input conditions. The Boolean product terms are derived by converting the three terms that will produce a binary 1 for Y to three corresponding literals:

$$\overline{A}B\overline{C}, \ AB\overline{C}, \ ABC.$$

Now each of the above terms are ORed to yield

$$Y = AB\overline{C} + AB\overline{C} + ABC$$

Next employing the laws of Boolean algebra, the above function is reduced to its minimal form. Figure A-34 shows the logic diagram of the original expression.

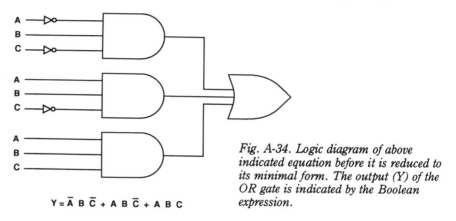

$$Y = \overline{A} \ B \ \overline{C} + A \ B \ \overline{C} + A \ B \ C$$

Fig. A-34. Logic diagram of above indicated equation before it is reduced to its minimal form. The output (Y) of the OR gate is indicated by the Boolean expression.

First using the Laws of Distribution yields:

$$Y = ABC + B\overline{C} \ (\overline{A} + A)$$

Next the Laws of Complements

$$Y = ABC + B\overline{C}(1)$$

Now the Law of Intersection

$$Y = ABC + B\overline{C}$$

Next the Law of Distribution

$$Y = B(AC + \overline{C})$$

And finally the Laws of Absorption to yield

$$Y = B(A + \overline{C})$$
$$Y = BA + B\overline{C}$$

The logic diagram indicates two AND gates, both with a common B input. Separate A and $\overline{C}$ inputs are applied as shown in FIG. A-35.

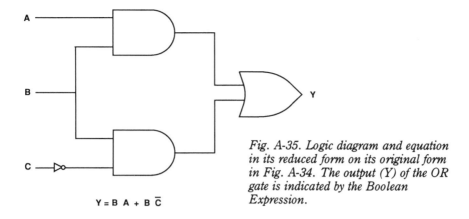

$$Y = B \, A + B \, \overline{C}$$

Fig. A-35. Logic diagram and equation in its reduced form on its original form in Fig. A-34. The output (Y) of the OR gate is indicated by the Boolean Expression.

Karnaugh Maps

In addition to Boolean Algebra-related techniques for reducing a Boolean function to its minimal form, several other techniques have been developed through the years probably beginning with Venn diagrams followed by Veitch diagrams, Karnaugh maps, and the Quine-McClusky method.

The Karnaugh map, developed by G. Karnaugh in 1952, is comprised of an arrangement of squares containing a 1 for an uncomplemented variable and a 0 for a complemented variable. The squares are so ordered that the difference between any two adjacent squares represents a one variable change. Figure A-36 shows a two-variable Karnaugh map while FIG. A-37 presents a three-variable map. From these figures, it is clear that a map of two variables must contain four cells and a map of three variables must contain eight cells. Generalizing, a map of n variables must contain 2^n cells.

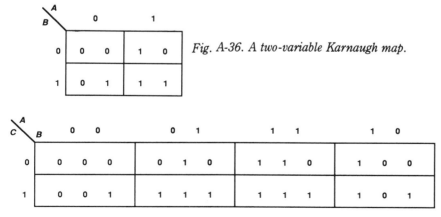

Fig. A-36. A two-variable Karnaugh map.

Fig. A-37. A three-variable Karnaugh map.

The advantage of the Karnaugh map in dealing with Boolean functions is that basic patterns can be instantly recognized. In addition, they provide all possible variable combinations and minimal terms. It is the recognition of these basic patterns that provides for minimization of the Boolean function. Consider the function previously reduced using Boolean algebra techniques.

$$Y = AB\overline{C}D + ABC\overline{D} + B\overline{C}D + \overline{A}BC\overline{D}$$

Figures A-38, A-39, A-40 and A-41 show the mapping of this function into their individual matrix terms. Beginning with the terms $AB\overline{C}D$, a 1 is inserted in the columns where A is 1 and B is 1 and in the row where C is 0 and D is 1 as shown in FIG. A-38. For the term $ABC\overline{D}$, a 1 is inserted in the column where A is 1 and B is 1 and the row where C is 1 and D is 0 as presented in FIG. A-39. The next term $B\overline{C}D$, 1 is inserted in the row where C is 0 and D is 1 and in the columns where B is 1 as indicated in FIG. A-40. The last term $\overline{A}BC\overline{D}$ has 1 inserted in the column where A is 0 and B is 1 and in the rows where C is 1 and D is 0 as illustrated in FIG. A-41.

Fig. A-38. Inserting 1s in column where A is 1 and B is 1 and row when C is 0 and D is 1.

CD \ AB	OO	OI	II	IO
OO			I	
OI	I	I	I	I
II			I	
IO			I	

A B $\overline{\text{C}}$ D

Fig. A-39. Inserting 1 in column where A is 1 and B is 1 and in row where C is 1 and D is 0.

CD \ AB	OO	OI	II	IO
OO			I	
OI			I	
II			I	
IO	I	I	I	I

A B C $\overline{\text{D}}$

CD＼AB	OO	OI	II	IO
OO		I	I	
OI	I	I	I	I
II		I	I	
IO		I	I	

B C̄ D

Fig. A-40. Inserting 1s in row where C is 0, D is 1, and columns where B is 1.

CD＼AB	OO	OI	II	IO
OO		I		
OI		I		
II		I		
IO	I	I	I	I

Ā B C D̄

Fig. A-41. Inserting 1s in column where A is 0 and B is 1 and in row where C is 1 and D is 0.

Now that the function is completely mapped as shown in FIG. A-42, the next step is to group the ones in such a way that a minimal expression results. First, as a general guideline, the grouping of ones should be as large as possible; the larger the grouping, the fewer number of literals in the corresponding term.

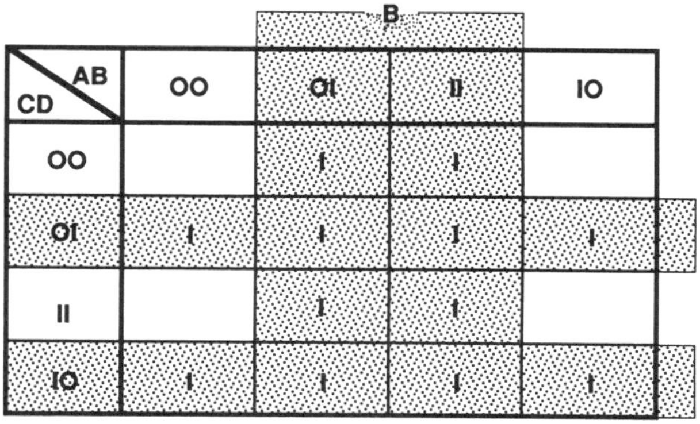

CD＼AB	OO	OI	II	IO	
OO		I	I		
OI	I	I	I	I	C̄D
II		I	I		
IO	I	I	I	I	CD̄

Y = A B C̄ D + A B C D̄ + B C̄ D + Ā B C D̄

Fig. A-42. Total mapping of Y = ABC̄D + ABCD̄ + BC̄D + ABCD̄.

Secondly, the minimum number of groupings should be used. This results in the minimum number of product terms in the expression. Thus the goal in grouping the one should be to gather as many ones as possible in such a way that the minimum number of groupings result.

A four-variable map requires four variables to define a cell. Thus in a four-variable map, the grouping of two cells will eliminate one variable, the grouping of four cells will eliminate two variables and the grouping of eight cells will eliminate three variables.

There are several approaches to reducing the map and consequently minimizing the Boolean expression. One approach calls for listing the coordinates of each cell that contains a one (1) and eliminates those that change during the listing. For example, considering the original expression, the coordinates of the first grouping listed as follows from FIG. A-43.

	Column 01					Column 11		
A	**B**	**C**	**D**		**A**	**B**	**C**	**D**
0	1	0	0		1	1	0	0
0	1	0	1		1	1	0	1
0	1	1	1		1	1	1	1
0	1	1	0		1	1	1	0

Fig. A-43. Grouping of 1s in columns 01 and 11 from Fig. A-42.

Because the literals A,C, and D changed during the listing of columns 01 and 11 they can be eliminated leaving only B.

Next consider the grouping in Row 01 (see FIG. A-44) by listing the coordinates of the 1s in that row:

	Row 01		
A	**B**	**C**	**D**
0	0	0	1
0	1	0	1
1	1	0	1
1	0	0	1

CD \ AB	OO	OI	II	IO
OO				
OI	I	I	I	I
II				
IO				

C̄ D

Fig. A-44. Grouping of 1s in row 01 from Fig. A-42.

CD \ AB	OO	OI	II	IO
OO				
OI				
II				
IO	I	I	I	I

C D̄

Fig. A-45. Grouping of 1s in row 10 from Fig. A-42.

Because the literals A and B changed during the listing they can be eliminated, leaving $\overline{C}D$.

Next, consider the grouping in Row 10 by listing the coordinates of the 1s in that row as shown in FIG. A-45:

Row 10

A	B	C	D
0	0	1	0
0	1	1	0
1	1	1	0
1	0	1	0

Because the literals A and B changed during the listing, they can be eliminated, leaving $C\overline{D}$.

Thus the original expression

$$Y = AB\overline{C}D + ABC\overline{D} + B\overline{C}D + \overline{A}BC\overline{D}$$

reduces to

$$Y = B + \overline{C}D + C\overline{D}$$

or

$$Y = B + (\overline{C}D + C\overline{D})$$

Applying De Morgan's theorem yields

$$\overline{Y} = \overline{B} + \overline{(\overline{C}D + C\overline{D})}$$

$$\overline{\overline{Y}} = \overline{\overline{B} + \overline{(\overline{C}D + C\overline{D})}}$$

and finally

$$Y = B(\overline{C}D + C\overline{D})$$

which agrees with the Boolean reduction performed on the same Boolean expression in the section that discussed Boolean algebra.

Now consider the first application (4-bit binary decade counter). Figure A-46 is a reprint of FIG. 6-3 with a few additional modifications to each of the four groups of six variable maps. A derivation of CLKOUT might be written as follows:

$$\text{CLKOUT} = \text{Map 1} + \text{Map 2} + \text{Map 3} + \text{Map 4}$$

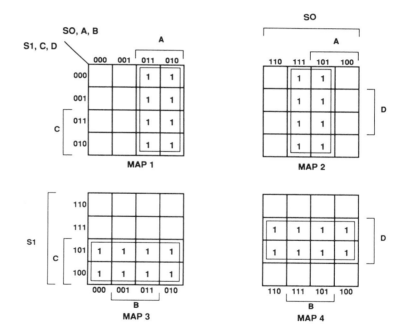

$$\text{CLKOUT} = \overline{S1}\,\overline{S0}\,A\,\cancel{XXX} + \overline{S1}\,S0\,\cancel{X}\,B\,\cancel{XX} + S1\,\overline{S0}\,\cancel{XX}\,C\,\cancel{X} + S1\,S0\,\cancel{XXX}\,D$$

$$\text{CLKOUT} = \overline{S1}\,\overline{S0}\,A + \overline{S1}\,S0\,B + S1\,\overline{S0}\,C + S1\,S0\,D$$

Fig. A-46. A reprint of FIG. 6-3, with a modification of SO, A, B and S1, C1, D indicated around the perimeters of the four maps.

First consider Map 1. Because there is a grouping of eight 1s, the *coordinates of each cell* containing a 1 can be written as follows

Map 1

S0	A	B	S1	C	D
0	1	1	0	0	0
0	1	1	0	0	1
0	1	1	0	1	1
0	1	1	0	1	0
0	1	0	0	0	0
0	1	0	0	0	1
0	1	0	0	1	1
0	1	0	0	1	0

This yields the term:

S1 S0 A B C D

However, those literals (columns) that changed can be eliminated from the above expression. These literals are B, C, D, leaving:

S1 S0 A

S0, S1, and A did not change and can be written in complement or uncomplemented form as follows:

$\overline{S0}\ \overline{S1}\ A$

Note S0 and S1 contained all zeros so they are written in complemented form.
    Now consider Map 2

Map 2

S0	A	B	S1	C	D
1	1	1	0	0	0
1	1	1	0	0	1
1	1	1	0	1	1
1	1	1	0	1	0
1	0	1	0	0	0
1	0	1	0	0	1
1	0	1	0	1	1
1	0	1	0	1	0

This yields:

S1 S0 A B C D

However, those literals (columns) that changed can be eliminated from the above expression. These literals are A,C,D, which leaves:

S1 S0 B

Now again S0, S1, and B did not change and can be written in complemented and uncomplemented terms as follows:

$\overline{S1}$ S0 B

Now consider Map 3:

Map 3

S0	A	B	S1	C	D
0	0	0	1	0	1
0	0	0	1	0	0
0	0	1	1	0	1
0	0	1	1	0	0
0	1	1	1	0	1
0	1	1	1	0	0
0	1	0	1	0	1
0	1	0	1	0	0

This yields:

S1 S0 A B C D

However, those literals (columns) that changed can be eliminated from the above expression. The literals are A,B, and D did change, which leaves S0,S1, and C which can be written in complemented and uncomplemented form $\overline{S0}S1C$. Now consider Map 4:

Map 4

S0	A	B	S1	C	D
1	1	0	1	1	1
1	1	1	1	1	1
1	0	1	1	1	1
1	0	0	1	1	1
1	1	0	1	0	1
1	1	1	1	0	1
1	0	1	1	0	1
1	0	0	1	0	1

This yields:

S1 S0 A B C D

However, those literals (columns) that changed can be eliminated. These literals are A,B,C. S1,S0, and D did not change and can be written in uncomplemented form:

S1 S0 D

Recalling that

CLKOUT = MAP 1 + MAP 2 + MAP 3 + MAP 4

and substituting the individually derived terms leaves:

CLKOUT = $\overline{S0}$ $\overline{S1}$A + $\overline{S1}$ S0 B + $\overline{S0}$ S1 C + S1 S0 D

The reduction of Boolean expressions to their miminal form can be performed by most PLD software packages, thus eliminating the need to work through the Boolean reduction operations and Karnaugh map procedures manually. Today's software packages contain a variety of proprietary reduction algorithms. The discussion of Boolean algebra and Karnaugh maps was given to provide an insight into the minimal form reduction process for instructional purposes and in case of the need to apply these techniques.

SEQUENTIAL CIRCUITS

Sequential circuits are circuits whose output is dependent upon not only the states of the inputs but also upon the previous conditions or states in the circuit. The main element of a sequential circuit is memory, the most common of which is the flip-flop. The output of a sequential circuit is determined by the states of memory elements and the states of the inputs.

Sequential circuits are commonly broken down into synchronous sequential circuits and asynchronous sequential circuits. The term *synchronous* implies that a constant frequency or repetitive clock pulse is used to step an operational counter or controller through its various states. The period of the clock pulse determines the speed of the circuit. *Asynchronous* sequential circuits are circuits that are not controlled by a common clock line. Consequently, they operate freely at a speed determined by the various propagation delays that are encountered by the various gates and flip-flops in the circuit. An input applied to this circuit will not cause all elements to change simultaneously due to factors related to RC time constants and the transistor switching characteristics that make up the circuit.

When synchronous circuits are compared with asynchronous circuits, the synchronous circuits are generally more reliable. However, speed is normally less in a synchronous circuit. For the reduced speed, however, synchronous circuits are normally free of race conditions. This is because the clock speed selected is normally slow enough to permit all logic levels to settle into their final states before they are reactivated by the following clock pulse. In addition, synchronous circuits are more predictable in their timing. The tradeoff between these factors for synchronous circuits suggest their use unless speed is the main factor in circuit operation. The prime advantage of an asynchronous circuit is speed; however, the short delay times encountered at the logic elements are not always predictable.

Some circuits combine both synchronous and asynchronous characteristics. For example, one part of the circuit (asynchronous) might be engaged in the exchange of control signals between sections while the sections themselves might be controlled by a (synchronous) clock pulse.

Flip-Flops

Logic circuits fall roughly into two general classifications of the logic gates studied previously that can be thought of as decision making devices and of the memory devices that store a bit of data. This section addresses the most popular memory device (the flip-flop) and expands the discussion into flip-flop applications such as registers and counters.

The term *latch* and *flip-flop* are often used interchangeably. Technically speaking, a latch is an asynchronous device implying that it can be triggered based upon previous sequential events. A flip-flop, on the other hand, is a synchronous device that is driven by a clock pulse.

Set-Reset (SR) Flip-Flop. The set-reset (SR) flip-flop has found wide applications in the design of various counters. In general, this flip-flop is made up of a couple of cross-connected NAND gates as shown in FIG. A-47. However, other variations are comprised of cross-connected NOR gates. The set and reset functions are implemented by momentarily shorting the collector to ground of one of the two transistors that comprise the SR flip-flop. Momentarily grounding removes the base current flowing through the transistor that causes the transistor to cut off. The cut-off transistor stores a binary 1, and the conducting transistor stores binary 0, that is, the nonconducting transistor will rise to V_{CC} or 1 and the conducting transistor will go to ground. Thus the SR flip-flop circuit is alternately set and reset by momentarily shorting the off transistor to ground. An industry standard symbol for this flip-flop is shown in FIG. A-48. Inspection of this flip-flop indicates its versatility; set (S), reset (R), clock pulse (CP), clear (C), and preset (P). The input applied to the S and R inputs are transferred to the outputs Q and $\overline{Q}$ during the positive transition of a clock pulse.

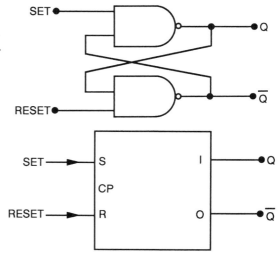

Fig. A-47. Basic construction of flip-flop using NAND gates.

Fig. A-48. Symbol of RS flip-flop.

The SR flip-flop has found application in various counters such as in a 4-bit shift register (the 7494) that converts parallel loaded values to serial stream (see FIG. A-49). To facilitate parallel ones transfer from two sources, two parallel load inputs (PL_0 and PL_1) with associated parallel data inputs (D_{0a} D_{0d} and D_{1a}-D_{1d}) are provided. To accommodate these extra inputs, only the output of the last stage is available. The asynchronous master reset (MR) is active high.

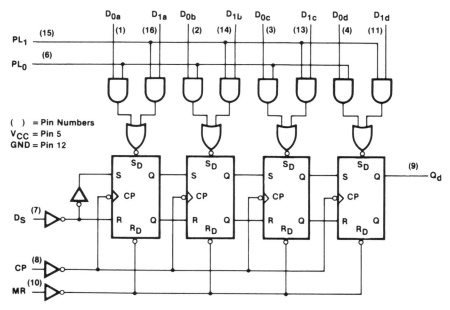

Fig. A-49. Logic diagram of 4-bit shift register (4-bit parallel to serial converter 7494). Courtesy of Signetics Corporation.

When MR is high, it overrides the clock and clears the register, forcing Q_d low.

Four flip-flops are connected so that shifting is synchronous; they change state when the clock goes from low-to-high. Data are accepted at the serial D_s input prior to this clock transition. Two parallel load inputs and parallel data inputs allow an asynchronous ones transfer from two sources. The flip-flops can be set independently to the high state when the appropriate parallel input is activated. Parallel inputs D_{0a} through D_{0d} are activated during the time the PL_0 is high, and parallel inputs D_{1a} through D_{1d} are activated when PL_1 is high. If both sets of inputs are activated, a high on either input sets the flip-flops to high. The register should not be clocked while the parallel load inputs are activated. The parallel load and parallel data inputs will override the MR if both are activated simultaneously. However, for predictable operation, both signals should not be deactivated simultaneously. Table A-20 shows the mode select function for the 7494.

Although this flip-flop has several variations, the truth table shown in TABLE A-21 is worth reviewing.

Positive logic is employed wherein a binary 0 refers to ground and a binary 1 + V_{cc} (the voltage applied to the circuit, for example using TTL, 5 volts). When both S and R are grounded, it is impossible to determine the state of the flip-flop because the previous state is unknown, implying the flip-flop could be either in a set or reset condition. Thus the table can be interpreted as X can be either a binary 1 or binary 0 while the $\overline{X}$ indicates the complement value. Applying a binary 1 to the reset input will cause the flip-flop to reset and $\overline{Q}$ will be at

Table A-20. Mode select function table for 4-bit
shift register (7494). Courtesy of Signetics Corporation.

OPERATING MODE	INPUTS							OUTPUTS			
	PL_0	PL_1	D_{0n}	D_{1n}	MR	CP	D_S	Q_a	Q_b	Q_c	Q_d
Parallel load	H	L	L	X	X	X	X	Q_a	Q_b	Q_c	Q_d
	H	L	H	X	X	X	X	H	H	H	H
	L	H	X	L	X	X	X	Q_a	Q_b	Q_c	Q_d
	L	H	X	H	X	X	X	H	H	H	H
Reset (clear)	L	L	X	X	H	X	X	L	L	L	L
Shift right	L	L	X	X	L	↑	l	L	q_a	q_b	q_c
	L	L	X	X	L	↑	h	H	q_a	q_b	q_c

H = HIGH voltage level.
h = HIGH voltage level one setup time prior to the LOW-to-HIGH Clock transition.
L = LOW voltage level.
l = LOW voltage level one setup time prior to the LOW-to-HIGH Clock transition.
q_n = Lower case letters indicate the state of the referenced output one setup time prior to the LOW-to-HIGH Clock transition.
X = Don't care.
↑ = LOW-to-HIGH Clock transition.

		Inputs		Outputs	
		S	R	Q	$\overline{Q}$
Table A-21. Generalized truth table for RS flip-flop.		0	0	X	$\overline{X}$
		0	1	0	1
		1	0	1	0
		1	1	0	0

$+V_{cc}$ and Q at ground. Applying a binary 1 to the set input will cause the flip-flop to set (Q will now be at a binary 1 and $\overline{Q}$ at a binary 0). Lastly, when both set and reset are at binary 1, am ambiguous state results and both Q and $\overline{Q}$ will settle to binary 0.

The T Type Flip-Flop. The T type flip-flop is characterized by the fact that it changes state any time it receives an input trigger pulse. The symbol for this flip-flop is shown in FIG. A-50 and its truth table shown in TABLE A-22. This type of flip-flop has found applications in BCD counters and frequency dividers.

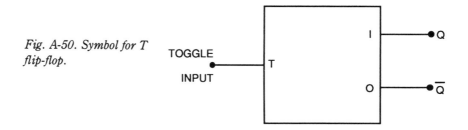

Fig. A-50. Symbol for T
flip-flop.

Q (T)	Q (T + 1)
X	$\overline{X}$

Table A-22. Truth table for T-type flip-flop.

The Type D Flip-Flop. The type D flip-flop is another popular type of flip-flop that has many applications in digital circuitry. Basically this flip-flop is comprised of four NAND gates as shown in FIG. A-51. Gates 2 and 3 represent the input gating while gates 4 and 5 represent the latch section. Its basic purpose is to store one bit of data.

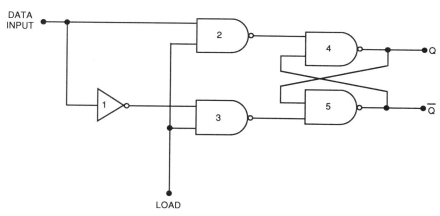

Fig. A-51. NAND gate configuration for D-type flip-flop.

The data input line receives the input data depending on the state of the load line. When the load line is a binary 1, the flip-flop accepts data present at the input line, but when it is a binary 0 data is not accepted by the flip-flop. If a binary 1 is present at the input line and the load line is a binary 1, the flip-flop sets 1. If the input line is a binary 0 and the load line is a binary 1, the flip-flop resets. The presence of either a binary 1 or binary 0 at the input line has no effect on the state of the flip-flop when the load line is a binary 0.

The type D flip-flop has found applications in industry as buffers and drivers. Figure A-52 shows the logic diagram of the 74373, wherein the user has a

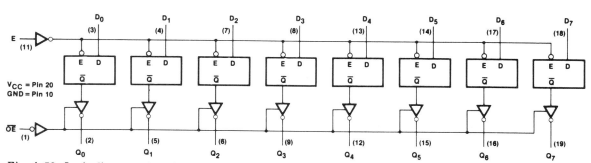

Fig. A-52. Logic diagram of octal D flip-flop with three-state outputs (74373). Courtesy of Signetics Corporation.

choice of 8 D-type flip-flops. Tri-state outputs are provided for driving high capacitive or low impedance loads. The flip-flops (or latches) are termed *transparent*. This means that while the enable (E) latch is high, the Q outputs will follow the D inputs. When the enable is brought low, the outputs will not follow the D inputs. Table A-23 shows the mode-select function table of the 74373. It is instructive to point out that the Output Enable (OE) does not affect internal operation of the latches and flip-flops. New data can be entered and old data retained while the outputs are off.

A second application of the type D flip-flop is in the design of shift registers. Figure A-53 shows the logic diagram 74164 shift register with eight Hex-type D flip-flops. Its mode select function table is shown in TABLE A-24. The versatility of this flip-flop is seen in closer examination.

*Table A-23. Function table of octal D flip-flop
with three-state outputs (74373). Courtesy of Signetics Corporation.*

| OPERATING MODES | INPUTS | | | INTERNAL REGISTER | OUTPUTS |
	$\overline{OE}$	E	D_n		Q_0-Q_7
Enable and read register	L	H	L	L	L
	L	H	H	H	H
Latch and read register	L	L	l	L	L
	L	L	h	H	H
Latch register and disable outputs	H	L	l	L	(Z)
	H	L	h	H	(Z)

The 74164 is an 8-bit edge-triggered shift register with serial data entry and an output from each of the eight stages. Data are entered serially through one of two inputs (D_{sa} or D_{sb}). Either input can be used as an active high enable for data entry through the other input. Both inputs must be connected together or an unused input must be tied high.

Data shifts one place to the right on each low-to-high transition of the clock (CP) input, and enters into Q_0 the logical AND of the two data inputs (D_{sa}, D_{sb}) that existed one setup time before the rising clock edge. A low level on the master reset (MR) input overrides all other inputs and clears the register asynchronously, forcing all outputs low.

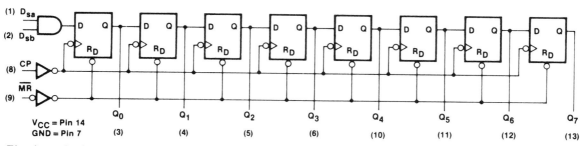

Fig. A-53. Logic diagram of shift register containing 8 D-type flip-flops with serial entry and parallel Exit (74164). Courtesy of Signetics Corporation.

Table A-24. Mode select-truth table for shift register containing 8-D-type flip-flops with serial entry and parallel exit (74164). Courtesy of Signetics Corporation.

OPERATING MODE	INPUTS				OUTPUTS			
	$\overline{MR}$	CP	D_{sa}	D_{sb}	Q_0	Q_1	—	Q_7
Reset (Clear)	L	X	X	X	L	L	—	L
Shift	H	↑	l	l	L	q_0	—	q_6
	H	↑	l	h	L	q_0	—	q_6
	H	↑	h	l	L	q_0	—	q_6
	H	↑	h	h	H	q_0	—	q_6

H = HIGH voltage level.
h = HIGH voltage level one setup time prior to the LOW-
    to-HIGH Clock transition.
L = LOW voltage level.
l = LOW voltage level one setup time prior to the LOW-
    to-HIGH Clock transition.
q = Lower case letters indicate the state of the refer-
    enced input (or output) one setup time prior to the
    LOW-to-HIGH Clock transition.
X = Don't care.
↑ = LOW-to-HIGH Clock transition.

A standard symbol for a generic type D flip-flop is shown in FIG. A-54 and a typical truth table in TABLE A-25 although other type D flip-flops may vary. Note that ambiguous conditions occur as long as the T (or Loadline) is binary 0. When T is binary 1, the output of the D flip-flop follows the input to the D input line.

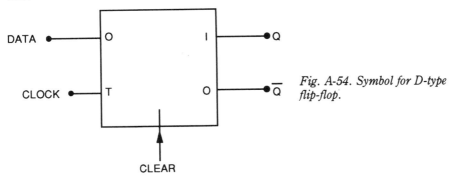

Fig. A-54. Symbol for D-type flip-flop.

D	T	$\overline{Q}$	Q
0	0	X	$\overline{X}$
1	0	X	$\overline{X}$
0	1	0	1
1	1	1	0

Table A-25. Truth table for D-type flip-flop.

The JK Flip-Flop. As stated previously, SR and D flip-flops find application where storage is required such as in a storage register. The T-type flip-flop is particularly applicable when toggle or complement characters are needed such as in counters or frequency dividers. The JK flip-flop combines all of the characteristics of the SR, D, and T flip-flops into one package. This flip-flop can perform both storage and toggling functions.

First, the JK flip-flop can be set and reset with set and reset inputs, regardless of what is applied to the JK inputs (binary 1 or binary 0) or the state of the clock. In this mode, it can serve as an SR flip-flop.

Secondly, the JK flip-flop can perform as a T type flip-flop by applying appropriate inputs to the JK lines. The flip-flop will alternately set and reset as the clock transitions occur. When this capability is combined with the fact that the JK flip-flop can be set or reset from a separate input, it functions as a D-type flip-flop. JK flip-flops are produced in several variations, however most are designed around a *master-slave* configuration. Generally data may be loaded into the master selection while the clock is high (binary 1) and transferred to the slave as the clock transistors from the high to the low. Consider the 7473 whose logic diagram and function table are shown in FIG. A-55 and TABLE A-26 respectively.

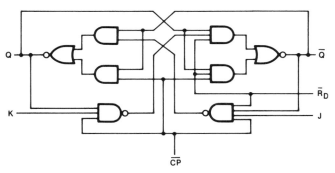

Fig. A-55. Logic diagram of dual JK flip-flop (7473). Courtesy of Signetics Corporation.

The 7473 is a dual flip-flop with individual J, K, clock, and direct reset inputs. The 7473 is positive pulse-triggered. JK information is loaded into the master while the clock is high and transferred to the slave on the high-to-low transition. For the 7473, the J and K inputs should be stable while the clock is high for conventional operation.

The 74LS73 is a negative edge-triggered flip-flop. The J and K inputs must be stable one setup time prior to the high-to-low clock transition for predictable operation.

The reset ($\overline{R}_D$) is an asynchronous active low input. When low, it overrides the clock and data inputs, forcing the Q output low and the $\overline{Q}$ output high.

The symbol for a JK flip-flop is shown in FIG. A-56 and a typical truth table is shown in TABLE A-27. Inspection of this truth table shows that the outputs Q and $\overline{Q}$ are the outputs that exist after the clock pulse transitions from high to low with the designated JK inputs. Where the flip-flop output is represented by an X indicates that the X can be either a binary 1 or binary 0 which in turn depends on the previous JK inputs.

*Table A-26. Function table of dual JK
flip-flop (7473). Courtesy of Signetics Corporation.*

OPERATING MODE	INPUTS				OUTPUTS	
	$\overline{R}_D$	$\overline{CP}^{(b)}$	J	K	Q	$\overline{Q}$
Asynchronous Reset (Clear)	L	X	X	X	L	H
Toggle	H	⊓	h	h	$\overline{q}$	q
Load "0" (Reset)	H	⊓	l	h	L	H
Load "1" (Set)	H	⊓	h	l	H	L
Hold "no change"	H	⊓	l	l	q	$\overline{q}$

H = HIGH voltage level steady state.

h = HIGH voltage level one setup time prior to the HIGH-to-LOW Clock transition.[a]

L = LOW voltage level steady state.

l = LOW voltage level one setup time prior to the HIGH-to-LOW Clock transition.[a]

q = Lower case letters indicate the state of the referenced output prior to the
HIGH-to-LOW Clock transition.

X = Don't care.

⊓ = Positive Clock pulse.

NOTES

a. The J and K inputs of the 7473 must be stable while the Clock is HIGH for conventional operation.

b. The 74LS73 is edge triggered. Data must be stable one setup time prior to the
negative edge of the Clock for predictable operation.

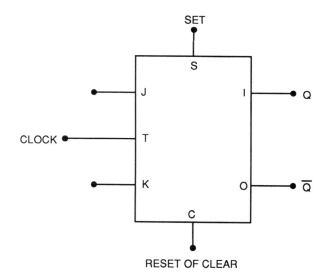

*Fig. A-56. Symbol for JK
flip-flop.*

J	K	Q	$\overline{Q}$
0	0	X	$\overline{X}$
0	1	0	1
1	0	1	0
1	1	$\overline{X}$	X

Table A-27. Truth table for JK flip-flops.

Registers

One of the often required operations in digital systems is the need to shift bits within a register. In fact, most digital systems contain a great deal of parallel-to-serial and serial-to-parallel data conversion. The data could have been placed in the register through a serial load process wherein each bit would shift in a specified direction for each clock command given or a parallel load wherein all bits would move into a register simultaneously for a given clock pulse command. Even though shift registers are used primarily for serial-to-parallel and parallel-to-serial data conversions, it is also commonly used for two other applications.

Shift registers can be tied in a loop causing various bits sorted in the flip-flops to be continuously calculated around this loop, which suggests its usability as frequency divider. Without a loop configuration, a bit can be permanently lost. This type of configuration is known as a *ring shift register*. A single bit stored in the register can be circulated continuously. As this cycle would repeat itself through n flip-flops, the corresponding waveforms would indicate for every n input pulses the output of any of the n flip-flops would be one pulse. This suggests that a ring shift register of n flip-flops produces frequency division by n. The period of any of the n flip-flops is n times the period of the input shift pulses. A circuit consisting of four flip-flops divides by four, and a circuit consisting of seven flip-flops divides by seven. However, a binary counter with the proper feedback connection could reduce the number of flip-flops for this particular application.

Also, the application of a shift register can be used as a *sequencer* when the register is connected in a ring. A series of pulses shifted from each other for a time period would equal that of the shift signal. This application is useful when you want a sequence of operations controlled by the sequencer to occur.

Shift registers are commonly classified as synchronous or asynchronous and refer to how registers are set and reset. Synchronous reset implies all flip-flops are reset simultaneously. Asynchronous reset implies that each flip-flop can be reset individually. A synchronous register implies that all flip-flops are loaded simultaneously in response to single clock source. Asynchronous loading implies that the inputs at each gate are all loaded simultaneously with the application of a single clock pulse applied to the flip-flop.

Generally, synchronous implies simultaneously while asynchronous implies individually. More precisely, a JK flip-flop can be considered a synchronous device since the J and K input data is not transferred to the output until the clock line triggers. The T and SR flip-flops can be considered asynchronous because they trigger the moment a signal other than when the clock line triggers. The asynchronous flip-flops are normally triggered by the preceding flip-flop while synchronous flip-flops are triggered only by the master clock.

As an example of a synchronous device, consider the industry standard parallel load—an 8-bit shift register 74166 whose logic diagram is shown in FIG. A-57 and mode select function table in TABLE A-28.

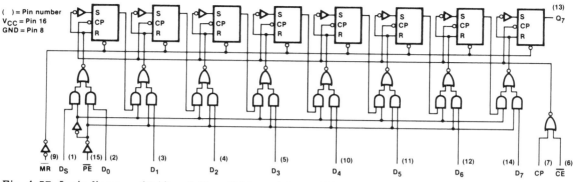

Fig. A-57. *Logic diagram of 8-bit serial/parallel in serial out shift register (74166). Courtesy of Signetics Corporation.*

Table A-28. *Mode select-function table for 8-bit serial in/parallel in/serial out shift register (74166). Courtesy of Signetics Corporation.*

OPERATING MODES	INPUTS					Q_n REGISTER		OUTPUT
	$\overline{PE}$	$\overline{CE}$	CP	D_S	D_0-D_7	Q_0	Q_1-Q_6	Q_7
Parallel Load	l	l	↑	X	l–l	L	L–L	L
	l	l	↑	X	h–h	H	H–H	H
Serial Shift	h	l	↑	l	X–X	L	q_0-q_5	q_6
	h	l	↑	h	X–X	H	q_0-q_5	q_6
Hold (do nothing)	X	h	X	X	X–X	q_0	q_1-q_6	q_7

H = HIGH voltage level.
h = HIGH voltage level one setup time prior to the LOW-to-HIGH Clock transition.
L = LOW voltage level.
l = LOW voltage level one setup time prior to the LOW-to-HIGH Clock transition.
q_n = Lower case letters indicate the state of the referenced input (or output) one setup time prior to the LOW-to-HIGH Clock transition.
X = Don't care.
↑ = LOW-to-HIGH Clock transition.

These parallel-in or serial-in, serial-out shift registers have a complexity of 77 equivalent gates on a single chip. They feature gated clock inputs and an overriding clear input. The parallel-in or serial-in modes are established by the shift/load input. When high, this input enables the serial data input and couples the eight flip-flops for serial shifting with each clock pulse. When low, the parallel (broadside) data inputs are enabled and *synchronous loading* occurs on the next clock pulse. During parallel loading, serial data flow is inhibited. Clocking is accomplished on the low-to-high level edge of the clock pulse through a two-input NOR gate to be used as a clock-enable or clock-inhibit function. Holding either of the clock inputs high inhibits clocking; holding either low enables the other clock input. This, of course, allows the system clock to be free-running and the register can be stopped on command with the other clock input. The clock inhibit input should be changed to the high level only while the clock input is high. A buffered, direct clear input overrides all other inputs, including the clock, and sets all flip-flops to zero.

The logic diagram for industry standard 74165 is shown in FIG. A-58 which might be considered an asynchronous device. Table A-29 shows its related mode select function table. This register is an 8-bit parallel load or serial-in shift register with complementary serial outputs (Q_7 and $\overline{Q}_7$) available from the last stage. When the Parallel Load (PL) input is low, parallel data from the D_0-D_7 inputs are loaded into the register asynchronously. When the PL input is high, data enters the register serially at the D_S input and shifts one place to the right (Q_0 -> Q_1 -> Q_2, etc.) with each to-positive clock transition. This feature allows parallel-to-serial converter expansion by tying the Q_7 output to the D_S input of the succeeding stage.

The clock input is a gated-OR structure that allows one input to be used as an active LOS Clock Enable (CE) input. The pin assignment for the CP and CE inputs is arbitrary and can be reversed for layout convenience. The low-to-high transition of CE input should only take place while the CP is high for predictable

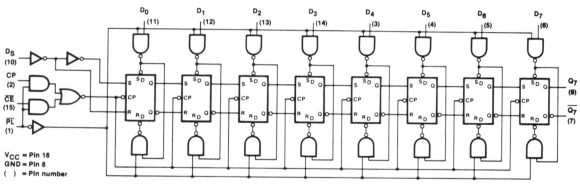

Fig. A-58. Logic diagram of 8-bit serial/parallel in serial out shift register (74165). Courtesy of Signetics Corporation.

Table A-29. Mode select-function table for 8-bit serial in/parallel in serial out shift register (74165). Courtesy of Signetics Corporation.

OPERATING MODES	INPUTS					Q_n REGISTER		OUTPUTS	
	$\overline{PL}$	$\overline{CE}$	CP	D_S	D_0-D_7	Q_0	Q_1-Q_6	Q_7	$\overline{Q}_7$
Parallel load	L	X	X	X	L	L	L–L	L	H
	L	X	X	X	H	H	H–H	H	L
Serial shift	H	L	↑	l	X	L	q_0-q_5	q_6	$\overline{q}_6$
	H	L	↑	h	X	H	q_0-q_5	q_6	$\overline{q}_6$
Hold "do nothing"	H	H	X	X	X	q_0	q_1-q_6	q_7	$\overline{q}_7$

H = HIGH voltage level.
h = HIGH voltage level one setup time prior to the LOW-to-HIGH clock transition.
L = LOW voltage level.
l = LOW voltage level one setup time prior to the LOW-to-HIGH clock transition.
q_n = Lower case letters indicate the state of the referenced output one setup time prior to the LOW-to-HIGH clock transition.
X = Don't care.
↑ = LOW-to-HIGH clock transition.

operation. Also, the CP and CE inputs should be low before the low to high transition of PL to prevent shifting the data when PL is released.

Counters

One of the most widely used devices in a digital circuit is a binary counter whose main purpose is to record the number of pulses that occur at its input. Various applications call for various types of counters. An up counter counts up to some number beginning with zero and upon reaching that number, it recycles to zero. A down counter starts at some given number and counts down to zero and recycles to start at its original number. Counters are also classified as synchronous and asynchronous. Synchronous again implies all flip-flops are triggered by a master clock while asynchronous implies that the flip-flops are not triggered by a master timing source.

As an example of an asychronous counter, consider the industry standard 7493 ripple counter as shown in FIG. A-59 and its corresponding function table in TABLE A-30.

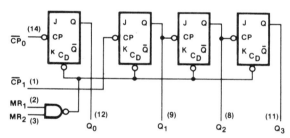

Fig. A-59. Logic diagram of a binary ripple counter (7493). Courtesy of Signetics Corporation.

( ) = Pin Numbers
V_{CC} = Pin 5
GND = Pin 10

COUNT	OUTPUTS			
	Q_0	Q_1	Q_2	Q_3
0	L	L	L	L
1	H	L	L	L
2	L	H	L	L
3	H	H	L	L
4	L	L	H	L
5	H	L	H	L
6	L	H	H	L
7	H	H	H	L
8	L	L	L	H
9	H	L	L	H
10	L	H	L	H
11	H	H	L	H
12	L	L	H	H
13	H	L	H	H
14	L	H	H	H
15	H	H	H	H

Table A-30. Function table for binary ripple counter (7493). Courtesy of Signetics Corporation.

NOTE
Output Q_0 connected to input $\overline{CP}_1$.

This counter is a four-bit, ripple-type binary counter. The device consists of four master-slave flip-flops internally connected to provide a frequency divide-by-two section and a divide-by-eight section. Frequency division is determined by the connection between flip-flops and the relationship 2^n. Both T and JK flip-flops can be used in frequency divider applications. Note from the logic diagram the first flip-flop stands alone; its output Q is not fed to the second flip-flop. This single flip-flop provides frequency division by

$$2^n = 2^1$$

where n is the number of cascaded flip-flops.

The remaining flip-flops produce frequency division by eight because their repetitive Q output is fed to the following flip-flops and the relationship is $2^3 = 8$. Each section has a separate clock input to initiate state changes of the counter on the high-to-low clock transition. State changes of the Q outputs do not occur simultaneously because of internal ripple delays. Therefore, decoded output signals are subject to decoding spikes and should not be used for clocks or strobes.

A gated AND asynchronous master reset ($MR_1 \bullet MR_2$) is provided which overrides both clocks and resets (clears) all the flip-flops.

Because the output from the divide-by-two section is not internally connected to the succeeding states, the device can be operated in various counting modes. In a 4-bit ripple counter, the output Q_0 must be connected externally to input CP_1. The input count pulses are applied to input CP_0. Simultaneous divisions of 2, 4, 8, and 16 are performed at the Q_0, Q_1, Q_2, and Q_3 outputs as shown in the function table. As a 3-bit ripple counter the input count pulses are applied to input CP_1. Simultaneous frequency divisions of 2, 4, and 8 are available at the Q_1, Q_2, and Q_3 outputs. Independent use of the first flip-flop is available if the reset function coincides with reset of the 3-bit ripple through counter.

Synchronous counters in general are more desirable than ripple counters. Figure A-60 shows the industry standard 74160 and its related mode select function table in TABLE A-31 as an example of a synchronous counter.

This synchronous, presettable counter features an internal carry look-ahead for application in high-speed counting designs. Synchronous operation has all flip-flops clocked simultaneously so that the outputs change coincident with each other when so instructed by the count-enable inputs and internal gating. This mode of operation eliminates the output counting spikes that are normally associated with asynchronous (ripple clock) counters. However, counting spikes may occur on the (RCO) ripple carry output. A buffered clock input triggers the four flip-flops on the rising edge of the clock input waveform.

These counters are fully programmable. The outputs can be preset to either level. As presetting is synchronous, setting up a low level at the load input disables the counter and causes the outputs to agree with the setup data after the next clock pulse regardless of the levels of the enable inputs. Low-to-high transitions at the load input of the 74160 should be avoided when the clock is low if the enable inputs are high at or before the transition. The clear function for the 74160 is asynchronous and a binary low at the clear input sets all four of

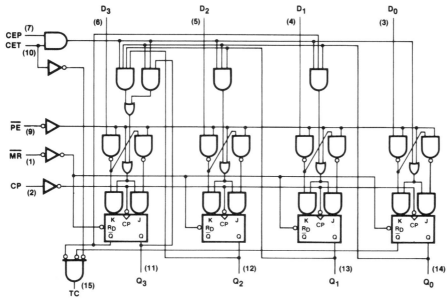

Fig. A-60. Logic diagram of the 74160 synchronous counter. Courtesy of Signetics Corporation.

Table A-31. Mode select function table for
74160 and 74161. Courtesy of Signetics Corporation.

OPERATING MODE	INPUTS						OUTPUTS	
	$\overline{MR}$	CP	CEP	CET	$\overline{PE}$	D_n	Q_n	TC
Reset (Clear)	L	X	X	X	X	X	L	L
Parallel Load	H	↑	X	X	l	l	L	L
	H	↑	X	X	l	h	H	(a)
Count	H	↑	h	h	$h^{(c)}$	X	count	(a)
Hold (do nothing)	H	X	$l^{(b)}$	X	$h^{(c)}$	X	q_n	(a)
	H	X	X	$l^{(b)}$	$h^{(c)}$	X	q_n	L

the flip-flop outputs low regardless of the levels of clock, load, or enable inputs. In contrast, the clear function for other members of this family of counters (74162, 74163, 74LS162A, 74LS163A, 74S162, and 74S163) is synchronous. A low level at the clear input sets all four of the flip-flop outputs low after the next clock pulse, regardless of the levels of the enable inputs. This synchronous clear allows the count length to be modified easily as decoding the maximum count desired can be accomplished with one external NAND gate. The gate output is connected to the clear input to synchronously clear the counter to 0000 (LLLL). Low-to-high transitions at the clear input of the 74162 and 74163 should be avoided when the clock is low if the enable and load inputs are high and load inputs are high at or before the transition.

A synchronous counter is generally more desirable than a ripple counter because logic gates that compose a flip-flop influence propagation delay within the circuit. These delays are usually caused by threshold levels and capacitive charges. For example, the JK flip-flop composed of four or five levels of logic gates which in turn increase propagation delay. These delays could be significant in very high frequency circuits. Further, the propagation delay can yield ambiguous states within the counter, which in turn could result in errors. The problem of propagation delay is made even worse when several flip-flops are required in the counter.

Traditionally, this problem has been corrected to some extent by decreasing the counting frequency. However, the time interval between counter states is lengthened and made much greater than the propagation delays of the individual flip-flops.

Three factors that affect how fast and what number would be practical for a counter arrangement are the input frequency, the propagation delay of the flip-flops, and the number of flip-flops contained in the counter. A balance must be reached between these factors to prevent the occurrence of ambiguous states.

A formula has been developed for determining the number of flip-flops that can be cascaded before ambiguous conditions begin to occur. The number of flip-flops (N) is equal to the quantity produced when the period of the input clock pulse T is divided by the propagation delay of the flip-flop T_d less one. The formula is:

$$N = [\ (T/T_d)\ - 1]$$

This formula has also found useful applications in determining the maximum number of flip-flops that can be connected in a ripple counter without introducing ambiguous conditions caused by too much delay.

Synchronous counters overcome the problems associated with this type of ripple or asynchronous counter. Recall that in a synchronous counter all the toggle inputs on the flip-flops are tied together and triggered from one common clock source and the pulses to be counted are all tied to this common toggle line. When a pulse does occur on this line, all flip-flops switch with the input pulses to be counted.

STATE MACHINE

State machines represent a class of sequential circuits or systems and form the basis for almost all control logic design. The following discussion was provided by the Altera Corporation, to whom I am extremely grateful.

State machines can be operated synchronously wherein a single synchronizing input signal (commonly referred to as the clock) causes all state transitions to occur synchronously where any predefined input transition can trigger a state transition. Asynchronous machines do not have a clock and false transitions can cause problems in some cases in the operation of the machine.

The two categories of state machines Mealy State Machines and Moore State Machines are differentiated by the influence of the input upon the output. Figure A-61 illustrates the basic difference between these machines. In a Mealy

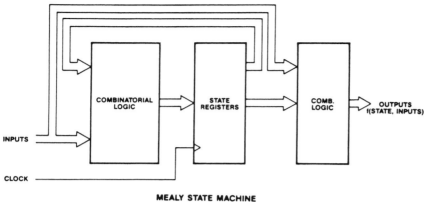

MEALY STATE MACHINE

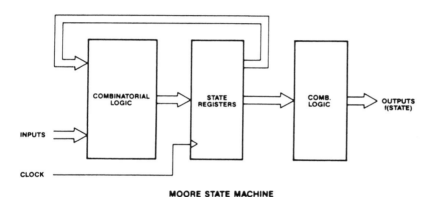

MOORE STATE MACHINE

Fig. A-61. Basic difference between Mealy state machine and Moore state machine. Courtesy of Altera Corporation.

machine, note that the outputs at any given time are a function of the current machine state and current inputs. This configuration permits multiple output combinations for any given state. A Moore machine, on the other hand, yields outputs which are a function of the current state and previous input history as held in the state but are not directly affected by input values. In reality, Moore machines are a subclass of Mealy machines.

Programmable Logic Devices

PLDs employ architectures that implement canonical state machine structure quite well. Figure A-62 shows a general PLD block diagram. The benefits of PLDs when used for state machine include:

- High gate count
- High flip-flop count
- Programmable I/O

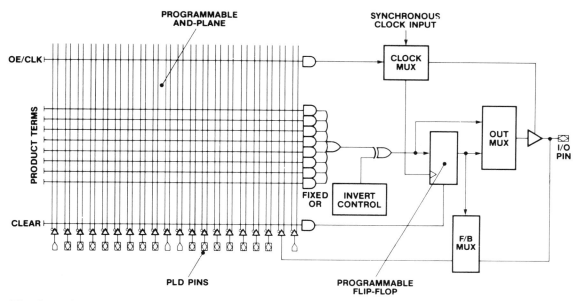

Fig. A-62. *General PLD block diagram. Courtesy of Altera Corporation.*

- Programmable flip-flop
- Structured architecture

Not all devices provide all of these benefits (older PALs do not support programmable I/O and flip-flops), but the overall fit is a good one for many state machine applications.

In targeting a state machine design for a PLD, key resources include flip-flops, I/O, and product terms. Product terms represent single-term logical ANDs of any PLD inputs and/or flip-flop outputs. The connections into these terms can be any set of complemented variables as defined by the user in the design. Because product terms represent a measure of the combinatorial logic capability available in a PLD, their total number and distribution is an important consideration.

FPLAs, as stated in Chapter 1, have both programmable AND and programmable OR logic planes. As a result, product terms can be distributed in any fashion among state variable (flip-flop) inputs and machine outputs. Product terms can even be shared between flip-flops or outputs. Programmable AND/fixed-OR PLDs (such as PALs) have a fixed number of product terms associated with each flip-flop. Eight product terms is a good average. If more than the allotted number of product terms is required for a given function, one or more cells may be used to expand the product term count at the cost of an additional array delay.

More advanced PLDs have programmable flip-flop types, wherein the type (D/T/JK/SR) of flip-flop can be selected by the user on a cell-by-cell basis. This can be very valuable when designing state machines, because certain functions require less product terms when implemented with D flip-flops instead of T flip-flops. The converse can also be true. More discussion on flip-flop type is in the State Machine Synthesis section.

Altera EPLDs provide a user-configuration selection of features from which any state machine can benefit. Figure A-63 shows a comparison of Altera's EPLDs with other popular PLDs used for state machine applications. The Altera EPLD family concept allows the user to select the device appropriate for the problem and still obtain, in most cases, a single-chip solution.

DEVICE	INPUTS	OUTPUTS	POSSIBLE STATES	P-TERMS	FLIP-FLOP TYPE
82S105	16	8	64	48	SR
PLS167	14	6	64	48	SR
16R8	16	8	16+	64	D
22V10	11(21)	10	32+	120	D
EP600	4(20)	16	256+	128	D/T/JK
EP900	12(36)	24	4K+	240	D/T/JK

+ = Half Used for State Variables/Half for Output Functions.

Fig. A-63. Comparison of Altera's EPLDs with other popular PLDs used in state machine applications. Courtesy of Altera Corporation.

There are several guidelines for state machine design. State machine design provides a high-level approach to synchronous logic design. The first design consideration is power-up zero—that is, all flip-flop outputs should be cleared to a logical 0 on power up. Every state machine must begin in a state which all state variables are set to zero. It is necessary to define in an "all zero" power-up state in the state table. All Altera EPLDs automatically clear all flip-flop outputs to a logical 0 on power.

Trap Illegal States

State machines should be designed so they cannot get stuck in an illegal state. Either all possible combinations should be defined in the STATES section of the state machine file, or the machine should reset any time an illegal state is entered. The following code, added to the state machine file, clears the machine when an illegal state is entered:

```
NETWORK:
CLEAR = NORF(ILLEGAL, CLOCK,GND,GND)
EQUATIONS:
ILLEGAL = /(STATE0 + STATE1 + ... + STATEN);
```

The clear variable in the network section provides the asynchronous clear function to the machine. The input to the register (ILLEGAL) is defined as the

NOT of all the possible legal states. Thus, if an illegal state is entered, ILLE-GAL = 1 and all state variables are reset to 0.

Asynchronous Inputs

To assure reliable operation of any state machine, care should be taken when using asynchronous inputs. An asynchronous input signal, which might violate a state register setup time, can cause a machine to enter an illegal state. Whenever possible, the inputs to a state machine should be synchronized with the machines' clock so that all signals are guaranteed to meet the input setup times.

When synchronization of inputs is not possible, it is necessary to adhere to the following rules:

1. Asynchronous inputs that determine the next state must be twice as wide as the state-machine clock. If an asynchronous input lasts for less than two clock periods, there is some probability it will be missed by the machine.

2. A state should change by only one bit in moving from one state to a next if the change depends on asychronous inputs. If more than one state register changes value between states, the asynchronous input might meet the setup time on one register, but miss the setup time of the other register. The machine would then enter an illegal state.

3. State transitions should never depend on more than one asynchronous input. If a multi-way branch depends on several asynchronous inputs, both branches could appear valid. The machine would then enter an illegal state.

Reducing Product Term Constraints

As the complexity of a state machine increases, product term demands increase as well. When product term needs exceed the number available in a device, the A+PLUS software offered by Altera produces the error message, "Too Many P-Terms".

When this message occurs, the state machine, as it now stands, will not fit into the selected EPLD. Either a new device must be selected, or the design must be slightly modified.

The SAM family of EPLDs by Altera has been optimized for state machine applications and offers the surest relief from product term limitations. The first member of this family, EPS448, can implement up to 448 states with no practical limitation on the sequencing complexity. It also offers 768 product terms to help define transition conditions.

If a general-purpose EPLD is chosen, the following techniques will help fit the machine.

Change State Variable Assignments. If the machine will not fit, first change the state variable assignments for all buried state variables. Different state variable assignments can result in simpler equations for a given machine. As a general rule, try to minimize the number of 1s or minimize the number of transitions for a given column in the state assignment section.

Adding State Variables. Adding a buried state variable doubles the number of possible states but the equations leading to each state variable can be simplified. After adding the state variable, try to change the state variable assignments as described.

Remove Large Counters and Shift Registers. The LogiCaps schematic capture program provides a powerful complement to the state machine software. For fast and efficient design, they should be used together with each being used where it is most applicable.

Partition State Machine. When faced with a large state machine of 10-30 states that must fit into an EPLD, the machine should probably be partitioned into two smaller machines. Partitioning eases design entry and simplifies the excitation equations for each machine. As state machines grow, a more effective approach is the SAM family which can easily implement state machines with up to 448 states.

State Machine Synthesis

This section discusses general state machine design concepts. Specific design issues, such as using a particular device's microinstruction set to full advantage, is not covered.

The state machine design process begins with thoroughly defining "what the machine does." Writing a verbal description of what job the machine performs in the overall system is a good way to start. Describing other blocks it will communicate with and associated inputs and outputs defines the external interface characteristics. Noting critical timing constraints and required sequences of operations (rudimentary states) describes the internal operation of the machine.

Next, the process of translating the design into one of the standard state machine documentation forms mentioned earlier can begin. In general, ASM notation and high-level language descriptions are preferred for larger designs, particularly those with greater than ten states.

Initially, the state machine description should be generated without undue worry about state minimization or overall efficiency. Comprehensiveness of the description is the first goal. Minimization techniques (to be described next) will be employed to compact the design as a second step.

State Minimization. State minimization is a process of reducing the total number of states in a state machine to a minimum. Minimization is based on a process of identifying *equivalent states* and combining them into a single state. Two (or more) states are said to be equivalent if the state machine generates identical output sequences for all input sequences applied, given any of the equivalent states as a starting point. The states are therefore not *distinguishable*.

The process for discovering equivalent states is an iterative search for states that produce identical output sequences for all input sequences. Using a state table notation is the clearest means of presenting state information for this analysis. Figure A-64 shows a simple state machine before and after reduction. The process involved consists of:

1. Locate all states that generate the same output for all input vectors (directly from the initial state table) and construct initial state groups. This grouping is called a *partition*.
2. Analyze each group over all input combinations to determine if the next states reachable from the group are equivalent as measured by the previous partition. If different, a new partition is required the group is subdivided.
3. The process is continued until the partition at step 1 + 1 is the same as the partition at step 1. At this point, the states are minimized. The states in each group are equivalent and can be reduced to a single state.

Unminimized Machine

PS	NS. OUTPUT	
	INPUT = 0	INPUT = 1
S0	S4,0	S2,0
S1	S2,0	S0,0
S2	S1,0	S6,0
S3	S6,0	S0,0
S4	S5,1	S1,0
S5	S4,0	S3,0
S6	S3,0	S6,0

Initial	=	(S0,S1,S2,S3,S4,S5,S6)
1st Partition	=	(S0,S1,S2,S3,S5,S6) (S4)
2nd	=	(S0,S5) (S1,S2,S3,S6) (S4)
3rd	=	(S0,S5) (S1,S3) (S2,S6) (S4)
4th	=	(S0) (S5) (S1,S3) (S2,S6) (S4)
5th	=	(S0) (S5) (S1,S3) (S2,S6) (S4)

Fig. A-64. Simple state machine before and after reduction. Courtesy of Altera Corporation.

Minimized Machine

PS	NS. OUTPUT	
	INPUT = 0	INPUT = 1
S0	S4,0	S2/6,0
S1/3	S2/6,0	S0,0
S2/6	S1/3,0	S2/6,0
S4	S5,1	S1,0
S5	S4,0	S3,0

For the example shown in FIG. A-64, the first partition isolates S4 (the only state from which a one output can be obtained). S0 and S5 are isolated from S1-S3 and S6 in the second partition because they have S4 as a possible next state. S1 and S3 are isolated from S2 and S6 in the third partition because they have S0 as a potential next state. Finally S0 and S5 are divided because they have S2 and S3 as possible next states, which are not grouped together in the previous partition (implying S2 and S3 are distinguishable).

This process can become tedious for large designs. Most designers utilize the technique on smaller submachines before integrating them into a larger design. The minimization process remains manageable when approached this way.

State Machine Partitioning. Partitioning complex state machine designs into smaller machines can utilize state machine device resources more effectively. For example, PLD devices have a fixed number of product terms per macrocell. For complex machines, the equations for a state variable input can require a large number of product terms. By partitioning a large state machine into smaller state machines, the individual equations can be reduced in complexity, albeit at an increase in total number of state variables.

Figure A-65 shows a state machine that can be divided into two simpler state machines. The idea behind this partition is that only one of the two submachines is active at any one time, the other being idle. Control transfer is passed back and forth between machines each time the original dividing line is crossed.

In FIG. A-65, states SA and SB are these idle states. Transitions leaving the idle states are dependent on both the original transition equation and current state of the other submachine. The holding transitions for the idle states have equations that are simply the logical inverse of all transitions leaving each idle state. Figure A-66 summarizes the state machine partitioning rules.

Mealy-Moore Machine Transformation

Mealy machines can be converted to equivalent Moore machines. The rules for this transformation are straightforward: for each transition into a state in the Mealy machine with a different output value, define a separate state in the Moore machine. The Moore machine produced has identical input-output behavior to the original Mealy machine. Figure A-67 illustrates this process for a simple state diagram.

Even though a Mealy machine might be synchronously clocked, outputs from the machine can respond to input transitions without reference to the clock. If such a Mealy machine has been designed, conversion may affect A.C. timing. This should be analyzed once the design is completed for any system impact.

Mealy/Moore conversion can mean an increase in the number of required states for the machine. Conversion is frequently employed when designs originally targeted for PLD-based state machines are redesigned for implementation in a PROM-based or microcoded sequencer design.

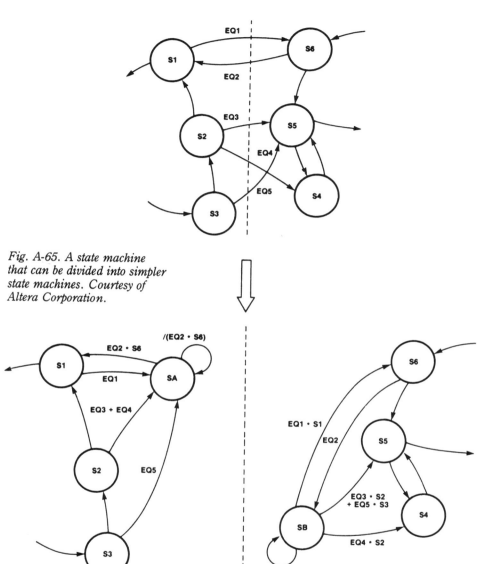

Fig. A-65. A state machine that can be divided into simpler state machines. Courtesy of Altera Corporation.

Implementing the State Machine

The final steps of implementing a state machine are:

- Minimizing transition logic.
- Select a target device or set of devices.
- Select flip-flop type (optional).
- Assign state variables (optional).
- Enter design.

1. Transitions leading into an idle state keep the same equation as the corresponding transition from the original machine.

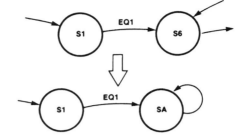

2. Transitions leading out of an idle state have the equation from the corresponding transition from the original machine, logically ANDed with the state (of the other machine half) that the transition originally came from.

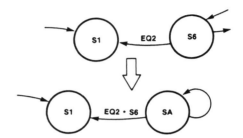

3. Multiple transitions that have the same source and destination states may be replaced by a single transition with an equation that is the logical OR of the two original equations.

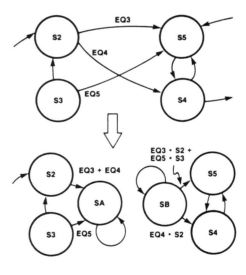

4. The idle states have a hold equation that is the logical inverse of all equations for transitions leaving that state logically ORed together.

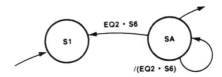

Fig. A-66. A summary of state machine partitioning rules. Courtesy of Altera Corporation.

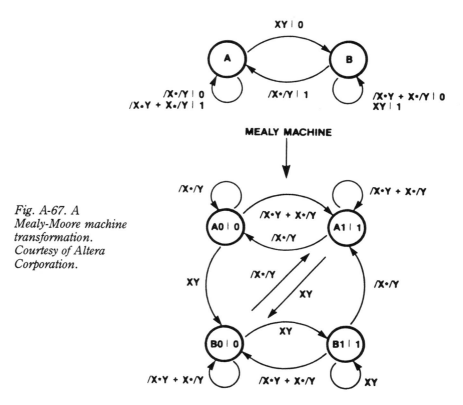

Fig. A-67. A Mealy-Moore machine transformation. Courtesy of Altera Corporation.

Minimizing transition logic can be done by hand or by a logic compiler such as A + PLUS (Altera Programmable Logic User System). Flip-flop type is relevant only if an SSI/MSI implementation or PLD with programmable flip-flop type is available, such as Altera's EP600/900-1800 family. State variable assignment is also required only in SSI/MSI designs or PLD designs. PROM or microsequencer designs map states onto memory locations and do not have state variables requiring definition. Where programmable devices are the target vehicle, the last step is to enter the design into the logic compiler for that device. After design processing, the compiler generates a JEDEC programming file to allow programming of the state machine component.

Flip-Flop Types. For state machines targeted for SSI/MSI or PLD implementations, flip-flop type can be an issue in selecting the minimal state machine implementation. As mentioned earlier, several Altera EPLDs allow the selection of either D, T, JK or SR operation for the device macrocells. Depending on the state machine, either D or T flip-flops can give the minimal design. It can be shown that JK (and therefore SR flip-flops) give results no better than these.

Figure A-68 shows the excitation table for the various flip-flops. In the table, a 1 means a variable must be excited, a 0 means the variable must not be excited, and an X means the excitation does not matter. Note that D and T

STATE VARIABLE TRANSITION	FLIP-FLOP TYPE			
	D	T	J	K
0 → 0	0	0	0	X
0 → 1	1	1	1	X
1 → 0	0	1	X	1
1 → 1	1	0	X	0

Fig. A-68. Flip-flop excitation functions. Courtesy of Altera Corporation.

columns all have two 1s in their transition specifications. J and K columns only have one 1. At first glance, these seem as though they might require fewer excitation terms. However, because both J and K inputs are required for any such flip-flop, the number of 1s is in fact two for both J and K inputs, and no economy is obtained over D or T flip-flops.

By analyzing state transition expressions in a state machine description, it is possible to determine the optimal flip-flop type for a given design. To assist the designer, Altera's ASMILE state machine language processor automatically performs optimum flip-flop selection during the compilation of a high-level state machine specification.

Selecting State Assignments. *State assignment* is the process of associating specific state variable codings to the various states in a state machine. For a state machine with M states, N state variables are sufficient assuming 2^N is greater than or equal to M. A clever state assignment can minimize required transition logic.

For example, T flip-flops can be used as state variables. Transition logic complexity is probably reduced if states that have a high degree of connectivity (transitions between them are functions of many product terms) have state variable codings that are as similar as possible. This means the codings might differ in only one or two state variables. The amount of variable toggling required to transition is therefore reduced. This is illustrated in FIG. A-69.

As mentioned earlier, increasing state variables can reduce individual flip-flop transition function complexity. Particularly if state variables are used as machine outputs, adding variables can be a very stable way to simplify the design. In the degenerate case (used quite frequently for simple machines), each state can be represented by a single state variable.

Microcoded Sequencers

Microcoded Sequencers provide a single-chip microcoded state machine vehicle. The benefits of this approach include user programmability, higher performance, less p.c. board area, lower power, and a consistent architecture allowing the development of optimized design tools.

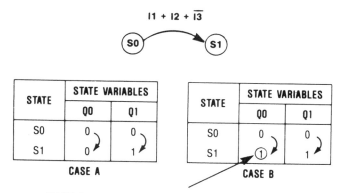

Fig. A-69. State variable assignment. Courtesy of Altera Corporation.

These devices range from simple PAL plus PROM devices, to devices such as Altera's SAM family which integrate all the functionality present in a bit-slice-based design. The SAM device, with nearly 500 words of user-programmable microcode EPROM, stack and loop counter represents the state-of-the-art in this area.

A microcoded sequencer (as with any state machine) responds to external inputs in order to select its next state. As discussed earlier, bit-slice microcontrollers have a single input that can be tested for state and a branch executed based on the result. One step up from this approach is logically masking multiple external inputs with a predefined AND mask and testing the result under microinstruction control. One of two possible next states is selected based on the outcome of the test. Both of these schemes allow only two-way state branching in a single clock.

The most advanced approach, utilized in Altera's SAM device family, inputs multiple external signals into a PLD front-end of the microsequencer. This PLD is coded with user-defined transition equations that are functions of current machine state and inputs. The output of the PLD selects one of four destination states, giving four-way single-clock state machine branching. In addition, these transitions functions are prioritized, implementing the priority implied in a state transition statement such as

IF (expression 1) THEN State _A
ELSEIF (expression 2) THEN STATE_B
ELSEIF (expression 3) THEN STATE_C
ELSE STATE_D

STATE_D is a default transition that is executed if none of the above expressions is true. This multi-way branch capability, combined with SAM's 15-level stack, counter and microinstructions gives an excellent vehicle for complex designs.

FEATURE	29PL141	14R21	SAM
Memory Words	64	128	448
Outputs	16	8	16
Inputs	7	8	8
Loop Counter	YES	NO	YES
Stack	2×6	None	15×8
Branching	2-Way	4-Way	4-Way
Instruction-Based	YES	NO	YES
Package	28/0.6	20/0.3	28/0.3

Fig. A-70. Microcoded sequencer comparison. Courtesy of Altera Corporation.

Figure A-70 shows a features comparison for Altera's SAM device compared to the other available single-chip microsequencer options. The SAM devices achieve higher density, higher performance, and lower power than any other available option.

Appendix B

Listing of Product Services

Altera Corporation
3525 Monroe Street
Santa Clara, CA 95051
(408) 984-2800

ANVIL Software
427-3 Amherst Street
Nashua, NH 03603
(603) 891-1995

Atmel Corporation
2125 O'Nel Drive
San Jose, CA 95131
(408) 441-0311

Cypress Semiconductor Corporation
3901 N. First Street
San Jose, CA 95134
(408) 943-2666

Data I/O Corporation
10525 Willows Road NE
P. O. Box 97046
Redmond, Washington 98073-9746
(206) 881-6444

Exel Microelectronics Inc.
2150 Commerce Drive
San Jose, CA 95131
(408) 432-0502

Gazelle Microcircuits Inc.
2300 Owen Street
Santa Clara, CA 95054
(408) 982-0900

Gould Electronics Inc.
2300 Buckskin Road
Pocatello, ID 83201
(208) 233-4690

Harris Corp., Semiconductor Division
P.O. Box 1239
Melbourne, FL 32902
(407) 724-3576

INLAB, Inc.
2150-I West 6th Ave.
Broomfield, CO 80020
(303) 460-0103

Intel Corporation
1900 Prairie Road
Folsom, CA 95630
(916) 351-8080

International CMOS Technology
2125 Lundy Avenue
San Jose, CA 95131
(408) 434-0678

Kontron Electronics
630 Clyde Avenue
Mountain View, CA 94039
(415) 965-7020

Lattice Semiconductor Corporation
5555 Moore Court
Hillsboro, OR 97124
(503) 681-0118

Logical Devices, Inc.
1201 NW 65th PL
Ft. Lauderdale, FL 33309
(305) 974-0967

National Semiconductor Corporation
P.O. Box 58090
Santa Clara, CA 95052-8090
(408) 721-5000

PLX Technology Inc.
625 Clyde Avenue
Mountain View, CA 94043
(415) 960-0448

Ricoh Corporation
3001 Orchard Parkway
San Jose, CA 95134
(408) 434-6700

SAMSUNG Semiconductors
3175 North 1st Street
San Jose, CA 95134-1708
(408) 434-5400

SGS Semiconductor Corporation
1000 E. Bell Road
Phoenix, AZ 85022
(602) 867-6100

Signetics Corporation
811 Arques Avenue
P.O. Box 3409
Sunnyvale, CA 94088
(408) 991-2000

Sunrise Electronics
524 South Vermont Avenue
Glendora, CA 91740
(818)914-1926

Texas Instruments Inc.
P.O. Box 225012
Dallas, TX 75265
(214) 462-4111

Xllinx Inc.
2100 Logic Drive
San Jose, CA 95124
(408) 559-7778

JEDEC Standards

The Joint Electronic Device Engineering Council (JEDEC) operates under the Electronic Industries Association (EIA) administrative and legal procedures and publishes JEDEC standards and publications. Copies of the JEDEC Standard 3-A (Standard Data Transfer Format between Data Preparation System and Programmable Logic Device Programmer) can be obtained from:

Electronic Industries Association
Engineering Department
1722 I Street NW
Washington, DC 20006
(202) 457-4900

Appendix C

Package Drawings

20 PIN DIP CERAMIC

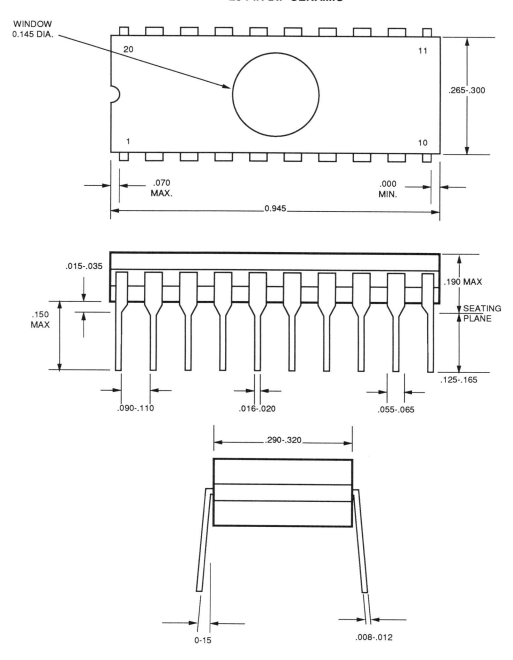

20 PIN DIP PLASTIC

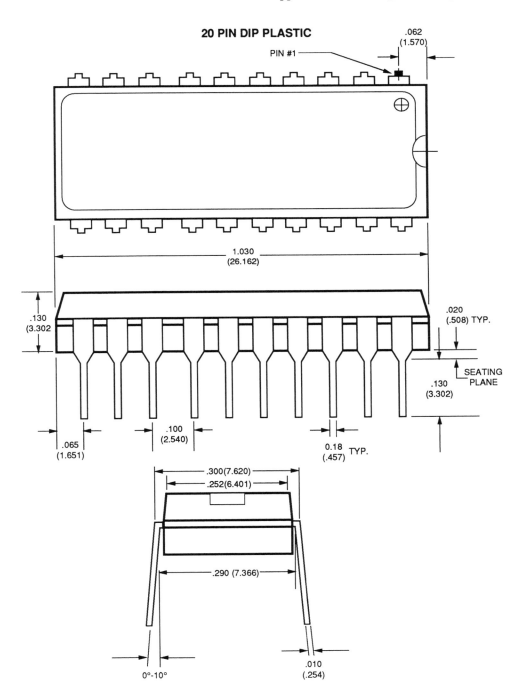

24 PIN DIP CERAMIC

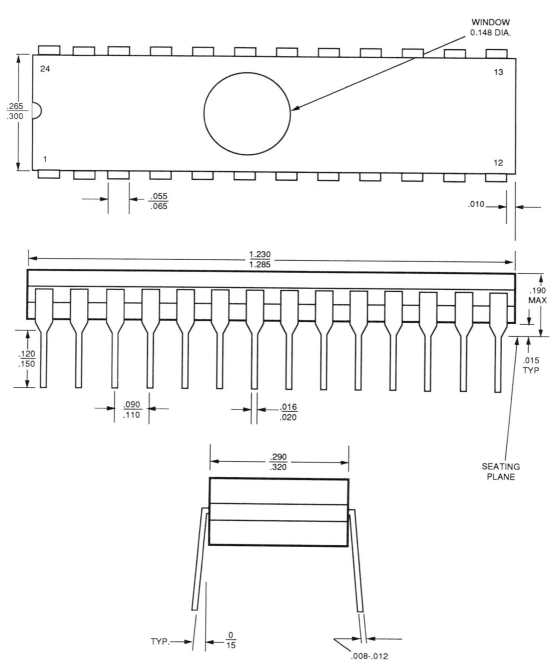

24 PIN DIP PLASTIC

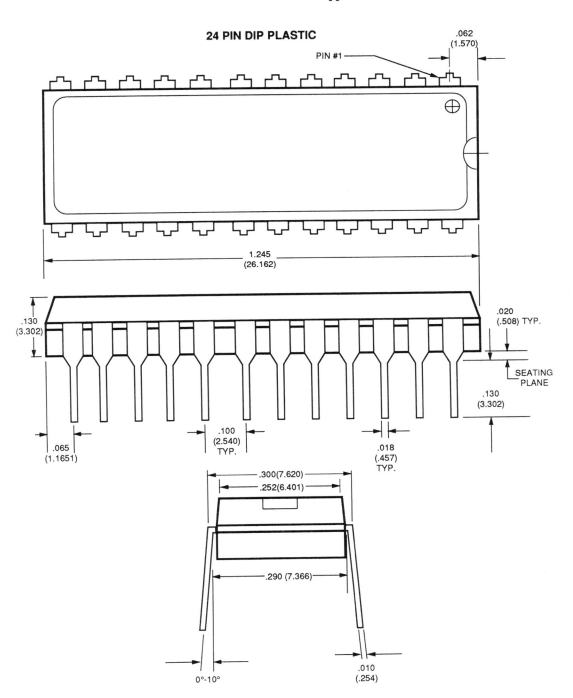

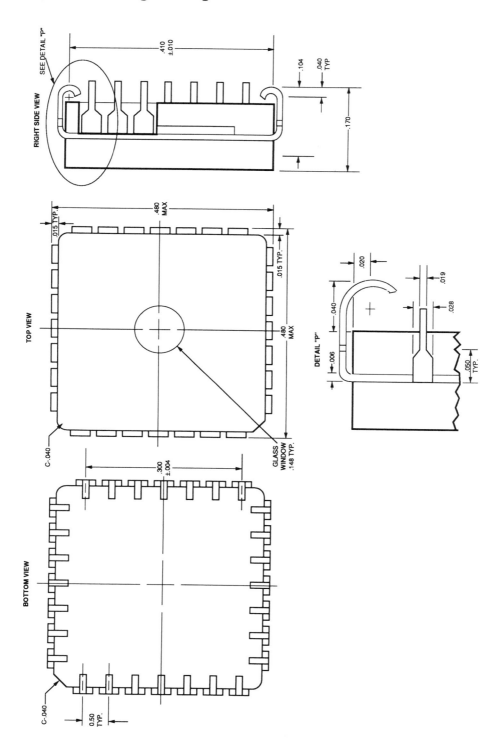

28 PIN JLCC CERAMIC

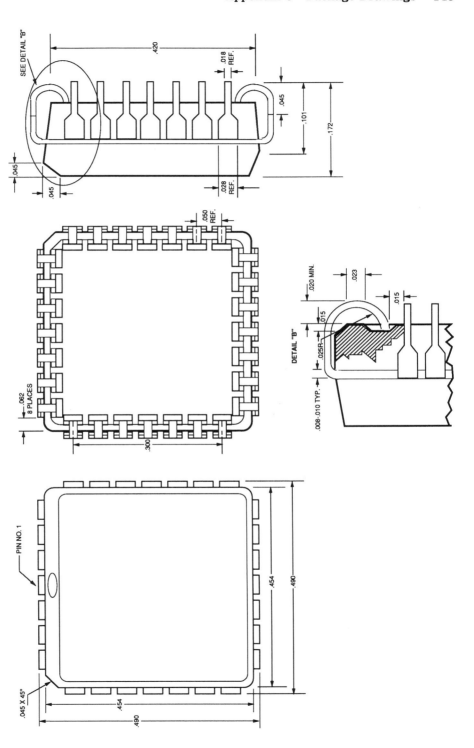

28 PIN LCC PLASTIC

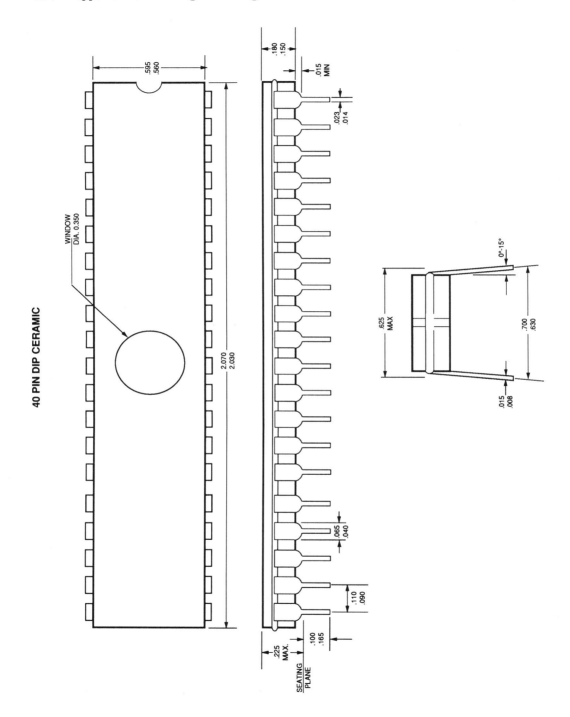

40 PIN DIP CERAMIC

WINDOW
DIA. 0.350

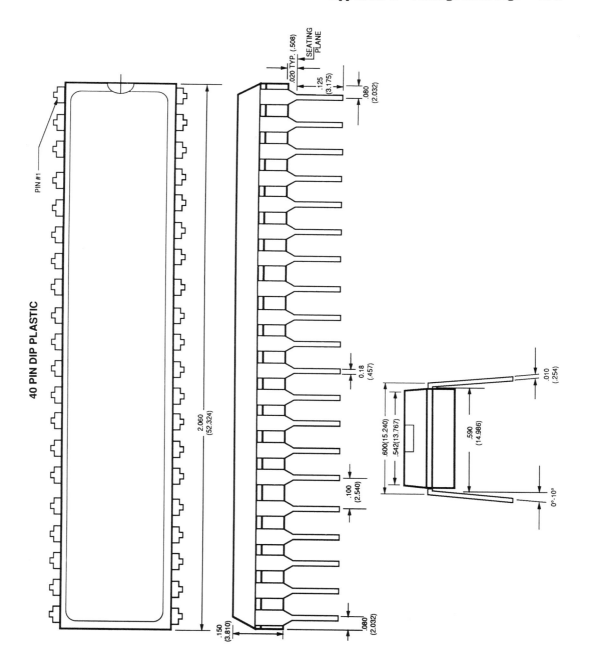

40 PIN DIP PLASTIC

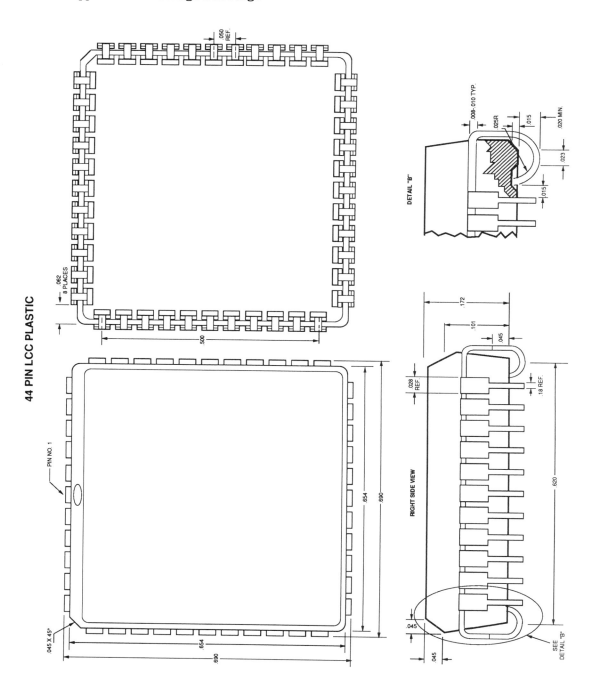

44 PIN LCC PLASTIC

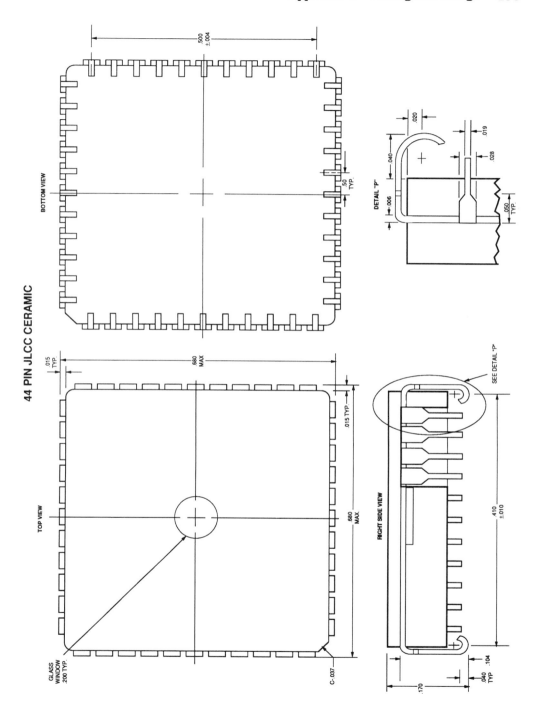

44 PIN JLCC CERAMIC

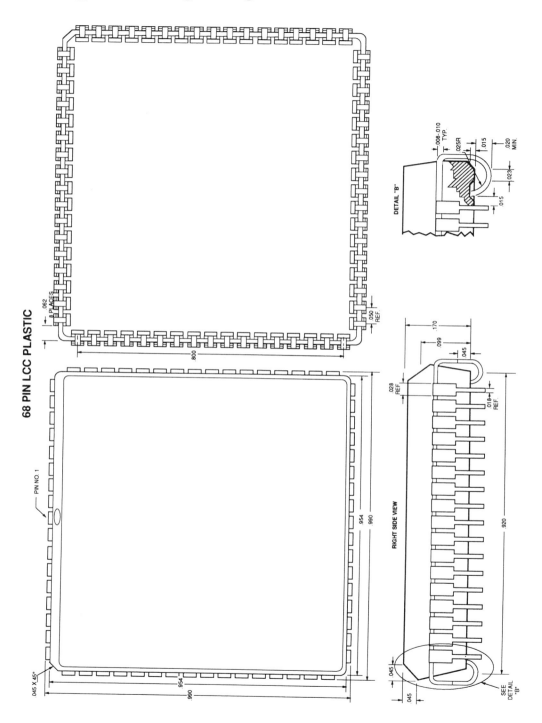

68 PIN LCC PLASTIC

PIN NO. 1

.045 X 45°

.990
.954

.990
.954

.800

.062
8 PLACES

.050
REF.

DETAIL "B"

.008-.010
TYP.

.025R

.015

.020
MIN

.023

.015

.015

RIGHT SIDE VIEW

.170

.099

.045

.028
REF.

.018
REF.

.920

.045

.045

SEE
DETAIL
"B"

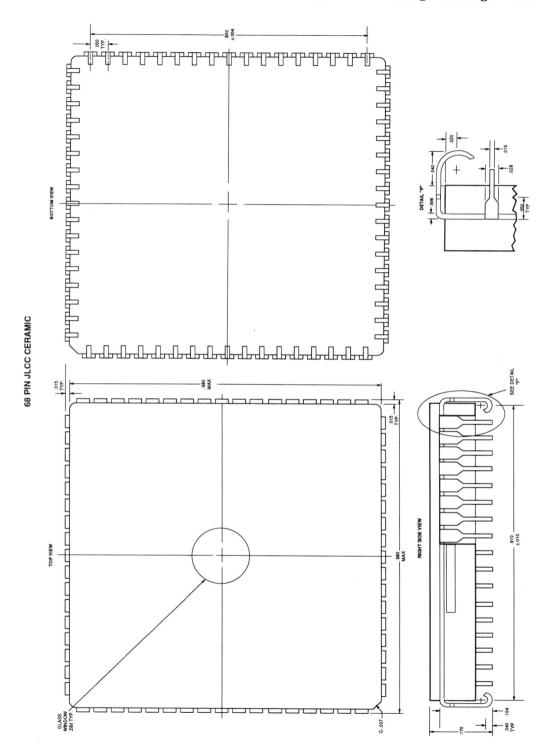

68 PIN JLCC CERAMIC

BOTTOM VIEW

TOP VIEW

RIGHT SIDE VIEW

DETAIL "P"

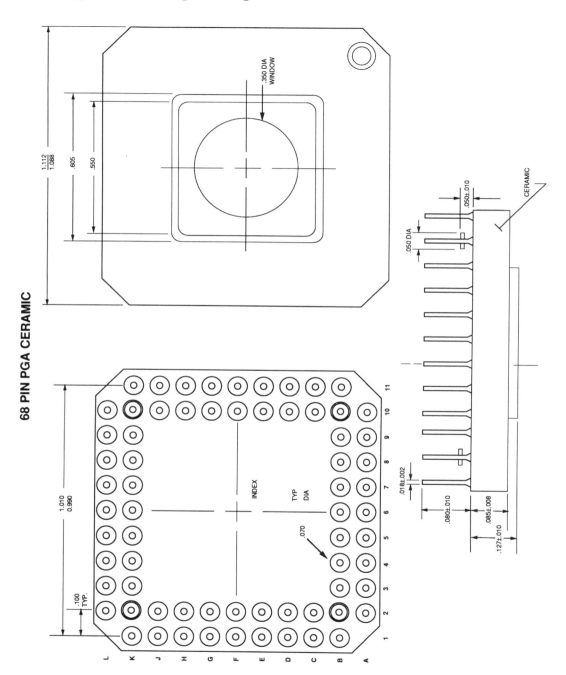

68 PIN PGA CERAMIC

Glossary

ABEL   Advanced Boolean Expression Language. An advanced CAE tool for PLD design.

ASIC   Application-Specific Integrated Circuit. Any IC that is designed to fit an application either by programming mask-customizing or custom designing.

asynchronous   The occurance of events triggered by previous events, as opposed to a repetitive clock cycle that can be thought of as synchronous events.

behavioral description   A description that addresses the functionality of the design without reference to either its underlying structure or the physical layout of the chip or board.

bit   The smallest unit of information in a binary system such as an on or off signal (Binary digIT).

Boolean equations   A logic equation expressed using the conventions of Boolean algebra.

CAD   Computer-Aided Design. CAD tools automate the process of generating engineering drawings.

CADAT   Computer-Aided Design and Test. A tool that provides software breadboarding and simulation of logic designs.

CAE   Computer-Aided Engineering, using a computer and software tools to design or assist in design.

CAM   Computer-Aided Manufacturing. CAM tools automate manufacturing operations, such as production testing and printed circuit board layout.

clock   A device that generates a constant series of on and off (0 or 1) pulses that is used to regulate the speed and operation of a circuit.

compilation   Conversion of a structural description to a physical layout for a chip or board.

counter   A circuit that counts pulses normally from a clock source.

DASH   A CAE tool that allows you to design circuits schematically, using a graphics workstation.

DASH-ABLE   A CAE tool that translates a DASH schematic design into an ABEL source file.

design vectors   Information used by the ABEL simulator to verify that a logic design functions as you intended.

EPLD   Erasable Programmable Logic Device (a specific PLD architecture).

F_{MAX}   Maximum operating frequency in cycles per cycle. Normally given units of Hz, where one Hz is defined as one cycle per second.

Fault grading   A process of analyzing and reporting the location and polarity of all possible faults in a PLD.

Fixed-function device   Any IC having an unalterable function (not programmable); an example is a 7400 quad NAND gate.

flip-flop   A circuit that can assume both of two states, binary 1 and binary 0, although not at the same time.

FPLA   Field-Programmable Logic Array. A PLD having both a programmable AND array and programmable OR array.

FPLS   An FPLA with registers (flip-flops) added.

fuse map   A representation of the fuse states (intact or blown) in a PLD, usually referring to the data that reside in the PLD programmer's RAM.

high-level equations   Equations that use arithmetic or relational operators (such as < or >).

high-level synthesis   Synthesis performed at the algorithmic level of design.

I_{CC} (supply current)   The current that occurs at the V_{CC} supply terminal when the circuit is in operation.

IFL   Integrated fuse logic (a specific PLD architecture).

Ioh   The current forcing condition used to test the logic high-level Voh.

Iol   The current forcing condition used to test the logic low-level Vol.

JEDEC file   A standard format for the transfer of logic design information, usually from a CAE tool to a PLD programmer.

output macrocell   The circuits that configure a PLD output to be any one of a multitude of different configurations.

PAL   Programmable Array Logic. A PLD having programmable AND array but a fixed OR array.

PLD Programmable Logic Device. Any IC that can be user-programmed to implement a logic function. It contains an uncommitted logic array.

PLD-CADAT A tool that provides PLD models to the CADAT simulator.

PLDtest A CAE tool providing fault grading and automatic test vector generation.

product term Boolean equations can be written in a "sum of products" format, as in Y = A * B + C * D. Product terms in this case are A * B and C * D. Miniterm is a synonym for product term.

PROM Programmable Read-Only Memory. A PLD having fixed AND array, but programmable OR array.

security fuse A PLD feature that secures programmed PLD after it has been programmed to prevent outside intrusion by other personnel.

seed vector Design vectors are also referred to as seed vectors when used in the context of PLDtest.

state diagram A graphic representation of a synchronous digital circuit, or state machine.

state machine A logic function defined by its clock selection and state assignments coupled to its state variables and transition definitions.

state variable A named variable assigned to or manipulated by state assignments.

synchronous The occurrence of events at the same time relative to a repetitive or cyclic clock signal.

test vector A set of inputs together with the expected outputs that are used to test ICs under actual in-circuit conditions.

t_{PD} (propagation delay time) The time interval during which the nonregistered output changes from one defined level (high or low) to the other defined level specified on the input and output voltage waveforms.

Index